UNDERSTANDING
AMERICAN GOVERNMENT
AND POLITICS

MANCHESTER
1824

Manchester University Press

D0317844

UNDERSTANDING POLITICS

Series editor **DUNCAN WATTS**

Following the review of the national curriculum for 16–19 year olds, UK examining boards introduced new specifications, first used in 2001 and 2002. A-level courses are now divided into A/S level for the first year of sixth form studies, and the more difficult A2 level thereafter. The **Understanding Politics** series comprehensively covers the politics syllabuses of all the major examination boards, featuring a dedicated A/S-level textbook and four books aimed at A2 students. The books are written in an accessible, user-friendly and jargon-free manner and will be essential to students sitting these examinations.

Already published

Understanding political ideas and movements
Kevin Harrison and Tony Boyd

Understanding British and European political issues
Neil McNaughton

Understanding US/UK government and politics
Duncan Watts

Understanding A/S level government and politics
Chris Wilson

Understanding American government and politics

A guide for A2 politics students

• *second edition* •

DUNCAN WATTS

Manchester University Press

Manchester and New York

distributed exclusively in the USA by Palgrave

First edition published 2002 by Manchester University Press

This edition published 2005 by
Manchester University Press
Oxford Road, Manchester M13 9NR, UK
and Room 400, 175 Fifth Avenue, New York, NY 10010, USA
www.manchesteruniversitypress.co.uk

Distributed exclusively in the USA by
Palgrave, 175 Fifth Avenue, New York,
NY 10010, USA

Distribued exclusively in Canada by
UBC Press, University of British Columbia, 2029 West Mall,
Vancouver, BC, Canada V6T 1Z2

British Library Cataloguing-in-Publication Data
A catalogue record for this book is available from the British Library

Library of Congress Cataloging-in-Publication Data applied for

ISBN 0 7190 7327 8   *paperback*
EAN   978 0 7190 7327 4

This edition first published 2006

14   13   12   11   10   09   08   07   06   10   9   8   7   6   5   4   3   2   1

Typeset
by Northern Phototypesetting Co. Ltd, Bolton
Printed in Great Britain
by CPI, Bath

Contents

Comparative boxes:
Britain and the United States

Acknowledgement

Manchester University Press and the Politics Association wish to thank Professor the Lord Norton of Louth for reading this text and for his helpful observations. Any errors are, of course, the responsibility of the author and/or publisher.

THE POLITICS ASSOCIATION

is a registered educational charity, committed to the diffusion of political knowledge and understanding. It produces a wide range of resources on government and politics, and on citizenship. Members receive the journal, *Talking Politics*, three times a year.

Further details can be obtained from the Politics Association, Old Hall Lane, Manchester, M13 0XT, Tel./Fax.: 0161 256 3906; email: politicass@btinternet.com

US presidents and their parties

	President	Party	Term
1	George Washington (1732–99)	Federalist	1789–97
2	John Adams (1735–1826)	Federalist	1797–1801
3	Thomas Jefferson (1743–1826)	Democratic-Republican	1801–9
4	James Madison (1751–1836)	Democratic-Republican	1809–17
5	James Monroe (1758–1831)	Democratic-Republican	1817–25
6	John Quincy Adams (1767–1848)	Democratic-Republican	1825–29
7	Andrew Jackson (1767–1845)	Democrat	1829–37
8	Martin Van Buren (1782–1862)	Democrat	1837–41
9	William Henry Harrison (1773–1841)	Whig	1841
10	John Tyler (1790–1862)	Whig	1841–45
11	James K. Polk (1795–1849)	Democrat	1845–49
12	Zachary Taylor (1784–1850)	Whig	1849–50
13	Millard Fillmore (1800–74)	Whig	1850–53
14	Franklin Pierce (1804–69)	Democrat	1853–57
15	James Buchanan (1791–1868)	Democrat	1857–61
16	Abraham Lincoln (1809–65)	Republican	1861–65
17	Andrew Johnson (1808–75)	Union	1865–69
18	Ulysses S. Grant (1822–85)	Republican	1869–77
19	Rutherford B. Hayes (1822–93)	Republican	1877–81
20	James A. Garfield (1831–81)	Republican	1881
21	Chester A. Arthur (1830–86)	Republican	1881–85
22	Grover Cleveland (1837–1908)	Democrat	1885–89

President	Party	Term
23 Benjamin Harrison (1833–1901)	Republican	1889–93
24 Grover Cleveland (1837–1908)	Democrat	1893–97
25 William McKinley (1843–1901)	Republican	1897–1901
26 Theodore Roosevelt (1858–1919)	Republican	1901–9
27 William Howard Taft (1857–1930)	Republican	1909–13
28 Woodrow Wilson (1856–1924)	Democrat	1913–21
29 Warren G. Harding (1865–1923)	Republican	1921–23
30 Calvin Coolidge (1871–1933)	Republican	1923–29
31 Herbert Hoover (1874–1964)	Republican	1929–33
32 Franklin Delano Roosevelt (1882–1945)	Democrat	1933–45
33 Harry S. Truman (1884–1972)	Democrat	1945–53
34 Dwight D. Eisenhower (1890–1969)	Republican	1953–61
35 John F. Kennedy (1917–63)	Democrat	1961–63
36 Lyndon B. Johnson (1908–73)	Democrat	1963–69
37 Richard M. Nixon (1913–94)	Republican	1969–74
38 Gerald R. Ford (b. 1913)	Republican	1974–77
39 Jimmy Carter (b. 1924)	Democrat	1977–81
40 Ronald Reagan (1911–2004)	Republican	1981–89
41 George H. W. Bush (b. 1924)	Republican	1989–93
42 William Jefferson Clinton (b. 1946)	Democrat	1993–2001
43 George Walker Bush (b. 1946)	Republican	2001–

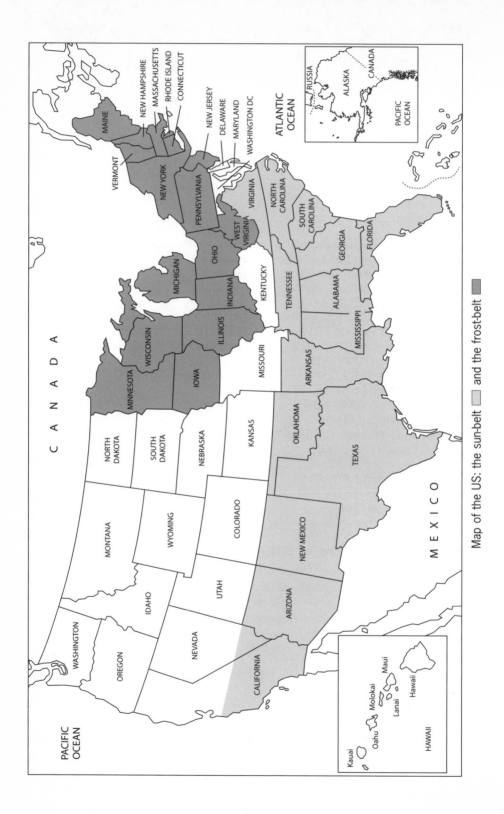

Map of the US: the sun-belt ☐ and the frost-belt ☐

Introduction: the setting of American politics

A knowledge of the social and economic environment of any country is important in achieving an understanding of its government and politics. So too is an appreciation of the ideas and values that have mattered and continue to matter for those who inhabit that country. Many students will know little of American human and economic geography, or indeed of its political culture. So here we are concerned with finding out more about the influences on American politics, and the factors that shape attitudes and events today.

In this section, we are concerned with examining those features of the United States, ranging from its size and landscape to its population and religion, which have a bearing on its political activity. Given its vast extent, it is inevitably a country of great diversity; and differences in race, gender, religion and social class have an impact on the way in which voters behave.

Geographically, the United States is a huge land mass, exceeding that of all but three nations in the world: Canada, China and Russia. It borders Canada in the North and Mexico in the South, and on its west and east coast lie two oceans, the Pacific and the Atlantic, respectively. It is a land endowed with considerable resources, ranging from coal to precious metals, and it is also rich in farmland. Nature has been generous and enabled America to develop as a country remarkably self-sufficiently. Areas have their own regional economic concerns, and political attitudes reflect these regional differences. Some parts of the country are well suited to ranching and agriculture, others to mining or manufacturing. The political perspectives of the automobile worker in Detroit are far removed from those of the farmers of Kansas, for example.

Geographical isolation

The country is not only vast, but also geographically rather isolated. Having only two immediate neighbours, it faces little threat of invasion or conquest. Moreover, as it is cut off from other continents, it has been able to keep itself aloof from many struggles in Asia, Europe and elsewhere, unless they are conflicts where key American interests are perceived to be involved. Between the two world wars, the country adopted an isolationist stance, whereas after World War II it assumed a global role including the leadership of the free, Western world. At times, as in Vietnam, it has chosen to involve itself in conflict, and during the era of the Cold War its military machine was much involved in overseas struggle. Sometimes, it has been more reluctant to meddle in other countries' affairs, and this has enabled it to develop its own distinctive political traditions and concentrate on its own internal development.

Isolationist voices have always periodically been raised, particularly from politicians more remote from the European scene (such as in the Midwest). After the experience of Vietnam and with the Cold War over, there is again a greater wish for America to 'play in its own backyard'. Many Americans display a sense of anxiety when presidents take them into commitments, such as those in Somalia and Bosnia, from which little credit is likely to emerge.

Sectional differences

Of all the sectional differences within the US, the most obvious is that which separates the American South from the rest of the nation. Traditionally, the South has been more rural and agricultural and the North more industrial, but the issue at the root of the distinction between them was slavery. Lincoln and the Republicans were opposed to slavery, and it was over this issue that the eleven southern states broke away to form the Confederacy in 1860–61. Their secession led to the Civil War, fought between the forces of the Union and those of the Confederalists.

The secession made the Democrats the party of the South, and after the Civil War was over the distinction between North and South remained. These differences were strengthened by the policies pursued during the era of Reconstruction, by differing economic interests, and above all by the continuing racial problem. Today, a further difference can be ascribed to military establishments, for most of the military facilities are based in the South, which tends to mean that on matters of national defence the South takes a more conservative viewpoint.

In religion, the South remains distinctive. There are strong Protestant leanings in the 'Bible Belt' and religious **fundamentalism** is widespread. Above all, however, it is the treatment of black Americans (African Americans) that has proved

> **fundamentalism**
> The interpretation of every word of the Bible as being literally true.

to be the key issue over the last century. Although black slaves were freed after the Civil War, they were still the victims of segregation, intimidation and discrimination; they were long denied basic rights, such as the franchise (right to vote). Since the 1960s, things have greatly changed. In 1960, in a southern state such as Mississippi, only one in twenty blacks were registered to vote. Today, many more blacks than whites remain unregistered, but that is true all over the country and it is not specifically a southern issue. With the advent of more civil rights and the spread of educational opportunity, the South has become less backward even if it still lags behind the rest of the nation in educational achievement and per capita income.

The South has changed significantly over the last generation. It is no longer true to speak of the 'solid South', as the Democrats used to do. It is now less cohesive as a society, and certainly less committed to the Democratic cause. In recent presidential elections, the Republicans have outperformed the Democrats, and in 2004 the Democratic presidential candidate, John Kerry, was able to make little headway in the region; in state and local elections, however, the Democrats continue to do well. White voters seem to have become disenchanted with Democratic presidential aspirants, but the voting rights won by blacks have been a reinforcement of the Democratic position, especially at local level.

No other region has such a cohesive identity as the South, but there are nevertheless other sectional differences. The West has tended to be more isolationist (as it is further from Western Europe), as well as more committed to the alleged virtues of rugged individualism and less federal intervention. Such a sense of self-sufficiency made this obvious territory for Ronald Reagan in the 1980s, for he was identified with the attitudes and values of the West.

California is a state with a special importance, not least because of its 55 representatives in Congress. No candidate for the presidency has much chance of success unless he or she can win its vote in the Electoral College – Nixon, Reagan and Clinton, among others, all carried the state. In 1992, it was suffering badly from a recession that helped to tilt it away from the Republican incumbent and towards the Democrats.

The population and where it lives

The diverse American population has grown by leaps and bounds, as the figures below indicate. In 2005, there were more than 293 million people living in the US.[1] The population growth of 32.7 million between 1990 and 2000 represented the largest census-to-census increase in American history.

Interim projections[2] suggest that numbers will continue to grow during the next half century, albeit at a reduced rate after 2030. By the mid-century mark, figures will touch 420 million. The country beginning to emerge will be a profoundly different America, more diverse in population. Whites, excluding

Latinos, will see their influence and numbers diminish from a 70% share of the population today to a bare majority of fractionally over 50% in 2050. The beginnings of that change are already under way. Within the next decade, minorities will account for one third of the population, because of immigration. By 2030, there will be what William Frey,[3] a demographer at the Brookings Institute in Washington, calls the 'racial generation gap', as the predominantly white generation of **baby boomers** makes way for a younger, more diverse population: 'It's the future versus the past. These old white baby boomers are being phased out and are fading away after 2030.' However, there will be plenty of company for these ageing baby boomers as they enter their twilight years.

> **baby boomers**
> Baby boomers were born in the baby boom in the United States, between 1945 and 1955.

Not only is the population growing, it is also ageing. The median age of the population is 36, the highest it has ever been. The number of elderly Americans (counted as being those over 65) is now just over 12% of the total. By 2050, their numbers will have swollen from today's 35 million to 87 million, from 12% to 20% over the age of 65. There will also be a large population of octogenarians, and the number of people aged 85 and older is expected to reach 21 million. This is politically significant, because the political outlook and concerns of this ageing population are likely to be a factor in determining election results and shaping public policy in future decades. The ageing baby boomers are going to be more concerned with security and pensions than schools or language training, which are likely to be more important to immigrants.

The growth in population

Year	Population
1900	76,212,168
1930	123,202,660
1960	179,323,175
1990	248,709,873
2000	281,421,906

The population of every state grew between 1990 and 2000, but not at an even rate across the country. Nevada was the fastest growing (up 66%), North Dakota the lowest (up 0.5%). Overall, the population of the West (particularly California and Nevada) is increasing most rapidly, followed by the South. By contrast, the Northeast and Midwest are barely increasing in size, as many inhabitants migrate to the South and West. More Americans today are seeking the warmth and other attractions of the so-called sun-belt (the bottom 40% of the country), and deserting the frost-belt, those states in the Northeast (see map on p. xii). States such as Florida have an appeal for retired people, but also for those tempted by the job opportunities in an area of new industries and substantial economic growth.

These changes in the distribution of the population are reflected in changes to the regional pattern of congressional representation. Eight states acquired more seats in the US House of Representatives and ten states lost members. The Northeast and Midwest each lost five seats, whereas the South and West each gained five seats. (see p. 125 for details of congressional apportionment).

The 2000 census revealed that nine of the largest cities had lost inhabitants in the previous decade, a continuation of an established pattern of suburbanisation that has characterised the last few decades. For many years, America was a predominantly rural society, but in the late nineteenth and early twentieth centuries, there was a movement of population from rural to urban parts as workers sought jobs in the expanding towns and cities. More recently, the trend has been away from urban centres and out to suburban areas, as new housing developments have grown up and new connecting roads have been built. In Los Angeles, four times as many people live in the metropolitan outskirts as actually in the city itself. Members of the better-off white community of some city centres have been keen to move out, so that their offspring can attend an all-white school and avoid the prospect of being 'bussed' to an integrated one. The population that remains in inner cities now tends to comprise poorer whites, blacks and assorted racial minority groups. This is fertile territory for the Democratic Party. The suburbs (although they vary greatly in wealth and quality of life) tend to be places where the predominantly white people enjoy higher income levels, and vote Republican.

The top ten cities with 100,000 or more population, having the largest black majorities (size in %)

City	% black majority
Gary (Indiana)	85.3
Detroit (Michigan)	82.8
Birmingham (Alabama)	74.0
Jackson (Mississippi)	71.1
New Orleans (Louisiana)	67.9
Baltimore (Maryland)	65.2
Atlanta (Georgia)	62.1
Memphis (Tennessee)	61.9
Washington (DC)	61.3
Richmond (Virginia)	58.1

Fourteen of the cities that have a population exceeding 100,000 now have a black majority, places ranging from Atlanta in Georgia to Detroit in Michigan, from Gary in Indiana to Washington DC. Apart from the African American population, there are many other racial minorities in this land of immigrants, ranging from Asians to Hispanics (persons of Spanish-speaking descent, who can technically be of any race) and Jews.

**Main groups in the population of the United States
(rounded to nearest million)**

Year	White	Black	Hispanic	Total
1970	178,000,000	23,000,000	n/a	201,000,000
1980	180,000,000	27,000,000	15,000,000	222,000,000
1990	187,000,000	31,000,000	22,000,000	240,000,000
2000	212,000,000	36,000,000*	35,000,000	283,000,000

Figures adapted from those provided by US Census Bureau.
* Includes black Americans of more than one racial group.

Racial groups

As the table indicates, some 75% of Americans are white and just under 13% are black). Numbers of **Black Americans** increased faster than the total population between 1990 and 2000, at a rate of nearly 16%, whereas overall population increase was 13.2%. The black population has for much of the last one hundred years sought to improve its position in American society. Freed as a result of the Civil War, it was long denied full participation and recognition. Its struggle to advance its position and achieve civil rights has been an important feature of postwar politics. The freedom rides and sit-ins, the marches and boycotts, posed problems for white Americans as they finally had to concede a greater measure of equal treatment than they had ever contemplated before.

Until the twentieth century, most blacks lived in the South, and 54% still do so; 19% live in the Midwest, 18% in the Northeast and 10% in the West. In the South, ten states have a black population of over a million and the population of four states and Washington DC is more than a quarter black. However, early in the twentieth century many left that area to seek a better lifestyle in the large cities of the West, Midwest and Northeast. Washington DC has the highest proportion of blacks (66% of the population), but many other cities have a large African American population, much of which is often to be found in poorer quarters; New York has 2.3 million and Chicago 1.1 million. In places as far apart as Los Angeles and Detroit, riots have from time to time broken out in the ghettos (densely populated slum areas, inhabited by a deprived minority group) as a result of deprivation and discrimination.

Issues of racial division and race relations have bedevilled America for much of its short history, and although blacks have achieved greater rights and political power they tend to be worse off, with an average income substantially below that of the white population, and one-third of the black population lives below the poverty line. It is a matter of political contention whether the black population should be helped by policies such as **affirmative action**, which provide certain groups with greater opportunities to achieve a range of positions long denied them.

One of the fastest-growing groups in the United States is the Hispanic population, which grew by 57.9% between 1990 and 2000. There are currently over 35 millon (12.5%) **Hispanics** or 'Latinos' (as some Hispanics prefer to be called). For the first time they outnumbered African Americans in 2003. Indeed, as a significant minority of black Americans are also Hispanics, the historic primacy of primarily English-speaking blacks was already at an end by the turn of the century. Hispanics tend to be undercounted in surveys, a situation made more possible by the number of illegal immigrants ever year. Most Hispanics have a Mexican origin, but those reporting 'other origins' are the fastest growing group (up 96.9% between 1990 and 2000).

The origin of the Hispanic population (%)

Origin	%
Mexican	58.5
Puerto Rican	9.6
Cuban	3.5
Others, of whom largest group are Central American, South American and Dominican	28.4

Mostly better off than African Americans, half of all Hispanics live in just two states, California (11.0 million) and Texas (6.7 million). They account for 24.3% of the population in the West, the only region in which Hispanics exceed the national level of 12.5%. Nearly two-thirds of the Cuban element live in Florida. A majority of Miami residents are Hispanic, but in cities from Dallas to Houston, Los Angeles to New York, they are also well represented.

Hispanics are expected to number 103 million by 2050 and will account for nearly a quarter of America's population, up from about 13% today. They are a young population, their relative youthfulness being reflected in the size of the under-18 population (35.0%, against an overall figure of 25.7%) and in its median age (26, as against 36).

Hispanics hardly form a coherent group, and come from diverse places. As mentioned above, most of them have a Mexican origin, but there are also many Puerto Ricans who have left their overcrowded island for the mainland with the hope of improving their position in life. Those from Cuba are a signif-icant group. They or their parents and grandparents fled from Castro's communist revolution in 1959. They tend to be more professional and middle-class, and do not share many of the social and political attitudes of the Mexican Americans and Puerto Ricans.

Inspired by the example of black activism, Hispanics have drawn closer together, but the diversity of their origins has prevented them from becoming a solid national grouping. They tend to be poorer than whites and many have not qualified as citizens. Their campaigning has been done via local groups that fight for better conditions rather than through large, nationwide associations. But they are becoming more organised and many are now acquiring citizenship. As they stand on the verge of being America's largest minority group, it is likely that issues of concern to their various sub-groups will gain greater prominence on the nation's political agenda. They may be still seriously under-represented in American institutions, but there have been recent signs of an emerging Latino-led radicalism, particularly among those who carry out many of the lowest-paid and dirtiest jobs in the US. In the words of one writer: 'The long history of political marginality is finally coming to an end. Latinos, all political pundits agree, are the sleeping dragon of US politics.'[4]

The votes of Hispanics are crucial in some states, Texas, California and Florida among them. In the light of what happened in 2000 (see pp. 174–5), Florida is a particularly interesting political battleground, not least because John Ellis (Jeb) Bush, the president's brother, is the governor. His articulate son could well prove to be the next member of the Bush dynasty to take the political stage. Born in Mexico to his mother Columba, George P. Bush could be one of the first Hispanics to become a well-known figure in public life.

Of the **Asian Americans**, many originally settled in California and the western states having journeyed from China and Japan. More recent immigrants have come from the Philippines, South Korea and Southeast Asia (especially Cambodia and Vietnam), but the area of settlement remains broadly the same: California and Hawaii, as well as the capital, Washington DC. There are more than 10 million Asian Americans, nearly 12 million if we include those who reported being Asian and at least one other race. They arrived in substantial numbers in the 1970s and 1980s, and the rate of increase has accelerated. The number of Asian alones rose by nearly 50% in the decade to 2000. Today, round half of them live in the West (49%), followed by 20% in the Northeast and 19% in the Midwest. Fifty-one % live in just three states – California, New York and Hawaii.

In the past, the Chinese and especially the Japanese were the victims of regular discrimination; in 1942 many of the latter were interned in camps because of their 'doubtful' allegiance. Since then, much of the anti-Asian prejudice has disappeared. Most Asian groups have advanced in American society, though there are occasional outbreaks of hostile feeling.

America's Asian and Hispanic population is set to triple over the next fifty years. Waves of immigration from Asia and Central America are likely to keep the country young and vital.

The **Native American population** was originally called 'Indian' by the explorers and colonists who found it. By prior usage, the land belonged to the Native Americans, but these tribal peoples were gradually displaced as the settlers moved westwards and the buffalo herds on which the Native Americans depended were wiped out. These people were eventually granted certain reserved areas, and many of the present Native Americans still live in or near these reservations, in Arizona, New Mexico and Utah. In a sense, it is wrong to group these Native Americans together, for they include representatives of many tribes whose cultures and lifestyles were once very different. Only about 2.5 million Native Indians and Alaskan Natives remain, the two groups generally being categorized as American Indian for census purposes. Forty-three % live in the West, the next largest group living in the South (31%).

Generally they experience inferior standards of living, the reservations being enclaves of social disadvantage. Native Americans are much more likely to live in poverty; they also earn less and achieve less via the educational system. Some leave their reservations because of the low quality of life there, and inhabit towns and cities such as Chicago and Los Angeles. However, those who have left have in many cases yet to become integrated into American society, and lack the occupational skills and cultural background to sustain themselves. They are prone to a variety of social problems, ranging from alcoholism and family disintegration to, at worst, suicide. Only recently have activist Native Americans begun to organise and press for changes in their quality of life.

Other than the Native Americans, all Americans are immigrants. The poor and oppressed from different parts of the world gathered in the country, so that it has developed as a land of diversity. In theory, all of those who entered the United States could benefit from the **American Dream**, according to which every enterprising person could improve his or her position in a land of opportunity.

Not all groups have benefited equally from this possible social mobility, but individuals of any race and background have been able to change their lifestyle and prospects, and via education, occupation and intermarriage have altered their status. America is often seen

> **American Dream**
> The widespread belief that by hard work and individual enterprise even the most poor and lowly Americans can achieve economic success, a better way of life and enhanced social status, in a land of immense opportunity.
> According to the Dream, there are no insurmountable barriers which prevent Americans from fulfilling their potential, even if many individuals and groups do not do so.

as a '**melting pot**', and groups from different
backgrounds and of differing cultures have been
able to mix with members of other groups, and
have become assimilated into the American way
of life.

> **melting pot**
> The process by which people
> of diverse lands, cultures,
> languages and religions are
> blended or assimilated into
> American society.

The religious mix

Given the diversity of races represented in the United States, it is inevitable
that many varieties of religious belief are to be found. There is no national or
'established' church for the whole country, though there were until the 1830s
established state churches. Religious allegiances are active at all levels of
society, and religious beliefs, language, symbols and values are important to
Americans. These impact upon politics, as faith groups seek to organise voters,
and play an active part in the selection of candidates and the appointment of
judges.

Religious beliefs feature strongly in policy debate. Candidates for office
routinely acknowledge the Almighty in their speeches and discuss issues in
moralistic terms. In the 2000 election, both
George W. Bush and his Democrat opponent, Al
Gore, frequently referred to their status as '**born
again' Christians**. In 2004, like the president, the
Democratic candidate John Kerry was willing to
parade details of his personal faith. Every
president from Jimmy Carter onwards has claimed
to have been 'born again'.

> **born-again Christians**
> Christians who claim that their
> religious life has been
> dramatically altered by a
> conversion experience that has
> made them see issues very
> differently.

Unlike many countries, the United States does not include a question about
religion in its census, so that information concerning religious allegiance has
to be taken from survey and organisational findings. These indicate that the
US has a greater number of religious groups than any other country in the
world (well over 1,200). The top organised religions are Christianity (82% of
all Americans, by far the largest), Judaism, Islam, Buddhism and Hinduism.
The 2002 edition of the *World Christian Encyclopedia*[5] suggests that there are
5.6 million Jews, 4.1 million Muslims, 2.4 million Buddhists and 1 million
Hindus. There has been a substantial growth in Islamic belief and Buddhism
among both Native Americans and the immigrant population in recent years.

Today, there are many more faiths than ever before, part of a remarkable
upsurge in religious feeling. Religious toleration is a long-standing tradition,
extending to groups with all manner of idiosyncrasies and eccentricities. It
applies to the growing number of Islamic supporters, some of whom have been
associated with more radical black political attitudes. Adherence to the

Muslim faith poses a challenge to some traditional attitudes and values, the more so since the attack on the Twin Towers (see p. 15), which placed many American Muslims in an uncomfortable and unenviable position. But as yet America has been spared the kind of religious tension that has bedevilled many other parts of the globe.

Within the Christian church, there are many different denominations. Fifty-two % of all Americans classify themselves as Protestants, 24% as Catholic, 2% as Mormon (Latter-Day Saints). Most Protestant denominations have European roots. Among adherents, the largest group belong to the Baptist church, which itself has many offshoots; the Methodists, Lutherans, Presbyterians and Episcopalians are also well represented. Comprising approximately a quarter of the population, Roman Catholics outnumber any single Protestant group.

Religious affiliations in the United States

Religion	Number	%
Christian denominations		
Roman Catholic	50,873,000	24.5
Baptist	33,830,000	16.3
Methodist/Wesleyan	14,150,000	6.8
Lutheran	9,580,000	4.6
Presbyterian	5,596,000	2.7
Other religions		
Jews	5.600,000	1.9
Muslims	4,100,000	1.5
Buddhists	2,400,000	0.9
Hindus	1,000,000	0.4

Adapted from www.adherents.com/rel (based upon information gathered by the Pew Research Centre, 2002) and from D. Barrett, *World Christian Encyclopaedia*, Oxford University Press, 2001.

This is the national picture, but the number of members of each particular sect varies widely from state to state. Baptists are very strong in Alabama, Georgia and Mississippi, and comprise more than half of the population in those states. The South has a strong Protestant majority. There are clusters of very firm allegiance in other areas, so that whereas Catholics are well represented in Connecticut, Massachusetts and Rhode Island, the Mormons (numerically small in the country as a whole) dominate the religious life of Utah, with 70% membership. In New York State, as one would expect, there are members of any sect and none; in New York City, 14% of the population is Jewish.

The importance of religion in American life

Religious groups operate at all levels of the political system, seeking to ensure that those who would attain political power share their beliefs. Religion has shaped and informed the character of political movements. It can be a powerful catalyst of social change. In the Civil Rights Movement of the 1950s and 1960s there were many prominent church ministers, notably Martin Luther King (see p. 308). The black church played an influential role in communicating ideas and information. Jesse Jackson was a younger member of the crusade for social justice and equal rights, and remains influential in the Democratic Party.

The **Religious Right** (many of whose members are part of the Christian Coalition) is an increasingly significant force in the Republican Party. On issues such as abortion and school prayer its contribution to discussion and action has had a considerable effect on politicians and voters. In 2004, its members played a significant role in the victory of George W. Bush in the presidential election.

Religious Right
A broad movement of Christians who advance conservative moral and social values. It first attracted attention as the Moral Majority, but later became known as the Christian Coalition. Highly active in the Republican Party, it seeks to take America back to its true heritage and to restore the godly principles that made the nation great. Most of its members emphasise that they have been 'born again'. They tend to be fundamentalist and are unquestioning in accepting Christian doctrines.

A candidate's religion can be a factor in determining his prospects, though the choice of Senator John F. Kennedy showed that a Catholic could be chosen despite some initial reservations. In 2004, the Democrats again nominated a Catholic, John Kerry. Whereas in 1960, some 80% of Catholics who voted did so for Kennedy, today they are less likely to vote as a bloc. But on an issue such as abortion or stem cell research, the words of any candidate are listened to with much interest by church leaders. The stand adopted may influence the prospects of election in certain states.

Broadly speaking, Jews (although they tend to be prosperous and better educated than members of other minority groups) are more likely to be Democrats than Republicans, as are Catholics and members of minority denominations. The fact that the Democrats were willing to choose Catholics in 1928 and 1960 as presidential candidates meant that many of that religious leaning were well disposed towards the party. It is perceived as being more accessible to them; they are welcome to join. Protestants, especially outside the South, incline strongly towards the Republicans, which is seen as the natural home for White Anglo Saxon Protestants – often referred to as WASPS.

Religious belief and practice are important in American family life and in the political process. God is alluded to in many public speeches, and religion is taken seriously. Americans are likely to believe in God, pray, attend a place of worship. More than two thirds of all Americans belong to a church or synagogue; more than half say religion is 'very important' in their lives; and more than 40% go to a religious service at least every week. This amounts to a remarkable level of religiosity, suggesting that America has resisted some of the secularising influences familiar in European nations. In Europe, only citizens of the Irish Republic exhibit a similar degree of religiosity to that of the Americans. The scale and intensity of belief are such that they influence the discussion of many issues from abortion to gay rights, from pornography to school prayer. Religious belief can also influence the conduct of foreign policy, as we see in Chapter 10.

Education, social class and economic inequality

America is much less preoccupied with social class than is Western Europe, and the Marxian division of bourgeoisie and proletariat has never been much applied to American society. Sociologists often talk of socio-economic status (SES) as a convenient tool by which to analyse the population, and this SES measurement is decided on the basis of education, income and occupation. The usual difficulty about any such categorisation applies, namely that people whose income places them in one stratum have a higher status than some who earn more than they do.

Whereas 'subjective social class' refers to the position in society in which a person places himself or herself, 'objective social class' depends on the position assigned by a social scientist. Many people assume that they are middle class, as befits a land in which people believe that they can achieve whatever they want if they seize their opportunities. In fact there are many people whose occupation and income place them lower down the social scale. Such persons may also wish to distance themselves from organised labour in the trade union movement, which has an unfavourable connotation for many Americans. Overall, the emphasis on class-based analysis fits the American experience less comfortably than in other countries, for the ethos of individualism and enterprise does not sit easily alongside any notion of class solidarity.

About one third of Americans have stayed on and attended some kind of college, and education is valued in the United States as both a desirable thing in itself and a necessary precondition for a successful economy in which skills and training are assuming ever-greater importance. However, the learning experience is not evenly shared, for there has traditionally been a much greater likelihood that blacks and Hispanics will not complete their high-school course. Most younger blacks do finish their high-school education, but relatively few go on to college; Hispanics are less likely to stay with their courses than blacks, and their drop-out rate is high even in the early years. Such differences in achievement have an impact on job prospects and earnings levels, and on the likelihood of political participation in adulthood.

In the early years of the Republic, agriculture was by far the most common occupation, but in the twentieth century America became the leading industrial country in the world. The invention of new machines and of techniques of mass production along with the superabundance of natural resources paved the way for economic success as an industrial nation. Today, commentators often describe the country as being in a postindustrial phase, in which success and rewards depend more on skill and training than on the old industrial structure in which labour and management were often in conflict.

White-collar work has grown rapidly as more and more people enter the professions and management of some kind, whereas the numbers employed in manufacturing have diminished and those in farming have been dramatically reduced. In 1800, 83% of the labour force was employed in agriculture; today the figure is below 3%. Many people work in government, and education and defence are areas in which 3.5 million and 3 million people work, respectively. Blacks are more often engaged in the service industries or, if more educated, in clerical work; Hispanics often work as labourers, operators and on the farms.

Income levels vary enormously, as one would expect in a land in which enterprise and initiative are encouraged. The wealthiest 5% of Americans earn 19% of the income; the poorest 20% earn only 4%. Twelve and a half % of Americans (just under 36 million) live in poverty, as defined by the official poverty line of an income of $17,029 for a family of four (in 2000). The wealth gap has been widening in recent years, most obviously between white households and Hispanic and African American families.[6] The median net worth of white households in 2002 was $88,651, or over eleven times greater than Hispanic families ($7,932) and over fourteen times greater than African American ones ($5,988). Hispanic and black Americans are much less likely to participate in politics, although they are the people who most depend on government help via federal and state welfare programmes.

A sense of unity, despite diversity

America is a multilingual, multiracial society of great social diversity. Yet many of the immigrants and their descendants have taken on board many traditional American values, such as a commitment to liberty and equality. There are forces that bring Americans together and give them a sense of common identity.

Part of this sense of national unity can be explained by the pursuit of the American Dream, by which, in a land of opportunity, all may prosper – if they are sufficiently enterprising. The Dream is often referred to in American literature and has been a theme of many a Hollywood film. Former President

Clinton spoke of it as the 'dream that we were all raised on'. It was one based on a simple and powerful idea: that 'if you work hard and play by the rules you should be given a chance to go as far as your God-given ability will take you'. Americans are valued as individuals, according to what they make of their chances in life.

Adversity has also helped to bring them together. War and the threat of war often serve to bind a nation, and in World War II Americans of all types could recognise the service and patriotism of others from a different background. So too in September 2001 and thereafter, the terrorist attacks on the World Trade Center, which destroyed the well-known image of the Twin Towers on the New York skyline and killed nearly 4,000 people of diverse backgrounds, also had the effect of uniting New Yorkers and their fellow Americans. They were determined both to hunt down those who perpetrated the outrage and to show the world that the spirit of the city could not be crushed.

Finally, shared values, a common culture, the prevalence of the mass media and intermarriage serve to blur the differences between different groups, for we have seen that in the melting pot of modern America all national groups are to some extent assimilated into the mainstream of American life. They come to accept and embrace American values, and to share a common attachment to democratic ideals and processes.

Common values: the political culture of the United States

The term 'culture' refers to the way of life of a people, the sum of their inherited and cherished ideas, knowledge and values, which together constitute the shared bases of social action. **Political culture** is culture in its political aspect. It emphasises those patterns of thought and behaviour associated with politics in different societies, ones that are widely shared and define the relationship of citizens to their government and to each other in matters affecting politics and public affairs. Citizens of any country or major ethnic or religious community tend to have a common or core political culture, a set of long-term ideas and traditions that are passed on from one generation to the next. As Heywood[7] explains, 'political culture differs from public opinion in that it is fashioned out of long-term values rather than simply people's reactions to specific policies and problems'.

> **political culture**
> The widely shared underlying political beliefs and values which most citizens of a country share about the conduct of government and the relationship of citizens to those who rule over them and to one another.

Political culture in the United States derives from some of the ideas that inspired the pioneers who made the country and the **Founding Fathers** who wrote its constitution. It includes faith in democracy and representative government, the ideas of popular sovereignty, limited government,

> **Founding Fathers**
> The men who attended the Philadelphia Convention in May 1787 and devised the American Constitution.

the rule of law, equality, liberty, opportunity, support for the free market system, freedom of speech and individual rights. But of course at different stages in history, the existing political culture serves some individuals and groups better than others. Until the 1960s, the prevailing political culture suggested that women and ethnic minorities were not full members of the political community. Not surprisingly, these two groups sought to change the political culture. They wanted to see ideas of equality and opportunity applied to them as much as to other groups. Since then, there has been a 'rights culture', as activists have sought to demand the rights they regard as their due.

Political culture is not an unchanging landscape, a fixed background against which the political process operates. Attitudes evolve and change over time, for there are in society often a number of forces at work which serve to modify popular attitudes, among them migration and the emergence in a number of liberal democracies of a substantial underclass. Both can be a cause of greater diversity in popular attitudes, for immigrants and those alienated from majority lifestyles may have a looser attachment to prevailing cultural norms. In the words of one author,[8] 'culture moves'.

American political culture is tied up with **American exceptionalism**, the view that American society and culture are exceptional in comparison with those of other advanced industrial countries. In a sense this is true of all societies and cultures, and one might equally point out that there are several things that they have in common with each other. But supporters of this 'exceptionalist' viewpoint suggest that there are several features peculiar to US politics and society that distinguish the country from other Western democracies. A number of American politicians and writers have

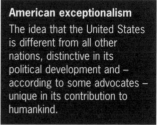

> **American exceptionalism**
> The idea that the United States is different from all other nations, distinctive in its political development and – according to some advocates – unique in its contribution to humankind.

reinforced this idea that theirs is a 'chosen people' that has made a special contribution to humankind and whose actions have been guided by a 'special providence'.[9] In his second inaugural speech in January 1997, Bill Clinton echoed such thinking, in his listing of his country's many achievements:

> What a century it has been. America became the world's mightiest industrial power, saved the world from tyranny in two world wars and a long cold war, and time and time again reached across the globe to millions who longed for the blessings of liberty. Along the way, Americans produced the great middle class and

security in old age; built unrivalled centres of learning and opened public schools to all; split the atom and explored the heavens; invented the computer and the microchip; made a revolution in civil rights for minorities; and extended the circle of citizenship, opportunity and dignity to women.

It was the Frenchman **Alexis de Tocqueville**[10] who first wrote of American exceptionalism, back in 1835. He saw the United States as 'a society uniquely different from the more traditional societies and status-bound nations of the Old World'. It was 'qualitively different in its organising principles and political and religious institutions from . . . other western societies', some of its

> **Alexis de Tocqueville (1805–59)**
>
> A liberal French aristocrat, writer and politician who visited the United States as a young man, was impressed and wrote *Democracy in America.*

distinguishing features being a relatively high level of social egalitarianism and social mobility, enthusiasm for religion, love of country, and ethnic and racial diversity.

One of its characteristics is a strong belief in **liberal individualism,** dating back to the ideas of the English political philosopher John Locke (1632–1704), who wrote of people's inalienable natural rights. By contrast, the culture of the Old World has emphasised ideas of hierarchy and nationality. What Hames and Rae[11] refer to as **messianism** is another characterisitc. Americans tend to see themselves as the 'Last, Best, Hope of Mankind', a theme apparent in foreign policy, where some

> **messianism**
>
> The belief in America's exceptional world role or mission. Some Americans see their country as long-awaited liberators of other territories.

Americans are isolationists who reject the rest of the world as beyond redemption, while others are idealists who want to save the world and make it better (i.e. adopt American values and goals).

Sometimes, the different values identified conflict with each other. If liberal individualism is one element of the American outlook, stressing as it does freedom from overbearing governmental interference, the Republican strand is another. As we see below, it is associated with the idea of political involvement by a concerned and interested citizenry, what Welch[12] describes as 'a marked tilt towards participation'. At times, the dislike of central government and fear of 'governmental encroachment' are more influential than the commitment to the ideal and practice of participation.

What are the key elements of American political culture?

Analyses of political culture are inevitably replete with generalisations that must be regarded with a degree of scepticism. There is and can be no definitive listing of shared political values and the ones suggested in any contribution often tend to overlap with each other. At times, they have been ignored or at least denied in regard to certain social groups. But none the less, we can point to a number of shared American interests and concerns. Among these are:

1 **Liberalism** – a recognition of the dignity and worth of the individual and a tendency to view politics in individualistic terms. Classical liberals believed in government by consent, limited government, the protection of private property and opportunity. They also stressed the importance of individual rights, some of which were regarded as 'inalienable'. Americans have great faith in the common sense of the average citizen and believe that all individuals have rights as well as responsibilities. Everyone should have the chance to fulfil their destiny, and no individual or group should be denied recognition of their worth or dignity. Individual liberties must be respected and their opportunities for economic advance unimpeded. By contrast, collectivist policies and solutions (those based on the idea that the state – on behalf of its citizens – should acknowledge society's collective responsibility to care about those in need) have never been embraced (see Chapter 8).

The word 'liberal' derives from the Latin *liber*, meaning 'free' or 'generous', implying qualities such as liberty and tolerance. The Americans have a strong attachment to liberty, as symbolised by the statue erected in its name. The War of Independence was fought in its name, and the Constitution, like the American Revolution, proclaims this commitment. The late Clinton Rossiter,[13] a renowned American political scientist, saw liberty as the pre-eminent value in the American political culture: 'We have always been a nation obsessed with liberty. Liberty over authority, freedom over responsibility, rights over duties – these are our historic preferences.'

2 **Equality** – the words in the Declaration of Independence are clear enough: 'We hold these truths to be self-evident, that all men are created equal.' As a relatively young nation, America lacks the feudal past that was a feature of many European countries. There has always been a strong belief in social equality, and although there are sharp inequalities of income and wealth, the divisions are not associated with a class system as they have been in Britain. The equality Americans favour is not equality of outcome, but rather of worth. They do not want a society in which all are reduced to the same level, for this would conflict with their belief in the opportunities they value in the American Dream. They do believe that every American is entitled to equal consideration, equal protection under the law and equal rights, even if at times there has been considerable reluctance to acknowledge that this applies to African Americans as well as to whites.

Equality is more about prospects of advancement than about result. No one should be limited by his or her social background, ethnicity, gender or religion. All should have the chance to climb the ladder of success and share in the American Dream, in a land of opportunity. Even those of humble origins can still rise to greatness, so that Bill Clinton, the lad from Hope in Arkansas, could reach the White House.

3 **Democracy** – a belief in government by the people, according to majority will. Today, this might be seen as similar to liberalism, with its emphasis on personal freedom and rights, but at the time of the writing of the American Constitution in 1787 there was far more support for liberalism (as set out in the writings of John Locke) than for democracy, seen as rule by majorities and mobs.

Liberalism and democracy have roots in an older classical republican tradition. This dates back to the days of ancient Rome and in particular to the writings of the Roman consul and writer Cicero. The speeches and writings of the Founding Fathers often employed republican imagery and symbols, and statues of George Washington have often shown him wearing Roman costume. The ancient Romans believed in the idea of a self-governing republic ultimately ruled by a knowledgeable and involved citizenry. In this sense, the term 'republic' refers to a form of government that derives its powers directly or indirectly from the people. In a representative democracy, Americans could select representatives to govern and lay down the rules by which society operates. For the Founding Fathers, 'republic' seemed preferable to 'democracy', with its overtones of demagogy and mass rule.

Such fears have long disappeared and there has, throughout much American history, been a strong consensus in support of democracy and the values that underpin it, including:
- **a deep interest in the exercise of power**, who has it, how it was acquired and how those who exercise it can be removed;
- **a general acceptance of majority rule**, but also respect for minority rights so that minorities can have the opportunity to become tomorrow's majority. Pluralism in society, involving the existence and acceptance of distinctive groups and political toleration, has been important as the country has become more ethnically and religiously diverse, and people have adopted new lifestyle arrangements;
- **a firm commitment to popular sovereignty**, the idea that ultimate power resides in the people themselves;
- **strong support for the rule of law**, with government being based upon a body of law applied equally and with just procedures. The principle of fairness applies, with all individuals entitled to the same rights and level of protection, and expected to abide by the same codes of behaviour. No one

is above the law, for, in the words of Chief Justice Marshall,[14] 'the government of the United States has been emphatically termed a government of laws, not of men';

- **a dislike and distrust of government and a fear of the tyrannical rule and exercise of excessive authority that can accompany it**, not surprising in a land whose pioneers tamed the wilderness, created new frontiers and tried to build themselves a better future. Americans have always had a wariness about those who exercise power over them – a distrust which has roots in Lockean liberalism, but was primarily based upon the experiences of the colonists in their dealings with King George III in the late eighteenth century. This suspicion of government and things associated with it may be a factor in the low turnouts in many elections.

  At the approach of the new millennium, the number of Americans who expressed 'confidence in Washington to do what is right' was 29%, down from 76% in 1964. Nearly two thirds claimed to feel 'distant and uncon-nected' with government. Many Americans are indifferent to what goes on in Washington. It seems remote from their experience and – many might add – the policies that emerge from the capital are often wasteful, ineffective and ill-judged. Such anti-government feeling is widely held, even if its intensity varies considerably. At the one end of the spectrum are moderates who are wary of overbearing Washingtonian attitudes and too much interference. At the other, there are strong devotees of states' rights who much resent the intrusion of central government and who wish to see far more decision-making conducted at state or local level.

- **a liking for politicians who seem to articulate the thoughts and feelings of the common man**. Populists who have railed against the special interests, the East Coast establishment or communists have often found a ready response. Anti-politicians à la **Ross Perot**, and those who blend religion and politics in the fashion of Jesse Jackson, have at times found themselves backed by a surge of popular enthusiasm.

> **Ross Perot**
> A billionaire Texan businessmen who had created and managed a highly successful computer firm and who in 1992 made known his interest in running for the presidency. In the November election, although he failed to win in any single state, he did very well, attracting some 19% of the popular vote. He stood again in 1996, as the candidate for the newly created Reform Party. This time, he made little impact.

Other features could be mentioned, such as love of God and of their country, eternal optimism and idealism. As we have seen, religion (see pp. 11–13) matters in American life in a way that it does not in most of Europe. The Declaration of Independence affirms that all men are 'endowed by their Creator' with certain rights, and ends with a recognition of the 'firm reliance on the protection of divine Providence' necessary to make the Declaration a success. Religious faith – the Christian faith – has been and remains all-important.

Intense admiration for and love of country is another American quality. Americans also tend to be very patriotic and to support emblems that help them to identify with their country. They acknowledge their Constitution, their anthem, their flag and other symbols of their nationhood. Morning in many schools begins with young Americans facing the flag and renewing their **Pledge of Allegiance**.

> **Pledge of Allegiance**
> 'I pledge allegiance to the flag of the United States and to the Republic for which it stands, one nation, under God indivisible, with liberty and justice for all.'

In particular, Americans respect the office of president, if not the behaviour of individual presidents. The figure in the White House operates as a focal point of their national loyalty and, especially in times of crisis, the president (always male so far, and referred to as such throughout this book) speaks up for the interests of all Americans. He and they possess the same vision. They want to build a better world for themselves and their families. They want a share in the American Dream. That Dream encompasses many of the values listed above – individualism, limited government, liberty and equal opportunities among them. It is in essence the belief that the United States is a land of opportunity for those prepared to work hard, get ahead and make a fortune. Americans are valued as individuals according to what they make of their chances in life.

Given the commitment to the American Dream and the ideas that underpin it, it is no surprise that **socialism** has never taken root in the United States. Indeed, for Seymour Lipset and Gary Marks,[15] its absence is a cornerstone of American exceptionalism. They point out that opinion polls in America continue to reveal a people whose attitudes are different to those of people in Europe and Canada. Americans do not favour an active role for government in the economy or a desire for large welfare programmes. They favour private efforts in business and welfare and rely more on philanthropic giving. The two writers point to the absence of those conditions that the left has always seen as a prerequisite for the development of any 'mass allegiance' to socialism, but draw attention to the diversity of explanations given for the failure of American socialism (see also pp. 249–51 for a more detailed analysis): 'Explanations for [socialism]'s weakness are as numerous as socialists were few. Some . . . attribute the weakness of socialism to the failures of socialist organisations and leaders. Another school ascribes socialism's bankruptcy to its incompati-

> **socialism**
> Socialists share a belief that unrestrained capitalism is responsible for a variety of social evils, including the exploitation of working people, the widespread existence of poverty and unemployment, gross inequality of wealth and the pursuit of greed and selfishness. Socialists would prefer to see a social system based on co-operative values and emphasise the values of community rather than of individualism. They also believe strongly in the need for a more equal and just society, based on brotherhood and a sense of social solidarity.

bility with America's core values, while still others cite the American Constitution as the decisive factor.'

In their analyses of the development of socialism, Karl Marx and Friedrich Engels (authors of the *Communist Manifesto*, 1848) contributed a Marxist perspective to the debate on the failure of American socialism. Marx had assumed that the working class was destined to organise revolutionary socialist parties in every capitalist society. He and Engels had, however, noted the respects in which the United States differed from European societies. Above all, it was a new nation and society, a democratic country lacking many of the institutions and traditions of previously feudal societies. It had a 'modern and purely bourgeois culture'. After Marx's death in 1883, Engels[16] gave more thought to the non-emergence of socialist movements on a mass scale. He attributed the 'backwardness' of the American workers to the absence of a feudal past. In his view, 'Americans [were] born conservatives – just because America is so purely bourgeois, so entirely without a feudal past and proud of its purely bourgeois organisation'.

CONCLUSION

The United States is a land of great diversity, even if there are factors that bind the nation together. Jews, Irish, Poles and many others have been part of successive waves of past immigration, leaving America as what Robert Singh[17] calls 'a kaleidoscopic mosaic of racial, ethnic, religious, regional and linguistic differences'. Some enthuse over the positive benefits of multiculturalism and multiethnicity, seeing it as an indication of vigour and energy. But diversity also creates special problems in a democracy, for it is associated with wide differences of opinion that can make it difficult to reach agreed solutions to political problems. Administering America presents a strong challenge to the governing institutions and those who run them. As de Tocqueville[18] observed more than 150 years ago: 'A confused clamour is heard on every side and a thousand simultaneous voices demand the immediate satisfaction of their social wants.'

De Tocqueville's words carry considerably more weight today. A distinguished historian and one-time adviser to President Kennedy, Arthur Schlesinger,[19] has written of 'the fragmentation of the national community into a quarrelsome spatter of enclaves, ghettos, tribes'. Others too fear fragmentation, the possibility of what alarmists refer to as a Balkanisation of the United States that could ultimately undermine the forces that pull it together.

REFERENCES

1 *The World Factbook*, CIA, 2004
2 US Census Bureau, March 2004 projection: other figures in the first half of the chapter are adapted from the official ones produced for the 2000 census, unless otherwise stated
3 W. Frey, Brookings Institute, as quoted in the *Guardian*, 19 March 2004
4 M. Davis, *Magical Urbanism: Latinos Reinvent the US City*, Verso, 2001
5 D. Barrett, *World Christian Encyclopaedia*, Oxford University Press, 2001
6 Pew Hispanic Centre, analysis of US census data, as quoted in the *Guardian*, 27 August 2004
7 A. Heywood, *Politics*, Macmillan, 1997
8 T. Rochon, *Culture Moves: Ideas, Activism and Changing Values*, Princeton University Press, 1998
9 W. Mead, *Special Providence: American Foreign Policy and How it Changed the World*, Knopf, 2001
10 A. de Tocqueville, *Democracy in America* vol. 2, reissued by Vintage, 1954
11 T. Hames and N. Rae, *Governing America*, Manchester University Press, 1996
12 S. Welch, 'Pressure Groups, Social Movements and Participation', in G. Peele, C. Bailey, B. Cain and B. Peters (eds), *Developments in American Politics 4*, Palgrave, 2002
13 C. Rossiter, *Conservatism in America*, Vintage, 1962
14 J. Marshall, judgement in *Marbury* v. *Madison*, 1803
15 S. Lipset and G. Marks, *Why Socialism Failed in the United states: It Didn't Happen Here*, Norton, 2000
16 F. Engels, letter quoted in 15 above
17 R. Singh, *American Government and Politics: A Concise Introduction*, Sage, 2003
18 A. de Tocqueville, as in 10 above
19 A. Schlesinger Jr, *The Disuniting of America: Reflections on a Multicultural Society*, Norton, 1992

USEFUL WEB SITES

www.americansc.org.uk The American Studies Resources Centre. A useful starting point for the discussion of all aspects of American government and politics, with links to many other sites.

www.census.gov Bureau of the Census. Statistics on the US and its citizens.

www.icpsr.umich.edu/GSS General Social Survey. Mass of polling evidence.

www.umich.edu/nes National Election Studies. More evidence from the polls.

The Constitution

2

Constitutions are important in all countries, for they set out the principles, rules and conventions according to which people should be governed. They normally outline the powers of the various parts of the governing body and the relationship that exists between them. Almost always, as in the case of the United States, they are written documents. Usually, they contain a declaration of rights, providing for civil and political liberties. However, the mere existence of a constitution and some written statement of freedoms is no guarantee that these will be respected.

In this chapter, we examine the drafting of the Constitution; its nature and contents; and the process by which it can be amended. We can then attempt some assessment.

POINTS TO CONSIDER

➤ How did the Articles of Confederation and the 1787 Constitution differ from each other?

➤ What are the main characteristics of the American Constitution?

➤ What is meant by the theory of a separation of powers and the notion of checks and balances?

➤ What role did the idea of a Bill of Rights play in discussions on the new Constitution?

➤ How easy is it to amend the American Constitution?

➤ How effectively has the US Constitution adapted to changing circumstances?

➤ Why do Americans attach such importance to their Constitution?

➤ What issues of constitutional reform have been debated in recent years and why has the cause of constitutional reform not aroused greater enthusiasm?

➤ What are the similarities and differences in the constitutions of Britain and the United States?

THE CONSTITUTION IN THEORY

In drafting the Declaration of Independence (1776), Thomas Jefferson helped produce a classic justification for breaking the British connection. To Jefferson and those around him, the only legitimate basis for government was the consent of the governed, a revolutionary sentiment at the time and an ingredient missing from the relationship between Britain and the colonists:

> We hold these truths to be self-evident, that all men are created equal, that they are endowed by their Creator with certain unalienable Rights, that among these are Life, Liberty and the Pursuit of Happiness. – That to secure these rights, Governments are instituted among Men, deriving their just powers from the Consent of the Governed, – That whenever any Form of Government becomes destructive of these ends, it is the Right of the People to alter or to abolish it, and to institute new Government.

The colonies – or the United States as they called themselves – drafted a compact that bound them together as a nation whilst hostilities were still raging. This agreement was known as the Articles of **Confederation** and Perpetual Union. It was adopted by a Congress of the States in 1777, and signed in July 1778. Not until March 1781 did these Articles become binding, when Maryland finally ratified them.

Confederation
A political system in which there is a loose alliance of self-governing states, with a weak central government to bind them together.

The Articles provided for a loose association, and established a confederal government that had only modest powers. On many key issues – including defence, finance and trade – it was at the mercy of decisions made by the state legislatures. This proved to be unsatisfactory, and George Washington recognised the weakness of the union that hung by only 'a rope of sand'. The new nation was near to chaos, for it lacked political and economic strength. The Confederation was inadequate for the task of governing such a diverse area, and there was no stability in the arrangements which had been agreed.

In particular, Congress, the main institution in the Confederation, had insufficient power to fulfil its duty, 'the management of the general interest of the United States', for it was too beholden to the thirteen colonies and lacked any means of enforcing its views. It was especially difficult for Congress to gain acceptance for a common foreign policy, for any agreements made might not be enforced by other states. Disillusionment with the existing governing arrangements was rife. This was the background to the drawing up of the American Constitution.

The Philadelphia Convention, 1787

In 1787, the legislative body of the Republic, the Continental Congress, put out a call to all the states inviting them to send delegates to Philadelphia on 25 May 1787. The meeting was to be held in Independence Hall, where the Declaration of Independence had been adopted eleven years earlier. The delegates met to consider 'the situation of the United States, to devise such further Provisions as shall appear to them necessary to render the Constitution of the federal Government adequate to the emergency of the Union'. They were authorised to amend the Articles, but in the event they cast them aside and proceeded to draw up a charter for a more centralised form of government. It was this Constitution that was completed on 17 September 1787, and formally adopted on 4 March 1789.

Inevitably, there were disappointments with the outcome of the deliberations, and some delegates departed before the signing ceremony (of the thirty-nine who did sign, few were completely satisfied with what had been accomplished). The settlement had to be a compromise, given the obvious differences between large and small states, and between those who wanted and those who baulked at an extension of federal power. Benjamin Franklin articulated the viewpoint of those who had doubts but still gave their acquiescence: 'There are several parts of this Constitution which I do not at present approve, but I am not sure I shall never approve them.' Acceptance was justified because 'I expect no better and because I am not sure that it is not the best.'

It was in theory desirable for every state to ratify (give formal approval to) the new document, but the convention delegates realised that this would be difficult to achieve quickly. They boldly declared that the proposed Constitution should become effective when nine had given their approval. Delaware was the first to sign, followed by Pennsylvania and New Jersey, and then by Georgia and Connecticut, where comfortable majorities were achieved. There was a fiercely contested struggle in Massachusetts over the absence of any Bill of Rights, but in early 1788 it too narrowly endorsed the document. In June 1788, the ratification by Maryland, New Hampshire and South Carolina meant that nine states had given their support, enough to see the document accepted.

The nature of the Constitution

The US Constitution is written and explicit. The document is relatively short and straightforward. It sets out the basic structure and functions of the various branches of government – executive, legislative and judicial – and the relationship between them. The Constitution is designated as the 'supreme law of the land', and this was taken to mean that in any conflict with state constitutions or state laws, the federal Constitution and federal laws take precedence. Over the succeeding two centuries and more, decisions by the Supreme Court have confirmed and reinforced this idea of constitutional supremacy.

The Constitution is the framework against which all political activity occurs, and laid down within it are the answers to key questions of governmental organisation. It explains the method of election for the federal executive and legislature, and the system of appointment to federal offices (including the Supreme Court). It itemises the powers of the central government, and denies certain powers to the states while giving them others. It provides certain civil, legal and political rights for the citizens that may not be taken away. It sets out the procedure for its own amendment.

The Constitution sets out the general political ideas, but its first three articles describe the three branches of the national government: legislative, executive and judicial, each with its own duties and responsibilities. The powers of the president are outlined, as are the topics on which the legislative branch can make laws, and as is the structure of the federal courts. Since its introduction, the Constitution has changed in a number of respects, but its underlying principles remain unaltered. These are:

- The three branches of government are separate and distinct, and the powers given to each of them are carefully balanced by the powers granted to the other two. Each branch therefore acts as a check upon the potential excesses of the other (see 'The separation of powers', p. 28–9).
- The Constitution, and the laws passed under its provisions, and any treaties entered into by the president which have the approval of the Senate, take precedence over all other laws, executive acts and regulations.
- All free men are equal before the law and are equally entitled to its protection (but not slaves and women, until the passage of the Fourteenth Amendment). Similarly, all states are equal, none being entitled to special treatment from the federal government.
- Each state must acknowledge the laws passed by other states.
- State government must be republican in form, with final authority resting in the hands of the people.
- The people must have the right to change their form of government by legal means defined in the Constitution itself.

The Founding Fathers who devised the Constitution had several clear-cut objectives in mind, and these were set down in the fifty-two–word preamble to the principal document. They may be summarised as:
- 'to form a more perfect Union';
- 'to establish justice';

- 'to insure domestic tranquillity';
- 'to provide for the common defence';
- 'to promote the general welfare';
- 'to secure the blessings of liberty to ourselves and our posterity'.

CHECKING POWER: CHECKS AND BALANCES IN THE AMERICAN SYSTEM

The federal system

The framers of the Constitution wanted a stronger and more effective national government than they had experienced previously. But they were aware of the dangers of excessive central control. They needed to balance the efficiency and good order that might come from central control against the liberties of the subject, which might be threatened by an all-powerful administration in Washington, DC. The answer was to establish a federal system, in which certain powers would be allotted to the national government and others reserved for the individual states. (See Chapter 3 for a full discussion of federalism in theory and practice.)

The separation of powers

All political systems need to have machinery to perform three basic tasks, which are the three arms of government – the executive, to make decisions and put laws into effect; the legislature, to create and pass laws; and the judiciary, to adjudicate in cases of dispute or to determine whether the law has been broken.

Montesquieu (1689–1755), the French philosopher who wrote *L'Esprit des lois*, argued that each arm needs to be separate, so that no one person can take control of all three functions of government. His influence is to be found in the work of the Founding Fathers, who drew up the US Constitution, for they instituted a number of checks and balances to prevent any danger of a powerful individual or group from dominating the whole structure by concentrating power in too few hands. In the forty-seventh essay in the collection published as *Federalist Papers*, James Madison (later to become the fourth president) quotes Montesquieu to that effect: 'There can be no liberty where the legislative and executive powers are united in the same person or body of magistrates, or if the power of judging be not separated from the legislative and executive powers.'

Some writers have questioned the appropriateness of the term 'separation of powers' in the case of the American Constitution. Richard Neustadt[1] pointed out that in the USA it is the institutions that are separate, rather than the powers. In his view, rather than having created a government of 'separated powers', the Founding Fathers created a system of 'separated institutions sharing powers'. The distinction is a valid one, for what they did was to devise a system in which each of the three branches of government can act as a brake on and balance to the others. In the case of the president and the two houses of Congress,

Amending the Constitution

The framers of the Constitution recognised the need to make provision for amendment of the document, should this become necessary. As the nation developed and circumstances altered, change would become necessary, but it must not be so easy that it opened up the possibility of ill-conceived changes,

a further check is introduced by virtue of the fact that each of them serves for different terms of office and are elected by different constituencies. In the words of Alan Grant: 'Negativity is the chief characteristic of the separation of powers doctrine as it is concerned with producing limitations and constraints on government rather than looking at the positive use to be made of such authority.'[2]

Having separated the three branches of government, the delegates of the Philadelphia Convention allowed a certain amount of participation in, and checking of, the activities of one branch by the others. Thus, key presidential appointments have to be confirmed by a majority of the Senate, all legislation the president wishes to see enacted has to pass through Congress, and the Supreme Court can declare the president's actions and policies (and those of Congress) to be 'unconstitutional' (though this last idea was not made explicit in the Constitution). The president has the opportunity to reshape the Supreme Court by making nominations in the event of vacancies, and can veto bills passed by Congress that are considered to be unnecessary or undesirable.

Other checks and balances

As we have seen, many checks and balances are written into the Constitution – although some have developed subsequently. Two examples of more recent checks are:

1 Political parties

The president and members of Congress belong to political parties, and therefore there are bonds between those who share the same affiliation. This may help the president pass his or her legislative programme through Congress, for if Congress has a majority of members who share the president's political allegiance then there are likely to be common legislative goals.

2 Congressional committees

Although neither the president nor the cabinet secretaries may belong to Congress, executive branch officers may be questioned in committee about their work and responsibilities. Like parties, committees do not feature in the American Constitution.

Over the years, the system of checks and balances can be seen to have been effective in several ways: presidents have vetoed more than 2,500 acts of Congress; Congress has overridden more than 100 of these; the Supreme Court has ruled more than forty federal laws 'unconstitutional'; the House has impeached several federal officials; and the Senate has refused to confirm several nominations.

or so unduly difficult that any proposal could be blocked by a minority of the nation. The answer was a dual process. Congress was given the right to initiate an amendment, by a two-thirds majority vote in each chamber; or the legislatures of two thirds of the states could request Congress to summon a national convention to discuss and draft amendments, a method never yet employed. Whichever procedure was adopted, there must be approval from three quarters of the states before any amendment entered into force.

This was the direct procedure for amending the constitution. It can also be changed by judicial interpretation, for in a landmark ruling, *Marbury v Madison* (1803), the Supreme Court established the doctrine of judicial review, which is the power of the Court to interpret acts of Congress and decide on their constitutionality or otherwise. This doctrine enables the Court to offer its verdict on the meaning of various sections of the Constitution as they apply in changing economic, social and political circumstances, over a period of time. In other words, without any substantive changes in the Constitution itself, the thrust of constitutional law can be changed.

In the same way, congressional legislation can also broaden and change the scope of the Constitution, as also can the rules and regulations of the various agencies of the federal government. Everything depends upon whether such legislation and rules conform to the intentions of those who devised the Constitution.

More than 5,000 amendments have been suggested, but only thirty-three have been submitted to the states. Twenty-seven alterations to the Constitution have been made so far, and it is likely that there will be further revisions in the future. Most of these changes were made in the very early period after it was adopted: the first ten were made in the first two years.

Subsequent amendments have covered a wider range of topics, among them the method of electing the president, the outlawing of slavery, the right of Congress to levy income tax, and the direct election of US senators. Most recently:
- **The Twenty-Fifth Amendment (1967)** provided for filling the office of vice-president when it becomes vacant in mid-term. The president must make a nomination which then requires majority approval in both chambers. (The procedure was to be used shortly afterwards, in 1973, when President Nixon required a new vice-president on the resignation of Spiro T. Agnew, and again the following year when, on the elevation of that vice-president – Ford – to the presidency, a new second-in-command was needed.)
- **The Twenty-Sixth Amendment (1971)** lowered the voting age to 18.
- **The Twenty-Seventh Amendment (1992)** concerned congressional salaries; no pay rise under consideration can come about until an election has intervened.

This amendment emerged in an unusual manner. A student at Texas University was working on a paper dealing with the proposed Equal Rights Amendment, and came across an amendment which was suggested as part of the original Bill of Rights. Six of the original thirteen states had ratified it, and later on another three had done so. The student launched a ratification movement, and found six more states that were willing to do so. Anti-Congress sentiment increased in the late 1980s and early 1990s, and in this atmosphere the movement for ratification gained ground, and finally – in May 1992 – Michigan became the thirty-eighth state to give its approval. This showed that even when two hundred years had elapsed it was still possible for a proposed amendment to be put into effect.

Overall, amendment of the Constitution has been rare. Relatively few amendments have been introduced and ratified. The thirteen proposals initiated in the house during the first six years of Republican control of Congress from January 1995 all failed to achieve the necessary majorities in the Senate, only two (flag desecration and the balanced budget) having passed the lower chamber with the necessary majority. Even these issues tended to be ones of broader national policy, albeit with constitutional implications, rather than straightforward issues directly affecting some aspect of institutional arrangements. Term limits do fall into this category, but despite being a high-profile part of the Republican 'Contract for America' programme in the November 1994 election, they have failed to materialise.

Why has so little constitutional change come about?

One answer is that in comparison with peoples of other nations, Americans have been broadly contented with that which the Founding Fathers devised. Many regard their constitution with considerable awe and reverence, their deference emerging in poll findings and other expressions of popular opinion. These indicate that Americans are both familiar and content with their constitutional arrangements. Indeed, according to US historian Theodore White,[3] the nation is more united by its commonly accepted ideas about government as embodied in the Constitution than it is by geography.

On becoming president in 1974, Gerald Ford observed that 'our constitution works'. He was speaking in the aftermath of the **Watergate crisis**, which led to the downfall and ultimate resignation of President Nixon. Nixon was judged to

Watergate crisis
The collective name for a series of abuses that began with a break-in at the Democratic national headquarters in the Watergate building, Washington, DC, but later involved revelations of many other acts of wrong-doing, ranging from wire-tapping to 'misleading testimony'. As the episode unfolded, it became evident that President Nixon was personally involved. This led to his becoming the first and only president to resign in disgrace.

have been involved with a cover-up and various illegal operations, and thereby to have abused his position. As the Americans firmly believe in the idea that 'we have a government of laws, not of men', Ford and many other Americans saw his removal as a vindication of their constitution. It had served to protect freedom, restrain the behaviour of those in high office and define the limits of executive power.

Given such widespread approval of the form of government, it is not surprising that America has not shown the same interest in constitutional reform that has characterised other nations. Very few people publicly advocate radical changes in the structure of government established in 1787. Those who would tamper with it have to make a strong case for change and tend to talk in terms of restoring it to its original glory rather than making fundamental alterations.

Other than a broad measure of popular satisfaction with the Constitution, there are other factors that help to explain the fact that the original document has survived more or less intact:

- The most obvious is the relative difficulty of achieving change. The fate of the Equal Rights Amendment shows that the hurdles created more than two hundred years ago are difficult to surmount. In the two attempts to outlaw flag desecration in the Senate, it was possible to muster sixty-two and sixty-three votes in favour, in 1995 and 2000 respectively. This was an impressive figure, but still five and four votes short of what was needed. Even if the Senate had passed the measure, then the hurdle of getting thirty-eight states to ratify the change would have been a hard one to get over.
- The very lack of clarity in the wording of the Constitution means that the vague phrases can be interpreted over time in accordance with the needs of the day. The language is retained, but the values mean different things in different eras. Congress is allowed to 'provide for the common defence and general welfare of the United States', a broad remit that enables the document to adapt to changing circumstances, without formal amendment to its language.
- In particular, the ability of the Supreme Court to make 'interpretative amendments' means that the Constitution is kept up to date. When the Bill of Rights (the first ten amendments to the Constitution) was introduced, it applied only to the national government. But over time, its provisions were extended by court judgements to the states. Phrases such as 'due process' and the 'equal protection of the law' have been instrumental in allowing this adaptation to changing circumstances.

Assessment of the Constitution

Without flexibility of the type we have seen, it is unlikely that the arrangements made more than two hundred years ago would have survived in a country that has changed dramatically. The diversity of the nation has increased, the country has spread westward across the entire continent, a stream of migrants has been absorbed, the population has soared, new resources have been exploited and all sorts of differing interests have developed, be they those of the east-coast ship owners who favoured free trade, the midwest manufacturers who wanted protection for their goods from foreign competition, farmers who wanted low freight charges or railroad operators who wanted high ones: Texas ranchers and Oregon lumbermen all have their own priorities and concerns. Yet the essential unity of the nation has grown stronger. That this has happened is in no small part because of the success of the working arrangements drawn up in 1787, which had enough built-in flexibility to cater for changing circumstances.

Americans pride themselves on having the world's oldest written constitution, and many still marvel at the wisdom of the Founding Fathers in devising a document that has stood the test of time and been capable of adaptation to changing conditions and circumstances. An American writer[4] has captured some of the appeal that it has for many Americans:

> Along with the flag, the Constitution stands alone as a symbol of national unity. America has no royal family, no heritage of timeless and integrative state institutions or symbols, no national church. Add to that America's history of being peopled by diverse religious, national and racial stocks, many of whom came long after the founding, and one can see how the Constitution could become such a focus of national identity and loyalty. There is precious little else to compete with it as an integrative symbol and evocation of America . . . Unlike the flag . . . which has changed dramatically over the years, with the constantly expanding number of states, the Constitution has endured virtually unchanged . . . This is, surely, another important source of its status as the focus of American identity, its stability and unchanging quality.

Disadvantages and advantages of the Constitution

Not all writers have supported the various provisions of the Constitution. It has been found deficient by some critics, who have been exasperated by the diffusion of power that was basic to its operation. The young Woodrow Wilson, then a professor of government but a future president, wrote his analysis, *Congressional Government*, in 1890, and therefore before the extension of federal and presidential power occurred in the 1930s. He argued that the American arrangements made it difficult to achieve coherence in policy-making or responsible government. In his view, there were too many people involved in the evolution of policy and there was too little likelihood of progress being achieved.

Wilson lamented the absence of strong parties. He particularly disliked the low quality of Congressional debate, which – largely because of party discipline – in his view lacked coherence. Too much discussion took place in obscure committees, headed by entrenched and autocratic senior members, a point not effectively addressed until the 1970s. He much preferred the British system of government, with its clear allocation of power and responsibility.

A common point of criticism is the failure of the Constitution to permit quick and decisive action, except in times of crisis. One can understand why an American president might envy a British prime minister, whose ability to achieve his or her programme within a parliamentary session is so much greater. But this was how

The Constitution in Britain and the United States: a comparison

Most constitutions are written down and embodied in a formal document. Britain does not have such a statement describing the framework and functions of the organs of government and declaring the principles governing the operation of such institutions. Yet it obviously has institutions and rules determining their creation and operation, and the British Constitution consists of these – found as they are in a variety of sources, mostly written down somewhere. It is more accurate to speak of Britain not having a codified constitution in which all the main provisions are brought together in a single authoritative document.

Written constitutions are normally produced following a period of internal dissension and upheaval, as in the US after the War of Independence. The US has the oldest written constitution in the world, but Britain has the oldest constitution of any kind. Britain has been relatively free from internal turmoil and has not been successfully invaded since 1066. It has not been found necessary to create a constitutional document to signify a break with the past and a wish to chart a new course. Britain has a remarkably long and unbroken constitutional history.

There are advantages in having a written constitution, notably:
- it provides a clear statement of the position on what is and what is not constitutional;
- it has an educational value, helping to curb the behaviour of those in government office;
- it is easier for the courts to interpret what is constitutional behaviour where a document lays down clear limitations on institutions and individuals;
- a written constitution is difficult to amend or tamper with, because the procedure for so doing is normally difficult.

Many Americans are thought to be much clearer about their constitutional position than people in Britain. Children in the US are brought up to revere the work of the Founding Fathers, and as they grow up they have a clear idea of how their system of government works. Their Constitution is easily available, and being short (seven articles, ten pages) it is readily accessible. The British lack this simplicity and ease of access. Anyone asked to

the Founding Fathers wanted it. They were not looking for speedy action. They preferred to create machinery that would function at a slower pace, once all interests had had a chance to expound their viewpoints and to influence the outcome of the debate on any issue. This is what characterises the American approach: the fact that particular groups can frustrate the pace of advance where they think that change would damage their interests.

Writing a few years before Wilsons, the British Liberal statesman William Gladstone, saw things differently. He described the American Constitution 'as the most wonderful work ever struck off at a given time by the brain and purpose of man'.[5] For all of its alleged defects, many writers and commen-

find the British Constitution would be hard-pressed knowing where to look for it. Yet there are disadvantages in having a written, codified constitution:

* Constitutions do not necessarily provide a clear protection for people's rights. American experience proves this, for the original document recognised slavery, and while the 15th Amendment passed in 1870 provides that: 'The right of citizens to vote shall not be denied or abridged by the US or by any states on account of race, colour or previous condition of servitude . . . Congress shall have the power to enforce this by appropriate legislation', yet in many states blacks were excluded on grounds of illiteracy from exercising their democratic right to vote until the 1960s.
* Constitutions can be inflexible and rigid, incapable of being easily adapted to the needs of the day. Whereas the British Constitution is adaptable and has evolved according to circumstances, a formal document can be difficult to amend, and therefore may act as a barrier to much-needed social change. Several US presidents have been attracted to the idea of gun control as a means of combating crime, but they have run into fierce opposition from the National Rifle Association (see p. 278), which reminds people of the statement in Article 2 of the Bill of Rights (see p. 37). The Supreme Court was similarly able to restrict some of the New Deal on the grounds that it was a breach of the Constitution, restricting states' rights and giving too much power to the president.
* Constitutions can be hard to change. In America, the fate of the Equal Rights Amendment (see pp. 320–1) illustrates the difficulty in gaining adequate support.

In Britain, there was until recently no widespread demand for or interest in devising a written constitution, although there are now some groups such as Charter 88 that campaign for one. The present constitution seems to work generally well, having survived several hundred years and provided the British people with a stable history and protection for their freedoms. However, to a greater extent than in the United States, there has been support for a number of constitutional reforms. The Blair government came to power in 1997, committed to action in several areas. As a result, measures ranging from the introduction of the Scottish Parliament, the Human Rights Act and the Freedom of Information Act have been passed, as part of a substantial package of constitutional changes.

tators might still agree with him over a century later. The Constitution has now survived for over two hundred years, and proved its durability over years of extensive and often rapid economic and social change. It may have been amended twenty-seven times but, after all, ten of these modifications were made at the beginning of its existence, and in any case the amendments and their subject matter suggest that there has been no fundamental alteration in its character.

In other words, the Constitution remains much as it was originally written. The whole **New Deal** was carried through with no attempt to amend the Constitution, and leaders who wish to innovate use the wording of the Constitution rather than seek to get it changed. Political fashion and practices have made the system viable in the twenty-first century, and presidents now rely on the Supreme Court to interpret their actions favourably.

> **New Deal**
> The programme introduced by President Frankliin D. Roosevelt in the 1930s to combat the depressed condition of the US. Several 'alphabet laws' (named after their initials) were passed to achieve the '3Rs' of relief, recovery and reform. The package greatly extended the role and authority of the federal government.

It may well be that if the framers of the Constitution were alive today, they would be surprised at the way in which its practical operation has evolved, for it has provided the political framework for a society immeasurably different from the one they knew. For instance:

- The Founding Fathers had fears about democracy and felt that the principle needed to be controlled, but subsequently the American system has become markedly more democratic. Politicians quickly saw merit in accepting the guidance of the electorate, and the importance of the popular will has become much greater than was ever intended.
- The balance of power has tipped in favour of the federal government at the expense of the states, most evidently since 1933 when President Roosevelt began his New Deal programme to lift the country out of serious economic depression.
- The presidency has become more powerful, and although it was envisaged as being remote and above the political fray it has in fact become the most identifiable institution and an essential part of the political battleground. However rigid a written constitution may appear to be, in the American case it is as flexible as most citizens wish it to be.

What has remained, as the Fathers envisaged, is the built-in conflict between the various institutions. They wanted no part of the machinery to acquire excessive power at the expense of the others, and created a system in which it was difficult to get all parts moving in the same direction and at the same speed. They were happy at the prospect of disputation between the federal government and the states, and between the institutions of the federal government. In this, their wishes have remained intact.

THE CONSTITUTION IN ACTION: THE PROTECTION OFFERED BY THE BILL OF RIGHTS

Much of the early opposition to the Constitution itself was not centred on resistance to increased federal power at the expense of the states, but more on anxiety that the rights of individuals were insufficiently protected. There was widespread agreement that a set of constitutional amendments must be drafted to provide specific guarantees of individual rights, although this would not happen until after a government under the new Constitution had been established.

THE BILL OF RIGHTS

The first ten amendments to the Constitution were added as a block by the Congress in September 1789, and ratified by eleven states by the end of 1791.

The first ten amendments to the Constitution and their purpose

Protections afforded fundamental rights and freedoms
• Amendment 1: Freedom of religion, speech, press and assembly; the right to petition the government.

Protections against arbitrary military action
• Amendment 2: The right to bear arms and maintain state militias (National Guard).
• Amendment 3: Troops may not be quartered in homes in peacetime.

Protection against arbitrary police and court action
• Amendment 4: There can be no unreasonable searches or seizures.
• Amendment 5: Grand Jury indictment is required to prosecute a person for a serious crime. No 'double jeopardy' – a person cannot be tried twice for the same offence. It is prohibited to force a person to testify against himself or herself. There can be no loss of life, liberty or property without due process.
• Amendment 6: The right to speedy, public, impartial trial with defence counsel, and the right to cross-examine witnesses.
• Amendment 7: Jury trials in civil suits where the value exceeds 20 dollars.
• Amendment 8: No excessive bail or fines; no cruel and unusual punishments.

Protections of states' rights and unnamed rights of the people
• Amendment 9: Unlisted rights are not necessarily denied.
• Amendment 10: Powers not delegated to the United States or denied to states are reserved for the states or for the people.

The Bill of Rights was ratified in 1791, but its application was broadened significantly by the Fourteenth Amendment to the Constitution, which was ratified in 1868. A key phrase in the Fourteenth Amendment – 'nor shall any state deprive any person of life, liberty, or property, without due process of law' – has been interpreted by the Supreme Court as prohibiting the states from violating most of the rights and freedoms protected by the Bill of Rights.

The contents of the Bill of Rights

James Madison did much of the drafting of the ten amendments. He was unconvinced about the adequacy of the existing protection and wanted to see clear constitutional guarantees of the liberties of the people. Those that he laid down in 1791 included a list of civil, religious and legal rights that remain intact today, in the same form in which they were originally set out. The first four set out individual rights, the next four deal with the system of justice, and the last two are broader statements of constitutional intention.

The new document applied to the federal government only, for many Americans were unworried about possible tyranny in their own states. It was the central government of which they were suspicious, although this fear has proved largely unfounded and many infringements of liberty have occurred at state and local level.

The Fourteenth Amendment, adopted in 1868, includes a 'due process' clause, and this does apply to the states. Since it lays down that no person can be deprived of life, liberty and property without the due process of law, this was seen as meaning that states were bound by the Bill of Rights in the same way as the national government was. For many years, the Supreme Court did not so rule, but in 1925, in a landmark judgement in *Gitlow* v. *New York*, it was decided that:

> For present purposes, we may and do assume that freedom of speech and of the press – which are protected by the First Amendment from abridgement by Congress – are among the fundamental personal rights and liberties protected by the due process clause of the Fourteenth Amendment from impairment by the States.

The ruling was of profound importance, and once it had been accepted that freedom of speech and of the press were protected at state and local level by the First Amendment, so it was inevitable that other provisions of that same Amendment would be enforceable in the same way. Those rights laid down in 1791 – including rights of religion, assembly and petition – are now applicable to all levels of government.

Although the First Amendment has been accepted as binding, this is not true of all of the other nine. A minority on the Supreme Court wished to proceed from the 1925 decision to make all freedoms protected by the Bill of Rights binding on the states. In other words, this would mean that the Bill of Rights would be incorporated fully into the Fourteenth Amendment.

This has not been the predominant opinion. The majority has taken the view that some provisions of the Bill of Rights should be included, in other words selective incorporation. Gradually the number of those original amendments that have come within the scope of the Fourteenth Amendment has been extended. Today, only the Second, Third, Seventh and Tenth do not apply at state and local level – along with the Grand Jury requirements of the Fifth. Other liberties not in the Bill of Rights also receive protection today – among them the right of association, the right of privacy, the right to be presumed innocent and the right to travel freely.

Once much of the Bill of Rights was interpreted as being applicable at all levels, judges in state courts began to place more emphasis upon its provisions than upon those set out in state constitutions. More recently, however, there has been a more conservative leaning among the Supreme Court justices, and this has led to a greater interest in the protection offered by state guarantees. Justice Brennan became concerned about the way in which the Court was narrowly interpreting the scope of the Bill of Rights. Back in 1977 he urged judges in state supreme courts to take up the challenge, noting that: 'State constitutions . . . are a font of individual liberties, their protection often extending beyond those required by the Supreme Court's interpretation of federal law.'[6]

CONCLUSION

The American Constitution is based upon key, underlying principles, notably:
- separation of powers, and checks and balances;
- limited government;
- judicial review;
- federalism (of which more in the next chapter).

These principles remain intact, but as a result of formal amendments, judicial interpretation and legislation, the Constitution has been much modified. The changes made have enabled it to endure and retain acceptance, in a country whose circumstances are differ substantially from those of the late eighteenth century.

Documents depend upon their implementation and interpretation. At different times, the US Constitution has been differently applied. Sometimes its provisions have been ignored, much to the detriment of minority groups for whom the Bill of Rights has proved to be an inadequate form of protection.

NB For full information on the protection offered in the area of civil liberties and rights, see Chapter 11.

REFERENCES

1 R. Neustadt, *Presidential Power: The Politics of Leadership*, Wiley & Sons, 1960
2 A. Grant, *The American Political Process*, Dartmouth, 1994
3 T. White, 'The American Idea', *New York Times Magazine*, June 1986
4 I. Kramnick, 'Editor's Introduction' to J. Madison, A. Hamilton and J. Jay, *The Federalist Papers*, Penguin, 1987
5 J. Brooke and M. Soresen (eds), *The Prime Minister's Papers: W. E. Gladstone*, HMSO, 1971
6 W. Brennan, 'Constitutional Adjudication and the Death Penalty', *Harvard Law Review* 100:2, 1977

USEFUL WEB SITES

www.nara.gov/education/cc/main.html National Archives Classroom web site. Many key historical documents on American government can be found here, notably the Declaration of Independence, the Constitution, etc.

www.access.gpo.gov/congress/senate/constitution/toc.html Congressional Research Service, Library of Congress. Online copy of the Constitution, annotated with commentary and relevant Supreme Court cases, etc.

www.constitutioncenter.org National Constitution Center. A useful starting point for study of the Constitution.

www.americanstrategy.org/foundations.html An introduction to American constitutional history.

www.lcweb2.loc.gov/const/fed/fedpapers The *Federalist Papers*, originally published 1788.

SAMPLE QUESTIONS

1 Has the American Constitution been an aid or an obstacle to good government?

2 Do the checks and balances written into the American Constitution still work today?

3 Should the American Constitution be rewritten?

4 Does the written constitution of the United States make the country harder to govern than Britain?

5 Discuss the view that the main difference between the US and UK constitution is that one is flexible and the other is not.

Federalism in theory and practice 3

Even the most authoritarian government would find it difficult to take all decisions at the centre. It would be impractical for any set of ministers to understand the needs of every area and to involve themselves in the minutiae of its public administration. Hence the need to allow some scope for regional or local initiative.

The Founding Fathers well understood that the structure and character of the governmental system that they were creating for the United States would shape the path of the country's development. It was important for them to strike the right balance between nationalism and states' rights. Since the Philadelphia Convention, that balance has changed and developed, and the emphasis on Washington, DC, has markedly increased. Yet in recent decades, there has been a movement to return power to the states, a tendency broadly encouraged by presidents from Reagan to Clinton.

POINTS TO CONSIDER

➤ Why did the US move away from its original system of 'dual federalism'?

➤ To what extent was there a conservative backlash against the growing power of Washington in public affairs in the 1970s and 1980s?

➤ Why has there been a resurgence of the states since the early 1980s?

➤ What label would you give to American federalism today?

➤ Have the dangers and complexities of the modern world made it inevitable that national rather than regional or local government is the main focus of power in any political system?

➤ What are the benefits of American federalism?

➤ Is local/state government better than national government because it is closer to the people?

➤ What are the differences between federalism and devolution? Is Britain experiencing 'creeping federalism'?

The system of government devised by the Founding Fathers at the Philadelphia Convention (1787) resulted from the compromises necessary to reconcile conflicting political and economic interests. Federalism was seen as a 'halfway house' between the concept of a centralised unitary state, which was unacceptable to thirteen states jealous of their independence, and the idea of a confederation, which would have been a weak association of autonomous states.

As Alan Grant has written:[1] 'It arose out of a desire to bolster national unity whilst ... accommodating regional diversity.' The Constitution does not mention the words 'federalism' or 'federation', but the United States has always been recognised as a major example of this compromise form of unity. Other nations later adopted the federal principle, which Zimmerman[2] describes as 'a government system in which constitutional authority is divided between a central and state or provincial governments'. Wheare[3] wrote more elaborately of federalism as 'the method of dividing powers so that the general and regional governments are each, within a sphere, coordinate and independent'.

In other words, powers are divided between a general (that is, a national or federal) government, which in certain matters is independent of the governments of the associated states, and state governments, which are in certain matters independent of the general governments. Every American citizen is therefore subject to two governments that act directly upon the people; the system was not designed as a pyramid structure with the federal government

---

The division of power in American federalism: some examples

Delegated powers (powers delegated to federal government)
- Declare war
- Make treaties
- Coin money
- Regulate interstate and foreign commerce

Concurrent powers (powers shared by the federal and state governments)
- Levy taxes
- Shape public health
- Regulate auto safety
- Control drugs

Reserved powers (powers reserved for state governments)
- Draw electoral districts
- Regulate intra-state commerce
- Create local units
- Determine police powers

at the apex, the states below it and then local government at the bottom. The Constitution lays down the binding division of power. In constitutional terms, the federal and state governments are seen as being of equal status within their own distinctive realms of authority. The Supreme Court settles any disputes about the division of powers between them. Its judgements are accepted as binding on the federal and state governments.

The relationship entails that no state may unilaterally secede from the Union, and a state cannot be expelled against its will. The interests of smaller states are protected in most federations by equal representation, or by additional members to those warranted by the size of their population. An important part of the Philadelphia compromise was to secure the support of the less populous states by giving them equal representation in the Senate – two seats per state.

Types of governmental systems: getting the terms right

In **unitary states**, legal power flows from one source, for instance the queen-in-Parliament in the United Kingdom and the Knesset in Israel; most European governments are of the unitary type. Power is concentrated in national government, and the operation of lower tiers of government derives not from a written constitution but from the centre. In Britain, local authorities exist but they do so at the behest of Westminster, and they are entirely subordinate to it. Some devolution of power is possible (as in the case of Northern Ireland, Scotland and Wales), but this does nothing to breach the idea that control derives from Parliament; local and devolved power can be revoked.

Devolution involves the idea that there should be some redistribution of power away from the centre to subordinate assemblies that can, if necessary, still be overridden by the parent authority. It usually springs from dissatisfaction with centralised government when ministers appear to be unwilling to recognise local needs.

In **confederacies**, the regional authorities exercise much of the power, and central control is relatively weak. Historically, the best example of a confederacy was probably that found in the United States under the Articles of Confederation, but many years later the eleven southern states seceded from the Union in the American Civil War and they too declared themselves to be a Confederacy. Switzerland today is often described as having confederal administration, its twenty-six cantons exercising much of the power in the country.

In **federal states**, power is shared between different tiers of government, a federal (central) government and regional governments – known as states in the US and *Länder* in Germany. Under federalism, the states have guaranteed spheres of responsibility, and the central government conducts those functions of major importance that require policy to be made for the whole country. Both tiers may act directly on the people, and each has some exclusive powers. Federalism thus diffuses political authority to prevent any undue concentration at one point. Under federalism, it is still likely that there will also be a system of local government, although it can vary significantly in form. In the US, the federal government has little role in regulating the functioning of this tier, which falls under the direction of the states.

The benefits of federalism today

With the growth of the federal government since the New Deal (see p. 36), it might have been expected that the states would become mere appendages of Washington. Yet despite the development of 'co-operative federalism' (see p. 47) and the fact that states were no longer 'co-ordinate and independent' as Wheare envisaged, in practice many writers could see them as a still important, indeed vital, part of the system. To Daniel Elazar,[4] the states 'remain viable because they exist as civil societies with political systems of their own'.

Each state has its own distinctive history and traditions, and Americans identify with their state as well as with the nation as a whole; states are broadly popular as a form of government. In recent years, most of them have improved the quality of their services and the personnel who deliver them. Political institutions have been reformed and more efficient management of programmes has been introduced. They have, particularly in some cases, acted in an innovatory manner, and have been a testing-ground for experiments whose results others can follow.

States also provide an opportunity for involvement in the political process to many citizens, and have been a training ground for national leadership. It is through securing election in a particular state that national politicians build up their reputation, either by serving in the legislature, by becoming governor of the state or by representing the state in Congress.

The fifty states are important in their own right, and they are preferable to a more centralised system that would be unsuitable for a country of the size and regional diversity of the United States. Although there are ways in which the federal government can directly intervene to force the states into adopting certain programmes and policies – as happened over the ending of racial segregation – nevertheless the central powers are limited. The relationship between Washington and the states is more one of negotiation and compromise than one of coercion.

Americans think of their states as being important. Until well into the nineteenth century, they identified first with, say, Virginia and second with the United States. The motto of Illinois reflects the ambiguity of loyalty even today: 'State Sovereignty, National Union'. States are still a powerful reference point in American culture, and it is state laws that citizens encounter more frequently than any enactments of the federal government. Many federal laws are actually implemented through the states, which modify them to suit their circumstances.

Federalism today has particular appeal to the many Americans who have become increasingly sceptical about the desirability of federal intervention. They show greater distrust of politicians who work in federal government than was the case forty years ago. They often feel that Washington is too remote from their experience. They have more confidence in their state governments, for the politicians who run them are more in touch with the people. Several opinion polls have pointed to this preference for state over national government and to the widespread belief that state administrations are better able to handle responsibility for several areas of policy. In answer to the question of which government they trusted to perform certain tasks, most Americans told interviewers for the *Washington Post*[5] that they felt that the state was preferable to the federal administration on 'running things' (70%–27%), establishing rules on welfare entitlement (70%–25%), setting rules for workplace safety (55%–42%), setting Medicaid and Medicare regulations (52%–43%) and setting environmental rules for clean air and water (51%–47%). Only on issues such as conducting foreign policy, protecting national security and safeguarding civil rights did the federal tier come off best.

The development of federalism in the twentieth century

The influence of the federal government was much strengthened in the twentieth century, as the US became a world power. This led to huge increases in the budget and a massive expansion of personnel, both civilian and military. As a major contractor and provider of jobs, the federal government's decisions vitally affect the well-being of the states and of the people.

The Great Depression of the 1930s greatly increased the expectation that the federal government would intervene to deal with the major social and economic ills of the country. Washington's attempts to ease these problems by direct works programmes, and by various schemes of assistance for businessmen, farmers and whole areas in dire need, filled a vacuum. Given the scale of the task confronting the country, the states were unable to act themselves, as a result of the strain on their finances as well as out of an ideological unwillingness in some cases to do so.

Some rurally dominated state legislatures neglected the urgent difficulties afflicting the nation's urban areas, and not surprisingly the city administrations turned to the federal government for a lead. The lack of a positive response by many state governments to the crisis of the cities only served to increase the tendency towards centralisation. Indeed, the very nature of the problems faced in a highly complex industrialised society provides a challenge to the federal system. The federal government has also often stepped in to co-ordinate governmental programmes when problems have cut across state boundaries.

Such a combination of economic and social factors led to pressure over a century and a half for a change in the political and constitutional relationships within the federal system. Several methods have been adopted which have served to increase the influence of Washington over the states:

1 **Constitutional amendments**. Some amendments since 1787 affected the federal system – for example, the Fourteenth Amendment provided the 'equal protection' of the law to all citizens, and the Sixteenth gave the federal government the right to raise graduated income tax.

2 **Decisions of the Supreme Court**. At times, Court decisions have allowed a considerable expansion of national intervention by emphasising the broad and permissive character of some clauses in the Constitution – for example, the congressional power to 'tax for the common defence and general welfare of the United States'.

3 **The financial relationship**. After the passage of the Sixteenth Amendment on income tax, the financial base of the federal government was expanded. This led to a considerable increase in the size of its budget. Americans now pay the majority of their taxation to Washington, a smaller amount to the states and slightly less again to their local governments.

With the demands for more education, health and welfare, police protection and environmental services from hard-pressed local and state governments, the federal government increasingly stepped in with more financial aid. The dependence of the states on federal financial resources to support their services has inevitably coloured the relationship.

Since the Great Depression, the main financial assistance has been in the form of **grants-in-aid**. Some existed before 1900, but most have developed since the 1930s, and this has led to federal supervision in areas not normally in its power. In other words, it is money 'with strings attached'. The federal government began to lay

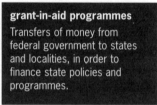

grant-in-aid programmes
Transfers of money from federal government to states and localities, in order to finance state policies and programmes.

down minimum standards and to inspect the results of its funding, and matching funds had to be provided by the states to qualify for federal aid. The more a state was prepared to develop programmes, the more it was likely to receive national funds or contracts.

Differing conceptions of federalism

In the US, there are, in addition to the national government in Washington, DC, fifty states and more than eighty-seven thousand units of local government. How to balance the relationship between these elements has been at the heart of discussion about federalism every since the passage of the Constitution. Several descriptions have been used to describe that relationship, which has fluctuated in different periods of American history.

Before the New Deal, America had a system of **dual federalism**. The Constitution had created two levels of government that were supposed to be independent, each with its own clearly defined sphere of influence and responsibility. The concept was interpreted in different ways, between those on the one hand who wanted a more nation-centred form of federalism and those on the other who wanted a more state-based form. The version which emerged triumphant was the nation-centred one, the issue being finally resolved on the battlefields of the Civil War in the 1860s, in which the Lincoln approach of keeping the country united was vindicated.

The label 'dual federalism' applies to the situation that existed in the nineteenth and early twentieth centuries. Such a model is a conservative one, for those who have supported it (right through until the present day) would prefer to see a strictly limited role for Washington. Supporters stress the importance of 'states' rights', a large and secure place for the states within the federal system. Some writers would argue that such a situation never really existed in anything like its pure form. From as early as the nineteenth century, the federal government was 'stepping in' to provide grants for improvements on expensive and necessary items such as road building.

Dual federalism proved to be inadequate to meet the needs of the Great Depression of the early 1930s. Franklin D. Roosevelt's energetic response to the deteriorating economic situation was to deploy the resources of the central government in a series of interventionist measures known as the New Deal, 'an extraordinary assumption of federal authority over the nation's economy and a major expansion of its commerce and taxing powers'.[6] More and more decision-making moved to Washington, with numerous grant-in-aid programmes bringing federal, state and local tiers into close, if not always harmonious, co-operation.

The New Deal programme inaugurated the era of **co-operative federalism**. This emphasised the partnership of different levels of government in providing effective public services for the nation. As Cummings and Wise put it,[7] the two levels were 'related parts of a single government system, characterised more by cooperation and shared functions than by conflict and competition'. Writing in 1966, Grodzins[8] did not view the American system as a 'layer cake' of three (national, state and local) distinct and separate planes, but rather as a 'marble cake', an inseparable mixture of differently coloured ingredients. In the nature of the relationship, the federal government supplements, stimulates and assist states, rather than pre-empting them. The distinguishing features of co-operative federalism were, then, a sharing of responsibilities over many governmental functions and the recognition that all the players were partners rather than adversaries.

The 1960s witnessed a marked expansion of the role of the federal government in initiating programmes and gaining state/local compliance. President Kennedy had promised to 'get the country moving again' with the use of federal money. The policy was vigorously taken up by his successor. In his **Great Society** programme (including such initiatives as the War on Poverty scheme), President Lyndon Johnson spoke of **creative federalism**, a more active form of co-operative federalism. This involved a massive expansion of federal aid, with grants to state governments increasing from nearly $7.5 billion in 1960 to $32 billion in 1978. Much of the funding came in the form of **categorical grants**, money being offered with the proviso that the recipient organisation carried out a specific task in such a way as to comply with detailed federal requirements.

Great Society

An innovative programme introduced by President Johnson to provide support for disadvantaged groups. The vision was of a society in which poverty and injustice could be eliminated via a programme of federal intervention and support for states and local authorities.

categorical grants

Grants made from the central government to states and localities for specific, often narrow, purposes and to be used in specified ways. There is normally a clear procedure for applying, implementing and reporting back on the use of the money.

The growing use of categorical grants

Year	Number of grants
1900	5
1930	15
1960	132
1971	530

Creative federalism was not supposed to be a means of imposing programmes from the centre, although it did involve a great expansion in the role of the federal layer. The idea was that Washington, the top tier, would seek out and respond to local ideas and demands, and be able therefore to provide the type of service and the money which was wanted by those who lived in each locality. The role of state governments and legislatures was less important, and a wide-ranging series of civil rights and other measures imposed a greater degree of regulation upon state capitals. Johnson was able to work with his overwhelmingly Democratic Congress to carry out his programme. In the process, he was helped by a series of decisions taken by the federal judiciary, which was in a mood to end racial discrimination and segregation, protect civil liberties, reform criminal justice procedures and grant new rights to both the accused and the convicted.

Some writers, particularly those opposed to the Great Society vision, wondered whether what had happened by the end of that decade was that creative federalism had become **coercive federalism**, a situation in which there was, in Kincaid's words,[9] 'unprecedented federal reliance on conditions of aid, pre-emptions of state and local authority, mandates, court orders, and other devices intended to ensure state and local compliance with federal policies'.

Criticism of the growth in central power: the new federalism

States and localities had become ever more dependent on federal funding, and the conditions attached to the aid had become stringent. At the same time, the deteriorating state of the American economy led many people to believe that the country could not afford such vast and expensive social programmes. To Johnson's political opponents, the proliferation of policies and grants had brought about confusion and an excess of bureaucracy.

Conservatives never liked high-spending federal programmes, which, in their view, involved an unnecessary amount of regulation and encouraged the states to initiate schemes which they did not want or need, simply to obtain the available federal funds. These critics claimed that problems were better tackled locally by people who understood the needs of the area, rather than by wasteful and inefficient national programmes. They disliked the idea of federal interference in the affairs of states and local authorities, and argued the case for a preservation of 'states' rights'.

As a conservative president, Richard Nixon had the opportunity both to preach and practise his ideas of a **new federalism**. To him, the relationship between all tiers of government was in need of redefinition. Yet his approach was not essentially about curtailing the amount of money which reached the localities, but more about how it got there. Money was provided by a **block grant**; the need was identified locally and the money then spent.

> **block grants**
> Discretionary grants handed over by the federal government to states or communities. Recipients can choose how the money is spent within the broad area covered by the transfer.

Despite the efforts of President Nixon to stem the flow of power from the states to Washington, it was still commonplace for academics and commentators to speak of the erosion of states' rights until 1980. The growth of grants-in-aid, the expansion of federal regulations, and the decisions of the Supreme Court (especially on desegregation) had all signalled a decline of the states as a significant force. In the words of one exam question of the 1970s: 'States' rights' are no more than an empty slogan for those who do not like the government in Washington.'

In January 1981, in his inaugural speech, President Ronald Reagan observed that 'Our government has no special power except that granted it by the people . . . All of us need to be reminded that the federal government did not create the states; the states created the federal government. He cast himself firmly in the dualist mould, emphasising his determination to 'demand recognition of the distinction between the powers granted to the federal government and those reserved to the states or to the people'. For him, it was not enough merely to adjust the delivery systems. He wanted to tackle the basic problem, namely that government was trying to do too much.

The Reagan version of 'new federalism' was more radical in its intention and in its impact. His intention was to bring about a restructuring of the federal system. In his vision of the future, the federal government would withdraw from several areas, the states would gain the right to take more initiatives and operate more programmes (if they so wished), and city governments would lose much of the power they had accumulated. He had little sympathy for 1960s schemes designed to help the cities. Of the War on Poverty, he observed: 'I guess you could say poverty won the war.' For him, this all added up to a 'new federalism', which would reverse a situation in which 'our citizens feel they have lost control of even the most basic decisions made about the essential services of government . . . A maze of interlocking jurisdictions and levels of government confronts average citizens in trying to solve even the simplest of problems.'[10]

The changes on which he embarked included:
- a reduction of grants-in-aid;
- a merging of those grants directed to specific purposes into block grants, which allowed for far more state discretion;
- a removal of many federal regulations;
- an emphasis on urban and other problems being solved by a concentration on
  (a) achieving an increase in the overall prosperity and wealth of the country, and
  (b) encouraging local private/public initiatives;
- a recasting of welfare arrangements, by which the federal government would take care of Medicaid health funding, whilst the states would look after the AFDC (Aid to Families with Dependent Children) and food stamp programmes.

What had been created by the end of the 1980s was not a replica of the pattern which existed before the days of Roosevelt and the New Deal. Federal funding may have been reduced, but the Supreme Court decisions which did so much to change the nature of American federalism survived intact. National standards were also largely preserved. The number of regulations was reduced and they were imposed with less zeal than was once the case, but in areas such as environmental regulation there remains a strong federal role. Americans are now used to turning to their president in Washington for a response to pressing national problems, and whether they are worried by rising crime, the system of welfare or any other aspect of policy, they expect a lead from the White House (and Congress) – even if they do not like the policy which emerges. The outcome therefore is a situation that, in Kincaid's words,[11] is something of a paradox, combining 'federal dominance and state resurgence ... If the states are so resurgent, why is the federal government [still] so dominant? The main reason is that the federal government has established a significant regulatory role in most domestic policy fields.'

Bush, Clinton and federalism

At the beginning of the twenty-first century, states are more active than they were twenty years ago, and that is unlikely to be reversed. After Reagan had vanished from the scene, his successors had markedly less impact on the balance of the federal–state relationship. George Bush senior did not share the Reagan view of the appropriate role for government in the nation's life, and if anything there was a modest swing back to emphasising the role of Washington. But the scale of the budget deficit meant that there was unlikely to be a return to the heyday of co-operative federalism. In any case, in the words of David McKay,[12] 'Lower level governments had been taught to be more self-reliant and to cut spending and services rather than increase taxes or plead for aid from the federal government.'

When Bill Clinton entered the White House, many commentators initially viewed him as a centraliser in intergovernmental relations. After all, he believed in more active national leadership than did Bush or Reagan. But as he was a southerner, some hoped that the former Governor of Arkansas would be likely to be a defender of states' rights. After all, he came from an area where there was a history of resistance to federal demands, and he had a reputation as an innovator who understood and appreciated the role of the states in the federal system. Moreover, he was not a traditional high-spending Democrat of the Kennedy–Johnson variety. Indeed, in his State of the Union message in 1996, he was forthright about the change of circumstances, declaring that the 'age of big government is over'.

Once he was elected, one of Clinton's primary concerns was to cut the budget deficit that had grown dramatically in the 1960s and 1970s. By the time Nixon left office, more than a quarter of all spending at state and local level was provided from Washington. Jimmy Carter had begun to trim the amount of national support, but as we have seen it was Reagan who set about slashing it. Clinton continued in this vein, redirecting financial resources and responsibility for programmes back to the states, a process intensified after the Republican congressional successes of November 1994. He was more generous with federal money than Reagan had been and more so than his Republican opponents desired, but the increased funding was modest by the standards of his party predecessors.

Two examples that illustrate the willingness of Bill Clinton to devolve power to the states concern welfare policy and **unfunded mandates**. The welfare reform proposals introduced in 1996 ended the federal commitment to providing assistance to low-income mothers and children brought up by them, thereby shifting the burden of welfare entitlement from Washington to the states. Many Democrats had doubts about the cessation of a policy that had survived since the days of the New Deal, but whatever his personal reservations, the president signed the measure. He recognised the prevailing mood, as registered in the mid-term elections, and with a presidential campaign

> **unfunded mandates**
> Orders imposed by the federal government on state and local governments requiring them to carry out certain tasks, for which there has been no reimbursement of the costs involved. The high cost of such mandates became a cause of tension between the federal and state governments.

ahead he had no intention of obstructing welfare reform. A less significant but none the less useful symbolic change was the ending by Congress of unfunded mandates, those orders imposed by the federal government on state governments that required them to implement certain programmes without providing them with the means to so do. Other measures involving the relaxation of central control included the repeal of national speed limits, and allowing states and local authorities more freedom to decide how they wished to apply the terms of the Safe Drinking Act. Taken together, the measures indicate a federal retreat from social programmes on which uniformity was previously seen as desirable.

Francis[13] has labelled the policy of transferring programmes once under federal direction to the states '**devolutionary federalism**'. The concept of devolution is in some ways a dubious one to apply to the United States, for it is traditionally associated with the idea of a transfer of specific powers to a subordinate tier of government, under a unitary system. But in as much as the term points to a rebalancing of the federal system in such a way as to boost the power of the states, its use has been accepted by several writers.

> **devolutionary federalism**
> A variant of new federalism, the emphasis being on devolving responsibility for once federally run programmes to the states, which – being closer to the people – are thought to be better placed to respond to local needs.

Clinton stressed the importance of improved co-operation between the federal and state/local governments, and spoke of increased opportunities for local experimentation. Within two weeks of assuming office, he had invited the nation's governors to meet him so that he could listen to their complaints and ideas. Over the following years, he established a framework in which federal officials were able to loosen programme requirements to allow states and localities greater flexibility.

In the last few years, there have been numerous examples of states acting in an imaginative and more assertive fashion. They have advanced their own interests by effective lobbying in the national capital, have tried out different forms of revenue-raising and cost-cutting, and have developed alternative policy approaches. A spirit of innovation and vitality has spread through several state capitals, in many cases supported by both liberals and conservatives. As federal, state and local administrations vie with each other to provide the public services that the voters demand, the atmosphere is one of what Thomas Dye has called[14] **'competitive federalism'**. Washington is no longer seen as 'knowing best' and there has been a greater recognition of the role and importance of the states in producing effective government.

The Rehnquist Court has of late been instrumental in helping to shape the character of American intergovernmental relations. It has leaned to a more state-centred approach. In 1992, in *New York v United States*, the justices took the view that the national government could not 'simply compel' a state to take particular policy actions. In 1999, they decided that Maine was not subject to Federal Labour Standards legislation, and a year later in *Kimel v Florida Board of Regents* they went significantly further in exempting states from the requirements of federal laws designed to prevent age discrimination.

These developments show that the debate about the appropriate level of federal intervention is unresolved, for the relationship cannot be fixed for all times. As Woodrow Wilson wrote back in the early twentieth century, the matter is not for 'one generation, because it is a question of growth, and every new successive stage of our political and economic development, gives it a new aspect, makes it a new question'.[15] Arguably the devolving of power from Washington since the 1980s is the most significant change in the balance of the national–state relationship since the time of the New Deal. Federalism has proved to be a flexible system, suitable for the administration of a large and diverse country, and capable of adaptation to changing needs and interests as the situation requires.

The impact of George W. Bush on federalism

When George W. Bush assumed the presidency, he labelled himself a 'faithful friend of federalism', as might be expected from a Republican ex-governor. He drew on his experience as a governor in Texas to show what might be achieved at state level. He showed his leanings towards local initiative in his early days, by seeking out the advice and services of leading state officials. He quickly established a study group to see how the role of states might be advanced. His early implementation of the campaign promises he had made on tax cutting was justified on several grounds, but one of them was that if the central government had a reduced role and spent less of national programmes, then money could be left in the pockets of individual Americans.

Yet there are other factors which have conspired to distance the president from such a pro-devolution policy in the last few years, whatever the rhetoric he continues to employ. The business community is sometimes unenthusiastic about regulatory state laws that are often pro-consumer or pro-environment, and has urged congressional intervention to pre-empt state legislation. The Religious Right dislikes some features of state autonomy (not least Oregon's suicide law and Massachusetts's contentious policy on same-sex marriages) and would prefer to see a stricter moral code, more uniform in its application – Bush has himself argued for a constitutional amendment to outlaw gay marriages. And the president's strong backing for improved standards in education implied stricter central controls to an extent that worried some sympathetic state governors, who were fearful of the possible adverse electoral consequences of an increased federal role.

More seriously, perhaps, two issues have come to the fore on which federal leadership has been needed. Firstly, national security: the September 11 attacks on the Twin Towers, and their aftermath, have shifted the focus of attention away from the states and more to Washington, where policy-makers have been engaged in measures to safeguard the interests of all Americans. Second, after the 'good years' in which the economy has been performing well, recession may make it more difficult for states to fund programmes for which they have in recent years assumed responsibility.

States–local relations reviewed: yesterday, today and tomorrow

Relations between the states and the centre are at the very heart of federalism, for federalism seems to provide for an in-built tension between the two levels of government. Hague and Harrop[16] point out that in the United States

> the original federal principle . . . was that the national and state governments would operate independently, each tier acting autonomously in its own constitutional sphere. In particular, the federal government was required to confine its activities to functions explicitly allocated to it, such as the power 'to lay and collect taxes, to pay the debts and provide for the common defence and welfare of the United States'. In the circumstances of eighteenth century America, extensive coordination between federal and state administration was considered neither necessary nor feasible. This model of separated governments . . . has long since disappeared, overwhelmed by the demands of an integrated economy and society.

The experience of American history reveals that the nature of federalism has changed over time. There was a broad tendency towards central control from the beginning, and it accelerated with the greater state regulation following the establishment of the New Deal. The trend reached its peak in the 1960s. Sometimes this greater central power came about as a result of constitutional amendment; more often it was a response to prevailing economic and social conditions. Sometimes too the tendency towards central control was given a push by judicial decisions, so that clauses in the Constitution were interpreted widely to provide the federal government with a broad scope for legislation. The result was that in America the centre gained power at the expense of the fifty states, especially in the area of major economic policy.

The centralising tendency was arrested in the closing decades of the twentieth century. In practice, American federalism has experienced growing interdependence. There is a developing trend towards improving relations between federal, state and local governments and finding common ground between them. In several areas of policy, such as education and transport, policies are made, funded and applied on all tiers. States have regained much of their lost autonomy and are very important in their own right, but on occasion the national government steps in. When California experienced a serious electrical power shortage in 2000, Washington became inevitably involved as the state began to make demands on the supplies of surrounding states.

The states have enjoyed a resurgence and renewal in recent decades. This has come about as part of a backlash against the activist government of the Great Society years. The Johnson presidency had some important achievements to its credit, not least for the poor and ethnic minorities who were their main recipients. These achievements came at a time when state and local governments often seemed inert and inefficient. But the changes generated opposition and political opinion turned against them. Americans have always been lukewarm about 'big government', and opponents found increasing evidence that too many programmes had been badly run, were wasteful and undermined individual and local initiative.

There were several reasons for the state resurgence in the late twentieth century, among them:
- the strong performance of the Republicans in congressional and gubernatorial elections in recent years, encouraging the adoption of policies based on less federal intervention and more respect for states' rights;
- increased wariness of congressional politicians on Capitol Hill who had responsibility for introducing and passing federal laws. The choice of ex-governors rather than congressmen as presidential candidates over the last generation is an indication of a growing distrust of Washington politicians. These former governors – Carter, but especially Reagan and Clinton – have been well versed in state perspectives on the appropriate national–state relationship;
- a feeling that the federal government has failed to respond to assorted economic and social problems, so that the states have had to act on their own. The cutting of many grants-in-aids further enhanced the tendency towards state self-reliance, spurring state politicians to reform;

- the handing over of decision-making powers to the states on important subjects such as welfare, especially via the 1996 Welfare Reform Act. From then onwards, although there was a national framework, it was increasingly left to the states to decide whether to hand over money to individual claimants and the level at which help should be given;
- rulings of the Supreme Court, a number of which have supported the states in their attempts to make important inroads on topics such as the availability of abortion;
- the increased willingness – indeed enthusiasm – of some states to experiment with new policies. State administrations have been notably more vigorous and creative than they were in the heyday of 'big government'.

The degree of government interventionism has tended to vary according to economic necessities and the tide of popular opinion. As the economy became national, there was an increasing need for national leadership to sort out problems such as urban decline, worker protection and the regulation of large corporations; state activity seemed inadequate to meet the challenge. When government became too big, then many voters came to see the federal government as part of the problem, rather than as part of the solution.

Sometimes people have had confusing aspirations, wanting smaller but decisive national leadership. Even those who deride big government and Washington 'meddling' sometimes find themselves calling for leadership on key issues. Robert Dole, a presidential contender in 1996, illustrated the ambiguity in a remark on law and order. He upheld states' rights by saying that: 'Republicans . . . believe that our country's increasingly desperate fight against crime is an area where more freedom is needed at the state level.'[17] He went on to promise that the proposed 'crime bill will impose mandatory minimum sentences on those who use guns in the commission of a crime, and make sure the jails are there to lock them up'!

The relationship between states and the centre is not static. America has, as Gillian Peele[18] points out,

> a vibrant but complex system which displays enormous variety and contradiction . . . Bush may expect, or indeed, want to continue the rebuilding of a genuine partnership with the states. The evolution of the American system has, however, produced a complex labyrinth of relationships that are less than easily navigated. It is thus likely that although the American federal and intergovernmental system will continue to tilt away from Washington, change will be relatively slow and incremental.

In the past, textbook writers have concentrated on the national scene at the expense of what happens in the states and localities. Examiners still tend to see American politics in this way. Yet not to be aware of the revival in sub-national politics would be to underestimate seriously the importance of the trends of recent years and also to misinterpret the essence of American federalism. In the words of Hames and Rae,[19] 'states are the basic building-blocks of American life, and they remain highly individual and distinctive'. Some of the innovations for which they have recently been responsible are set out on p. 58.

State and local government in operation

The fifty states vary enormously, all of them having distinctive histories, constitutions, governmental institutions and policies. As we have seen, they have a substantial degree of autonomy, so that the quality of public service provision, the level of taxation and the degree of tolerance extended on matters sexual and social are very different in liberal Massachusetts and conservative Kansas. Robert Singh[20] points out that on sexual matters the variation is marked, there being laws theoretically forbidding adultery in twenty-four states, fornication in seventeen, oral sex fifteen and the sale (but not use) of marital aids eight:

> the state of Alabama allows sex with donkeys and corpses, but punishes oral sex between husbands and wives . . . Most of these laws are unenforced . . . and unenforceable. Nevertheless, the differences illustrate how domestic regulations can differ sharply even on the most intimate and private of matters, according to the particular state's moral traditions and political culture.

In general, matters that lie entirely within the borders of the fifty states are their exclusive concern. These include such things as:

- regulations relating to business, industry, property and utilities;
- the state criminal code;
- working conditions within the state.

All of the states are bicameral (that is, have two legislative chambers), except for Nebraska, which is unicameral. As with the federal government, the lower house is normally the larger of the two and generally senators or members of the upper house serve for four years, as against two for members of the lower chamber. Many of the states impose **term limits** on their legislators (see also pp. 152–4), largely because of the movement in recent decades towards greater professionalism in legislatures and the resulting development of **career politicians**. Until the 1960s, many state legislatures had only met in alternate years and even then had short sessions. Today, their

term limits
Restrictions on the number of terms for which a member of an executive position (e.g. governor) or an elected state representative may serve. In 1995, the Supreme Court prevented states from introducing limits on the length of time their federal legislators can serve, but within the state legislatures there are no federal requirements. Thirty-nine states have a limit on governorships, eighteen on legislators.

career politicians
People committed to politics, which they regard as their vocation. They know little else beyond the worlds of politics, policy-making and elections.

operation varies across America. Some states, such as California, are highly professionalised, with regular sessions and paid, full-time members. On the other hand, Kansas, Montana and seven other legislatures do not have annually paid members, but make payments for each day when the chambers are in session. They meet much less regularly.

Each state has an elected governor, but again the substance of the position varies considerably. All but two of the governors serve for four years. In New Hampshire and Vermont they have only a two-year term, but no limit on the maximum number of consecutive terms for which they can hold their position. There has been a trend towards greater gubernatorial power in recent years. In forty states, the governor has full responsibility for proposing the budget and, to the envy of most recent presidents, forty-one of the fifty also have some version of the line-item veto (see p. 89).

The fact that four of the last five presidents were at one time governors suggests the degree of respect that the office of governor now carries. In most states, there has been a greater recognition in recent years of the need to modernise gubernatorial authority, the more so as the states are now assuming some responsibilities that were once the prerogative of the federal government. This changed atmosphere has given governors a greater opportunity to make their mark, by introducing or urging the use of state initiatives in economic, environmental and social policy.

Innovation across American states

Several states have been active in Washington, DC, in recent years, lobbying on their own behalf and employing professional lobbying companies to help them in their bid for federal help. However, they have also recognised the need to become more self-reliant. This has led to more creative thinking, and some states have been fertile in devising initiatives:

- California has been restrictive on the rights of entry of illegal immigrants and the use of affirmative action programmes. These and many more policies have resulted from the widespread use of direct legislation, as described on pp. 222–6.
- Hawaii has introduced a British-style scheme of health care, and Oregon too has promoted a new system for the delivery health provision.
- Wisconsin has experimented with parental choice and a voucher system in state education.
- Several states have tried out different approaches to issues of law and order, the main common factor between them being that policies have generally veered towards 'toughness'. Texas is noted for its frequent use of the death penalty and its 'bootcamps' for young offenders; other states have employed policies ranging from 'zero tolerance' to registration of sex offenders.

Local government

In addition to its fifty state governments, America has a vast and complex maze of local governments. Generalisation is difficult, because they range from the extremes of small, rural, sparsely populated townships to huge, densely populated metropolitan areas, with cities, towns, counties and districts in between. Every American lives within the jurisdiction of the national government, a state government and perhaps ten to twenty local bodies. For instance, the six-county Chicago-Illinois metropolitan area has more than twelve hundred different governments, some serving the people in broad ways, others providing more specialised services.

Since the Reagan era, states have been willing to decentralise their governing arrangements to the local level ('second order devolution') and the smaller units encourage individual participation and promote the value of individualism. There is a strong tradition of grassroots democracy in America that fits in well with the widely shared belief that government should be kept as close to the people as possible. The very existence of so many governments to deal with so many different and necessary services seems to indicate that democracy flourishes in the localities, a situation far removed from British experience.

Yet the health of local democracy in America can be overstated. As in Britain, local politics is often poorly covered by the media and consequently the public often remains ill informed about what goes on. This in turn makes it difficult to hold those who represent them accountable. Moreover, levels of turnout in some elections are often very low. Some cities such as Birmingham, Alabama, have done much to encourage neighbourhood democracy by creating neighbourhood boards that have meaningful control over important policy decisions. In this way, voters can see that participation is worthwhile and they feel that it is worth the effort to take their involvement beyond voting alone.

Writing of Britain and the United States, McNaughton[21] gets the balance about right:

> In the USA, if anything, citizens are more interested in the politics of their state and their community than in the goings-on in Washington. Their daily lives are clearly affected more by the nature and performance of local government than those of British citizens. American local democracy is, therefore, more lively, more meaningful and more cherished than it is in the UK.

FEDERALISM AND DEVOLUTION IN BRITAIN AND THE UNITED STATES: A COMPARISON

Britain is a unitary state. As such, sovereignty resides at the centre, in Parliament, even if power may be delegated to other bodies. By contrast, America is a federal country in which sovereignty is divided between Washington and the regions, the division of responsibilities being set out in the Constitution. The constitutional position of the two countries is therefore very different. In practice, there are some similarities, now that Britain has gone down the route of creating devolved bodies in Scotland, Wales and Northern Ireland.

Devolution involves the ceding of power by Parliament to some new elected body. Bogdanor[22] defines it as 'the transfer to a subordinate elected body, on a geographical basis, of functions at present exercised by ministers and Parliament'. As such, it differs from federalism, which

> would divide, not devolve, supreme power from Westminster and various regional or provincial parliaments. In a federal state, the authority of the central or federal government and the provincial governments is co-ordinate and shared, the respective scope of the federal and provincial governments being defined by an enacted constitution . . . Devolution, by contrast, does not require the introduction of an enacted constitution.

It is important not to emphasise unduly the formal differences between unitary and federal systems, for in practice the distinctions are less clear cut than at first appears. In countries such as Britain or Spain that have devolved bodies and/or regional structures, no likely government would seriously contemplate reducing their autonomy. To do so would invite political difficulties. Power is actually more widely dispersed than the term 'unitary' implies. Similarly, in any federal structure, the federal government is bound to exercise enormous power, the exact extent of which varies from country to country. This is because any country needs strong, effective leadership, especially – but not only – in times of crisis. It is in recognition of this requirement in twenty-first-century America that examiners have sometimes asked whether the United States is becoming a kind of unitary state. So too have they asked whether Britain is moving in a more federal direction.

Yet whilst it is true that the old distinctions between the British and American systems are less clear cut than used to be the case, none the less by British standards America remains a very decentralised country in which political power is diffused. Even allowing for recent experiments in devolution, Britain is still much more centralised than even many other unitary states. The way in which national governments have removed the powers and in some cases terminated the existence of local government is an indication of that process. This could happen in Britain by the passage of national legislation, whereas in America, whenever Washington has attempted to increase its power at the expense of the states, there has usually been considerable state resistance. Local feelings and the tradition of self-government count for more in America than they do in Britain. The Constitution guarantees to the states a degree of independence and self-government never recognised by sub-national units in the United Kingdom, where the Scots and the Welsh had a long wait in the struggle for devolution. Federalism in America is very much alive today.

In Britain, the governmental motivation for decentralisation has not derived from an ideological belief that there was excessive centralisation that needed to be reversed. Rather, it has sprung from a recognition that it was necessary to concede some ground to the people in those areas of the country which have felt aggrieved, for otherwise electoral damage or social disharmony might come about. But whatever the motive, Blondel concludes:[23] 'one could argue that the regionalism which has been introduced in [Britain and Spain] constitutes an imitation of federalism – indeed, is federalism in all but name . . . the difference between federal and unitary states is becoming smaller, not only in practice but formally as well'.

America's constitutional arrangements, history and geography mean that it is almost certain to retain a federal system into the long distant future, the more so now that central and state government are acting in greater partnership with each other. Its arrangements provide for a more straightforward allocation of power between Washington and the states than exists between London and the national capitals, with their differing degree of autonomy. However, in a relatively small country such as Britain, there would be difficulties in making federalism work effectively.

Is Britain becoming a federal state?

The changes in recent years to the pattern of government in Britain seem to indicate a move in a more federal direction. Northern Ireland had a devolved assembly in the days before Direct Rule, so that the relationship between London and Belfast was essentially federal in character, with certain functions allocated to the national level of government and the rest to the provincial one. The new assembly formed as a result of the Good Friday Agreement (1998) has similar powers, so that Northern Ireland, Scotland and Wales all have devolved administrations, although in Northern Ireland the Assembly has been prone to suspension and in Wales it has strictly limited powers. Another development has been the introduction of an elected mayor for London and in some other towns and cities, an experiment based on the experience of American cities such as Washington and New York. Ministers have also allowed for the possibility that at some point in the future there might be elected regional assemblies, although at the time of writing, in early 2005, there is little evidence of any significant demand for them and the prospect has receded into the background.

Differing degrees of devolution have been accorded to the various elements of the United Kingdom. This is a move towards a Spanish-type structure, in which the peoples of some areas of the country have more control over their future than their fellow Spaniards elsewhere. Coxall and Robins[24] have envisaged the development from 'a unitary state to a mosaic of federal, devolved and joint authority relationships between core and periphery, with the English core becoming more decentralised as regional and urban identities find political expression'.

When commentators speculate on moves towards a federal structure in Britain, they do not usually imply a uniform division of power between Westminster and provincial units formally set out in a written document. Rather, they envisage a situation in which the policy of devolution is gradually applied to all parts of the United Kingdom, just as it is now applied to Scotland and Wales. Bogdanor[25] seeks to distinguish this from a strictly federal system, and refers to it instead as 'federal devolution'. This is happening at the very time that in the United States there has been a move towards 'devolutionary federalism'.

CONCLUSION

Federalism is a form of government that divides political responsibility. Its underlying ideas are that:

- too much political power is dangerous and it is therefore desirable that there should be diverse levels of government to prevent undue concentration
- particular powers are best assigned to particular tiers best suited to exercising them.

An understanding of federalism is crucial to unlocking the secrets of the American political system. It decentralises American politics, helps decide which president is elected, enhances judicial power and decentralises policies as well. In the distant past, the debates were about whether the national government should regulate the railroads or adopt minimum wage legislation. Today, they are about whether it should regulate abortion, determine speed limits on highways or lay down that 18-year-olds cannot legally drink alcohol. Policies relating to the economy, the environment and many other issues are subject to the centralising force of the national government and the dispersing force of the fifty states. Because of the overlapping powers of the two tiers of government, most discussion of policy is also a discussion about federalism.

The neat arrangements devised at Philadelphia have been adapted to changing circumstances at different periods in American history, because special situations have required a new approach. The broad drift has been towards a centralisation of power since the early days of dual federalism. But in recent years there has been a significant reversal and today it is meaningful to talk of states' revival and renewal.

REFERENCES

1 A. Grant, *The American Political Process*, Dartmouth, 1994
2 J. Zimmerman, *Contemporary American Federalism: The Growth of National Power*, Praegar, 1992
3 K. Wheare, *Federalism*, Oxford University Press, 1946 (reissued 1963)
4 D. Elazar, *American Federalism: A View from the States*, Harper and Row, 1984
5 *Washington Post* – ABC poll, fieldwork conducted in March 1995
6 J. Burns, J. Peltason, T. Cronin and D. Magleby, Government by the People, Prentice Hall, 1994
7 M. Cummings and D. Wise, *Democracy under Pressure*, Harcourt College Publishers, 2000

8 M. Grodzins, *The American System*, Rand McNally, 1966
9 J. Kincaid, 'American Federalism: The Third Century' in *Annals of the American Academy of Political and Social Science*, May 1990
10 R. Reagan, as quoted in G. Wasserman, *The Basics of American Politics*, Longman, 1997
11 J. Kincaid, as in 9 above
12 D. McKay, *American Politics and Society*, Blackwell, 2001
13 J. Francis, 'Federalism', in R. Singh (ed.), *Governing America: The Politics of a Divided Democracy*, Oxford University Press, 2003
14 T. Dye, *American Federalism: Competition Among Governments*, Lexington Books, 1990
15 Quoted in Wasserman, as in 10 above
16 R. Hague and M. Harrop, *Comparative Government and Politics: An Introduction*, Palgrave, 2004
17 R. Dole, as quoted in G. Wasserman, as in 10 above
18 G. Peele, 'Introduction: The United States in the Twenty-First Century', in G. Peele, C. Bailey, B. Cain and B. Peters (eds), *Developments in American Politics 4*, Palgrave, 2002
19 T. Hames and N. Rae, *Governing America*, Manchester University Press, 1996
20 R. Singh, *American Government and Politics: A Concise Introduction*, Sage, 2003
21 N. McNaughton, *Success in Politics*, John Murray, 2001
22 V. Bogdanor, *Devolution in the United Kingdom*, Oxford University Press, 1999
23 J. Blondel, *Comparative Government: An Introduction*, Prentice Hall, 1995
24 B. Coxall and L. Robins, *Contemporary British Politics*, Macmillan, 1998
25 V. Bogdanor, as in 22 above.

USEFUL WEB SITES

www.nga.org Site of the National Governors' Association, containing analysis of issues affecting the states and information on current policy initiatives.

http://newfederalism.urban.org The Urban Institute (a Washington think-tank). Monitors changes in federal social policies that affect the states and local governments.

www.voxpop.org:80/jefferson Issues of federalism debated.

In addition, the web sites of particular state and local governments can be consulted.

SAMPLE QUESTIONS

1 What is the role of the states in the American federal system?
2 Does the cry of 'states' rights' have any meaning in the US today?

3 To what extent has there been a change in the relationship between the federal and state governments, and why has any change come about?

4 To what extent has there been a shift in power away from Washington and towards the states since 1980?

5 'American federalism works well because, although the constitutional structure has been largely unchanged, in practice the system operates with flexibility and in a spirit of partnership.' Discuss.

6 To what extent would the Founding Fathers recognise the concept of federalism as it is practised in the United States today?

7 What are the advantages and disadvantages of American federalism as it operates today?

8 Outline the major consequences of American federalism.

9 'America has a federal and Britain a unitary form of government, but in reality the influence of the national government over the states and local and devolved authorities respectively is broadly similar.' Discuss.

10 Discuss the similarities and differences of American federalism and British devolution.

The executive

4

The president is the head of just one of the three branches of government, but he is – in the words of one writer[1] – the 'superstar of the American political game'. As the only nationally elected official other than the vice-president, he is the symbol of both the federal government and the nation. Much is expected of American presidents, but in reality there are limitations to the power that any modern president can wield. He is an 'emperor with few clothes'.[2] Power is his for a fixed term only and is held on trust from the people who elect him. It is checked by the restraints of a separate legislature and an independent judiciary.

In this chapter, we will examine the executive branch of government, analysing the development of presidential power, the differing perceptions of the role presidents should play, the help available to the President and the difficulties he experiences in controlling the federal bureaucracy.

POINTS TO CONSIDER

➤ What do we mean by 'presidential power' and why has this power tended to increase over the last hundred years?

➤ How then can we measure presidential success?

➤ What are the limits of presidential power?

➤ What is the current balance of power in the relationship between the president and Congress?

➤ Is the prime minister stronger within the British system of government than the US president within the American system?

➤ Has the position of vice-president grown in political significance in recent years and if so why?

➤ In what respects are the British and American Cabinets (a) similar and (b) dissimilar?

➤ In what ways does the federal bureaucracy both support and limit the presidency?

THE MODERN PRESIDENCY

The role of the president as outlined in the Constitution

The American Constitution has relatively little to say about what the American president can and should do. Key terms such as 'the executive' are not clearly defined. Furthermore, the functions set out are subject to restraints.

The actual powers outlined in the document are set out mainly in Article II:
- Article I:7: to veto congressional legislation;
- Article II:2: to act as commander-in-chief of the US armed forces;
- Article II:2: to grant pardons;
- Article II:2: to make treaties;
- Article II:2: to appoint ambassadors;
- Article II:2: to appoint judges;
- Article II:2: to appoint members of the executive;
- Article II:3: to comment on the State of the Union;
- Article II:3: to recommend legislation to Congress;
- Article II:3: to summon special sessions of Congress.

The Founding Fathers had in mind a presidency of which the holder would stand above the political process and act as a symbol of national unity. He would not depend directly on the people or any political party for his support. This would enable him to act as a kind of gentleman or aristocrat, remote from the political arena. Congress was supreme, as far as the actual government of the country was concerned. In the words of Maidment and McGrew,[3] the presidency would be 'the brake, the restraining hand of the federal government; it would provide the balance for the congress, and the House of Representatives in particular'.

It has not worked out in this way, for from an early stage presidents have stepped in to resolve national problems. In the twentieth century, wars and domestic crises provided the opportunity for assertive leadership from the man in the White House, so that there has been a broad, underlying trend towards greater presidential power. But as we shall see, the combination of weak presidents and variations in the national mood have meant that at different times the presidency has been a power-house and a motionless engine. There has been no continuous accumulation of power, more a waxing and waning of the degree of leadership and control.

The growth of presidential power

Presidential power has increased since the days of the Founding Fathers as people turned to the presidency for initiatives to get things done. Presidents filled the vacuum left by the inertia or inaction of Congress, the states or private enterprise. Presidential power is judged according to the ability of a president to achieve the identifiable goals he has set himself. Those presidents who set themselves clear priorities and manage to accomplish them are widely viewed as successful. Some do not set themselves clear objectives, or if they do so have difficulty in fulfilling them.

From 1933 to the 1970s: the imperial presidency

The modern presidency really began in 1933, for the Great Depression, created (or, at least, certainly accelerated) a fundamental change in political behaviour in the United States. The sheer scale of economic dislocation and hardship overwhelmed the states, and their inadequacy was revealed. The public and the special interests turned to the federal government to promote measures of recovery. The administration of Franklin D. Roosevelt was not reluctant to respond.

Since then, the American system has become a very presidential one and the political process now requires a continued sequence of presidential initiatives in foreign policy and in the domestic arena to function satisfactorily. Modern presidents impose themselves with far greater effect on the political environment than did their counterparts of the nineteenth century.

The early 1960s saw the peak of enthusiasm for presidential power. A broad spectrum of commentators welcomed its expansion, for post-1945 there was a consensus about domestic and foreign policy which encouraged a delegation of power to the president. There was a greater degree of agreement about the fundamentals of policy-making, and the level and extent of debate over public policy were less intense and robust than at other times.

Of course, there was dispute and division, but many things were agreed. The legacy of the New Deal, the great postwar economic expansion, the growing confidence over the management of the economy, the belief in the solubility of problems and the increasing claims on the federal government combined to create a feeling of well-being. It was felt to be prudent to allow the president a relatively free hand to lead his country. There was broad agreement that the federal government should have a significant role in the nation's economy and in creating and maintaining a welfare system.

The Johnson era (1963–69) was the high point of the postwar domestic consensus that was about to crumble. Till then, there was a belief that social ailments were amenable to the application of money, and this confidence in the power of economic growth and social engineering enormously enhanced the presidency. It seemed to be the only institution which could solve problems. It had the expertise to devise new policies; Congress did not, and looked to the president for a lead.

In foreign policy, the postwar consensus aroused even less dissent than its domestic counterpart. Few raised a voice against the direction of American policy after Truman had laid down the 'Truman Doctrine', which outlined America's place in the world and was to become the foundation of foreign policy to the late 1960s. America was the world's policeman and had abandoned its prewar isolationism, stationed troops abroad and played an increasingly interventionist role.

Congress had willingly accepted presidential leadership, and gave Truman and his successors more or less carte blanche in matters of national security. The nation was united, and congressmen had no desire to create an impression of disunity. A bipartisan coalition acquiesced in most presidential initiatives. Foreign policy was the president's policy, which received the almost automatic ratification of Congress. It was an unsatisfactory position, which opened up the possibility of the abuse of power.

Such abuses of presidential power did occur – the **Vietnam war** and Watergate were but the most significant. In 1974, many Americans became aware for the first time of the tremendous accumulation of power in the hands of the president. The 'separation of powers' principle had been incorporated into the Constitution to prevent a concentration of power in one part of

Vietnam war

The war began under Kennedy and escalated under Johnson to prevent communist North Vietnem from taking over South Vietnam and to contain the spread of communism in Southeast Asia. It ended with an American withdrawal in 1973, America's first defeat in war. In 1975, Vietnam was united under communist rule.

Watergate

Watergate is the collective label for a series of abuses of power that began with a break-in at the national headquarters of the Democratic Party in the Watergate Building, Washington, DC, in June 1972, as part of an attempt to find out the Democrats' election plans and thereby assist the chances of a Republican victory. As the story unfolded, many malpractices were uncovered. Several members of the Nixon administration were indicted and convicted on charges ranging from burglary and wire-tapping to 'misleading testimony' and 'political espionage'. It became apparent that Nixon had been taping conversations in the Oval Office and that he had been tapping the phones of his political enemies. When parts of the tapes were released, many began to become more than ever suspicious that the president had himself been involved. With talk of him being impeached, he resigned in August 1974, the first president to do so. He left the White House in disgrace.

the government. Watergate and the revelations of the misuse of power by the executive branch by several past presidents reminded people of the message spelt out by the Founding Fathers – a system that placed too much responsibility in the hands of one man must offer temptations for wrong-doing.

This growth of executive power did not happen suddenly under President Nixon. Arthur Schlesinger[4] argued that the concept of the constitutional presidency had given way by the 1970s to an **imperial presidency**, a revolutionary use of power very different from what had originally been intended. The presidency no longer seemed to be controllable via the constitutional checks and balances.

> **imperial presidency**
> A label for the increased authority and decreased accountability of the presidency, at its peak by the late 1960s/early 1970s. It signified an era in which there was a high-handed and often secretive handling of foreign policy issues and in which in domestic policy too presidents were able to evade the usual system of checks and balances.

The 1970s to the present day

In the aftermath of these concerns, power passed to two presidents, Ford and Carter, who were widely perceived as anything but 'imperial'. Neither projected the image of an assertive leader and both were rejected by the voters after one period in office. Observers began to refer to the limitations of the presidency rather than to the strength of the office, with Franck[5] writing of the 'tethered presidency', one too constrained to be effective of providing the leadership America required.

Ronald Reagan was the first postwar president since Eisenhower to complete two terms in office, and despite the lapses that occurred (in particular, Irangate – see box overleaf), he is widely perceived as having achieved much of what he wished to accomplish. After the setbacks of the 1970s, there was talk of a 'restored presidency'. Many Americans seemed to warm to the Reaganite style, which is why he has been immortalised in numerous ways, with an airport, an aircraft carrier and highways being named in his honour.

The Reagan years (1981–89) were eventful in foreign and in domestic policy. In external relations, the president began with a reputation as a Cold War warrior, deeply suspicious of the 'evil empire' of the Soviet Union. Yet in the second term, the unyielding attitude was softened, and his close working relationship with the Soviet leader Gorbachev helped to bring about an easing of international tension and an end to the Cold War. By 1988, the thaw in relations was well under way, and the most anti-communist president of recent years had reached an accommodation with the regime he had long detested.

At home, his agenda was to reduce the role of government in the lives of ordinary Americans, and he wished to return power to the states and downplay the influence of the federal government in Washington. His economic programme included a commitment to tax cuts, and the Reagan years witnessed an era of economic growth. There was also a huge expansion of the federal deficit, for lower taxes and increased military expenditure were not matched by cuts elsewhere of a proportionate nature. The US, the largest creditor nation in 1981, was the world's largest debtor eight years later.

The goal of substantially rolling back the sphere of influence of the federal government was not achieved. Federal expenditure actually increased marginally in the early years, though non-defence spending – such as that on education – suffered sizeable cuts. But what Reagan was able to do was to make many Americans feel good about themselves and their country. After years in which its reputation had taken a severe blow over episodes such as Vietnam and Watergate, he was able to restore morale and there was a resurgence of patriotic feeling and confidence about the future.

Irangate

President Reagan's style of leadership was relaxed and detached, and he did not involve himself in anything but the broad generalities of policy. His aloofness from day-to-day activities had certain benefits, but carried the disadvantage that he was sometimes ill-informed and out of touch with events occurring in his administration.

The Iran–Contra affair, the major crisis of his presidency, occurred as a result of his method of managing the nation's affairs. Two officials within the National Security Council, John Poindexter and the more junior Lieutenant-Colonel Oliver North, were accused of pursuing a policy of selling arms to Iran in return for the release of American hostages detained in the Middle East. The proceeds of the arms sales were channelled to the Contras, rebel forces who were seeking to overthrow the left-wing Sandinista government of Nicaragua, which the US Administration wished to destabilise so that it could be overthrown.

Both operations, the arms for hostages and the diversion of money to the guerrillas, were illegal. Congress had refused to agree to military aid for the rebel forces in Nicaragua, though it was willing to grant humanitarian assistance and keen to see the regime toppled. Altogether, at least four main laws were breached, and the sale of weapons to states sponsoring terrorism was something that the president himself had publicly denounced.

George Bush was a Republican of a different kind to Reagan, and was uncommitted to the economic doctrines of the New Right. When he took over, he was confronted with the vast budget deficit, and contrary to his election promises he was forced to introduce increased taxation. He was not deeply interested in domestic problems, but found himself in office when many Americans began to worry about stagnation at home in domestic policy. His neglect of this area left him vulnerable to his political critics, and despite his successful conduct of the Gulf War abroad in 1991, he was unable to arouse popular enthusiasm when faced by the challenge of Bill Clinton and Ross Perot in 1992.

Unlike Bush, **Bill Clinton** was not initially faced by a Congress dominated by his political opponents, but the advantage was more apparent than real and his initiatives were rebuffed on several occasions. After the November 1994 elections, he was confronted by two Republican-dominated chambers, a situation which lasted throughout the rest of his presidency. Relations with Congress were often strained, the more so as the president became more deeply immersed in the problems which led to his impeachment (see pp. 83–4) But in the eyes of many Americans he remained a likeable and attractive figure, whatever his personal lapses.

The Clinton legacy will always be controversial, for his presidency was dogged by the character issue. He was a man of huge appetites that he did not seek to control. He behaved surprisingly imprudently for a man equipped with such astute political skills. His affairs and his evasions of the truth may be seen as character flaws. More seriously, they damaged his presidency and, some would say, the institution as well. In a recent survey of American presidential leadership styles, Fred Greenstein[6] has effectively summed up the mixed, paradoxical Clinton performance in this way: 'It is a tribute to Clinton's resiliency and political prowess that he has succeeded in serving two presidential terms. It is a commentary on his weaknesses that this talented political leader has not had more to show for his time in office'.

The George W. Bush presidency

Critics have caricatured George W. Bush as a know-nothing, verbally challenged and not very industrious politician who has risen well beyond his abilities. They have also assembled plenty of evidence to suggest that he has shifted American politics sharply to the right. If this is so, it is a far cry from the 'compassionate conservatism' that George W. advanced in the 2000 election campaign. At the time, the allegation was frequently made that there would be little to choose between the two candidates; whoever won, little would change.

After polling day, many Americans indeed hoped that George W. would recognise his limited mandate and seek to govern from the centre, as a man of the consensus. This did not prove to be the case, for he and his supporters were serious in their intent to mark a distinct break from the Clinton years. They soon won the support of the ultra-conservative Heritage Foundation, whose members were pleased to find many items on the Republican wish-list becoming reality. Its head[7] detected that the new team was 'more Reaganite than the Reagan administration'.

The Bush technique was to use the rhetoric of bipartisanship, humility and healing as a cover for the pursuit of a radically conservative agenda. The president's charm and seeming reasonableness earned him some admiration, as did some of his early initiatives. For instance, he:

- appointed Colin Powell, widely seen as a moderate, as his first secretary of state, and a black woman, Condoleezza Rice, as his national security adviser and then – in his second term – as Powell's successor;
- selected an ethnically diverse first Cabinet which included two black and two Asian Americans (one of the Asians was a Democrat, Norman Mineta), a Cuban American, an Arab American, and four women;
- tried to break down social barriers in Washington by inviting liberal critics to the White House and also meeting black American political leaders and visiting black churches and schools;
- opted for an educational policy which Democrats broadly support, the emphasis being upon improving provision in the poorest areas of the country, with extra funding and greater teacher accountability; he showed some willingness to negotiate over the principle and detail of his contentious educational voucher scheme.

The early charm offensive helped to blunt some Democrat criticism of the Bush agenda and performance, a task made easier because the last, scandal-ridden days of the Clinton administration demoralised the opposition. But behind the handshakes and smiles, the actions were tougher than the tone would suggest. Critics pointed out that the Cabinet might have been socially well balanced, but that its members were in several cases deeply conservative. They also noted the importance of business in the administration, with millionaires at the cabinet table; for instance, Condoleezza Rice has a Chevron oil tanker named after her, and chief of staff Andrew Card is a former leading lobbyist of General Motors. More partisan and controversial actions included:

- appointing hard-liners such as John Ashcroft as his first attorney general (Ashcroft's record includes strong backing for those who oppose abortion rights and affirmative action) and the hawkish Donald Rumsfeld as his defence secretary
- widening the already-large gap between the position of the haves and have-nots, by a redistribution of wealth in favour of the rich; measures include: (a) the programme of $1,600 billion tax cuts which primarily benefit more affluent Americans; and (b) the proposal to drop inheritance tax, to the benefit of the top 2% of Americans, who have estates worth more than $675,000;
- supporting faith-based social services, by offering aid to churches which perform welfare work; critics feared that this might lead to reductions in funding of secular social care;

- opposing a patients' bill of rights, which would have removed legal immunity from private health-care organisations;
- halting foreign aid spending on abortions, so that in future there will be no federal spending in support of international family planning organisations which back abortion;
- allowing prospectors to open up the Alaskan National Wildlife Refuge and relaxing environmental controls on old power plants;
- repudiating the Kyoto protocol signed by Bill Clinton on pegging green-house gas emissions;
- renouncing American support for the nuclear test-ban treaty, the anti-ballistic missile treaty and the ban on chemical weapons, and pursuing a costly and highly controversial national missile defence system known as Star Wars Two. Opponents believe that narrowly defined national security interests and the commercial interests of the biotechnology sector are being allowed to take precedence over responsible multilateral agreements and global collaboration.

A more assertive presidency

On September 11, 2001, there was a sudden terrorist attack on the World Trade Center in New York, a building that symbolised the business life of America. Hijacked aircraft crashed into the Twin Towers, causing thousands of deaths and massive destruction. Intelligence sources immediately pointed to Osama bin Laden and his Al-Qaida organisation as the guilty parties. Once the aggressor was confirmed, President Bush was under strong pressure from elements within the United States to act swiftly, but he did not take any drastic measures straight away. Acting in concert with the British government, he attempted to create an international coalition to wage war on international terrorism. The war aims that he set the US and its allies were to apprehend Bin Laden and destroy his network, both of which were long-term goals. As the air campaign in Afghanistan (where Bin Laden was hiding) got under way, it became apparent that there was another goal in destroying the Taliban regime.

The collapse of the Twin Towers jolted the Bush presidency into uncharacter-istic vigour. It moved into a higher gear and Bush became more focused and purposeful. Washington reorganised itself around the executive branch and Bush reorganised his administration around the struggle against terrorism. Almost at once, he persuaded Congress to approve a substantial recovery package that also made additional provision to allow for strengthening of the intelligence and security services. Congress also quickly passed an anti-terrorism bill that greatly increased the potential of executive power.

Having long been suspicious of the power exercised by 'big government' in Washington, many Americans rallied behind President Bush. They were in a mood to accept more assertive presidential leadership. They were unsure of what was happening to them and yearned for a sense of direction. This gave the president a chance to take a firmer grip upon events. He began to shape the political agenda, and his early actions were accepted with little dissent. Some commentators began to use phrases such as 'the revived presidency' or 'the reimperialised presidency'. War – in this case on terrorism – was the catalyst for change. It demanded personalised control from the man who symbolised the unity of the country.

In seeking to wage war on terrorism, the president engaged on a daunting task. In the short term, the crisis of September 11 served to boost presidential prestige. It matured the new incumbent of the White House into an international statesman. In its early days, what was an American tragedy proved to be the making of George W. Bush. In the words of a Washington correspondent, 'the sharpest learning curve in the history of the presidency has seen Bush mutate into a figurehead who has the people behind him'.[8]

But the short and successful war against the Taliban proved to be the first stage of a wider war on terror. Vice-President Cheney and others in the White House became obsessed with the link between international terrorism and the existence of weapons of mass destruction (WMD). Cheney became the Administration's most aggressive voice in favour of confronting Iraq, hyping the nuclear threat from Saddam Hussein. Saddam had long been a thorn in America's side, and Cheney and other hawks were keen to see America launch a pre-emptive strike against one of American's enemies. A 'coalition of the willing' was assembled to fight in Iraq, consisting primarily of American and British forces. On this occasion, world opinion was much less united behind the president, and at home the war soon generated opposition.

Many early supporters of military action against Iraq later became alarmed at the seeming lack of a plan for peacekeeping after the cessation of hostilities. The failure to find WMD, the excesses of some American troops and the continuation of insurgency against the occupation caused continuing disquiet. At the time of writing, in the first part of 2005, the outlook is unclear. A favourable scenario would see the establishment of an Iraqi government that commanded broad support, following the elections of January 2005. Given the antagonism that American forces have generated among significant sections of the Iraqi population, that picture may seem unduly optimistic.

The president faced internal criticism not just over Iraq. Many Americans were concerned that the Administration was undermining the constitutional rights and liberties of US citizens. The passage of the Patriot Act (see p. 304) enabled him to imprison citizens without charge and clamp down on a range of established freedoms. Conditions at Guantanamo Bay were a regular cause of criticism.

Differing verdicts on George W. Bush

Americans are not ambivalent about George Bush. People tend to like or dislike him with an unusually intensity. For some, he represents the ideal of presidential leadership, whereas others continue to regard him as an embarrassing usurper who had no right to be in the White House in the first place.

Republican and Democrat voters find them themselves in sharp disagreement about almost all aspects of the Bush presidency – on America's standing in the world, whether he has been too partisan, whether he has a good grasp of the issues and whether he has been to willing to inject his own moral and religious beliefs into politics. Whereas the pollsters find that Republicans see a man who is decisive, determined and strong, opponents see a person who is arrogant, cocky and bone-headed.

Bush represents the politics of certainty. He does not flinch when the arguments and numbers seem to be against him, for in his view government is about truth which re represents. He tends to paint stark visions of enemies and good guys. This simplicity and starkness appeal very much to some people, who in uncertain times are content to know that the person in the White House knows the answers.

Those who dislike him are deeply suspicious about his abilities and his motives. What to his admirers seems like moral clarity, to his detractors seems like simple-mindedness; certitude seems like self-righteousness; and piety like sanctimoniousness. As for his policies, even many Americans who originally backed the invasion of Iraq have subsequently developed doubts about not only the credibility but also the competence of the Administration. Whether the war came about because of a thirst for oil or out of crusading interventionist zeal, they are uneasy about the reasons for and direction of policy.

A mistake made by some of the president's critics is to underestimate him. Those with more insight recognise that however much they might doubt his competence and policies, he is a strong performer on the campaign trail. If his style does not travel well across the Atlantic, it goes down well in the United States. One liberal critic on this side of the Atlantic[9] noted in the mid-term election contest some of his qualities, and was surprised to find himself admitting to them. In particular, Bush:

- spoke fluently and without notes;
- mastered the common touch and – in his folksy, accessible way, mouthing rather simple sentiments – was surprisingly effective;
- looked and sounded relaxed;
- seemed surprisingly knowledgeable, whether talking about education or the war on terrorism;
- could be humorous;
- inspired loyalty among his followers, who admired him as a 'tough guy'.

Yet in November 2004, George Bush was re-elected, in the process winning more votes than any other presidential candidate had done before. His victory was decisive (see pp. 227–34), not just in the battle for the White House but also in the congressional elections, in which Republicans tightened their grip, adding seats in both the House and the Senate. Whatever the anxieties over

Iraq and the war on terrorism, the victory illustrated how difficult it is for any challenger to defeat a sitting president at a time when the country has troops abroad and national security is a live political issue. Allegations that during the Bush presidency nearly a million jobs had been lost, the budget surplus squandered, record deficits created, and 4.5 million Americans left without health insurance made less impact than might have otherwise been the case.

Following the attack on the Twin Towers, Bush adopted a different style which was well received by many Americans. He won substantial support for his security policies and initially his ratings in the opinion polls soared. Although the presidency had been weakened over recent decades, his response and reactions to it suggested that the political system could still respond to presidential leadership during times of adversity. Yet should the president's policy in Iraq fail to achieve its objectives, there might well be a reaction against the more assertive style of the post-September 11 era.

Presidential leadership and power today

As the size and influence of the United States in the world have developed, so has the machinery of government and with it the informal power and influence of the president. He is a national leader and by many is seen also as the leader of the Western world, the person who will represent the country on the global stage.

Factors in the broad growth of presidential power and influence: a summary

1 **The growth of 'big government' in years after 1933**, as Roosevelt became identified with increased federal intervention in the Depression.
2 **The importance of foreign policy**, with the development of an American world role after World War II.
3 **The personality and conception of the office held by the incumbent:** sometimes, a passive president seems appropriate for the times, as in the 1920s, whilst at other times an active presidency is required.
4 **The inertia of Congress and erosion of balance:** at times, Congress surrendered much influence, and allowed strong 'liberals' to achieve reform.
5 **The mass media:** the media can focus on one national office, for the president is news.

In discussing past presidents, commentators often refer to 'presidential leadership' and 'presidential power'. Sometimes, the two terms are used interchangeably. Yet there is a difference between them. Political leadership implies the capacity to chart the course of events, set out goals and persuade and inspire others to follow. It suggests influence. Power is the ability to achieve the goals. This implies command over the personalities, institutions and events involved. All presidents have a substantial degree of power, deriving from the office they hold, but there are serious limitations in the exercise of it. When they leave office, they lose power. Those who have exercised leadership and sought to reshape the political landscape in pursuit of what they see as the public good are the ones most often remembered.

Americans recall FDR, JFK and Ronald Reagan long after they left office. In recent decades, Americans have generally expected leadership. They want leaders who have a clear vision of where they are going. No other person in the political system can highlight issues as the president can.

Presidential powers are set out in the Constitution, but they are also influenced by political and personal considerations. They may be limited by circumstances. To exercise a high degree of power requires careful utilisation of the resources open to the president. If he has qualities of leadership, then his chances of 'changing the constellation of political forces about him in a direction closer to his own conception of the political good'[10] are much increased. Presidential leadership can focus attention on what needs to be done and help the White House to overcome any inertia and obstruction in the political system.

The nature of the presidency at a particular moment depends considerably upon the incumbent. Great men make great presidents. Personality is important to the style and impact of the presidency, but the active presidential leadership of the 1960s and the habit of congressional compliance are out of fashion.

Popular expectations of presidents

Many Americans want more from their president than somebody who is merely efficient while in office. They also want someone 'presidential', and look for someone who can embody the American creed and reflect the 'spirit of the people'. Like the flag and the Constitution, the president is a symbol of national identity. Some have been successful in capturing the public's imagination and winning their support, as Kennedy and Reagan were able to do. If they can do this, then their influence and informal power will increase as well.

In the age of television, the personality and style of leadership of anyone who would be president have become all-important. The need to perform well is crucial, and Reagan, for all of his seeming lack of familiarity with some key issues and his occasional verbal stumbles, was a man who embodied the American Dream. His resolute optimism, his old-fashioned values and his promise to help America 'stand tall' after the malaise of the 1970s were very popular. His background as a film and TV actor enabled him to communicate well (his supporters called him 'the Great Communicator'), so that he represented a merger between the worlds of entertainment and politics.

How Americans evaluate their presidents varies over time. In part, it depends on who has recently been president and who is the present incumbent. In different eras, Americans have a different idea of what their president should be like. At times, they demand vigorous leadership, but they may then become troubled by the consequences of that assertiveness and yearn for a less active presidency. After a while, such inactivity can be portrayed as weakness and ineffectiveness. In Wasserman's words:[11] 'Americans have swung back and forth in how powerful they want their presidents . . . [they] have walked a thin line between too much and too little power.' Wasserman illustrates this by pointing to the worries felt by many citizens about the abuse of power by Nixon, yet the perception only a few years later that Jimmy Carter was too weak to solve the nation's difficulties. In actual fact, it was the reaction against Vietnam and Watergate (as well as changes in the organisation of Congress) that made it difficult for Carter to stamp his authority on the legislature.

Qualities often admired in presidents are honesty, as well as decision-making ability, judgement, intelligence and toughness. Yet although the average voter seems to value credibility and truthfulness as admirable qualities for anyone in the White House, the example of Bill Clinton shows that even if they distrusted him when it came to truth-telling, many of them none the less admired him for other reasons. They recognised that he was a creative, resourceful and smart politician, a man with fine rhetorical skills who excelled on the public platform. Ironically, some of his best approval ratings came at the very time when the Lewinsky scandals (see p. 84) were exposing aspects of his more irresponsible behaviour.

The reputation of past presidents

American historians have often compiled lists of presidents whom they admire or consider great. Greatness is difficult to define. For some, it conjures up an impression of idealism in thought or action. Others think of the accomplishment of heroic deeds. Judgement, integrity, talent, vigour of mind and vision are other qualities that might be identified as important criteria. Experts tend to place more faith in intellectual capacity, experience and ability to impart a sense of direction than do members of the public, who, as we have seen, regard honesty as especially important. Landy and Milks[12] make the point that: 'The great presidents were great because they not only brought about change, but also left a legacy – principles, institutional arrangements and policies that defined an era . . . When decisive action was required, they took it . . . the need to execute requires presidents to be willing to flout the popular will.'

In early 2000, the findings of a survey of fifty-eight American history professors were published for the public affairs TV channel C-Span. Ten qualities were tested, ranging from crisis leadership to moral authority, from vision to administrative skills, and from the pursuit of equal justice to performance in the context of the times. The top ten in the rankings were (in order) Lincoln, Franklin Roosevelt, Washington, Teddy Roosevelt, Truman, Wilson, Jefferson, Kennedy, Eisenhower and Lyndon Johnson, whose reputation has risen steadily in recent years. Almost without exception the presidents considered 'great' by academic commentators have been 'leaders'. Most of the more passive ones have been long forgotten or remembered only because of the futility or scandals of their administrations.

The presidency is what its holder makes of it, being as large and important, or as weak and as insignificant, as the holders of the office. Academics have tended to divide past presidents into 'active' leaders of the nation or 'constitutional or passive' ones. The two views of presidential power can be seen in contrasting the approach of past incumbents and reactions to them.

Theodore Roosevelt remarked in his *Autobiography* that he

> declined to adopt the view that what was imperatively necessary for the nation could not be done by the president unless he could find some specific authorization to do it. My belief was that it was not only his right, but his duty to do anything that the needs of the nation demanded, unless such action was forbidden by the Constitution or by the laws . . . I did not usurp power but . . . did greatly broaden the use of executive power.

He was of the Lincoln school and like him a Republican. Roosevelt favoured a policy of active leadership, setting out national goals. Others of this type have wanted to make a mark on the national scene, not being content with mere stewardship of the presidency. Roosevelt, Truman, Kennedy and Johnson were of this type, as was Bill Clinton.

By contrast, the leaders of Lincoln's own party in the two chambers of Congress gave a warning in what has become known as the Wade–Davis manifesto: 'the authority of Congress is paramount . . . if [the president] wishes our support he must confine himself to his executive duties – to obey, and to execute, not to make laws'. Those who take this view have a custodial view of the presidency, by which the incumbent confines himself to carrying out those powers expressly mentioned in the Constitution and leaves Congress to take the lead in deciding what is to be done. Examples included Harding and Coolidge in the 1920s – significantly, they were both Republicans, many of whom tend to have a more sceptical view of the role of government.

Some writers[13] have detected a third variety, referred to as the 'Eisenhower type'. Exponents of this style combine elements of both the views described above. They tend to delegate responsibility (and thus shield themselves from blame when things go wrong), using the rhetoric of being 'above the political battle' to conceal a more active engagement with the political process. This has been called the 'hidden-hand' approach, and its adherents have sometimes been willing to take a decisive stand and wield a surprising degree of power. Nixon tried to convey the impression of being a national figure and statesman beyond the heat of battle, whilst at the same time using the White House as a centre for powerful and partisan leadership.

Most modern presidents have by inclination been more activists than stewards. Bill Clinton began his period in office by taking several initiatives, helped as he was by his majority in both chambers of Congress. But his intentions were stalled in November 1994 and the political agenda was increasingly set on Capitol Hill rather than in the White House, with Clinton reacting to policies rather than shaping them. Some of his later 'triumphs' were more by way of fending off the impact of congressional inroads into social programmes than as a result of his preferred lines of action. Not surprisingly, some commentators wrote of the 'constrained presidency'. Yet in his case his qualities as an effective campaigner, with a knack for appealing over the heads of congressmen to the nation at large, often enabled him to stage a comeback. He was able to use the presidential office as a pulpit from which to preach his values on issues that mattered to him, such as the family, race and even religion.

Presidential success?

It is unclear what constitutes presidential success. The views of academics (see pp. 78–9) and the voters do not necessarily coincide, the two groups not sharing the same priorities. Success depends on what the president is supposed to do. If the criterion is dynamism and/or creativity, then Eisenhower was not a success. But in other respects, given his more limited conception of the role as that of a steward of national affairs, he was arguably successful, being a popular national leader who was suitable for the mood of the times.

Certain eras require more vigorous leadership and legislative action than others. By the criterion of the proportion of his legislative programme achieved, President Johnson was an undoubted success. But he presided over a country that was becoming increasingly troubled and divided, and his memory has been tarnished by the events in Vietnam. Bill Clinton was able to speak to the hearts of many Americans at times of crisis and presided over eight years of economic success. Yet he stained the presidency as a result of his personal conduct and harmed his party's prospects in the 2000 election.

Fred Greenstein[14] has singled out six characteristics that might be used in assessing the effectiveness of president leadership:
  • **effectiveness as a public communicator**: the ability to convey ideas to party, public and the international community;

- **organisational capacity**: effectiveness in planning and executing policies – in other words, the skills exhibited as manager of the executive branch;
- **political skill**: the ability to persuade Congress, mobilise support and campaign effectively;
- **political vision**: the ability to articulate clear goals;
- **cognitive skills**: the ability to understand a range of key issues;
- **emotional intelligence**: the character and temperament to work under pressure.

The list is not exhaustive and some of the criteria might be questioned, much depending on the qualities sought after in a political leader. Others that might be added in the light of earlier comments are the abilities to achieve legislative goals, to maintain steady judgement in an international crisis and to preside over a strong economy. Some might add the ability to maintain popularity and to get re-elected.

The limitations on presidential power

Several presidents from Franklin Roosevelt to Bill Clinton have at times spoken of the constraints under which they operated whilst in the White House. They have complained about the difficulties they experienced in carrying out policy, particularly on the domestic front. Clinton's failure to restructure health care was an obvious example, but so too was George W. Bush's difficulty in achieving reform of the tax system in his first administration. Sometimes, these problems were because of the president's personal deficiencies as leaders. Carter was little versed in the methods of Washington politics and failed to understand the rudimentary facts about the policy-making process. A congressman[15] produced his impression of the exchanges between the president and speaker Tip O'Neill, which went as follows:

> O'Neill: A fine speech, Mr President. Now here's a list of members you should call, you know, to keep the pressure on. We need their votes.
> Carter: Tip, I outlined the problem to the people of the United States of America. It was rational, and my presentation was also rational. Now the American people are the most intelligent people in the world, Tip, and I am sure that when they see their Representatives think my program over, they will see that I was right.
> O'Neill: Lookit, Mr President. We need you to push this bill through. This is politics we are talking here, not physics.
> Carter: It is not politics, Tip, not to me. It's what is right and rational and necessary and practical and urgent that we do . . . Say, do you like my sweater?
> O'Neill: [later to a congressional colleague] That guy is hopeless. It's gonna be a long winter.

On leaving office, Lyndon Johnson – who was far more adept at manipulating the levers of power than Carter – pointed out to his successor, Richard Nixon, some of the realities of political power. Johnson observed: 'Before you get to the presidency, you think you can do anything. You think you're the most powerful leader since God, But when you get in that tall chair, as you're gonna find out, Mr President, you can't count on people. You'll find your hands tied and people cussin' you.'

In *Presidential Power*, first published in 1960, Richard Neustadt[16] pointed to the limitations on the power of the president, as well as to the strength of his position. Neustadt was writing before the days of the 'imperial presidency', but even at that time took the view that the presidency was actually rather weak in US government, being unable to effect significant change without the approval of Congress.

Neustadt soon found himself in demand by the president-elect, John F. Kennedy, and began his advisory role with a memo suggesting how the new president might approach his term in office. As a liberal who believed in an activist presidency such as that of FDR, Neustadt urged Kennedy to get to off to a good start, creating 'a first impression of energy, direction, action and accomplishment'. But it was Neustadt's diagnosis of how a president might overcome the limitations of his role that has been much quoted. Neustadt concluded that 'the power of the presidency is the power to persuade, its professional reputation and its public prestige'. In a system in which there is shared power, the president must do his best to bargain with rival power centres to get what he believes to be needed.

In a revised edition of *Presidential Power* (1990), Neustadt confirmed his earlier findings. Indeed, he detected a further blow to presidential power. The Cold War had contributed to the increase in post-1945 presidential power. With its disappearance, the role of commander-in-chief might be more fraught with problems than it was when Neustadt had first written that: 'Presidents will less and less have reason to seek solace in foreign relations from the piled-up frustrations of home affairs. Their foreign frustration will be piled high too.'[17] In the later work, he reiterated his emphasis upon the importance of the personal qualities of the incumbent. It takes, in Neustadt's view, a person of extraordinary temperament to make a really significant impact and achieve all the goals he sets for himself.

Among the specific factors which Neustadt's work highlighted are:

1 Congress (see also p. 93 below)

The president needs congressional support, and in the more assertive mood of Congress in recent years' incumbents have found this difficult to achieve even with their own party in control. Faced by a hostile Congress, Bush and Clinton (in his last six years) had difficulties in carrying out aspects of their programme, resulting in 'gridlock', a situation in which the two branches of government were locked in conflict.

The tendency of Congress to appoint special prosecutors to probe every aspect of a president's affairs, and the relentless media interest which this creates, have a paralysing impact on presidential policy. Investigations drag on, seemingly for partisan reasons, and – as Clinton found to his costs (see box overleaf) – there is always the ultimate horror of the threat of **impeachment** at the end of the road.

> **impeachment**
> The process by which Congress can remove officers of the national government, including the president. The House votes on a charge or series of charges, and a trial on the charges is then conducted in the Senate.

2 The Supreme Court

The Court can damage a president and negate a particular activity, as it did to FDR over his 'Court-packing' scheme (see p. 169) and to President Nixon over the Watergate tapes. During the Clinton presidency too, it became clear that proceedings could be brought against an incumbent, with the president and his closest staff being compelled to give evidence under oath.

3 The Constitution and constitutional amendments

Any president seeking to bring about a measure of gun control faces the difficulty that the right to bear arms is written into the Constitution. In developing his New Deal programme, President Roosevelt found that the same document could be used as a barrier to social progress.

Some amendments to the Constitution in the last few decades of the twentieth century have weakened the presidency. The Twenty-Second Amendment limited the president to two terms of office, and the Twenty-Fifth provided for the removal of a person physically or mentally unfit.

4 The federal system

Whereas points (1) and (2) above are limitations which derive from the operation of the 'separation of powers' principle, there are hurdles for any president which reflect the operation of the idea of federalism. The fifty states have a large degree of fiscal and legislative autonomy, which acts as a check on the role of the federal government and therefore of the president, who has to negotiate with state representatives in several areas of decision-making.

5 The mass media

Television can be a source of power to a telegenic president, but it can also act as a 'double-edged sword'. It can damage his reputation, for a poor performance or gaffe (e.g. Ford's in the presidential debates of 1976 – see p. 204) is seen by so many viewers that credibility is undermined. Press

IMPEACHMENT: THE CLINTON EXPERIENCE

Article II:4 of the American Constitution states that: 'The President, Vice President and all civil officers of the united States, shall be removed from Office on Impeachment for, and Conviction of, Treason, Bribery or other high Crimes and Misdemeanours.' Impeachment, then, involves a charge of misconduct against an officer of the national government being laid. In the case of the president, he is then committed for trial and, if convicted, removed from office.

In the process of impeachment, the House acts as the prosecutor and the Senate as judge and jury. Any member of the House may initiate impeachment proceedings by introducing a resolution to that effect. The House Judiciary Committee conducts proceedings in the lower chamber and then decides in favour of or against impeachment. It delivers a verdict to the whole House, which requires a 50% vote to impeach. If the process goes ahead, the case is then tried in the Senate, the chief justice presiding on this occasion. A two-thirds vote of those present is needed to secure a conviction and subsequent removal.

Impeachment is one of the most potent checks upon the abuse of power. It can also be a means of undermining a president's authority. But – being a rather partisan, cumbersome and time-consuming means of ensuring accountability – it has only sparingly been used. Charges have been considered by the House against more than sixty officials, including nine presidents. But in only seventeen of these cases has the issue resulted in a Senate trial. Only two of the nine cases involving a president have got that far: those of Andrew Johnson in 1868 and Bill Clinton in 1999. The Senate failed to convict Johnson by just one vote, whereas in the Clinton case the Senate was at least twelve votes short of the necessary number. The case of Richard Nixon's obstruction of justice in the Watergate inquiry never reached the Senate, for he resigned as president in August 1974. Had he not done so, he might well have been the first incumbent of the White House to be impeached successfully.

The impeachment of Bill Clinton

Clinton was not impeached for sexual misconduct, although the case against him originated in a case of sexual harassment concerning Paula Jones. As part of the Clinton deposition (testimony), he was asked about his relationship with Monica Lewinsky, a former White House intern. Clinton's answers were untruthful and the perjury involved enabled the (Republican) prosecutor, Kenneth Starr, to recommend that the president be impeached. (The Jones case was eventually settled out of court. If this had happened earlier in the proceedings, impeachment might have been avoided.)

journalists can be vigilant in exposing presidential wrong-doings, as over Vietnam, Watergate, Irangate and Whitewatergate/Monicagate. The press was generally indulgent towards President Kennedy's personal indiscretions, but in the post-Watergate atmosphere it has been more disposed 'to seek out the dirt' in the private lives of politicians.

Four articles of impeachment were laid before the House Judiciary Committee, which in December 1998 voted to approve further action on all of them, namely:

- **article 1**, charging perjury before Ken Starr's federal grand jury;
- **article 2**, charging perjury in the Paula Jones deposition;
- **article 3**, charging obstruction of justice in the Paula Jones case;
- **article 4**, charging failure to respond to the eighty-one questions posed by the House Judiciary Committee during the impeachment inquiry.

The whole House decided to go ahead on two counts, articles 1 and 3. House Representatives handling the prosecution in the Senate emphasised how the obstruction of justice involved in the third article involved a threat to the rule of law that the president had sworn to uphold. They professed concern that if he was allowed to escape punishment, this set a bad precedent. It would permit one system of justice for the powerful, another for other people. Some Democrats might have agreed with the view that he had behaved badly and violated his oath, but the majority of them – and a few Republican moderates – were unconvinced that this amounted to 'high crimes and misdemeanours'. As Senator Jeffords put it: 'I am gravely concerned that a vote to convict the President on these articles may establish a low threshold that would make every president subject to removal for the slightest indiscretion, or that a vote to convict may impale every president who faces a Congress controlled by the opposing party. In other words, this would be a potentially devastating precedent.'

The Senate agreed and voted to reject both articles, with ten Republicans defecting from the party line on the perjury count and five on article 3.

Why did the impeachment proceedings fail?

As we have seen, some Republicans could not accept that the gravity of the offences merited such a drastic punishment as was being proposed. They realised too that the way in which the charges were brought by a near-obsessed special prosecutor and passed by a Republican-dominated House smacked of undue partisanship. It seemed like a Republican witch-hunt against Clinton. If this was the public perception, then their party might suffer for its behaviour at the polls. Beyond this, senators were only too aware of the public mood. The President's personal popularity was increasing, at the very time impeachment proceedings were being debated. To impeach him would have been particularly risky for the Republicans, bearing in mind that many Americans did not seem sufficiently troubled to want to be rid of him. They were able to distinguish between the flawed man (whose failings were well known to them at the time of his re-election in 1996) and the successful president who was presiding over a seemingly strong economy.

6 Pressure groups

Individual groups achieve prominence at particular times. Today, a Republican president has to contend with the Christian fundamentalists, pro-lifers and big corporations. A Democrat has to deal with the labour unions and environmentalists. In Bill Clinton's first few months in office, the clashes between groups concerned over 'gays in the military' inflicted serious damage on his reputation.

7 Public opinion

Levels of popular support can fluctuate, as they did for George Bush senior (high at the time of the Gulf War, then down as the state of the domestic economy failed to impress Americans). Clinton retained a high degree of public approval, in spite of his personal misdemeanours. He was able to bounce back after the disastrous 1994 elections and to win re-election. Many have been less fortunate, and this can be damaging not only because of the need to win re-election. A president who is losing popular backing or at least acquiescence may find that opposition in Congress, the media and the bureaucracy will increase, so that other checking mechanisms come into play.

8 Bureaucracy

The president has plenty of constitutional authority, but the problem is sometimes how to get the bureaucracy to work for him. He needs to be able to persuade as well as to direct, but even then he can find that his will is frustrated by bureaucrats who tend to see the world through a lens which is focused largely on their own departments. No modern president seems to have been able to stop the growth of bureaucracy, so that the majority of the agencies created since the 1930s have survived intact into the twenty-first century.

There are other factors, ranging from the power of the federal reserve to determine interest rates to the current mood of detachment, some say neo-isolationism, which affects the conduct of foreign and defence policy: one area in which presidents – as commanders-in-chief – have always given a lead. The American writers Burns et al.[18] make a series of fair observations when they write of

> one of the persisting paradoxes of the American presidency . . . on the one hand, the institution is too powerful, and on the other, it is always too weak. It is too strong because in many ways it is contrary to our ideals of government by the people and decentralization of power. It is too weak because presidents seldom are able to keep the promises they make. Of course, the presidency is always too strong when we dislike the incumbent. And the president is always too constrained when we believe a President is striving to serve the public interest – as we define it.

Neustadt, as quoted above, makes the point that the power of the president always did depend upon personal leadership rather more than the formal position: 'powers are no guarantee of power'. This was true in the days of the imperial presidency. Indeed, it is easy to overstress the power of presidents before Watergate and to overemphasise the decline or difficulties of the presidency from the 1970s onwards. John Hart[19] reminds us that FDR, the first of the so-called modern presidents, was untypical in the power that he exercised:

> None of his successors faced anything like the enormity of the Depression of the early 1930s, and none took over the White House during a national emergency so clearly and unambiguously defined. Neither has any post-FDR president had such a comparable level of public support for presidential initiative and leadership. As the beneficiary of a landslide election victory in a realigning election (one in which the voters opted for a complete change of direction and which resulted in a permanent shift in popular support), a strong coat-tails effect in the congressional races, and as head of a political party that behaved as a 'cohesive office-seeking team', FDR enjoyed a political environment that none of his successors have shared, and most could only fantasise about.

In other words, the Roosevelt presidency was the exception rather than the rule. Personality, ability and circumstance all play their part in determining presidential power, but whoever is in the White House operates in a system which specifically denies too much power to the executive.

The differing roles of the president

Head of state

The president is the symbolic head of state and as such a focal point of loyalty. He has ceremonial functions, ranging from visiting foreign countries to attending important national occasions. These opportunities for favourable media coverage give him an advantage over his opponents, for he can be seen to speak and act in a 'presidential' manner.

Chief executive

The ability of the president to carry out or execute laws is laid down in Article 2 of the Constitution – 'The executive power shall be vested in a President of the United States.' He is the head of a vast federal bureaucracy, employing nearly three million civilians in the executive branch.

Chief legislator

Although the president is not part of the legislative branch of government, he has the constitutional rights to recommend measures to Congress. In the twentieth and early twenty-first centuries, presidents have increasingly found themselves in the position of producing a package to encourage the legislature. They have used the State of the Union address every January to present their annual programme, and today most measures passed by Congress have their origins in the executive branch. As we have seen, much depends on the political situation. A president without a congressional majority – such as Bill Clinton in his last six years – is in the position of responding to and attempting to modify measures, rather than initiating them. In general, presidents are more successful in securing their legislation in the earlier than in the latter years of their term.

In this role, presidents make extensive use of arm-twisting techniques to impose their will or fend off policies that they dislike. This may involve invitations for senators and representatives to attend the White House or a round of golf ('killing opposition by kindness') or threats to obstruct public works projects in a congressman's district. Senator Byrd[20] of West Virginia gave an indication of the sort of meeting that might occur:

> [President] 'I respect you for your opposition to that funding [for the Contras in central America], but I wish you would see your way to vote with us next time on that. Can you do it?'
> 'Well, I will certainly be glad to think about it, Mr President . . .'
> 'Well, Bob, I hope you will. And by the way, that money for the heart research center in Morgantown that you have worked for, I will bet your people love you for that . . . I have given a lot of thought to that. Be sure and take another look at that item we have, funds for the Contras.'

In addition to subtle and more blatant arm-twisting, presidents can also use the presidential veto (see box below) as a means of blocking unwanted policies.

The presidential veto

After passing through both houses of Congress, bills are sent to the White House for the president to sign. If the president fails to act within ten days (excepting Sundays), a bill automatically becomes law. But in the last ten days of a session, a failure to act amounts to a **pocket veto**; in other words, as Congress is not sitting and cannot fight back, the bill is effectively killed.

When a president vetoes a bill within the allotted time, Congress can override the decision, as long as two thirds of those present in each chamber support the initiative. Presidents know that Congress only very rarely successfully overrides their vetoes, so that the mere threat of using the power is often enough to enable them to extract concessions from the legislature. As long as the power is sometimes used, the threat is a credible one. Presidents vary in their use of the veto, some using it extensively, as the figures suggest:

Number of vetoes and overrides for selected presidents 1933–2001

President	Number of bills vetoed	Number and % of vetoes overridden
Roosevelt (1933–45)	635	9 (1.4%)
Eisenhower (1953–61)	181	2 (1.1%)
Johnson (1963–9)	30	0 (0.0%)
Nixon (1969–74)	43	7 (16.3%)
Reagan (1981–9)	78	9 (11.5%)
Clinton (1993–2001)	37	2 (5.4%)

Figures adapted from those available from the Research Division, Congressional Quarterly, Washington, DC.

Head of party

The president is the leader of his party, a role which itself involves several duties. The president:
- tries to fulfil its programme, the platform on which he was elected;
- is its chief fund-raiser and campaigner;
- appoints its national chairperson;
- distributes offices and favours to the party faithful.

As party leader, the president's control is limited, the more so given the decentralised nature of American political parties. He can use party identification to gain support in Congress, if they are of the same party, but in the case of Bill Clinton this did not guarantee support even in the first two years when he had a congressional majority. If members of either chamber oppose the president, there is little he can do about it, other than appeal directly to the people over their heads. The president has no formal disciplinary sanctions.

Presidents vary in their attempts to keep the party within their control. President Carter placed little emphasis on this party responsibility, which did little to ease his relations with Congress. At first, Clinton was more aware of party feelings

For many years, critics of the procedure argued that the presidential veto was a blunt weapon, for the president either had to sign or reject an entire bill. Knowing this, congressmen sometimes attached extra (and unpalatable) provisions **(riders)** to a bill which they knew the president really wanted. By so doing, they were trapping him, for he either had to sign the whole bill with the unwanted features, or lose it altogether. After much discussion, Congress finally passed a **line-item veto** in 1996, giving the president the power to veto 'objectionable' parts of an appropriations (expenditure) bill, whilst agreeing to the rest of it. This innovation was soon tested in the Supreme Court. In *Clinton* v. *New York* (June 1998), the judges were asked to decide whether Bill Clinton's rejection of some aspects of a tax bill was legitimate. They concluded that the line-item veto was unconstitutional, in that it violated the requirement that any bill must pass both houses and be signed by the president in the same form. If the President was allowed to strike out particular features, then in effect a new bill was being created.

The loss of the line-item veto means that presidents are left with one weaker power which they can employ if they are unhappy with a piece of legislation. Having signed the bill, they can withhold the funds **(impoundment)** appropriated by Congress for its implementation. Generally, impoundment has been used sparingly, but President Nixon used it regularly against a Democrat-dominated Congress, both as a means of controlling spending and as a means of controlling its behaviour. Congress responded by passing the Budget and Impoundment Control Act in 1974 (see p. 143). This laid down restrictions on the presidential use of impoundment. What remains is a much weakened alternative to the defunct line-item veto.

PRESIDENTS AND THE MAKING AND HANDLING OF FOREIGN POLICY

Crisis management

The president's roles as chief diplomat and commander-in-chief are related to another presidential responsibility: crisis management. A crisis is a sudden, unpredictable and potentially dangerous event. Most occur in the realm of foreign policy. Crises often involve hot tempers and high risks. Quick judgements are needed, despite the availability of only sketchy information. Whether it is American hostages held in Iran or the discovery of Soviet missiles in Cuba, a crisis challenges the president to make difficult decisions. In origin, crises are rarely the president's doing, but handled incorrectly they can be the president's undoing.

With modern communications, the president can instantly monitor events almost anywhere. Moreover, because situations develop more rapidly today, there is a premium on rapid action, secrecy, constant management, consistent judgement and expert advice. Congress usually moves slowly (one might say deliberatively), is large (making it difficult to keep secrets) and is composed of generalists. As a result, the president – who can come to quick and consistent decisions, confine information to a small group, carefully oversee developments and call upon experts in the executive branch – has become more prominent in handling crises.

Throughout the twentieth and early twenty-first centuries, crises have allowed presidents to become more powerful, and crisis management is a natural role for most who assume the presidential position. Most have been only too willing to step in to the vacuum and seize their chance to lead, whether it be Kennedy over the Cuban missiles, Bush senior over the Iraqi invasion of Kuwait, Clinton over Bosnia, or George W. Bush over the terrorist attacks on Washington and New York in September 2001.

The machinery of foreign policy

Presidents have their own style of management, and their own priorities. Some wish to be more involved with the detail of foreign policy than others, and wish to centralise decision-making on all aspects of foreign and national security matters into their own hands. The foreign policy-making machine in the United States is a vast one, with the president at the apex of the structure. He appoints key personnel such as the secretary of state and the defense secretary, and the heads of important agencies such as the Central Intelligence Agency (CIA).

In its original form, the Department of State was not concerned with overseas policy alone, but over the years most of its domestic workload was gradually transferred elsewhere. The department retains the Great Seal of the United States, and if the president or vice-president resigns it is to the secretary of state that the resignation is officially submitted. The main work of the department is concerned with:

- promoting of the security interests of the US and its allies;
- protecting foreign trade and commerce;
- helping negotiate and enforce treaties and other agreements with foreign countries;
- administering the Agency for International Development, the Peace Corps, and most non-military aid to foreign nations;
- maintaining friendly contacts between the US and other countries, including such things as arranging the reception of new foreign ambassadors by the president and advising on the recognition of new foreign countries and governments;
- informing the American public about developments in the field of foreign policy, by publishing appropriate documents, official papers and other publications;
- protecting American citizens, their welfare and property abroad. This last function involves the supervision of the Foreign Service of the United States, including the ambassadors and administrative, consular, economic and political officers who manage the country's foreign relations. It is also concerned with the treatment of any Americans abroad, and it issues passports for their visits and processes visa applications for those entering America.

In the Executive Office (see pp. 94–9), the president has his own advisers, and the special assistant for national security affairs (SA) has a highly significant position in the presidential team. Presidents like the advice and support of the SA, who is not only conveniently located (in the White House), but also owes prime loyalty to the person who chose him or her for the position. By contrast, the secretary of state – once appointed – has a department to represent, the views of which can shape his or her own in a way which the president may not like.

The National Security Council, created by the National Security Act of 1947 (see p. 99), meets irregularly to advise the president on foreign and defence policy. By the terms of the statute, it comprises the president, vice-president and the secretaries of state and defence, along with advisers such as the heads of the CIA and the joint chiefs of staff. Originally, the position of SA was little more than that of a secretary to the National Security Council, but it has grown vastly in scope. Today, some presidents prefer to rely on an informal group of advisers and the SA, rather than the statutory body.

Despite intentions to the contrary, Ronald Reagan allowed his SA unprecedented freedom of manoeuvre, and in the Iran–Contra affair his office operated what was in effect an independent foreign policy. The State Department and Congress were in the dark about the way in which the SA and some members of the National Security Council were engaged in trading arms with Iran in return for the release of American hostages, just as they were about using the proceeds of arms sales to supply the Contra guerillas in Nicaragua with weaponry – and thus evade a congressional ban on such a distribution of military supplies. 'Irangate', as it became known, illustrated the difficulties of establishing democratic control of the SA and his or her office. It also showed how powerful that office is, for the SA has special access to the president. Whatever they may say before assuming office, presidents like this source of extra and independent advice, for it frees them from the bureaucratic preoccupations of any department or agency.

and the need to 'manage' his legislative colleagues, but his policies came unstuck. By the time he was seeking re-election in 1996, there was an air of detachment between the presidential and congressional wings of the party.

Chief diplomat

The president has the power to develop relations with representatives of foreign powers, appoint ambassadors to those countries, and sign treaties that become effective once the Senate has consented by a two-thirds majority. As we have seen, in the postwar years, presidents have become the initiators and executors of foreign policy. Although Congress officially declares war, there is presidential primacy in this area, and this has provided incumbents with a formidable source of influence and power, doing much to enhance or diminish their political stature at home.

Commander-in-chief of the armed forces

Closely related to the role of chief diplomat is the position of commander-in-chief, for it is the ability to use the might of the armed forces that makes a president's foreign policy credible. Presidents have very extensive powers in wartime, deciding when to intervene abroad. They have embarked on intervention in wars from Korea to Vietman and beyond, deploying troops as necessary. In practice, much of the authority is delegated to the secretary of state for defence, who in turn normally delegates command to leading figures in the military establishment.

In reaction to presidential warmaking in Vietnam, Congress passed the **War Powers Act** in 1973 to curb presidential freedom. However, its effectiveness is questionable, and presidents from Reagan to Clinton have basically ignored the limitations it was designed to impose upon them. It is often mentioned at times when troops are deployed, but in 1991 during the war with Iraq President George H. Bush described it as being 'unconstitutional', and three years later, in sending troops to Haiti, his successor also did not seek congressional approval for his intervention. Neither was there much congressional oversight of the war fought by President George W. Bush in Afghanistan.

> **War Powers Act**
> Imposed a 60–day limit on the time for which a president can keep American troops abroad without congressional approval. Without such authorisation, the troops have to be withdrawn; overall, 90 days can be allowed, to enable the withdrawal to be carried out successfully.

Originally the Act was passed over President Nixon's veto. Ever since, Congress and a succession of presidents have failed to reach agreement over its status and relevance. In recent years, some congressmen have recognised that the attempt to control presidents in this way was ineffective and perhaps not even prudent. Whilst some would like to strengthen the Act to give it more teeth and others would wish see it made more workable, there are many who would prefer to scrap it altogether. Members of the latter group accept that in an age of fast-moving crises on the international scene, it is unwise to undermine the president as he performs his role on America's behalf.

Others

The late Clinton Rossiter,[21] an American political scientist, listed other presidential roles: 'Voice of the People' in American affairs, 'Protector of Peace' (intervening in race riots, etc.), 'Manager of Prosperity' and 'Leader of the Western World'.

The presidency and Congress

The Constitution places a joint responsibility on the president and Congress to govern the nation, and real leadership is only easy to bring about when both bodies (and sometimes the Supreme Court as well) are facing in the same direction. Sometimes, as we have seen, Congress has the upper hand, but in the last sixty years of the twentieth century presidents were usually in control despite attempts to lay down specific restraints. The politics of shared power has often been stormy, and conflict can easily arise – whether over Watergate, the Iran–Contra affair, the confirmation to the Supreme Court of Clarence Thomas (see p. 164) and of many other recent nominations, Whitewatergate and Clinton's health proposals.

In recent decades, one major area of contention has been over the conduct of foreign policy. Initiatives are usually launched by the president, but Congress still has an overseeing role. It has the power to raise taxes to fund a conflict, to create and maintain armed forces, to regulate arms sales and to sign treaties. It has the power also to make war. Johnson never formally declared war against North Vietnam, but the hostilities there led to Congress reassessing its position. The Nixon presidency saw a struggle between the White House and Capitol Hill over the control of foreign policy.

A hostile Congress can make life difficult for any president, by refusing his nominations, failing to fund his programmes and refusing approval to treaties he has carefully negotiated. If he has public support, he is much less likely to meet this degree of obstruction, and he can take to the media to rally public support on his side. Congressmen will watch the popular reaction with interest. Theodore Roosevelt was an exponent of the 'bully pulpit' approach, for he saw the opportunities for inspirational leadership if he could get his message across to the nation at large – as though it was a religious congregation. Wilson, Kennedy, Franklin Roosevelt and Reagan all knew how to 'preach' to the nation, and strengthen their position by winning acquiescence and support.

The President and the Prime Minister: a comparison of Britain and the United States

For years, it has been a regular part of discussion on the British and American systems of government to compare the two offices and to decide which is the more powerful, the prime minister or the president.

An obvious difference is that in Britain the ceremonial and political roles are separated, so that the queen is the titular head of state while the prime minister is the chief executive or political head of the government. In America, the roles are combined in one person, a consideration that imposes considerable demands on the incumbent, but means that he has many opportunities to appear on social occasions and attract favourable media coverage.

The prime minister is relieved of certain time-consuming duties, such as receiving ambassadors and dignitaries from abroad, and there may be an advantage in separating the ceremonial and efficient roles, pomp from power. Yet wearing both hats gives the president a dimension of prestige lacking in the office of prime minister, for the prime minister is only a politician whereas the president is both in and above the political battle, more obviously representing the national interest.

The holders of both offices have a similar responsibility for the overall surveillance and direction of the work of executive departments of government, and there are advantages of the prime minister over the president and vice versa. The prime minister is part of a plural executive, and he or she and the Cabinet are collectively responsible to the House of Commons. He or she may, of course, have acquired a real ascendancy over his or her colleagues, and the impact of Margaret Thatcher's tenure in office showed the extent of prime ministerial dominance. Yet the British Cabinet is bound to be concerned in most major decisions during the lifetime of a government.

In the US, the Cabinet is much less significant, and several presidents – whilst not formally dispensing with the Cabinet – have been casual about holding meetings and have treated its suggestions in a cavalier manner. Their cabinet colleagues tend to be people drawn from the world of business, the ranks of academia or other professions, and return there once their term in office has expired; they have no personal following of their own in Congress or in the country. Cabinet members in Britain have a greater political standing in their own right, and are less easily ignored; they may be contenders for the party leadership.

A key factor in the comparison of prime minister and president is that the former is a more powerful party leader. He or she leads a disciplined party, whereas the president does not.

SUPPORT FOR THE PRESIDENCY

The Executive Office of the President

As presidential responsibilities widened in the years following the Great Depression, it became increasingly difficult for the president to cope with the

This means that whereas the president can find difficulty in getting proposals enacted into law, perhaps because of states' rights or the views of Congress or the Supreme Court, the prime minister, given a reasonable majority, is likely to get most of his or her programme through. In as much as the reputation of a government may depend on what it can achieve, the prime minister has far more chance of implementing the proposals he or she wants. Margaret Thatcher could reform the health service along the lines she favoured, whereas a few years later Bill Clinton could not. As Walles[22] observes: 'Whereas a Prime Minister . . . with the support of party, is ideally placed for authoritative action, a President . . . often lacking the full support of his party in the legislature . . . is poorly placed to translate policies into working programmes.'

In the area of foreign policy, both presidential and prime minister are generally in charge of the direction of the Government's external relations. On their own or through the appropriate departments, they declare the tone of the nation's foreign policy. There are differences in their position, however, for the president must get any treaty approved by two thirds of the Senate, and if the policy requires legislative back-up the president may have difficulty in getting this through the Congress.

On the other hand, whereas the president may decide administration policy alone in conjunction with the secretary of state, a British prime minister is much more likely to put his or her policy before the Cabinet, where views can be expressed. There may be individual opportunities for the prime minister to bypass the full Cabinet and take key decisions in a cabinet committee, but in most cases the prime minister appoints a foreign secretary with whom he or she is in agreement or whom he or she feels can be imposed on.

The prime minister is of course always liable to be defeated in the House, and therefore may not see out his or her term. Similarly, as with Margaret Thatcher, the incumbent of Number Ten can be removed when in office. Both cases are rare. The occupant of the White House has a guaranteed fixed term in office, unless he does something very wrong, as over Watergate. The advantage in security of tenure is with the president, although when it comes to choosing the date of the next election (and manipulating the economy to create the 'feel good' factor), the advantage is with the prime minister.

Within the two political systems, the prime minister has the edge, because of his or her leadership of a disciplined, centralised party in a political culture which is orientated towards party government. This enables him or her to get things done. But the president has the greater power overall, for he or she is the leader of a more significant country in international terms, with enough nuclear capacity to wipe out civilisation.

demands of the job. He lacked the necessary support, a point noted by the President's Committee on Administrative Management, in 1937: 'The president needs help', it proclaimed.

A Commission on the Organisation of the Executive Branch of the Government, set up by President Truman and headed by Herbert Hoover, reported twelve years later. It was troubled by the lack of clear lines of authority from the president down to the civil service, and felt the modern president faced an impossible task unless there was an extensive regrouping of executive departments and agencies into a number of smaller, non-overlapping units, and an increased use of the Cabinet. These changes would give the president the chance to achieve an effective supervision of the governmental activities for which he was constitutionally responsible.

Both analyses drew attention to the burdens of the presidency, and argued the case that because executive power was centred on one person he needed help from better support services rather than from other people. The Cabinet might have seemed a possible choice to relieve the burden. But as the officers who serve in it are non-elected and therefore lack political or moral authority – and in any case, are not usually front-rank politicians – they have little incentive to relieve the president of any duties. In particular, they have little experience of managing relations with Congress. In other words, even if the president wished to make greater use of the Cabinet, several of its members have little interest in offering the necessary backing, for their reputation does not depend on the president's political success. Each secretary looks after his or her patch; however, the president looks after his own duties, but also has to answer for any of their shortcomings.

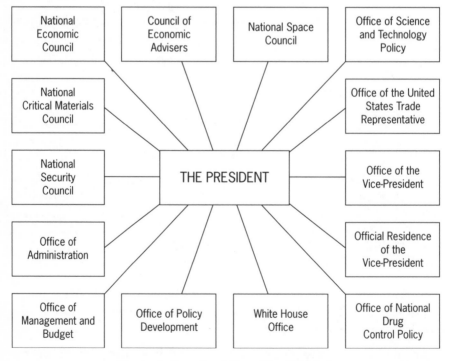

Figure 1 Executive Office of the President

Source: Based on an illustration from a US Government Manual, 1995–96.

The president is in a solitary position, with overall responsibility for the activities of an enormous governmental machine which he must direct and co-ordinate. To do this, the president requires information about operations, assessments of policy needs and means of ensuring that his or her decisions and those of Congress are efficiently carried out, in the ways and spirit in which they are intended.

The establishment and operation of the Executive Office

As a result of the recommendations of the 1937 Committee, Roosevelt agreed that new machinery should be established. Two years after it reported, an enlarged presidential office was created, far larger in scale than had existed previously. Instead of a few clerks and secretaries, there was to be a new Executive Office of the President. In the words of Clinton Rossiter,[23] the presidency was converted 'into an instrument of twentieth century government . . . it gives the incumbent a sporting chance to stand the strain and fulfil the constitutional mandate as a one-man branch of our three-part government'. In his view, the innovation saved the presidency from paralysis, and the Constitution from radical amendment.

From the earliest days, it was obvious that the new office would be highly significant, but even so the extent of its eventual impact on American government could not have been judged. At the time, it comprised barely 1,000 staff, whereas at the beginning of the twenty-first century the total exceeds 5,000. The extent of its operations and of its importance, however, is not to be judged by numbers alone, but more by the centrality of its position in the workings of the executive branch. It has become what Maidment and McGrew[24] call 'the principal instrument of presidential government'.

The modern president relies on the Executive Office to come up with the background information, detailed analysis and informed policy recommendations that are needed to enable him to master the complexities of a task. It has taken its place at the heart of the administration, giving the president the advice he depends upon, conducting many dealings with Congress, and helping to publicise and supervise the implementation of presidential decisions. The president is freed to deal with top-level matters of the moment and to engage in future planning.

The component parts of the Executive Office change from president to president, for it is the president's personal bureaucracy. Individuals have varied in the use made of it and amended its internal organisation to reflect their own priorities, interests and needs. New parts of the office have been established, some have been developed or transformed from their original character, and others have become redundant.

The Executive Office is an umbrella under which exist a number of key agencies which cover the whole range of policy areas and which serve the president directly. The Office of Management and the Budget already existed in 1939, but otherwise only the White House Office has been there since the

ELEMENTS OF THE EXECUTIVE OFFICE

The White House Office

The president's closest aides, his personal staff, work in the White House Office, the nerve centre of the Executive Office. Of those located in the White House, only a few dozen of the most senior advisers will see the president regularly. There are special assistants to advise on foreign and domestic affairs, speech writers, liaison officers who maintain contact with Congress, and, of course, the press secretary. There is nowadays a special counsellor to the president, and also many whose services are more concerned with basic personal needs, such as a personal secretary, a social secretary and a physician.

The office ensures that urgent priority issues reach the president's desk quickly, and members seek to ensure compliance by the departments with presidential policies, and so obtain for the president control over the federal administration. These assistants obtain their real authority from their closeness to the president, and the trust which he places in them. By deciding who should see the president and the issues to prioritise, they have much discretionary power. The danger is that the office can so 'protect' the president that he becomes remote from the political world. He becomes surrounded with 'yes-men' who say what they think the president wants to hear, and thus prevent him from making a balanced assessment.

Under Kennedy, several members were used more to help the president carry out the tasks he set himself, rather than to act as key advisers. In contrast, other presidents have given this inner circle enormous influence, so that some administrations are remembered in terms of the president himself and the immediate associates with whom he surrounded himself – Nixon had Haldeman and Ehrlichman, Carter had Jordan and Powell, and Reagan had Baker (later his secretary of state), Deaver and Meese. During the Nixon presidency the size of the White House Office grew substantially, with well over 500 personnel. Nixon downgraded his Cabinet, and so to get the co-ordination of policy which he required he established the post of counsellor to the president. The appointee was given the prime responsibility for co-ordinating the handling of home and overseas affairs, and was included within the Cabinet – a status denied to previous White House aides.

The Office of Management and Budget (OMB)

Nixon reconstituted the Bureau of the Budget into the Office of Management and Budget (OMB) in 1970, as a major managerial instrument for the president. Its main task is to prepare a federal budget to submit to Congress, and all appropriations requests from the departments come through the office for approval. The departments use their influence to retain maximum financial autonomy, and the President needs support if he is to keep

original machinery was set up. Elements have changed in different administrations, but central to the work of the office are the White House staff,
personal appointees who are likely to be the closest advisers for general and
particular policies (see box below).

overall control of their plans. The office can be a powerful instrument, for it also provides
a mechanism by which the president can co-ordinate governmental activities, and ensure,
in his role as manager of the executive branch, that programmes are carried out as
efficiently as possible.

The National Security Council (NSC)

Established in 1947, the National Security Council (NSC) was given the role of advising the
president on domestic, foreign and military matters relating to national security. Its function
is to consider policies on matters of common interest to the departments and agencies of
the government concerned with national security, and to make recommendations. Like the
Cabinet, the NSC does not make decisions for the president, but it provides evidence and
advice from which the president can come to his own conclusions. At times of crisis, the
council does not usually seem to be the place where key assessments are made.

The Council of Economic Advisers

Economic policy is increasingly important to the performance and reputation of any administration, and for presidents, few of whom are economic experts, assistance is needed.
Since 1946, a three-person panel of professional economists, the council of Economic
Advisers, has been appointed with the consent of the Senate to advise on key issues. Often
they are university academics, but new presidents select people of their own persuasion
and outlook. It is a purely advisory body, but it is an important counter to the Treasury and
the OMB, which have a narrower and more immediate focus. Such advice helps presidents
to bear in mind longer-term considerations in their economic thinking. One specific responsibility is to assist in the preparation of an annual economic report to be given by the
president to Congress; this outlines the Administration's view of economic trends.

The Office of Policy Development (OPD)

Since 1981, the Office of Policy Development (OPD) has had an important advisory role in
the conduct of domestic policy. President Nixon had his Domestic Council for this
purpose, but like some of his other innovations its reputation was damaged as part of the
general discrediting of Nixonian methods, following the Watergate revelations. President
Reagan's establishment of the new OPD is a further reflection of the presidential need for
systematic and coherent advice on matters of internal policy.

There are other bodies in the Executive Office, such as the Council on Environmental
Quality, the Office of Science and Technology Policy and the Intelligence Oversight Board.

Assessment of the Executive Office

It was because of the growing demands on the president that some help was necessary if he was to be equipped adequately for the necessary tasks. As the president's responsibilities grew, so did his need for expert assistance. At the time of the creation of the Executive Office few commentators realised just how important it would become. It is now far larger than in the year after its establishment, and its influence has grown even more dramatically than its number of personnel. What makes it so important for the president is that it is beholden only to him. Its members are appointed by the President, and they know that they owe their position to him and therefore seek to serve him loyally.

The Executive Office is the main instrument of presidential government, and all modern presidents rely upon it to a greater or lesser degree, for information, analysis and policy recommendations. In some cases, their dependence is greater than others, and certain key aides emerge as the linchpin of the administration. For them, their focus of attention is inevitably the presidency, as it must be. It is easy for them to become so obsessed by the protection of the president that they ignore the limitations of the office designed by the framers of the Constitution. In other words, the Executive Office – and especially those assistants who serve in the White House Office – can become out of touch with the viewpoints and requirements of those who inhabit other areas of the system of government.

The danger can be that, having appointed an advisory team of people who share his or her personal and political preferences, the president receives advice only from those who share the same outlook. Other people in different branches of the governmental process also have insights worthy of an audience, and some congressmen and bureaucrats may find that their route to the president is barred. Presidents can come to rely too much on those around them, and in that way allow themselves to become out of touch with the views of a wider section of the American public.

The vice-presidency

For many years the office of vice-president ('Veep') was viewed as little more than a joke. Its first incumbent, John Adams, wrote of it derisively to his wife in 1793: 'My country has in its wisdom contrived for me the most insignificant office that ever the invention of man contrived or his imagination conceived.' The majority of his successors would probably have shared his view, and a disillusioned John Nance Garner, Franklin Roosevelt's deputy, suggested that the office was not 'worth a pitcher of warm spit'. Even Walter Mondale,[25] Carter's mostly successful vice-president, referred to the job as 'handmade for ridicule and for dismissal. In the nature of it, you always look like a supplicant, a beggar, a person on a string.'

The office was only created as an afterthought by those who devised the Constitution. The document simply says that the vice-president will be chosen by an Electoral College, outlines the circumstances when he or she will be acting president and lays down that he or she will preside over the Senate. Given that there are so few formal responsibilities, some vice-presidents make little of it. One such occupant was Charles Dawes, who served under President Coolidge. Dawes declared that his position was 'the easiest job in the world'.

Choice of the vice-president

Presidential candidates want a running-mate who will be an asset to the ticket and boost their electoral prospects. Ideally the person chosen will balance the presidential candidate's own background and characteristics, so that geographical, demographic and ideological factors come into play. It may be that the choice will be pleasing to an area, to a group of voters or to some faction within the party. Kennedy, a northern liberal and a Catholic, chose Johnson, a Texan Protestant likely to appeal to southern conservatives. Nixon chose Spiro Agnew (a Maryland governor) to please the same group. Clinton chose Al Gore, for although they came from similar geographical backgrounds and shared many similar beliefs, Gore offered definite advantages which might extend the appeal of the ticket. In particular, he was seen as a 'Mr Clean', reassuring on the topic of 'family values', a subject on which Bill Clinton was thought to be vulnerable. George W. Bush opted for Dick Cheney, who had served as defence secretary in Bush senior's Cabinet and was expected to provide some experience and weight to the presidential challenge in 2000. Cheney had the experience of handling foreign affairs and national security issues that the presidential candidate so obviously lacked.

Responsibilities and role

The vice-president assumes some of the ceremonial tasks of the president, and represents him on formal occasions, whether it be the funeral of a foreign leader or the commemoration of some past event. The vice-president is formally the presiding officer of the Senate, refereeing its proceedings and interpreting the rules. Usually, vice-presidents put in few appearances, for there is little kudos to be won and little chance to exert political influence – given that he or she is not a member of the chamber. Otherwise, vice-presidents take on ad hoc assignments, their number and character depending on the use that the president wishes to make of them. Bill Clinton gave his deputy the task of conducting a national review of the workings of the federal democracy. Other presidents have been much less willing to use their running-mate than he was.

A frustrating role

For those with presidential ambitions, the post takes them that much nearer the White House, and there is always the chance that their services might be needed should a death or assassination occur, or electors choose them as the next president. About one third of vice-presidents eventually become president; five have done so since World War II: Truman, Johnson, Nixon, Ford and Bush senior.

Yet it is still difficult for vice-presidents to carve out a useful and distinctive role. The job is a frustrating one, particularly when the administration is nearing its end – even more so if it is unpopular. On the one hand, the 'Veep' is expected to remain loyal and act as a mouthpiece of the presidential team. On the other, he or she may wish to establish a distinct persona and, if things are going badly for the president, to show a degree of detachment. Hubert Humphrey was in such a dilemma over Vietnam, in the latter days of the Johnson presidency. Whatever Humphrey's personal reservations, he was unable to oppose official policy whilst he remained a member of the White House team. Al Gore faced a similar problem. In his case, there was no dispute over political direction, but he was embarrassed by the scandals which so damaged the Clinton reputation. Especially in the latter days, he kept himself as detached as possible when it was apparent that the administration was in political difficulty.

The office provides the incumbent with an opportunity to see the workings of government at the highest level, and gain a useful insight into the problems that arise and the way in which they are handled. But it is easy for the occupant to seem faceless and lacking independence of outlook. Few presidents would appreciate an outspoken understudy, or one who diverted too much attention from them. Many have preferred to keep their number two in the dark on key issues. Roosevelt took this isolation of his vice-president so far that he did not even tell his 'Veep' that America was developing the atomic bomb.

Nixon did not find work under Eisenhower fulfilling, any more than Johnson did under Kennedy. In both cases, the relationship was a poor one before they were ever chosen as running-mates. Nixon's own vice-president, the much-despised Spiro T. Agnew,[26] found it a 'peculiar situation to be in, to have . . . a title and responsibility with no real power to do anything'. Indeed, Nixon barely knew Agnew at the time he chose him as his running-mate. Having felt humiliated in the vice-presidential job himself, he inflicted even greater humiliation on Agnew. By most accounts, Agnew was scorned by the White House staff and given little of importance to do. Johnson too was snubbed by White House staffers, who reputedly mocked him behind his back as 'Uncle Cornpone'.

Presidents rarely feel that they can totally trust the person they have chosen to run with, for such associates have their own ambitions. It is usually a 'marriage of convenience' on the part of the president, rather than an expression of deep regard for the person selected. Political rather than personal considerations dictate the original choice.

The growing significance of the position

Until well into the twentieth century, the vice-presidential role was to act as what Cronin and Genovese[27] describe as 'ceremonial ribbon-cutters'. It was generally regarded as a 'semi-retirement job for party stalwarts, acting as a resting place for mediocrities or a 'runner-up'. Two constitutional amendments helped to raise the status of the office. The Twenty-Second limited the president to two full terms in office, and thereby increased the chances of the vice-president taking over. The Twenty-Fifth, in 1967, confirmed the previous practice of making the vice-president not an acting one but the real thing, in the event of a national emergency such as the incapacity of the president to fulfil his tasks. A procedure is laid down to determine if and when the deputy should take over, as it is to determine for how long and under what conditions he or she should exercise presidential duties. (In 1985, George Bush senior was the first vice-president to assume such responsibilities, when President Reagan had an operation for skin cancer.)

Although these amendments boosted the importance of the role, its influence still varies according to who is in the White House, For some presidents, their deputies can be useful in an advisory capacity on matters of politics and policy. Jimmy Carter made more use of Walter Mondale than had been usual in the past, because he needed the support of a Washington 'insider' who could give good advice based upon his knowledge and experience. Reagan allowed Bush to attend many meetings and to represent him in many engagements. However, activity and influence are very different, and whereas Mondale was allowed more say in the decision-making process, this was much less true of his successor.

During the Clinton administrations, it became fashionable for writers to describe Al Gore as 'probably the most influential vice-president in American history'. Not only did he preside over important projects such as the '**Reinventing Government**' initiative, he also took an active interest in issues ranging from the environment to science and technology. On foreign affairs, he was deeply involved in discussions such as policy towards the Middle East, Russia and South Africa, as well as issues of

Reinventing Government
An approach to civil service reform, adopted by the Clinton administration, that emphasised empowerment and decentralisation as ways of improving the performance of government agencies and programmes.

nuclear non-proliferation. On these and other matters, Bill Clinton valued his advice. Often, Gore would remain in the Oval Office when all other advisers had departed, so that his voice was the last the president heard. Gore is said to have been allowed considerable influence over the composition of the revamped Cabinet at the beginning of the second term, the idea being that this would give him influential supporters in key positions to help him prepare his bid for the November 2000 contest. Clinton seemed to feel less threatened by his vice-president than had some of his predecessors.

In several ways, the two men complemented each other, a point spotted by the labour secretary, Robert Reich,[28] who noted that: 'Al [Gore] is . . . methodical where B is haphazard, linear where B is creative, cautious where B is impetuous, ponderous where B is playful, private where B shares his feelings with everyone. The two men need one another, and sense it. Above all, Gore is patient, where B wants it all now.' For Gore, the position was a good training ground for the job he badly wanted. He used it as an opportunity to prepare himself for the presidency, carefully studying the operation of power at the highest level.

In the events leading up to war in Iraq, the same label of 'probably the most influential' was applied to Dick Cheney, who has been called 'the power behind the throne'. His is an unusual case, for if he qualifies as the most powerful ever vice-president, he is also among the least visible. As a running-mate, he was a surprise choice and had several apparent disadvantages. He is an uninspiring and rare public speaker and a mediocre election campaigner, lacking an obviously warm and appealing personality to charm the electorate. He brings little to the presidential ticket, coming from a small, conservative state that almost any Republican presidential candidate would expect to win. Moreover, ever since he was selected as vice-presidential running-mate by George Bush, there have been serious doubts about his health. After all, he has had four heart attacks and uses a 'pace-maker plus' to give his heart an electric shock should it lose its normal rhythm. A further potential source of weakness might be the fact that, according to polls, he is not trusted by a significant element of those interviewed. His recent past as chief executive at Halliburton oil services company at a time when it dabbled in questionable accounting make him appear as the embodiment of America's corporate ills.

However, as vice-president, from a Bush point of view, Cheney has several assets. He is uncommonly and fiercely loyal to his boss, and the president trusts him with absolute confidence. Particularly since September 11, Bush leans on Cheney for advice, seeing him as a heavyweight with *gravitas* who will deal with day-to-day issues effectively. Although Cheney is taciturn and rarely shows his cards in meetings, he uses private opportunities to speak his mind. His judgement and views command respect. His importance in the Bush administrations is recognised by admirers and critics alike. He is useful to the president in several ways, able to say things that the president may feel, but dare not publicly say. Whereas George Bush often speaks in terms of 'compassionate conservatism', his vice-president has licence to betray the innermost thinking of some Republicans around the White House. He famously derided environmentalism as a 'personal virtue' and broke the 'no gloating' rule after the fall of Baghdad. Above all, Cheney has one quality that endears him to the president. He does not covet the president's office. He does not need to be seen often in public, for he is not seeking to build a popular reputation as part of a build-up to some presidential bid. He has no political ambitions.

There has been discussion in recent years of 'a new vice-presidency'. Yet in spite of the developing trend towards providing vice-presidents with a more worth-while role, for much of the time they are effectively 'waiting in the wings' in case their services are called upon to assume the burden of the presidency. They stand in readiness to assume command, in the event of death (either through natural causes or assassination), of resignation or of removal from office. Nine presidents have failed to complete their allotted terms, eight through death, and one (Nixon) because of his forced resignation. The possibility of assassination is a real one: four presidents have been killed, two in the twentieth century (McKinley and Kennedy), and several others have been the victim of life-threatening attacks. Because of this, Vice-President Adams was right in his summary of the strengths and weaknesses of his position: 'I am Vice-President of the United States. In this, I am nothing, but I may be everything.'

Unsurprisingly, because the vice-president is a heartbeat away from the supreme office, there is often a tension between him or her and the president he or she serves. Henry Kissinger,[29] an eminent figure in the Nixon administrations, noted that the relationship between the occupants of the two posts was never easy: 'it is, after all, disconcerting to have at one's side a man whose life's ambitions will be achieved by one's death'. Lyndon Johnson[30] clearly was aware of this unusual aspect of his office, on one occasion admitting that whenever he was in the presence of JFK, he felt 'like a goddam raven hovering over his shoulder'. In his case, a tragic death forced him to make the transition from acting as a standby to assuming the awesome responsibilities of the presidency.

The Cabinet

The Constitution allows the president to invite the opinions of the main officers of the executive departments of government, but there is no mention of summoning them together as a Cabinet. Yet this has always happened, from George Washington onwards. The influence of **the Cabinet** has varied according to the tastes and

> **the Cabinet**
> Cabinet meetings comprise the president, the vice-president and the officers who head the fourteen departments, plus a few other officials whom the president considers to be of appropriate rank.

inclinations of the President. As a broad generalisation, it was a more powerful body before the 1930s than it has been subsequently. Yet the 'decline' has not been a continuous one, and from time to time individual presidents have promised to use such gatherings more. A very few have fulfilled their initial promise.

Abraham Lincoln is usually credited with the comment 'seven noes, one aye – the ayes have it', following a cabinet discussion in which his proposal was unanimously rejected by those around the table. True or otherwise, the remark indicates the view that most presidents have of the people they appoint to serve under them. Presidents tend to view them as spokespersons for their departments who have nothing to contribute on other matters.

This means that presidents lack the political support which the British Cabinet gives to the prime minister. The American Cabinet does not contain party notables, high-ranking members with a power-base and standing in their own right. Neither do cabinet members have a place in the legislature, and so they are of little assistance to the president in pushing his programme through Congress. An American Cabinet bears little relation to one operating in a parliamentary system. It does not work as a team as the British one does, and American and British Cabinets have little in common other than the name.

Some presidents have begun their presidency with the intention of using the Cabinet more. They have spoken of its value and how they intended to utilise the talents of those appointed to it. Truman spoke of 'a body whose combined judgement the president uses to develop fundamental policies of the administration'.[31] Reagan flattered his new appointees, saying that they were to be used rather like a board of directors in a corporation. He would discuss issues frankly with them and take on board their input when making decisions. In 1969, Richard Nixon saw the cabinet members as having an important role in policy-making. But whatever the initial promises, the relationship between president and cabinet officers tends to deteriorate within a year or so. Any honeymoon romanticism about the office begins to wear off and the more trusted White House staff come to outstrip the Cabinet in power and influence. In Truman's administration, 'important decisions were made by ad hoc groups consisting of cabinet officers and others. He did not wish to . . . formalise the meetings.'[32]

The number of meetings tends to decline as the years go by: by 1972, Nixon was down to eleven meetings in the course of the year. As Watergate enveloped his administration, he came to regard the Cabinet with intense suspicion and conceived a strong dislike for its individual members, whom he had originally appointed and praised as people capable of providing an 'extra dimension . . . superior and even great leadership'. He got rid of more of them than most of his predecessors. Those who retained their positions found the meetings boring and rather 'bland': 'Nothing of substance was discussed. There was no disagreement because there was nothing to disagree about. Things over which we might have disagreed were not discussed.'[33] Similarly, Jimmy Carter's good intentions were never fulfilled. The number of his cabinet meetings declined significantly and members felt that they lacked any proper agenda or coherent theme.

Especially in the early years of his administration, Reagan was keen on the idea of cabinet government, and at meetings was likely to go round the table and invite individual views. He also made use of cabinet councils of five or six cabinet members on topics such as economic affairs and human resources, and these worked with White House staff to provide a source of new ideas for the president – a system which was analogous to the British system of cabinet committees. Bill Clinton formed committees of cabinet and sub-cabinet members, as in the case of the National Economic Council. Again, the purpose was to integrate departmental heads and White House officials better around particular policy areas. The original precedent for such committees was the NSC, formed shortly after World War II with the intention of providing the President with quality advice on matters concerning the security of the nation against external threat.

Every Cabinet has its key players who matter more as individuals than as members of a collective team. John Foster Dulles was a key figure in the Eisenhower Administration; Warren Christopher and Madeleine Albright had the same status under Bill Clinton. Along with Dick Cheney, Donald Rumsfeld, Condoleezza Rice and Colin Powell were important personnel in the first four years of George W. Bush's presidency. Every Cabinet has its dominating personalities; sometimes the influence varies according to the personalities involved and the department they represent. Their influence depends more on their individual worth to the president than to their role as part of team. Presidents lack the time and often the inclination to deal with individual cabinet officers. Only those whose views are valued and who handle matters of national security and foreign policy are likely to gain regular access to the White House.

Choosing the Cabinet

One of the first tasks of a new president before the inauguration is the choice of the Cabinet, and the selection is watched by commentators eager to get an indication of the likely tone and style of the administration. The president can choose whom he wishes, although it is wise to nominate people who are likely to be acceptable to the Senate. The Cabinet is the president's personal creation, and he will seek out people felt to be useful, and effective within their departments. Few people can assume that they will be included, for it does not follow that prominent people in the presidential election campaign will be rewarded with a position in the Cabinet; other rewards may be awarded and preferred.

The president will want to include people who are loyal to him and to presidential programmes. Other considerations include the need to reward prominent politicians who helped the campaign nationally and within the president's state. There are often political debts to repay. Kennedy, as a northern liberal, was even prepared to include a southern segregationist within the cabinet – though this seemed to be in direct contradiction of his expressed support for civil rights. The choice did enable Kennedy to achieve a geographical balance, with representation of regions different from his own. A broad social balance is desirable, and recent presidents are aware of the need to acknowledge the existence within the US of women and of different racial groups such as the black and Jewish communities.

The president will also want people of administrative competence who may bring expertise and specialist knowledge to their work. It does not matter if they have not previously served in a government position, and many have no political background. There will sometimes be an attempt to persuade congressmen from either house to serve the Administration, but in most cases figures who have won re-election are unlikely to be interested in forsaking the legislature for administrative responsibilities which are lacking in influence over the overall direction of policy. Moreover, from their own experience they will know what it is like to grill members of the Administration, and may be unwilling to submit themselves to the procedure. Republican Cabinet appointees often come from a

---

Cabinets in Britain and the United States: a comparison

- In both countries, cabinet membership is usually around twenty, the British model traditionally being the larger of the two. There are 22 members of the second Bush cabinet (the president, 15 departmental heads and six of 'Cabinet rank'). The post-May 2005 Blair Cabinet has 23 members, but a further three ministers attend the meetings.
- In Britain, meetings are held regularly (every Thursday). American Cabinets meet irregularly, much depending on who is president and whether it is early or late in the lifetime of the Administration.
- In Britain, members are elected politicians, drawn from the House of Commons and answerable to it. Some are powerful figures in their own right, with a political standing in the party and country. They may even be potential rivals to the prime minister. US cabinet appointees have not been elected, are not figures of prominence within the party (occasionally, one or two may be members of the other main party), are not members of Congress and are not viewed as potential rivals.
- In Britain, the Cabinet is the main decision-making body. It takes decisions, coordinates policy, and acts as a court of appeal when agreement cannot be reached in

business background. Eisenhower, Nixon, Bush and Reagan all plucked people from the worlds of commerce and manufacturing. Those chosen may be elevated from obscurity, and when the Administration comes to an end they often return to such a status – having made little impact on the public mind.

The role and practice of American Cabinets

As we have seen, the Cabinet is not even mentioned in the Constitution, although the Twenty-Fifth Amendment lays down a procedure to be followed in case of the president's incapacity. Congress determines the lines of succession after the vice-president, and beyond the speaker and Senate president *pro tempore*, the Cabinet personnel are listed in order of status, starting with the secretary of state.

The Cabinet is an advisory body only, and in the final analysis the president consults whom he wishes and may choose to ignore what the cabinet members say – assuming they are consulted in the first place. As the president does not have to refer to the Cabinet in times of crisis, the sole responsibility for decision-making rests with him. The role can be a lonely one. The president may choose to seek out the advice of individuals whose counsel is trusted, but for many members there is little incentive to offer backing and support. There is no question of the president seeking and feeling the need to act upon the advice of all of the cabinet members. He may prefer to seek the advice of the White House Office and the OMB when advice is needed. Presidents use the Cabinet as they feel appropriate or necessary. They may choose to hold meetings regularly, as Eisenhower did, or perhaps allow the Cabinet to meet

cabinet committee. Even if the prime minister is very powerful, the role of the Cabinet is still a major one, although commentators debate the balance of power between the premier and his or her colleagues. Major issues come before the Cabinet and ultimately, prime ministers need cabinet backing. The president looks elsewhere for policy advice, co-ordination and support. He may choose to consult the Cabinet, but does not feel bound to do so. Discussions are frequently regarded as pointless or boring, often not dealing with the matters that might cause controversy.

- In Britain, the doctrine of 'collective responsibility' applies to cabinet members. In the US, there is no such doctrine and disagreement in public is more apparent. For instance, in the George W. Bush administration, the secretary of state and the defence secretary have taken a different line on European Union defence policy.
- In both countries, the tendency in recent years has been for the cabinet meeting to be bypassed. In Britain, those who allege that we have prime-ministerial government often point to the increased use of a Kitchen Cabinet of key advisers and to the tendency of strong prime ministers to consult with cabinet members on a bilateral basis. In the US also, matters tend to be resolved in small, informal groupings or between the president and the appropriate departmental secretary.

only irregularly, and consult individuals where they are likely to be in a position to contribute usefully. Kennedy regarded the Cabinet as an anachronism as a consultative body and felt that full meetings were usually unproductive. He posed the question which sums up the way in which many presidents regard cabinet discussion: 'Why should the postmaster sit there and listen to a discussion of the problems of Laos?' In other words, members can more usefully employ their time on the work of their own departments rather than engage in general discussions.

Cabinet unanimity does not exist in the sense to which we are accustomed. It may be desirable where it can be achieved, but it is not a constitutional principle such as 'collective responsibility' in Britain, which requires all ministers to support the decisions of Cabinet publicly or resign. Members do differ in their views, and may do so publicly, as happened at the time of the Vietnam War and at the time of the Argentinean dispute with Britain in the early 1980s. In both cases, spokespersons reacted in different ways when questioned about their reaction to policy decisions.

No cabinet member feels he or she has to rush to defend a colleague (or president) under attack, and when there are disagreements no one feels obliged to resign – though members may choose to do so, if they are at odds with the president. Disagreement is not in itself an automatic reason for resigning, and Congress would not call for resignation as cabinet members are not responsible to the legislature, only to the president.

The bureaucracy

Bureaucracy refers to what Burns et al.[34] describe as a 'professional corps of officials organised in a pyramidal structure, and functioning under impersonal, uniform rules and procedures'. By the term 'bureaucrats', we refer to people who operate in the executive branch, whose career is based in government service and who normally work there as a result of appointment rather than election; they work for presidents and their political appointees. They serve in government departments, and in the more than fifty independent agencies embracing some two thousand bureaus, which are sub-units of the agencies.

It is sometimes assumed that the Administration is primarily concerned with putting into effect decisions taken elsewhere, so that politics and Administration are separate compartments. According to this view, bureaucrats are the neutral instrument of elected politicians and their concern is only to pursue their tasks with the utmost efficiency, free from considerations of personal gain or political advantage. Such a view is naive, and the executive branch is deeply involved in politics at many levels.

Who is part of the federal bureaucracy?

- Some five million people work in the executive branch.
- Of these, 60% are civilians; the rest are military personnel.
- About 12% of them operate in Washington.
- The rest are based around the country.
- In California, there are more than a quarter of a million federal employees.
- Of the three million civilians, about one million work in the area of national security – for the air force, army, navy and various defence organisations – and nearly half a million work for the welfare agencies.
- There are some fifteen thousand different categories of federal employee. The majority are white-collar workers, ranging from inspectors and engineers to secretaries and clerks.

Much of the legislation which goes before Congress begins its life in the departments and many agencies of government, and pressure group activists and congressmen realise this and may seek to influence proposals from the Administration at an early stage. Equally, much discretion is granted to those who implement the law when enacted, and they seek to influence congressmen on matters such as appropriations. In the same way, they seek to influence other agencies and departments whose interests conflict with their own, and so administration and politics cannot be isolated from each other.

Key positions in the American bureaucracy are held by persons appointed by the president (see box overleaf), and because these are normally people who share his or her outlook this might be expected to result in presidential control of the bureaucratic process. Yet this often does not happen, for once in position, those appointed may 'go native' and become part of the administrative machine, rather than agents of the president's will. As with relations with Congress, presidents soon find out that it is important to persuade, for they lack the power to command. In the frustrated words of President Truman: 'I thought I was the President, but when it comes to these bureaucracies I can't make 'em do a damn thing.'

The importance of political appointments can be exaggerated. They may seem to provide the president with an opportunity to change the direction and character of government policy, but in reality the number of appointments which he can make amounts to only a small percentage of those who work for the federal bureaucracy. For his first administration, President Clinton was able to nominate 222 personnel in the Department of Commerce, less than 1% of those working in the department; overall, he chose less than 0.2% of the total civilian, non-postal federal workforce. Moreover, the appointments have to be made in the brief period between the day of the presidential election and

Inauguration Day. Inevitably, the presidents must concentrate their attention on appointments at cabinet level and leave many of the rest to other members of their team.

The American bureaucracy has a large degree of autonomy, each agency having its own clientele, power-base and authority. Much of that authority derives from Congress, which creates or destroys agencies, authorises and approves reorganisation plans, defines powers and appropriates agency funds. Yet even Congress is unable to control the operation of bodies once they are established, and many of them have a life of their own. Walles[35] sees the bureaucracy as 'an active and largely independent participant in the political process, negotiating and bargaining with Congress, groups and the presidency alike'.

The presidential power of appointment

At one time, political appointees made up the vast majority of the federal bureaucracy. Appointments were made on the basis of patronage, 'who you knew, rather than what you knew', and membership of the successful party was important in gaining government jobs. Andrew Jackson (1829–37) developed the patronage system to its maximum extent, for he believed that 'to the victor go the spoils'. By the 'spoils system', employment was given to members of the party that won political office, not just as a reward for political support but also as a way of ensuring that many offices were opened up to ordinary citizens.

The Jacksonian approach survived for several decades and it helped to make the federal bureaucracy responsive to the needs of the White House. However, it later came to be associated with corruption. Congress tackled this problem by passing the Pendleton Act (1883), which limited the number of political appointments that a president could make and established a merit system for about 10% of federal jobs. This stressed ability, education and job performance as the key criteria for appointment, rather than political background. The merit system now applies to some 95% of federal civilian jobs.

Today, the president has an opportunity to influence the nature of the bureaucracy via his power of appointment over the most strategically important positions in government. He can nominate more than three thousand senior civil servants to serve in the Administration, and these include the heads of the fourteen major departments (the secretaries), as well as assistant and deputy department secretaries, deputy assistant secretaries and a variety of other appointive positions. Nearly seven hundred of the top presidential appointments have to be confirmed by the Senate. Once in office, their tenure depends on how the White House judges their performance.

The president is likely to choose personnel whom he regards as loyal and competent, and who share his political outlook. Abernach[36] notes that whereas in the past many appointees had been people who had established good connections with interest groups or congressional committees, in the Reagan era 'ideology was the key'. Before coming to office, Reagan established an appointment system which ensured that appointees would be faithful to him and pursue his objectives of reduced governmental activity.

There are some two thousand federal agencies, which are not directly amenable to presidential command or congressional directive. There is no collectivity of purpose, and the decisions and actions of one body may easily conflict with those of another. The Federal Reserve Board, which supervises the private banking system of the US and regulates the volume of credit and money in circulation, may pursue policies which are at variance with those of the Administration, just as the secretary of the Treasury may publicly cross swords with the director of the OMB.

The types of organisation involved

The federal administration is organised around most of the same vital functions which exist in any other national bureaucracy. The administrative apparatus responsible for fulfilling them is divided into three broad categories:

1 Government or executive departments

The heads of departments (or ministries) are picked by the president and hold office at his pleasure. As we have seen, they constitute the American Cabinet, although they do not share collective responsibility for government policy as they do in Britain. There are fifteen cabinet-level departments, which vary greatly in size. They are subdivided into bureaus and smaller units, often on the basis of function. Within the Commerce Department, there is the Bureau of the Census, and others such as the Patent and Trademark Office.

By far the most important department is the State Department (see pp. 90–1), but others include the Treasury, the Defence Department, and the Justice and Interior Departments. Others include Agriculture, Commerce, Labour, Health and Human Services, Education, Housing and Urban Development, Transportation and Energy.

2 The independent agencies

In addition to the executive departments, which are the major operating units of the federal government, there are many other agencies which help to keep the government and economy functioning smoothly. As they are not part of the executive departments they are often known as 'independent agencies'. They are powerful and important bodies in the executive branch: *in* it but not *of* it. They include several types of organisation, and have differing degrees of independence. They carry out functions laid down in statute, but have a complex set of formal and informal relationships with president and Congress, unlike those of a normal executive department.

These agencies vary considerably in character and purpose. Some provide special services either to the government or to the people (the forty or so

executive agencies, such as the Veterans' Administration), whilst others are supervisory, monitoring sections of the economy (**regulatory commissions**, such as the Federal Reserve Board and the Environmental Protection Agency). Some have substantial independence, others rather less. In many cases, the agencies have been created by Congress to tackle areas or issues that are too complex to come within the scope of ordinary legislation.

The independence of regulatory commissions is considerably greater than that of the executive agencies, this substantial autonomy having been deliberately arranged by Congress. Regulatory commissions have a different function: they remove supervision of particular areas from presidential hands, and are run by independent boards of commissioners. Often there are only five to seven commissioners, who serve for a fixed term of anything varying from three to fourteen years.

Such commissions are part of the executive branch, but they are not under direct presidential control. When vacancies arise, the president appoints appropriate personnel. However, once their appointment has been confirmed by the Senate, incumbents have security of tenure, and remain in office until their term of office has expired. Commissioners are not responsible to the president for the work of the commission, and because of their autonomy they can pose considerable problems for any president. Such commissions are sometimes described as the 'headless fourth branch of government'.

Commissions have quasi-judicial and quasi-legislative functions, as well as executive ones. Their number grew considerably during the twentieth century, for as new problems arose so new machinery was needed to watch over developments and resolve problems as they arose. Congress established these commissions in a way designed to keep them free of White House influence. It has given them much power, but their relationship to the president is unclear. Any president will be concerned with their activities because of the way in which they regulate economic activity, but presidential power over them is limited, given their conditions of appointment.

A new president will be confronted with a complex array of commissions whose leading figures have been selected by a predecessor, and it may be two or three years before the new incumbent can tip the balance of agency thinking by making new appointments on the retirement of existing officials. President Kennedy felt particularly limited by the fact that eight years of Republican patronage under his predecessor, Eisenhower, meant that he was unable to get his own people in important offices, and direct policy along the lines he favoured. Crucially, the president lacks the power of dismissal over such appointees. Moreover, the legislation regulating the commissions requires that members should be drawn from both political parties, a further limitation on presidential control of their operations.

3 Government corporations

The United States avoided nationalisation of the type that was introduced in Britain by the postwar Labour government. However, the federal government has become involved in conducting numerous activities which are commercial or industrial in nature. For this purpose, the corporation has been seen as the most appropriate form to enable activities to be carried out according to commercial or industrial needs. The intention was to give those directing such corporations the same sort of freedom to take decisions as that enjoyed by a director of any private enterprise organisation. As such, they are a cross between business corporations and regular governmental agencies. Examples of corporations include the Panama Canal Company, the St Lawrence Seaway Development Corporation and the Tennessee Valley Authority (TVA).

These and other bodies have a huge annual turnover and are responsible for projects of massive importance. The attempt to allow them freedom of manoeuvre has not always worked, for as with British nationalised industries there is a temptation for the Administration and Congress to seek to exert control over the decisions taken. The 1945 Government Corporation Control Act was passed to integrate corporations more closely into the normal machinery of the executive branch.

Making the bureaucracy function better

Reform of the bureaucracy is difficult to achieve, for as soon as a proposal is made specific, its implications for particular groups are understood and they may then lobby against change. Efforts to make the bureaucracy more efficient and more responsive are regularly mentioned at election time, but they continue to run into difficulties. Ronald Reagan was deeply sceptical of bureaucrats and their work, and he committed to a series of changes. These included privatisation of some operations, contracting out, and handing over federal programmes to the states as part of the New Federalism project. The outcome was less dramatic than he had anticipated, but there were some successes, such as bringing in private-sector enterprise to root out inefficiency and waste. In as much as cuts in personnel were made in areas such as welfare, they tended to be balanced by increases in staffing in the Justice, Defence and State Departments.

The *Reinventing Government Report*, September 1993

In 1993, President Clinton gave Al Gore the task of reviewing the bureaucracy and making recommendations for promoting efficiency and flexibility, and improving morale. His National Performance Review (NPR) made several criticisms of the federal bureaucracy, including:

- the wastefulness of many governmental organisations;
- their traditional preoccupation with familiar working practices;
- the lack of incentive for them to experiment and innovate;
- the relative absence of penalties for inadequate performance.

The Gore Report (known as the *Reinventing Government Report*) made wide-ranging recommendations which among other things stressed the need to cut red tape, place more emphasis on customer service, give more authority to those operating at lower levels of employment, and prune unnecessary expenditure. The broad thrust of the review was accepted, but it was less easy to command agreement when individual measures were to be implemented. Critics made the point that many changes were impossible to achieve, for it was not in the interest of Congress or the White House to insist on measures which were upsetting to groups of voters across the country.

The NPR has had some modest successes, not least in pruning the number of federal employees by more than 300,000, transforming the Federal Emergency Management Agency into a highly efficient disaster-relief unit, and removing thousands of pages of governmental rules and regulations written in largely incomprehensible language. Progress was made and meaningful reform of the bureaucracy has occurred in recent years. But other factors have been at work besides the Gore review, notably:

- the ending of the Cold War. The reduction in personnel was at least in part related to the defence cuts which followed from the thaw in international relations;

THE BUREAUCRACY IN BRITAIN AND THE UNITED STATES: A COMPARISON

Government departments

Government departments are organised differently in the two countries. Their heads (secretaries of state, often known as ministers) have a more directly political role in Britain. They:

- are in most cases elected members of Parliament;
- not only run their departments, but take part in cabinet and cabinet committee meetings, have parliamentary duties such as answering questions and taking part in debates, and perform a constituency role as Members of Parliament;
- are able to introduce legislation in the likelihood that it will become law, because of the strength of party support;
- are used to the rough and tumble of party politics, in some cases becoming figures of party standing in their own right;
- may have already served in several other departments as a junior minister and perhaps taken charge of one or two;

- the fact that both parties supported the Government Performance and Results Act of 1993, which required every government agency to publicise its performance criteria, to enable Americans to have a more effective assessment of how well public bodies were performing;
- the political climate created by Republican stress on 'smaller government' following the 1994 mid-term elections. Promises were made to axe departments such as Housing and Urban Development (HUD) and Energy, but these were not abolished. More modest ambitions were to lessen the impact of the Food and Drug Administration and to privatise some NASA programmes; these were fulfilled. Overall, however, the changes made in the 1990s were fewer than many Republicans had wanted to see.

The term 'bureaucracy' conjures up an image of red tape and inefficiency, and in the 1990s it was fashionable for many Americans to deride 'faceless bureaucrats' whose actions were wide-ranging and difficult to control. Anti-government politicians (many of whom were to be found in the Republican Party) were able to capitalise on this mood and urge the need for smaller government. There are problems in large and complex bureaucracies, for those working in them tend to acquire expertise in their own area and in the immediate problems confronting them, and also to extend their sphere of activity. Presidents have always found difficulty in ensuring that federal employees at all levels relate their expertise to the wider public interest. In the twentieth century, they initiated eleven reviews to try and make bureaucracy more responsive and efficient, and less costly and intrusive.

- are liable to be reshuffled from time to time, collecting as they go a wealth of experience in office.

American secretaries:
- are not usually prominent party figures;
- often return to relative obscurity after they have served the president who appointed them;
- have no regular constituency or congressional duties, although from time to time they will talk to congressmen about legislation which they wish to see enacted and testify before congressional committees;
- are less sure of seeing their legislation on the statute book.

Below head of department level, there are key differences in the two systems. In Britain:
- Ministers are advised by permanent secretaries: career civil servants whose role is prestigious and powerful. They may serve for several years and acquire a wealth of knowledge and experience, derived from functioning under different party administrations. There is no comparable job in US government departments, for senior depart-

▶

mental figures such as heads, under-secretaries and assistant secretaries are political appointees of the incoming administration.

- Almost all senior civil servants are permanent employees who are expected to be loyal to the government of the day.
- Less use is made of political advisers, although governments of recent years have employed more than ever before. As we have seen, secretaries of American departments are surrounded by a coterie of appointees, political figures who help the departmental heads to impose their will on the career civil service below them.

British constitutional theory makes a clear distinction between the political role of ministers and the administrative role of civil servants. Under the convention of individual ministerial responsibility, each minister is responsible to Parliament for the conduct of his or her department. Ministers, the elected politicians, are in charge; civil servants, the appointed officials, advise on policy and the implementation of ministerial decisions. Traditionally, the British civil service has been known for having three characteristics:

1 **permanence:** unlike ministers, civil servants do not change at election time. This allows for continuity of administration between governments and the development of expertise.;

2 **neutrality:** civil servants do not allow their political opinions to influence what they do, and they carry out the policies of whatever party is in power. This enables an incoming government to have confidence in what they do.

3 **anonymity:** no one is supposed to be able to identify civil servants; this enables them to give impartial and frank advice without fear of public reaction. It is the minister who is responsible for taking the praise or blame for actions and policies.

In the last few years, the organisation of the British civil service has been overhauled and its character has undergone changes:

1 Much of the administration has been handed over from government departments to agencies established under the 'Next Steps' programme, and the vast majority of civil servants now work for appointed chief executives rather than elected government ministers. The agencies and their chief executives are not accountable to Parliament or to the electorate, as government ministers and their departments used to be.

2 A unified, career civil service no longer exists, many chief executives and top civil servants being brought in from outside Whitehall to introduce new thinking. The traditional permanence of the civil service, which underpinned its public service ethos and methods and its commitment to serving the needs of the government of the day, has been eroded, with the hiving off of officials into agencies, a new emphasis on market testing and contracting out, and the increased importance of political advisers. The Blair government has doubled the number of these advisers, in a bid to ensure that the political will of ministers is reinforced as they seek to impose a sense of direction on their departments.

3 Civil servants have also become less neutral and anonymous. A frequently encountered observation among critics such as Hennessy[37] is that there has been a 'politicisation' of the civil service, with many senior civil servants owing their positions to the preference of prime ministers from Thatcher to Blair for having people in top positions who share their outlook. Civil servants are:
   (a) alleged to tell ministers what they wish to hear, rather than offer unpalatable advice based on careful and impartial analysis;
   (b) said to be increasingly drawn into the political arena, being used by politicians to draft party political speeches, prepare briefings for party events and help ministers in their policy presentation;
   (c) more likely to be named if mistakes occur, as ministers have become ever more reluctant to assume responsibility for the mistakes of their officials.

Other bodies

The Next Step agencies are only one example of the way in which British governments are making more use of unelected persons of dubious accountability. A further development in Britain has been the growth in the number of quangos (quasi autonomous non-governmental organisations) in the last few decades. According to Hall and Weir,[38] the total quango count in 1996 amounted to 6,424 public bodies. These are involved in government, but operate at arm's length from it. They comprise many state-related organisations which are influential in making or applying government policy, are executive or advisory in character, and may have important regulatory functions. Examples include the Arts Council, the Countryside Commission and the Commission for Racial Equality, as well as NHS trusts and police authorities. The appointment of members to quangos has become another form of political patronage for whichever party is in power.

American civil servants also work in hundreds of agencies, ranging from those which are part of cabinet departments to others which operate independently. Others again are to be found in the regulatory commissions and government corporations. The profile of the federal bureaucracy is not a single, monolithic institution, but rather a network of hundreds of distinct organisations employing millions of individuals.

In some respects, therefore, the workings of the British bureaucracy in the last few decades have taken on characteristics more familiar in the United States. Some of the traditional differences have been removed, in that:
   • there has allegedly been a 'politicisation' of the senior civil service, with appointments increasingly made on a 'one-of-us' basis;
   • more use is made of political appointees or 'aides' to advise and bolster ministers;
   • more use is made of agencies and other unelected bodies;
   • appointment of key personnel in these agencies such as chief executives is in the gift of the government of the day.

CONCLUSION

Many Americans have an ambivalent attitude towards the presidency. Like the framers of the Constitution, they both fear and admire leadership. At times, they seem to expect their president to rise above the party battle and represent the broad consensus of the nation at large. At others, they expect to see him provide a lead, both to Congress and to the people.The presidency has been described by Malcolm Walles[39] as 'the focal point of the United States system of government'. The Constitution may have shared power between the executive and the legislature, but it is the president who symbolises the nation. When people think of the achievements or failures of any particular epoch, they see these in terms of presidential rather than congressional eras. The curtailment of the imperial presidency accelerated during the 1990s. It is a trend which is widening the gulf between the electorate's expectations and a president's capacity to deliver. Presidential aspirants scatter promises on the campaign trail, but find them increasingly hard to fulfil.

The president needs and gets support from a multitude of advisers – the vice-president, the Cabinet and the Executive Office of the President, which includes the smaller White House Office. The policies deriving from the decision-makers in the executive branch are implemented by the federal bureaucracy, which has grown in size as its responsibilities have expanded. All who work in the area of making and carrying out governmental policy spend their time trying to match the expectations of a demanding electorate.

REFERENCES

1 G. Wasserman, *The Basics of American Politics*, Longman, 1997
2 T. Hames and N. Rae, *Governing America*, Manchester University Press, 1996
3 R. Maidment and D. McGrew, *The American Political Process*, Sage/Open University, 1992
4 A. Schlesinger Jr, *The Imperial Presidency*, Houghton Mifflin, 1973
5 T. Franck, *The Tethered Presidency*, New York University Press, 1981
6 F. Greenstein, *The Presidential Difference: Leadership Styles from FDR to Clinton*, Martin Kessler Books (Free Press), 2000
7 As quoted in the *Guardian*, 20 August 2001
8 E. Vullami, *Observer*, 23 November 2001
9 J. Freedland, the *Guardian*, 5 November 2002
10 T. Cronin and M. Genovese, *The Paradoxes of the American Presidency*, Oxford University Press, 2004
11 G. Wasserman, as in 1 above
12 M. Landy and S. Milks, *Presidential Greatness*, University Press of Kansas, 2000

13 G. Wasserman, as in 1 above
14 F. Greenstein, as in 6 above
15 J. Beatty, as quoted in D. Mervin, *The President of the United States*, Harvester Wheatsheaf, 1993
16 R. Neustadt, *Presidential Power: The Politics of Leadership*, Wiley & Sons, 1960
17 R. Neustadt, *Presidential Power and the Modern President*, Free Press, 1990
18 J. Burns, J. Peltason, T. Cronin and D. Magleby, Government by the People, Prentice Hall, 1994
19 J. Hart, *The Presidential Branch: Executive Office of the President from Washington to Clinton*, Chatham House, 1995
20 R. Byrd, *New York Times*, 27 July 1985
21 C. Rossiter, *The American Presidency*, Harcourt Brace, 1960
22 M. Walles, *British and American Systems of Government*, P. Allan, 1988.
23 C. Rossiter, as in 21 above
24 R. Maidment and D. McGrew, as in 3 above
25 As quoted in D. Broder and B. Woodward, *Washington Post National Weekly Edition*, 2 February 1992
26 As quoted in 10 above
27 T. Cronin and M. Genovese, as in 10 above
28 R. Reich, *Locked in the Cabinet*, Knopf, 1997
29 H. Kissinger, *White House Years*, Little, Brown, 1979
30 D. Kearns, *Lyndon Johnson and the American Dream*, Harper and Row, 1976
31 Quoted in H. Goswell, *Harry S. Truman*, Greenwood Press, 1980
32 H. Goswell, as in 31 above
33 As quoted in 10 above
34 J. Burns et al., as in 18 above
35 M. Walles, as in 22 above
36 J. Abernach, 'The President and the Executive Branch', in C. Campbell et al. and B. Rockman (eds), *The Bush Presidency: First Appraisals*, Chatham House, 1991
37 P. Hennessy, *The Hidden Wiring: Unearthing the British Constitution*, Gollancz, 1995
38 W. Hall and S. Weir, *The Untouchables: Power and Accountability in the Quango State*, Democratic Audit/Scarman Trust, 1996
39 M. Walles, as in 22 above

USEFUL WEB SITES

www.whitehouse.gov Official presidential site for the White House. Useful for following the day-to-day activities of the president, including daily briefings and press releases.

www.whitehousehistory.org White House Historical Association. General overview of the presidency and the White House; offers a virtual tour of the White House, showing its objets d'art.

SAMPLE QUESTIONS

1 'The power to persuade': is this a valid description of presidential power today?

2 The presidency was described as 'imperial' in the 1960s, 'tethered' in the 1970s, 'restored' in the 1980s, and 'constrained' in the 1990s. How might we categorise presidential power today?

3 What factors determine the ability of a president to exercise control over Congress?

4 Assess the effectiveness of presidential power in relation to either (a) domestic or (b) foreign policy.

5 What factors determine the power of the president? In what ways are his powers limited?

6 How successfully do presidents direct and co-ordinate the work of their administrations?

7 Examine the evolution and present importance of the Executive Office of the President.

8 How important is the Cabinet in American government?

9 Which is the more useful to the president, the Cabinet or the Executive Office?

10 'In this, I am nothing, but I may be everything' (John Adams). Evaluate the role and importance of the vice-presidency, in the light of this remark.

11 Examine the part played by the federal bureaucracy in government and policy-making in the United States.

The legislature: Congress

5

Congress is a bicameral legislature, comprising two bodies: the Senate and the House of Representatives. They are law-making chambers, and both have broadly equal powers, making the Senate the most powerful upper house in the world. Both chambers are directly elected by the people. Although representation and law-making are the primary roles, Congress has other duties. For example, the Senate approves or rejects the US president's choices for the heads of government departments, Supreme Court justices and certain other high-ranking jobs. The Senate also approves or rejects treaties that the president makes.

In this chapter, we are going to investigate the role and status of Congress and its members in the American system of government, the way it is organised, the attempts at reform in the past and proposals for further reform in the future.

POINTS TO CONSIDER

➤ What is the make-up of Congress?

➤ Why might an ambitious American politician prefer to serve in the Senate rather than the House of Representatives?

➤ What are the major stages through which legislative proposals must pass before they become law?

➤ What factors influence members of Congress as they make legislative decisions?

➤ How important is the role of congressional committees?

➤ How might Congress be usefully reformed?

➤ What are the social characteristics of members of Congress? In what respects have they undergone change in recent years?

➤ In what ways do the duties and responsibilities of US congressmen coincide and conflict with those of Members of Parliament?

➤ How do the membership of Congress and Parliament compare in terms of age, gender, race and social background?

How Congress is organised

Congress is bicameral. In other words, it has two chambers:

- **The Senate** consists of two senators from each of the fifty states.
- **The House of Representatives** has 435 members. Members of the House of Representatives are elected from congressional districts of about equal population into which the states are divided (see the box opposite on apportionment). Every state must have at least one House seat. For example, Alabama has two senators and seven House seats, Delaware two senators and one House seat, and New York State two senators and thirty-four House seats. Representatives are often called congressmen or congress-women, though technically the term applies to senators as well.

The Democrats and the Republicans have long been the only major parties in Congress. In each chamber, the party with more members is the **majority** party, the other the **minority** one. Before each new session of Congress, Republicans and Democrats in each house meet in what is called a caucus or conference to choose party leaders and to consider legislative issues and plans.

Committees form an important feature of each chamber's organisation. They prepare the bills to be voted on. The committee system divides the work of processing legislation and enables members to specialise in particular types of issues. The majority party in each chamber elects the head of each committee and holds a majority of the seats on most committees.

The vice-president serves as head of the Senate and presides over its proceedings. In fact, he or she usually only appears on special occasions or to break a tie, and for everyday work the Senate elects a president *pro tempore* to serve in the vice-president's absence. The speaker of the House serves as presiding officer and party leader. He or she is chosen by the majority party, the choice then being ratified by the whole chamber. The speaker is the most important member of Congress, because of the broad powers the post provides within the assembly (see box on pp. 126–7).

A new Congress is organised every two years. Voters elect all the representatives at that time, and a third of the senators come up for election every two years. The Senate is therefore a continuing body because it is never completely new. The two chambers elected in November 2004 form the 109th Congress.

The 109th Congress: party representation in January 2005

	Democrats	Republicans	Independents
House (one vacancy)	201	232	1
Senate	44	55	1

The independent Senator Jeffords votes with the Democrats on procedural matters.

Apportionment of membership in the House of Representatives

Apportionment is the process of dividing the 435 members or seats in the House of Representatives across the country. A reapportionment has been made on the basis of each decennial census from 1790 to 2000 (except following the 1920 census), in line with the growth and decline of population in each of the fifty states.

The average size of a congressional district based on the 2000 census is 646,952, more than triple the average district size of 193,167 based on the census taken one hundred years earlier. Of the seven states with one seat, Montana is the largest, having a population of 905,316. Wyoming, which also has one seat, is the smallest district, having a population of only 495,304. Overall, in 2000, eight states were granted additional representation and ten lost out in the process of reallocation.

The drawing of House districts is up to the state governors and legislatures, who have often used these powers to advantage their own party and penalise their opponents. In the past, malapportionment (large differences in the populations of congressional districts) was common in many areas of the country. Districts could be devised in such a way that minority party districts included more votes than majority party districts, so that each minority party voter would count for less. In Michigan in 1960, the sixteenth district had 802,999 inhabitants whereas the twelfth had only 177,431.

The two main malpractices are packing (drawing up a district so that it has a large majority of supporters, to make it safe) and cracking (splitting up an opponents' supporters into minorities in a number of districts, in order to lessen their impact). Such practices are often referred to as gerrymandering, a technique named after Governor Elbridge Gerry of Massachusetts. It is said that one of the constituencies he created had the shape of a lizard. 'Why, this district looks like a salamander!', remarked an observer. 'Say rather a Gerrymander', relied an opposition 'wit'.

Malapportionment has long been criticised by reformers, who were supported in their efforts by a Supreme Court judgement in 1964 which held that legislative districts at both the state and national levels should be as close to equal in population as possible. Yet controversy continues, being notably a feature of the post-1990 census. Some states took the opportunity to create districts that were racially representative of the population, designing minority districts in which the minorities became the majority of the voting population. This happened in North Carolina's twelfth district, which snaked across thirteen counties in half the state, in a bid to include as many black voters as possible. This ploy by the controlling Republicans helped to lessen support in surrounding districts for the Democrats, because they contained fewer Democrat-voting minorities.

Figures on apportionment adapted from those provided by the Bureau of the Census.

Each House of Congress has the power to introduce legislation on any subject, except revenue bills, which must originate in the House of Representatives. The large states may thus appear to have more influence over the public purse than the small states. In practice, however, each chamber can vote against

The role of speaker in the House of Representatives

Members of the majority party in the House choose the speaker in a party caucus (gathering of party members) at the beginning of each two-year session of Congress. The person chosen is not necessarily the oldest or longest serving, but is usually someone who commands respect and has served a lengthy apprenticeship in other party offices in the House.

The speaker's is the only House role mentioned – although not described – in the Constitution. As presiding officer of the lower chamber, he or she fulfils several functions including opening each session, ruling on procedural matters, deciding who shall speak and referring bills to committees. Beyond this, the speaker has several powers of appointment, including membership of the Rules Committee and of ad hoc committees that may be created. The speaker is third in line to the presidency, should the president and vice-president resign, be impeached or be killed. Because of this, the speaker is expected to inform the White House of his or her whereabouts at all times. He or she also represents the House on ceremonial occasions.

The two most recent incumbents, at the time of writing in early 2005, have been Newt Gingrich and Dennis Hastert. Taking over in January 1995 after the Republican success in the mid-term elections of the previous November, Newt Gingrich became the first Republican speaker for forty years. His period of office was highly influential. He was concerned not only to make the lower chamber operate more efficiently, but also to introduce a system of party government within the chamber. Accordingly, he:
- ushered in several rule changes;
- tightened the co-ordination of activities among House leaders;
- limited the number of subcommittees within each committee and reorganised several committee jurisdictions;
- introduced greater cohesion among the Republicans, so that in the first hundred days of his speakership the 'Contract for America' programme was pushed through the House with an average of only five dissenting voices on thirty-three roll-call votes;
- handpicked committee and subcommittee chairs, often ignoring the claims of

legislation passed by the other house. The Senate may disapprove a House revenue bill – or any bill, for that matter – or add amendments that change its nature. In that event, a conference committee made up of members from both houses must work out a compromise acceptable to both sides before the bill becomes law.

The Senate also has certain powers especially reserved to that body, including the authority to confirm presidential appointments of high officials of the federal government as well as to ratify all treaties by a two-thirds vote. Unfavourable action in either instance nullifies the wishes of the executive.

In the case of impeachment of federal officials, the House has the sole right to bring charges of misconduct that can lead to an impeachment trial. The Senate

seniority; chairs were to be limited to six years' service in future, in order to prevent their becoming too powerful and independent;

- created task-forces of carefully chosen colleagues to consider issues and make proposals, and thereby bypass the characteristic blockages often found within the committee system;
- freed himself from the day-to-day business of running the House by handing over such tasks to the House Majority Leader, so that he was able to concentrate on determining the party agenda;
- used frequent media appearances to turn his office into a powerful position from which he could advance an alternative programme that was more conservative than that of the president.

By virtue of his forceful personality and the backing he received from several freshmen Republicans, Gingrich became the most powerful speaker of modern times. But his tenure did not last long and he did not achieve all that he hoped. Aspects of the 'Contract for America' programme (see p. 259) stalled because of opposition in the Senate. Moreover, his personal brand of leadership created enemies who disliked the concentration of power in his hands. This led to his downfall shortly after disappointing mid-term elections in 1998. After four years, the mantle of leadership was taken up by Dennis Hastert, a legislator with no national profile at the time.

The Hastert approach to the speakership has been more traditional in its mode of operation. More of a conciliator, he has sought a consensus. By spending more time in the chamber and involving himself in legislative details and procedures, he has opted for a 'return to regular order'.[1] Although at the time, his appointment was expected to be a short-lived affair, he has none the less outlasted his more high-profile predecessor.

As we have seen, the speaker is a highly influential figure, possessing considerable power via his or her control over the majority party and his or her influence over how the committee system operates. This is why more powerful holders of the office such as Gingrich have often been referred to as the equivalent of prime ministers.

has the sole power to try impeachment cases, and to find officials guilty or not guilty. A finding of guilt results in the removal of the federal official from public office.

The eighteen broad powers of the whole Congress are spelled out in the eighth section of the first article of the Constitution. The first seventeen are specific duties, but the eighteenth sets out the task of making 'all Laws which shall be necessary and proper for carrying into execution the foregoing Powers, and all other Powers vested by this Constitution in the Government of the United states, or in any Department or Officer thereof'.

THE POWERS AND STATUS OF THE HOUSE AND OF THE SENATE

The two primary functions of Congress are to represent the will of the people and to make laws for the country. The two tasks overlap, for if the laws do not represent the people's wishes then the law-makers may suffer defeat at the next election.

Which chamber has the higher status?

Whereas, in Britain, one chamber is dominant, this is not so in the United States. In powers, the US chambers are virtually co-equal, having some concurrent powers (as in the passing of legislation or in overriding a presidential veto) and some exclusive ones. Many commentators would argue that the Senate's responsibilities with regard to treaties and ratification of appointments, give it a greater degree of authority. Even the restriction that all bills on revenue raising must originate in the House is hardly a limitation, as the Senate has the same full power of amendment as it has with other types of bill.

Indicative perhaps of the Senate's higher status is the fact that candidates for the presidency and vice-presidency tend to come from the upper house (or after serving a period in office as a state governor). Few come from the House of Representatives. Senators tend to get higher levels of media coverage and so find it easier to build personal reputations. More of them are known nationwide, the names of Elizabeth Dole, Edward Kennedy, John Kerry and John McCain all being recognisable well beyond the confines of their states. Richard Pear[2] has elaborated in this way:

> Great senators have made the Senate great, and have influenced the course of American history in ways which can be recorded in the history books . . . [Some] sitting for safe seats have spent their lives in the Senate, becoming the embodiment of national or regional thinking on certain topics. Great senators are

The concurrent and exclusive powers of the two chambers

Type of powers	House	Senate
Concurrent (both chambers involved)	Pass legislation	
	Override presidential veto	
	Begin process of amending Constitution	
	Declare war	
	Confirm choice of newly appointed vice-president	
Exclusive	Introduce money bills	Confirm appointments and ratify treaties (known as the 'Advice and Consent' role)
	Initiate impeachment procedure	Stage impeachment trials
	Elect president, should there be deadlock in Electoral College	Elect vice-president, should there be deadlock on electoral college

competitors for the limelight with presidents. They know their power and can use it for long term objectives.

An important difference is the length of service of a senator and a representative. Senators have the opportunity to acquire a working knowledge of their subjects of concern, without the problem of constantly having to campaign for their return to Washington. They can take part in a genuine debate rather than speaking and listening with the likely reactions of the voters in mind. Also, they have been elected by the whole state rather than a district of it. For instance, senators Edward Kennedy and John Kerry represent the entire state of Massachusetts, whereas Ed Markey is the Democrat House representative for the Seventh District.

By comparison, members of the House are at a disadvantage. Maidment and McGrew[3] quote the example of one newly elected representative, who described his four years in the House in this way: 'The first two years, I spent all of my time getting re-elected.' Two years is perhaps too short a time in which to achieve anything substantial. For this reason, membership of the lower chamber is not a particularly satisfying form of activity, or a particularly honoured position. Every two years, there are some representatives who do not seek re-election, but return from whence they came. Some are put off by the nature of their work, which they may find unrewarding. Little can be achieved by a 'freshman' unless the committee on which he or she serves suddenly bursts into prominence, because of a sensational investigation or contentious bill. For many of them, the job leads no further. If they wish to advance their careers, they may well seek a seat in the Senate. Senators, by contrast, do not look for an opportunity to enter the House.

Americans are healthily sceptical about all those who represent them in Washington, and all politicians are held in low esteem. Americans tend to have a higher regard for those who have improved themselves by their own industry and perseverance in the fields of business, law and the other professions, rather than for those who operate in government.

The functions of Congress

The overall role of Congress is extensive. As with any other Western democracy, it performs a key representative task. People choose representatives to make decisions for them, and if they do not like the decisions made they can reject those previously chosen at the next election. In this way, a link between the people and the national government is formed, and the consent of the governed is achieved. Representation is a difficult concept, and is open to a number of interpretations, but it involves the basic idea that legislators are responsive to those who put them in their position (see also pp. 137–8).

The work in which Congress is engaged can be conveniently classified according to three main headings: legislation, investigation and finance. The legislative role is the prime function, for it affects the lives of the American people most directly. An efficient and responsive legislature has the power to further national goals at home and abroad, by the way in which it handles its law-making task.

Legislation

Bills are introduced by a variety of methods. Some are drawn up in standing committees, some by special committees created to examine specific legislative issues, and some may be urged by the president or other executive officers. Individuals and outside organisations may suggest legislation to congressmen, and individual members may themselves have ideas they wish to see pass into law.

Such is the volume of legislation proposed by senators and representatives that much of it has no chance of getting any further. It is introduced in the first

---

COMMITTEES IN CONGRESS: MAIN TYPES

In *Congressional Government*, Woodrow Wilson[4] (later to become a Democrat president) wrote that 'Congress in session is Congress on public exhibition, whilst Congress in its committee rooms is Congress at work.' Committees are indeed the principal means via which the House and Senate carry out their legislative duties. In the 107th Congress, there were 199 permanent committees and subcommittees. The smallest in the Senate is the Ethics Committee (6 members) and in the House the Administration Committee (13). The largest in the Senate is the Apppropriations Committee (28) and in the House the Transportation and Infrastructure Committee (75).

There are several types of committee, notably:

1 Standing committees

Standing committees are permanent, having fixed jurisdictions that operate from one session of Congress to another. These are the most important committees and the focus of much of the work performed by the legislature. In the House, the Rules Committee has a crucial role, with the power to delay or even stop legislation. The Ways and Means Committee raises money; the Appropriations Committee deals with how government spends that money. Many members of the House Budget Committee are drawn from these two bodies, with one member from each of the other standing committees. In the Senate, the Appropriations, Budget, Finance and Foreign Affairs Committees are prestigious. Membership of the committees mentioned is highly prized, and congressmen and senators may have to wait years to get assigned to them. Usually, congressmen serve on one or two standing committees only, whereas in the smaller Senate members are expected to serve on three or four.

Most standing committees spawn subcommittees. The House and Senate Appropriations Committees have thirteen of them each. The standing committees carry out the committee stage of the legislative process, holding hearings and taking evidence from witnesses who might be representatives of the Administration, pressure groups or even

place more as a way of securing the goodwill of lobbyists or constituents than with any expectation of further progress. After the initial introduction, the leadership sends bills to designated committees, where many of them die. Ninety % of those before a subcommittee get no further, for lack of time or lack of support. This is the justification for the existence of committees. They act as a screening mechanism for the flood of measures presented, and thereby prevent the Senate and House being overwhelmed.

For those bills with significant backing, the committee schedules a series of public hearings that may last for weeks or months, and allow for an outside

ordinary members of the public. These committees also conduct investigations within their broad policy area, ascertaining – among other things – why any problems occurred, whether legislation is working and what action might be taken. In the Senate, the committees additionally carry out the role of 'advice and consent' (see p. 128).

2 Select committees

These are temporary committees that cease to exist unless specifically renewed at the beginning of each new Congress. They may be asked to study or report on a particular topic, but they do not receive or report bills. Their investigations are often time-consuming and detailed, and tend to cover areas that would not be catered for in the investigative capacity of standing committees. An example taken from the Clinton years is the Senate Committee on Whitewater, established in the 104th Congress. It was given the task of uncovering any illegal activity in the president's involvement in a failed Arkansas real-estate project back in the 1980s.

3 Joint committees

Permanent bodies, these include members drawn from both houses and have continuing oversight over a particular area of policy. The Joint Economic Committee has the important tasks of studying and reporting on the president's annual economic report. Joint committees may also initiate legislation.

4 Conference committees

Again drawn from both houses, these are temporary committees charged with resolving the differences between legislative proposals dealing with the same topic. These differences come about because of amendments attached to the bill by one chamber but not the other, or because the two houses have passed different bills relating to the same subject. Before a bill goes to the president, it must be passed in identical language by both chambers.

input from interested bodies. The subcommittee then discusses and amends the bill, and – assuming there is a vote in its favour – it is sent ('reported') to the full chamber, where it is debated, and again a vote occurs. (In the House,

---

The Rules Committee

The House Rules Committee of only thirteen members is the most influential committee in the lower chamber. Comprising some of the most senior members of the House and having a 2:1 membership in favour of the majority party, it organises the timetable of the House and thereby effectively determines the fate of proposed legislation.

The committee decides on a rule, which sets the time limit for debate and states whether amendments can be allowed on the floor of the House. It may decide that there can be debate and amendments subject to the overall time available ('open rule'), or it may limit debate and insist that only members of the reporting committee may offer amendments ('closed rule', usually used only for tax and spending bills). Normally, without such a rule, the bill will not reach the floor.

Before Congress was reformed in the 1970s, the committee was even more powerful than is the modern one. The 'old guard' (a coalition of southern Democrats and Republicans) used their influence to block proceedings. The committee was then much disliked by liberals and those who wanted to see reform; they saw it as dictatorial and unrepresentative.

Today, the committee is less controversial and more representative of the membership of the majority party. If it wants a bill to be passed, the committee can expedite its passage, by sending it quickly to the floor of the House for immediate debate.

THE ROLE OF THE ADMINISTRATION IN LEGISLATION

The amount and character of legislation have changed significantly over the years. In the 1960s and 1970s, there was a burst of legislative action, but in the following decade the pace of change – especially on substantive issues – slowed down.

Federal governments cannot in theory make laws, and their proposals have no priority in congressional procedure. Presidents can propose legislation, but if congressional leaders prefer their own then the White House has no means of redress. Departments, in consultation with committee chairpersons and party leaders, draw up the measures seen as desirable. They are then introduced by sympathetic members.

Although most successful legislation now originates in the executive branch, the Administration cannot be sure of its passage in the form that it favours. Whereas, in Britain, the system of party discipline ensures that a government with a parliamentary majority may get its way, this is not the case in the US. Presidents cannot depend on congressional support, and Congress remains a major force in determining the shape and timing of legislation.

the bill will first go to the Rules Committee – see box opposite – which determines the time limits to be allowed and decides whether or not amendments from the floor will be permitted.)

Usually, both chambers consider their own bills, at approximately the same time. To succeed, the approval of both the Senate and the House is necessary. If there are differences in the versions passed, then a conference committee will seek a compromise.

The bill must have successfully endured the procedure of both houses, and have been approved in identical form, for it to become law. If this does not happen in the lifetime of one Congress, the attempt has failed: the whole process needs to be started again.

At this point, the bill goes to the White House for the approval of the president. He may sign it, veto it or do nothing. If Congress is sitting and he does nothing, then after ten working days the bill becomes law without his signature. If the Congress has adjourned and the president waits ten days before signing, then this is a pocket veto. Other than in this case, a vetoed bill is returned to the Congress, with the reasons for rejection. The presidential veto can be overturned, if both chambers can muster a two-thirds majority against it.

Figures produced by Professor Davidson[5] show that only about 3% of bills received by the president are vetoed, and only about 4% of all vetoes are overridden by Congress. Presidents may veto a bill for several reasons –

The president and Congress: co-operation in the legislative arena

The separation of powers and the divided government that it involves present an obstacle to policy-making. They set the scene for a continuous struggle, although the Constitution requires the two branches to work together. The Administration and Congress can legislate when the president and congressional leaders bargain and compromise. President Johnson was skilled in this process, for as an ex-Senate majority leader he understood the need for the White House to build bridges with his former colleagues. He urged his aides and cabinet members to get to know more about the key figures on Capitol Hill and what mattered to them. What was sometimes known as the 'Johnson treatment' 'ran the gamut of human emotions', from accusation and cajolery to tears and threats. Writing of the relationship with congressmen, two journalists, Evans and Novak,[6] noted the technique:

> Johnson anticipated them before [interjections] could be spoken. He moved in close, his face a scant millimeter from his target, his eyes widening and narrowing, his eyebrows rising and falling. From his pockets poured slips, memos, statistics. Mimicry, humor and the genius of analogy made The Treatment an almost hypnotic experience and rendered the target stunned and helpless.

But Johnson had more than personal skills working to his advantage. He was president at a time of strong Democrat majorities in both chambers. Some of his more recent successors would have been delighted to receive such party backing. Moreover, his opponents were less ideologically driven and cohesive than has been the case since November 1994. In today's circumstances, a president needs to be in regular consultation with his opponents, as well as his supporters. The Clinton experience, following the Republican victory in the mid-term elections of November 1994, showed that to rescue his legislative proposals, he needed co-operation and agreement. When he obtained this, his success record improved (other than in the year of impeachment proceedings), as the figures indicate:

perhaps because it differs from their own legislative preferences, or because they feel it is unconstitutional, costs too much, or is hard to enforce.

The legislative procedure of Congress has often been described as an 'obstacle course', for bills have to get past the appropriate standing committee, be given time by the Rules Committee and then survive the debate on the floor of the House or Senate. To have got this far, there must have been a substantial degree of support, but in the Senate this is no mere formality and the bill can always be subject to a **filibuster**, by which senators hold the floor of the chamber, speak at length and seek to delay proceedings to avoid a vote being taken. The aged Strom Thurmond holds the record: in seeking to delay the 1957 Civil Rights Act, he spoke for 24 hours 18 minutes!

filibuster
A device that enables a senator or group of them to kill a bill by the use of delaying tactics. As there is unlimited debate in the Senate, they can carry on talking for as long as they wish. Only a closure vote of 60% can end a filibuster, and there has not been a successful one for more than twenty-five years. The word 'filibuster' derives from the Spanish word meaning 'pirate, one who plunders freely'. Filibusters are part of the normal political process, a means by which a legislative minority can prevent a vote.

It is not surprising that few bills successfully navigate the procedure. In the 106th Congress (1998–2000), 5% of those introduced went on to become law. In the 107th Congress, the success rate dropped to 4% of the 8,948 bills introduced. The procedure is not without advantages. The separation of powers is there to stop the domination of one section of the governmental machinery by another, and the law-making process reflects this aim of preventing tyranny. It is impossible for the whips to force through changes at the wish of the executive branch, and there is no elective dictatorship of the type often said to exist in Britain. Instead, those who seek to get a bill passed onto the statute

Year	%
1993	86.4
1994	86.4
1995	36.2
1996	55.1
1997	56.6
1998	51.0
1999	37.8
2000	55.0

NB In his first two years, George W. Bush achieved a success rate of 87% and 88%. He had a thin legislative agenda that he pursued with modest vigour, whereas his predecessor had a more difficult ride, not least because Clinton had a busy programme on which he was seeking to drive a reluctant Congress to take action.

book need to build a consensus in its support, and if it does pass it is likely to have substantial backing.

However, in a crisis the machinery is less responsive than the situation demands. Franklin Roosevelt and Lyndon Johnson, each aided by a Congress controlled by his own party, were able to introduce a package of measures speedily, but their experience is untypical. The system offers a built-in advantage to those who would thwart legislation, which is why Denenberg[7] describes Congress as 'a bastion of negation'. The legislative procedure enables a dissenting minority to prevent the passage of bills by their obstruction at several access points – and thereby kill the proposal off.

The legislative process is lengthy and complex, there being so many obstacles that a bill may fail to overcome. It is not surprising that so few bills survive this 'legislative labyrinth' and become law, for the odds are stacked heavily against success. Because of the number of bills introduced, the standing committees – to which so much power is given – are overwhelmed. Much depends on the drive and forcefulness of the committee chairpersons. It also helps if the two chambers are under the control of the same party, as in the era of Republican predominance since November 1994. But even when the majority has been more cohesive, as in recent years, there is no certainty that members will vote with their parties in support of the legislative programme.

Investigation

One of the most important non-legislative functions of Congress is the power to investigate. This power is usually delegated to committees, either the standing committees, select (special) committees set up for the specific purpose, or joint committees composed of members of the two houses. As the legislative initiative in Congress has diminished in recent years, so the investigatory role has assumed a greater importance.

It is in the scrutiny of the executive that the extent of congressional power becomes most apparent. Two factors give Congress greater power than the British Parliament. The first is the separation of powers, which was designed to prevent undue concentration of power in one location, and which denies the executive the chance to sit in Congress. Second, the absence of strong party discipline means that congressmen can act as free agents, and act and vote as they please; they do not feel beholden to their party leaders for their advancement.

Investigations may be conducted to gather information on the need for future legislative action, to test the efficacy of laws already enacted, to inquire into the qualifications and performance of members and officials of the other branches of government, and to lay the groundwork for impeachment proceedings. Often, these hearings will involve the use of outside experts to assist in conducting the investigation, and to enable a detailed study of the issues involved.

Most of these hearings are open to the public, and they are widely reported in the media. Witnesses can be compelled to testify, and those who refuse may be cited for contempt; those who give false testimony can be charged with perjury. Investigations of a special type (such as that by the 1987 joint committee on the Iran–Contra affair) attract much publicity and through their findings can provoke much public and political controversy. Congress can examine anything it considers appropriate within the legislative sphere, and added to the overseeing aspect of investigation (i.e. acting as a watchdog on the executive), this indicates the power of the two houses in the political process. Investigations over the years have covered topics such as drug addiction, the Ku Klux Klan, foreign aid programmes, the American role in NATO, foreign commitments in China and Vietnam, and the possible abuses of power involved in the Watergate/Irangate operations. Whitewatergate and allied scandals were the subject of investigation during the Clinton years.

Finance

The presidential budget proposals may begin their existence in the White House, but they have to survive the detailed scrutiny of Congress. Most policies cost money, and thus require congressional authority to raise and spend it. Once the president and Congress are agreed upon a programme (authorisation), it is Congress that has to appropriate the funds to pay for its implementation. Such appropriations are processed by a committee in either house, and until the president signs the annual appropriations bill the original authorisation of expenditure amounts to nothing.

In recent years, the federal budget has been a continuing source of controversy between the president and Congress. The conflict originally dates back to the growth in the costs of federal programmes in the Great Society programmes of the 1960s, and in the years since then there has been an insufficient amount of revenue to match the expenditure. This has resulted in budget deficits, which by the 1990s were increasingly viewed with much alarm by many commentators and politicians.

Congress could accept the increase in military spending in the Reagan years, for it shared the goal of keeping America strong. It also liked the idea of low taxation. But the growing deficit could only be tackled by reduced spending in other areas, and this posed political difficulties for congressmen. A large part of the expenditure could not be cut without tackling the controversial social security and medical programmes, which used up so much federal money but were popular with recipients. These programmes and other entitlements such as pensions (adjusted for annual cost-of-living increases) were difficult to control.

Without cuts in defence spending, welfare and other areas, there was little scope for tax cuts unless the deficit was allowed to increase – which is what happened. The reason, as given by President Reagan's director of the OMB,[8] was that: 'Deficits create many winners and few losers . . . Every legislator is in a position to confer benefits on his or her favourite constituencies, and the incentive for any individual legislator to refrain from such behaviour is virtually non-existent.'

Representation

The House of Representatives was originally viewed by the framers of the Constitution as the body that would **represent** the wishes of the mass of the people. The Senate, not directly elected, was seen as a more detached, dispassionate body that could operate as a check upon the House, which was liable to be influenced by considerations of short-term popularity. When direct election of the Senate was introduced, the House lost its unique position as the body reflecting the mood of the mass electorate. Since 1913, both chambers can claim to be representatives of the people.

The importance attached to this function of representation is one of the distinguishing features of

representation
This has several meanings in political science. Usually, it means the authority to act on behalf of another, as gained through the process of election; in this sense, the representative acts to safeguard and promote the interests of the area represented. It can also mean the extent to which a representative mirrors or is typical of the characteristics of the person he or she formally represents – for example, is the House representative in that it has an appropriate balance of women and ethnic minority members? (see pp. 149–52.)

Congress, compared with other legislatures. The Senate and the House have always attached the highest priority to the attitudes and concerns of those who elected them, and other considerations such as party figure much less in their thinking. This leads us conveniently into a consideration of the roles and responsibilities of congressmen.

The work and responsibilities of members of Congress

Any Senator or Representative is concerned with five broad spheres of responsibility: the national interest; the constituency interest; the party interest; the lobbyists and the political action committees that supported his or her campaign; and his or her own personal convictions. In Congress, the congressman must seek to balance the importance of these spheres to him or her.

Several congressmen represent areas where their re-election is likely. They know that party discipline is much looser than in Britain, and the party label counts for less. Some of them may not feel particularly beholden to special interests. In other words, they can make up their own minds on issues, in the light of what they think is best for the country, best for their constituency and most in accordance with their own wishes. Independence of judgement in the light of their own conscience and beliefs is still a determinant of their vote.

Congressmen and party voting

Members of either chamber are required to vote on many occasions every year, more so in the House than in the Senate. In 2003, there were 675 House votes and 459 Senate ones. Among other things, the votes may cover bills in their various readings, amendments to them, budgetary details and (in the Senate) treaties or appointments made by the president.

In recent years, there has been an increase in party loyalty, against the background of a more intense ideological struggle. The attempt to drive through the Republican 'Contract for America' programme (see p. 259) inspired greater loyalty among majority party members than had usually previously been the case. So too it provoked greater unanimity among the Democrat minority. Contentious issues ranging from abortion to taxation and from gun control to school prayer have often been the cause of increased partisanship, as also was the failed attempt to impeach President Clinton. For all these reasons, there was a marked polarisation in party attitudes, and intraparty rancour and invective became more common.

Apart from the Republican takeover in November 1994, other factors too have contributed to greater party unity, among them:

- the break-up of the so-called Solid South (see p. 3) a few decades ago, meaning that the Democrats in Congress are altogether more homogeneous, being notably more urban-based and liberal;
- the declining influence of the liberal element within the Republican party, in an age when the Religious Right has been in the ascendancy. As party support has been increasingly concentrated in the South and West, so too has the conservative element been strengthened;
- the influence of ideologically based pressure groups, including think-tanks (see pp. 281, 294), that have tended to push parties in a more partisan direction. Since these groups often provide funding for election campaigns, their influence is important. As a price for their backing, they expect some adherence to their preferences. Such a pressure discourages party negotiators in Congress from the politics of bargaining and compromise.

For the reasons given, party voting (a situation in which the bulk of the members of one party vote with each other and against the opposition) has become markedly more common than it was a few decades ago, but it is by no means the norm, as the figures given below indicate:

Party voting in Congress

Year	House (%)	Senate (%)
1958	40	44
1963	49	47
1968	35	32
1993	65	67
1998	56	56
2003	52	67

NB The year of the greatest intensity of party voting was 1995, when on 73% of the possible occasions a party vote was recorded in the House, 69% in the Senate. In the last years of the Clinton presidency, in spite of the impact of impeachment proceedings in 1999, partisanship was actually at the lowest level recorded since the late 1980s, with only 43% of the House votes and 49% of those in the Senate being party votes. By then, Republican leaders lacked a clear majority in both chambers to push through their agenda, although there were still some highly partisan confrontations.

The more partisan atmosphere of recent years has not just been a feature of votes on the floor of the chambers. It also influences members' conduct in committees and in relationships with the White House.

The party has never claimed the allegiance of congressmen as it does that of the Members of Parliament (MPs) in Britain. MPs see support for the party, except on rare occasions, as a primary duty. In the United States the situation is different. As Walles[9] puts it: 'While party membership provides a natural starting point for action, ultimately it may well take second place to activity related to committee and constituency pressures.'

Parties are of course the route via which the senator or representative reaches Congress, but as Mayhew argues,[10] once the journey is successfully accomplished 'it is the pressure for re-election which colours congressional activity'. He distinguishes three forms of likely activity that to a greater or lesser degree might influence a congress member's behaviour in pursuing this goal:

1 self-promotion, via postal communication and diligent attention to social and other occasions in the constituency. Engagements include conducting surgeries with constituents, making tours around local factories, hospitals and schools, appearing on local radio stations, addressing lunches and giving interviews to local journalists;

2 credit-claiming, as members point to what they have done for their district (jobs, contracts, support for local industry etc.) and for individuals. This is especially relevant to the representatives, facing as they do the prospect of a re-election battle within two years, although no Senator wants to antagonise important interests within the state;

3 position-taking, undertaken to help promote a favourable image of what the representative really believes in – what Mayhew calls 'the public enunciation of a judgmental statement on anything likely to be of interest'.

The constituency 'welfare' role

Since about 1980, it has been constituency responsibilities that have come to consume much of the time of the legislators. They hire more staff to work in their state and local offices, make more trips to the constituency, receive and send more mail to the voters, and generally treat such work as a priority demand upon their time. For many members of congress, it has come to be a more important responsibility than drafting legislation.

In American government, there has always been talk of **pork-barrel politics**, by which Congressmen are judged according to the success with which 'they bring home the bacon'. It used to mean 'delivering the goods' in terms of bringing rewards to the constituency. Today, constituency service has a wider connotation than merely gaining 'pork' or advantages. It is also about assuming the role of welfare worker or ombudsman, as citizens feel that they need assistance in their dealings with those who work in government offices and who are part of what is seen as an unresponsive bureaucracy.

Helping constituents in difficulty is more likely to ease the path of re-election than speaking and voting on controversial issues. Christopher Bailey[11] has highlighted this change of emphasis,

pork-barrel politics
This is all about congressmen being able to secure advantages, for bills are pieces of legislation designed to produce visible (usually economic) benefits, such as defence contracts, local highways and post offices, for constituents. By the passage of legislation covering local projects, congressmen hope that they will find political favour with their constituents. If congressmen can serve on committees such as that dealing with transportation and infrastructure, there are ample opportunities for practising pork-barrel politics.

and quotes the example of a Democratic senator from Alabama, who observed:

> Many freshmen view their role differently than 25 years ago, when a Senator was only a legislator. Now a Senator is also a grantsman, an ombudsman, and a caseworker, and cannot ignore [these activities] . . . When we are asked by our constituents to help, we can't say we don't have time because we are focusing on national and international issues.

Bailey concludes that 'the increased emphasis on constituency service has transformed members from national legislators to narrowly focused ombudsmen'. He shows how many of them see themselves as lobbyists furthering the interests of their constituents in dealings with federal bureaucrats, by interceding on their behalf.

The danger of such an approach, in which Congress members see themselves as acting as advocates for the people, is that they may be tempted to act more forcefully on behalf of those who are the most influential persons in the community, particularly those who have contributed to campaign funds. The Ethics Committee of the House advises that the member must treat all constituents equally, 'irrespective or political or other considerations', and warns against favouritism or arm-twisting tactics. This has become the more important in recent years given the number of cases involving questions of ethics.

Bailey also makes the point that, in spending more time on matters of welfare and other matters of constituency service, Congress members may boost their reputations but do so at the expense of their effectiveness:

> By ensuring that grandma gets her social security cheque, the member may enhance his chances of gaining re-election, but the consequences are profound. Mismanagement and corruption within the federal agencies go unnoticed, and federal benefits are distributed on the basis of political clout rather than need. The cost to the taxpayer of the expanded notion of constituency service runs into billions of dollars, and the cost to the American people is a Congress filled with ombudsmen rather than legislators.

Congressmen are acutely aware of their prospects for political survival. They know that these depend to a large extent on their ability and effort, and accordingly they spend a large part of their time in discovering, assessing and acting upon the wishes of those who sent them to Washington. Maidment and McGrew[12] quote a Republican who described his task in the House as 'taking care of home problems, case work, not necessarily having anything to do with legislation at all. Taking care of constituents.' The member continues: 'if Senators and Representatives are to be believed, they are constantly looking over their shoulders for guidance. Few, if any, are willing to ignore the interests of their constituents. In that sense, the Congress is an extraordinarily representative legislative body. It is sensitive to the slightest shift in electoral opinion.'

The roles of congressmen: conflicts involved

There is no easy answer to the question of which is the most important respon-sibility of congressmen. Many voters expect that they will represent the wishes of the people of the district, for that is why they are sent to Washington in the first place. They are there to voice feelings 'back home', and not to take an independent line based on some perception of the national interest or personal feelings. If the needs of the US as a whole happen to be in line with those of the folks 'back home', so much the better, but if they are not then constituents will draw this to the attention of their elected representative.

In the eyes of the voters, this is not just a matter of constitutional theory, but one of tangible benefits which the congressman can and should be able to win. The title 'representative' is therefore not lacking in significance – congressmen do or should represent the people of their district.

Congressmen inevitably perceive their roles differently. This was highlighted by the findings of the final report of the Commission on Administrative Review (in the House, 1977), which analysed the responses of 140 representatives about what they saw as their most important responsibility. The priorities were:
- 45% the nation only;
- 28% the nation and district;
- 24% the district only;
- 3% unsure.

When a conflict arose between these differing pressures upon them,
- 65% professed to follow the dictates of conscience;
- 25% thought it depended on the issue;
- 5% wished to follow the wishes of the district;
- 3% were uncertain.

In practice, any congressman, senior or junior, must react according to the pressures of the moment. It is unrealistic to expect that he or she will ignore the chances of re-election in making a decision, and for that reason he or she is likely to pay heed to the prevailing mood of fellow citizens – especially those in his or her locality. Yet on many issues where there is no clearly expressed constituency view or obvious local involvement, the congress member can argue a more exalted case as a trustee of the national interest.

Congressional reform: the 1970s onwards

Congress can be, and often is, very parochial, run as it is by senators and repre-sentatives who have their own individual ambitions and constituency problems to preoccupy them. Because of this, it can seem as though it is more concerned with safeguarding its own interests and those of the members' localities than with acting for the general good. Several presidents have criticised the preoccupation with immediate local pressures that has prevented congressmen from seeing what needs to be done over the longer term. Since the 1970s, Congress has become much more assertive, but some writers (and some presidents) wonder if it has become any more constructive.

Legislative curbs

The struggle in the Nixon years over the bombing of Cambodia made Congress act. It overrode the President's veto and passed the 1973 **War Powers Act** (see p. 92), which reasserted congressional oversight of foreign policy by curbing the scope for the commander-in-chief to wage war abroad. Another limitation that Congress imposed was the **Budget and Impoundment Control Act**, which was an attempt made in 1974 to allow a more effective check on the president's budgetary and economic planning. Congressmen objected to the way in which the president impounded (refused to spend) huge sums of money set aside for social programmes. Both chambers set up their own budget committees, and a Congressional Budget Office, with its own specialist staff, was created, to boost their expertise, and enable them to seek out and acquire the sort of information that presidents tended to deny them.

The internal workings of Congress

Apart from the legislative control over the presidency, the other changes made were more to do with the internal organisation of Congress itself. The time was appropriate for an expansion of internal democracy.

Problems with the committee structure

Many younger congressmen felt that the workings of their chambers were beyond their control. Power lay with the committee chairpersons (see pp. 144–5), and in the hierarchical structure new entrants saw little chance of being able to play a significant part and wield real influence for many years. Yet they were elected to look after the position of their constituents, and could not do so as effectively as they wished if they did not have the backing of powerful committee chairpersons.

Congressional committees are very important, and the House in particular has always devolved much power to them. Even though there is more debate on the floor of the Senate, its committees too are very influential and have been described as[13] 'the nerve centre of its legislative process'. To serve on one of the more prestigious committees is an ambition of many congressmen, and the position of chair is regarded as especially influential.

Committee chairpersons

Chairpersons of committees occupy an important position in American government. They are key figures in the work of Congress, whether it be in investigation and scrutiny, in the examination of scandals and complex and/or controversial issues, or in the passing of legislation. After the majority party leaders, chairs are the most influential members. There is one-party domination of chairmanships. In both houses, all are currently in Republican hands.

As we have seen, the House Rules Committee, the Senate Foreign Relations Committee and several others are prestigious and membership is highly prized, with the chair much sought after. In the days of the seniority rule (see below), the position had great security of tenure, for the incumbent was usually experienced and respected, and often served for several years. Today, that situation has changed and there are some able, younger persons of more diverse backgrounds who achieve the chair. It can no longer be assumed that the chair will be reappointed from session to session, survival in part depending on the ability to command support within the ruling circles of the party. There is also today media coverage of committee hearings and media scrutiny of what goes on in committee, particularly in cases where there is a high-profile investigation under way. Power has also

Until the 1970s, Congress operated via a **seniority rule**, so that length of service was the main determinant of committee allocation. It favoured the congressmen who came from areas where their party always won, so that they would gain the opportunity for years of unbroken membership (as long as they could survive their party's primary election). For the Democrats, it paid to represent the South or the northern cities; for the Republicans, advancement came for those who hailed from the agricultural Midwest. Representatives and senators who were elected for these areas were accordingly overrepresented on committees.

> **seniority rule**
> The rule stating that the chair of a congressional standing committee will be the person of the majority party with the lengthiest unbroken period of continuous service on that committee. Reforms in the 1970s undermined the principle, as the Democrats in the House moved to elect their chairperson each session. But it remains the case that the more senior and experienced a person is, the greater the likelihood that he or she will become the chair. However, there are exceptions and these make the change significant and worthwhile.

The seniority rule applied especially to advancement within the committees, and those who became chairpersons were the most senior members of their party on the committee. This provided enormous influence, for it was the chairperson who determined the agenda for discussion and the number and composition of subcommittees. The Democrats were the victorious party in almost all of the congressional elections from 1930 to 1970, so that many chairpersons were unrepresentative, and often conservative, southern Democrats. This had a significant bearing on legislation, for too

been diluted by the greater number of subcommittee chairmanships, a rival source of influence.

None the less, chairpersons are key figures in the legislative process:

- They tend to be active and effective legislators, often experienced in making the system work.
- They appoint members to subcommittees.
- They have a major influence over the legislative agenda, determining the bills that will be considered and the priority attached to them.
- They also have influence over the amendments called and the order in which they are discussed.
- They direct financial resources.
- In the days of the iron triangles of the past (see pp. 282–3), the significance of the role was even greater, for between them the relevant departmental secretary, interest-group representative and long-serving committee chair could largely shape policy in areas such as agriculture, tobacco and nuclear power. President Johnson was adept at gaining the support of the 'inner circle' of senior members of Congress, when pushing his Great Society programme through the legislature.

much influence lay in the hands of those who represented rural – and white – America.

The old system had few defenders, but it had one main advantage. The existence of an 'inner club' of senior members whose attitudes and behaviour could be predicted meant that presidents knew whom to do business with. These people counted, for they had so much influence over congressional proceedings. If their approval was sought and won, then Congress could be managed. When reform finally came, this was not the case – as President Carter found to his cost. No longer were the reactions of Congress as coherent as they had once been. Anything could happen, without the strong will of senior chairpersons to steer legislation and impose control.

Reform of the structure

In 1973 the Democrats in the House decided, at a caucus meeting, to abandon the automatic use of the seniority system. In future, chairpersons would be nominated by the steering and policy committee of the party, and the nominees would then be subject to an election by secret ballot of all Democrats in the chamber. Most of the senior members were actually elected in the first elections, but there was now an opportunity for change. Two years later, with an influx of younger and more liberal representatives, three elderly chairmen were removed.

Another change prevented chairpersons of key committees from serving as the chair of other significant ones. Chairs also lost some of their control over the sub-committees, which became less beholden to the parent body. The Republicans saw the need to exhibit a similar 'democratic' interest, and implemented similar changes within their party.

Nowadays, less-senior members of Congress have more authority, subcommittee chairs are more independent and, especially in the Senate, subcommittee chairs may be offered to congressmen who have only served for one or two terms. Often, chairpersons are still chosen on the basis of seniority, with the longest-serving majority-party member on the committee being selected.

Since the 1980s, Democrats from the South have lost their disproportionate strength, and those from safe northern industrial areas have frequently been chosen. Whereas once the system discriminated against organised labour, civil rights and urban-based interests, that is no longer the case. Over time, women and members of racial minorities ought to benefit from the seniority rule as it now operates, whereas if there was a free choice without recognition for long service they might get selected only rarely.

Power in Congress has become more dispersed than ever before, and the seniority rule for choosing chairpersons is much less of a bone of contention than it used to be. In the Senate, most members who belong to the majority party chair a subcommittee, several a full committee. In the House, many Republican representatives now have such a responsibility.

Improved staffing

The formation of the Congressional Budget Office (via the Budget and Impoundment Control Act, p. 143) was an indication of the wish of many congressmen to improve their professionalism and acquire a new expertise. An Office of Technology Assessment had already been formed two years earlier, and the General Accounting Office and other research services were reformed to allow for the use of more analysts and experts.

The number of aides to congressmen in both houses has been increased, as has the staffing of committees. Maidment and McGrew[14] estimated that by the end of the 1980s there were some 40,000 staff serving members, committees and various support agencies. Congress ought to be able to perform its task with greater efficiency, having equipped itself with an increased capacity to handle and investigate presidential initiatives.

Letting the cameras in

Reforms of the legislative procedure in 1970 allowed each house to decide whether to televise its proceedings. A new generation of legislators was more comfortable than its predecessors with television, and eager for coverage of floor debate. Members quickly agreed to experiment with a closed-circuit debate. The House first opened its chamber to television in 1979; the Senate held out for a further seven years. But long before there were broadcasts of floor debate, television had been allowed to record more impressive and/or dramatic events on Capitol Hill, among them the State of the Union messages and Senate committee hearings such as those concerned with the possible impeachment of Richard Nixon.

Representatives and senators have learnt to exploit television by consenting to interviews, appearing on news programmes and crafting photo-opportunities with constituents. Some of them now devise a video version of their press releases, so that they can be sent – or beamed via satellite – back to local stations.

What more can and should be done?

By the start of the twenty-first century, the balance of power had significantly altered from the situation a generation earlier. Congress became assertive, and the change in overall party control in both houses (from Democrat to Republican) meant that there was a much greater willingness – indeed enthusiasm – to challenge presidential policy. As the continuing saga of Whitewatergate and alleged sexual lapses unfolded, great damage was done to Bill Clinton's authority, but also – some would say – to the presidency itself.

Congress now has the expertise and will that it has lacked for many years, and if it wishes to challenge the president it has the capacity to do so. Yet the reforms carried out, especially the weakening of the importance of seniority, have actually made it less easy to organise congressmen to act in concert and produce a united response. If anything, they are even freer to concentrate on acting in a way pleasing to their constituents, and are an easy prey to the special-interest groups that lobby for their support.

Much of what is done is designed to enhance the chances of re-election, and this does not make for effective long-term thinking. It does, however, ensure that congressmen think about the wishes and needs of those who elected them, and this helps to ensure that there is continuous accountability.

Criticism still surfaces from time to time of a 'do-nothing' or 'obstructive' Congress, which is portrayed as timid, obsessed with internal bickering, narrow-minded and self-interested. Those who seek further congressional reform ask:

1 **Is Congress efficient?** Congress has to deal with a vast number of complex bills, and criticism often relates to the pace of legislation. David Brinkley, a TV anchorman, expressed public frustration[15] when he said that 'it is widely

believed in Washington that it would take Congress thirty days to make instant coffee work'. There is much talk of a 'paralysis in Congress', brought about by the number of subcommittees and their overlapping jurisdiction. Again, with more independently minded members less committed to the party line, it is more difficult for leaders to create coalitions to get business conducted and the agenda kept on time. For instance, much-needed reforms on health care have been particularly difficult to achieve.

2 **Does Congress defend the national interest?** Are legislators so anxious to ensure their re-election that they neglect to think of the national interest? Are they willing to tackle controversial issues which may be unpopular with their constituents? One House Republican leader[16] suggested that congressional behaviour was too concerned with 'perpetuating the longevity and comfort of the men who run it'. Are those representatives too concerned with the views of special interests? Think of the way in which expensive congressional elections are financed. Are congressmen beholden?

3 **Is Congress representative?** In both parties, there is a notable overrepresentation of middle-/upper-middle-income groups. Women and racial minorities remain seriously underrepresented.

Such questions are often asked and the responses are invariably critical. If it is true that Congress does not often perform its legislative and investigative tasks as effectively as it should, this perhaps reflects the fact that it is, in Walles's words,[17] 'better organised for obstruction than for promotion'. The overlapping jurisdictions between committees and subcommittees provide opportunities for affected interests to delay or halt action. Walles suggests that the machinery seems 'ill-equipped to establish priorities which can be readily translated into action'.

Dominated by 535 sets of individual considerations, Congress can be an ineffective body, unable to devise policy initiatives coherently and pass them into law. It can sometimes seem that those 535 interests take precedence over the overall needs of the nation, and this is why major national problems – from tax reform to energy policy, from welfare to gun control – have been so difficult to resolve.

Congress is not rated highly in popular esteem. The public seems to admire its local representatives more than it approves of the legislature as a whole. In surveys, interviewees tend to advance similar criticisms to the ones considered above, notably that Congress is cumbersome, negative, slow to respond and too often beset by gridlock. This is certainly true of its legislative work, in comparison with many other legislatures around the world. But in other respects, members of legislatures in Europe might well envy the facilities, independence and influence of their American counterparts, who are less beholden to their party allegiance and able to exert important powers of oversight.

Legislatures in Britain and the United States: a comparison

Both countries are bicameral. Whereas the US has two elected chambers, in Britain only the lower house is elected. The House of Lords, as at present constituted, contains appointed life peers, bishops and archbishops, law lords and an elected element chosen from the ranks of the hereditary peerage. The Blair government has put forward proposals to eliminate the hereditary element altogether, but there is disagreement among MPs as to the composition of the chamber in the future. The majority of Labour MPs would like to see a predominately elected house, whereas the prime minister appears to favour a predominantly appointed body, perhaps with a small elected element. In America, the upper house is elected and based upon regional representation, the latter not as yet a feature of the British second chamber.

All four chambers have legislative responsibilities and in both countries criticism is often voiced about the effectiveness of law-making procedures. Congress is widely portrayed as an inefficient, 'do-nothing' legislature, whereas sometimes the allegation against the British House of Commons is that it has too vast a programme that – because of intense party whipping – it is able to force through Parliament and into law.

Fundamental to the comparison, of course, is the system of government. Under the separation of powers, Congress is designed to be an effective check upon the executive. In the traditional absence of strong party loyalty among its members, it has sought to curb presidential ambitions – particularly if a different party controls the two arms of government. Since the 1970s, Congress has been described as 'resurgent' and its ability to hold the executive to account has been strengthened, as a result of internal reforms and the passage of legislation.

The British Parliament is often said to be 'in decline'. Commentators write of 'the passing of parliamentary control' and sometimes seek to boost the power of the House of Commons, in particular, to act as an informed and effective critic of government. It is often alleged that instead of Parliament controlling the executive, it is now the executive that controls Parliament. Not all academics would accept that Parliament is as ineffective as its critics suggest. Philip Norton[18] regards it as 'not just significant' but also 'indispensable'.

'Legislative decline' is a theme much discussed in relation to many liberal democracies. Power has passed from the legislative to the executive, as governments have needed to be able to pass laws to please the mass electorates. However, whereas the broad trend in Britain has been inimical to Parliament, in the US it is the presidency that has been subject to numerous limitations in recent years.

Issues for consideration

Is Congress socially representative of the nation?

By this use of 'representative', we mean 'typical of a class'. Sociologists use the term this way when they speak about a 'representative sample' of the people. In the case of America, the suggestion is that congressmen should possess characteristics that are broadly similar to those possessed by the people as a whole. If this is the case, then Congress as a whole will be a microcosm or mirror-image of the nation.

Congress is not such a microcosm, for congressmen – judged by attributes such as socio-economic status, education, race, gender and age – are not representative of Americans as a whole. Like the House of Commons, Congress is overwhelmingly white, male, middle-class and middle-aged.

Most senators and representatives are professionals: lawyers, business people, accountants, journalists, doctors, teachers, university professors or farmers. Lawyers are a sizeable contingent: their numbers are lower than in the 1970s, but still almost 50% of the 109th Congress. Next come business and banking. There are few blue-collar workers, and the poor, the underclass of the big cities and others near the bottom of the social pile are unrepresented in this sense, although this does not mean that present congressmen are incapable of representing their interests. Some rich senators – Edward Kennedy among them – are active in seeking to protect the underprivileged, and can be vociferous advocates of their cause.

Black Americans and Hispanics are present in smaller numbers than is justified by their presence in the community. They and other ethnic minorities as a whole still have a long way to go to achieve anything like equality, as do women. In the 109th Congress, there are more women than ever before. Groups such as Jews and Catholics are now represented in greater numbers than in the past, but still underrepresented.

The social backgrounds of legislators in Britain and the United States: a comparison (based on the election outcomes 2001 and 2004, respectively)

* In general, legislatures in European democracies and the United States tend to be male, middle-aged, middle-class and white.
* The number of women has increased in most assemblies, although the situation is patchy. It is poor in the US and in some European countries, such as France, Greece, Ireland and Italy. In Britain, the representation of women moved forward in 1992 and significantly so in 1997 (120/635). It fell back slightly in 2001, to 118.
* Most representatives attain their position only after doing some other job and making a mark in their chosen careers. This may give them experience of life, but it also means that the voice of the young is largely excluded. Since 2001, the average age of Conservative members in the House of Commons has been 48, of Labour members 50. (Labour had 10 members who were under 30 at the time of the election in 1997, 4 after 2001.) In the US, it tends to be slightly higher, so that the average age of representatives at the start of the 109th Congress was 56 and of senators 60.
* The middle-class nature of elected representatives is more marked now than it used to

The profile of congressional membership in recent years

Members	105th Congress		107th Congress		109th Congress	
	House	Senate	House	Senate	House	Senate
Women	51	9	59	13	65	14
African American	37	1	36	0	42	1
Hispanic	18	0	19	0	26	2

NB To aid comparison, the figures for 1985–86 (the 99th Congress) were 22/2 women, 19/0 African American and 11/0 Hispanic.

Representatives and senators particularly are older than the average of all Americans. Senators are usually older than representatives, partly perhaps because of the minimum entrance qualification (age 30, as opposed to 25), but also because many senators build up a reputation over six years and then, as incumbents, are difficult for opponents to remove. They may survive for many years, as the example of Strom Thurmond illustrates. Originally elected in 1954, he remained a senator until the end of the 107th Congress, the month in which he celebrated his hundredth birthday (December 2002).

It is very doubtful whether any freely chosen assembly ever could constitute a cross-section of the electorate, for the choice is largely at the mercy of the voters. But having said this, the discrepancies between different groups and categories and their representation in Congress is clearly a considerable one.

This underrepresentation obviously matters to the groups who feel largely unrecognised. It becomes all the more important that if such groups are not well

be in Britain. Labour evolved as a party to represent the working classes in Parliament. In 1918, the Parliamentary Labour Party (PLP) had 87% working-class membership. Since the 1960s, the parliamentary party has been dominated by members with a university education and middle-class professions, many of them in higher education. Following the 2001 election, the manual worker element diminished to 12%, the lowest ever. The Conservatives have always found it difficult to get working-class candidates to stand, and if this happens it is usually in unwinnable constituencies. Business people, managers, lawyers and other professional employees (particularly from the communicating professions) are well represented in Britain. So too are the law, business and academia strongly represented in the US.

- Twelve British MPs elected in 2001 belonged to ethnic minorities, including two Muslims and three Sikhs; 21 Jews were successful. Hispanic and black Americans fare badly in Congress, but among religious groups again Jews are well represented.
- Of course, both countries use the 'first past the post' electoral system. This does not encourage the representation of minority groups, for everything is staked on one candidate in a single-member constituency. Parties encourage the choice of candidates who are likely winners and fear a possible loss of votes by deviating from the norm.

represented among the membership, then at least there need to be members who in their approach can show an empathy with those unlike themselves. There have always been legislators who – whilst socially untypical of and unlike those whom they seek to serve – can nevertheless imagine what it is like to be disadvantaged and are prepared to articulate their concerns for such people.

For the practice of their profession, congressmen need the education and skills normally associated with middle-class professionals. In a system reliant upon volunteers to come forward, it is unlikely that the least educated, those from the poorest backgrounds and the majority of people who do manual work are likely to put their names forward. Few would wish to forsake their existing lifestyle and live the life of a congressman, who spends much of the time in Washington, away from the family. That being the case, it is all the more important that those who are chosen as candidates, and who are victorious, should reflect in their own experience and understand the conditions and outlook of all 'walks of life'.

Should there be term limits for congressmen?

In the 1990s, there was renewed interest in 'term limits', although the debate on how long any incumbent should serve has a much longer history. The Founding Fathers considered limiting the period for which any member of the executive or legislature should sit, but decided to avoid setting a limit on the number of terms anyone could serve.

In the nineteenth century, however, it was customary for elected politicians to limit themselves. It was only in the twentieth century that congressmen began to exceed two terms in the House and one in the Senate. The development of the seniority rule for committee chairmanships inspired representatives to seek a longer term. The introduction of direct election for senators in 1912 encouraged them to seek an extra six years.

Recent developments

Term limits were approved in the 1990 elections in Colorado, and thereafter in several – mainly western – states. In the 1994 elections, the tenth item in the Contract with America (see p. 259), the Citizen Legislature Act, dealt with the issue. It urged the need for a first-ever congressional vote to place limits on career politicians and replace them with citizen legislators.

In 1995, the Supreme Court ruled in the case of *US Term Limits, Inc.* v. *Thornton* that states could not impose term limits on their congressional delegations, but the ruling did not apply to state legislators. Eighteen states now have limits on legislative service, but there is little uniformity in their application. Thirty-nine have limits on the period of gubernatorial service.

Why the interest today?

Several factors inspired the desire to curb career politicians from staying in power on Capitol Hill:

1 All politicians – and congressmen foremost amongst them – are increasingly viewed with disdain by many voters, who have a deep scepticism about the motives of those who serve them. They wish to 'throw the rascals out', and believe that they can 'clean up' a sleazy Congress by ensuring that fresh faces appear to replace older, seasoned Washington politicians who can 'play the system'. Yet despite this distaste for Congress and many congressmen, voters seem more than happy to re-elect their own representatives in either chamber, a point that leads to the second explanation.

2 In recent years, incumbents have been re-elected with great regularity. In 1994, no Republican incumbent was defeated in any gubernatorial, Senate or House race, and even the Democrats lost only two incumbent scalps in the Senate – though they lost 34 in the lower house. For a variety of reasons, incumbency presents an advantage over opponents, so that once elected some congressmen have stayed on Capitol Hill for a long (too long?) time.

3 Allied to the point about long-time career politicians is the feeling that there are too many incentives for congressmen to stay 'on the Hill'. Perquisites and salaries are generous: too lavish for the many Americans who have a much less comfortable life.

A beneficial change?

Against:

1 Term limits are unnecessary in that the American system provides a check on those in power through regular (in the case of the House, frequent) elections. The incumbent can be challenged from within his or her party in a primary election, and by the voters as a whole in the general election.

2 It seems undemocratic to impose limits on the electorate's right of choice, for limits on congressmen are actually limits on voters. They cannot reward able men and women who have given good service.

3 If there are problems of low ethical standards and scandalous or self-interested behaviour, the answer is to legislate against the evil or to vote against the offending congressman.

For:

1 Term limits would weaken the stranglehold of long-servers in Congress, people who command excessive influence by virtue of their seniority. Fresh faces may be talented, as well as less 'corrupted' by long service in the system.

2 A 'citizen legislature' would replace a chamber of career politicians.

Congressmen would be more in touch with those who elect them, and contain 'ordinary people'.

3 Applying term limits to congressmen is a logical extension of the curbs on presidential service. In thirty-one states, governors also have a limited period of office.

Are congressmen paid enough and do they have good facilities?

Members of both houses of Congress are paid $162,100 per year, as at January 2001. The figure is high by most American standards, although well below that of several corporate presidents, who earn many times as much. For many members of the public, the amount seems excessive and whenever there is an increase there are expressions of popular disquiet. In fact, the most recent amendment to the Constitution, the Twenty-Seventh, concerned this very issue. As law-makers debate and set their own levels of pay, there was a feeling that any such change should not take effect until an election has intervened, thereby allowing the public the opportunity to vote out those who had enhanced their own salary levels!

In addition, members have awarded themselves a variety of expense allowances, which are generally considered a necessary accessory to members' regular salaries. They range from generous staff assistance and accommodation to free use of video-recording facilities and sophisticated computer services. Congressional leaders receive additional remuneration. Once they leave office, they receive handsome retirement benefits.

Pay and facilities of elected representatives in Britain and the United States: a comparison

- In terms of accommodation, equipment, staffing, library assistance and other amenities, congressmen are notably better placed than their British counterparts.
- Each senator and representative has a suite of offices in a building connected to Capitol Hill by an underground railway, and the member has access to office equipment, gymnasia and many other facilities, as well as generous expenses.
- For many years, it was customary for MPs to lament their inadequate facilities, the vast size and splendour of the Palace of Westminster being little consolation for the conditions in which they had to operate. Today (January 2005) an MP has a salary of £57,485, as well as a range of allowances for office help and accommodation. Some members still voice criticism of the lack of constituency help they receive, whilst others feel that they could do with more research assistance at Westminster. The lack of office equipment and particularly of information technology services is frequently condemned, for the House makes no central provision for such facilities.

CONCLUSION

The effectiveness of Congress and the need for congressional reform have been periodically analysed in recent decades. The changes of the 1970s went some way towards enhancing Congress's powers and made it more assertive in relation to the presidency. Yet doubts about the performance of Congress and its members remain, as the preoccupation in the 1990s with 'term limits' indicates.

The public expects that Congress will be both responsive to popular needs and efficient. Many Americans lack confidence in the performance of those who represent them, and feel that congressmen are too swayed by lobbyists and party leaders and insufficiently committed to serving their interests. They also decry a 'do-nothing' Congress, complaining that it is often slow to identify, define and effectively tackle the problems facing the nation. But if Congress is sometimes slow to act, this may be because the American people themselves do not agree on what the problems are and how they should be resolved.

REFERENCES

1 A. Grant and E. Ashbee, *The Politics Today Companion to American Government*, Manchester University Press, 2002
2 R. Pear, *American Government*, MacGibbon & Kee, 1963
3 D. Maidment and D. McGrew, *The American Political Process*, Sage/Open University, 1992
4 W. Wilson, *Congressional Government*, rev. edn, Meridian Books, 1956
5 R. Davidson and W. Oleszek, *Congress and its Members*, Congressional Quarterly, 1998
6 R. Evans and B. Novak, *Lyndon B. Johnson: The Exercise of Power*, New American Library, 1966
7 R. Denenberg, *Understanding American Politics*, Fontana,1976
8 As quoted in C. Jillson, *American Government*, Harcourt Brace, 1999
9 M. Walles, *British and American Systems of Government*, P. Allan, 1988.
10 D. Mayhew, *Congress: The Electoral Connection*, Yale University Press, 1974
11 C. Bailey, 'Ethics as Politics: Congress in the 1990s', in P. Davies and F. Waldstein (eds), *Political Issues in America*, Manchester University Press, 1991.
12 R. Maidment and D. McGrew, as in 3 above
13 G. Wasserman, *The Basics of American Politics*, Longman, 1997
14 R. Maidment and D. McGrew, as in 13 above
15 D. Brinkley (TV anchorman), as quoted in T. Conlan, M. Wrightson and D. Beam, *Taxing Choices: The Politics of Tax Reform*, Congressional Quarterly Press, 1990.
16 J. Rhodes (one-time House Republican leader), *The Futile System*, EPM Publications, 1976

17 M. Walles, as in 9 above

18 P. Norton, *Does Parliament Matter?*, Harvester Wheatsheaf, 1993

USEFUL WEB SITES

www.thomas.gov Named after Thomas Jefferson, the Library of Congress site that offers a comprehensive look at Congress in the past and today; useful information about current activities.

www.cq.com *Congressional Quarterly*. The authoritative site of the weekly magazine covering congressional activities, committees etc.

www.house.gov (House of Representatives) and **www.senate.gov** (Senate) Both give valuable details about the work of the two chambers, reports about current legislation, the activities of Congressmen, their conditions etc.

www.vote-smart.org Vote Smart. An easy-to-understand guide to current legislation going through either chamber.

SAMPLE QUESTIONS

1 Why is the US Senate more powerful and prestigious than the House of Representatives?

2 Examine the role of Congress in making the law. Is Congress an efficient law-making body?

3 Discuss the view that Congress is more effective at representation than it is at law-making.

4 What reforms might lead to an improvement in the public perception of Congress?

5 Should Congress be more socially representative of the nation?

6 Discuss the view that the real work of Congress is done in its committee rooms.

7 Why is Congress a more powerful legislature than the British Parliament?

8 Compare the background and roles of MPs and congressmen. What might an MP like and dislike about the American legislature?

The judiciary: the Supreme Court   6

The judiciary wields considerable political power in the US and for this reason must be considered in any discussion of the political process. Its members may not act overtly in the manner of a politician seeking election or re-election, but in a more passive way their influence is highly significant. They do not take the initiative, but rather wait for cases to be brought before them. At that stage, in the light of the facts presented, they can make judgements that may have important political implications.

In particular, the Supreme Court has a key role in making the Constitution relevant to modern needs and circumstances. It is not bound by past precedent, and it can specifically or implicitly overrule, ignore or modify judgements made in previous cases. Its decisions have important political significance. In this chapter, we examine the judiciary in general, but our attention will be particularly directed to the Supreme Court, its history, judgements and personnel.

POINTS TO CONSIDER

➤ How have recent presidents differed in their approach to the appointment of federal judges?

➤ Why is the presidential choice of justices in the Supreme Court considered so important?

➤ What principles should guide judges as they interpret the American Constitution?

➤ Has judicial activism gone out of fashion?

➤ How and why did the idea of judicial review develop in the United States?

➤ What have been the main differences in the approach to issues concerning civil rights of the Warren, Burger and Rehnquist Courts?

➤ Has the Supreme Court become too powerful?

The range of state and federal courts

There are today two parallel systems of courts in
the United States that between them cover the
range of **civil and criminal** cases. There are the
state court systems established under the
individual state constitutions: these decide
actions and settle disputes concerning state laws.
There is also the federal judicial system, which
has become more important as the country has
expanded and the amount of legislation passed
by Congress has increased. In effect, there are
therefore fifty-one different judicial structures.

civil and criminal law
Civil law relates to private and
civilian laws, and deals with
relationships affecting
individuals and organisations
(e.g. family or property
matters). Criminal law relates
to crimes against the state. It
is concerned with such things
as theft, violence and murder.

The practice of state courts may vary significantly, for it is the essence of federalism that the states may run their own affairs in the way best suited to their
own wishes and requirements. Differences of operation and terminology are
inevitable, and this makes general comment on their structure more difficult.
For instance, judges are elected in approximately three quarters of the states,
whilst in others they are appointed.

States are responsible for passing and enforcing most of the civil and criminal
law of the United States. For every person in a federal prison, there are at least
eight in a state prison. The vast majority of cases are resolved in state
municipal or justice courts in town and cities, with a right of appeal to the
state appeals courts or, in a small minority of cases involving the interpretation
of the state constitution or basic constitutional rights, to the state supreme
court.

Federal courts enforce federal law and state courts enforce state law, but the
relationship between the two systems is more complex than this. The federal
Constitution is the supreme law of the land, and if state law conflicts with it
or with federal laws made under that Constitution, then state law gives way.
This is made clear in the 'supremacy clause' of the Constitution (Article VI).
Because of it, decisions made in the federal courts can have a broad impact on
those made in the state courts.

We are primarily concerned with the federal judicial system, the structure
of which is relatively simple. There are three layers of courts. At the bottom of
the pyramid are the district courts, above them are the circuit courts of appeal
and at the apex of the system is the Supreme Court, the highest court in the
land.

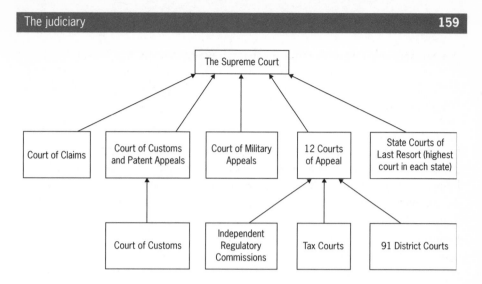

Figure 2 The structure of the federal judiciary

The appointment of judges in federal courts

Federal judges are appointed by the president, who is advised by the Department of Justice and the office of the deputy attorney-general. This power of appointment is highly significant. As Vile[1] puts it: 'No president can afford to ignore either the partisan advantages of such appointments or the fact that the men he appoints will be able, to say the least, to give a particular emphasis to the way in which policy is carried out.'

The power of appointment gives the president the opportunity to influence the balance of opinion in the courts. By 1940, Roosevelt had achieved a Democratic majority among federal judges, but the high point was reached during the presidency of Johnson, when more than 70% were of his party. In his 1980 election campaign, Reagan undertook to choose conservative judges who would abandon the social activism of many earlier appointees. His overt concern with the ideological stance of judges was in line with the Nixon approach, but a departure from the usual practice whereby party label was a more important consideration. For Reagan, Republican leanings alone were not a sufficient guarantee of suitability.

In his two terms as president, Ronald Reagan made 368 federal judicial appointments, 4 to the Supreme Court, 6 to special courts, 76 to circuit courts and the rest to district ones. Like presidents before him, he made partisan appointments, but two factors were particularly significant about his choices:
1 He had the opportunity to appoint more lower-court judges than any of his predecessors since Franklin Roosevelt – Reagan filled about half of all the judgeships at that level.

2 His appointees were singularly conservative by nature, much more so than most previous Republican nominations. This was a deliberate decision by the president to choose people of a different legal philosophy to those who had in the past sat on the bench.

George Bush senior followed a similar approach in his selection of another 185 judges. The effect of the appointments made in the twelve years from 1981 to 1993 was to transform the type of personnel who sat in judgement on legal issues. Overwhelmingly, the nominees were young, white males who were deeply conservative. Few women, African Americans or members of other minority groups were selected, but in one respect the choices were unusual for Republican administrations. More Roman Catholics were chosen than usual, probably because the Justice Department was in sympathy with the Catholic stance on the controversial matter of abortion, and saw a chance to win some popularity with the Christian Right on the topic.

Appointments made in the Clinton era were quite distinctive. As a result of a rush of retirements, he was able to nominate almost a quarter of all federal judges, and he used the opportunity to diversify the composition of the judiciary. Almost all of his nominees were Democrats, but many of them were more moderate and less ideological than some party members would have liked. The tables below illustrate the different approach of recent presidents and give an early indication of the type of the background of judges appointed by George W. Bush.

Presidential appointments to the federal judiciary

1. Party affiliation of appointees under selected presidents

President	Party	Party appointees (%)
Roosevelt	Democrat	97
Kennedy	Democrat	92
Nixon	Republican	93
Reagan	Republican	94
Bush sr	Republican	89
Clinton	Democrat	88

2. A profile of appointees under selected presidents

Characteristic	Reagan	Bush sr	Clinton	Bush jr (Jan. 2001–Dec. 2002)
Female	28	36	110	18
Black	7	12	62	9
Hispanic	15	8	24	6
Asian	2	0	5	6
Total appointees	368	185	376	100

Figures adapted from those provided by T. Cronin and M. Genovese, *The Paradoxes of the American Presidency*, Oxford University Press, 2004

The Supreme Court

Courts tend to have a reputation for conservatism. Often, they resist the tide of innovative enthusiasm, interpreting the law as it is, guarding precedents and securing rights that have been traditionally recognised. The American Supreme Court has at times acted in a remarkably radical way, and rather than reacting to the wishes of politicians it has sometimes forced them to deal with great issues of the day. In particular, it was the Court that was instrumental in the drive to establish the rights of black Americans on a firmer footing in the postwar era. By so doing, it was effecting a major change – one resisted by a large section of the population.

The Court has not regarded the American Constitution as fixed and unalterable, but rather as an evolving body of ideals. It has preserved the fundamental principles which underpin the whole political system and create its basic character, but it has sought to reformulate them at various times in a way which makes them relevant to the problems of the day. It was not expected to exhibit such extraordinary influence when the Constitution was devised.

The Constitution said little about the judiciary, and the status of the Court is only briefly sketched. Judicial power was vested in one Supreme Court 'and in such inferior courts as the Congress may from time to time ordain and establish', but it was unclear as to how important the main Court was to be. Few specific powers were set out, but the document did not seek to limit its role. The expectation in the very early days of the Republic was that the court would play a lesser role in the newly established governing arrangements than the other two branches of government.

Much of the Court's present-day influence stems from a series of remarkably vigorous interpretations of the law and Constitution by the fourth Chief Justice, John Marshall, who was the leading figure on the bench from 1801 until his death in 1835. He established the Court's pre-eminence in judicial matters, and helped to make it a major influence in American politics. His contribution was threefold. He:

- helped to establish the independence of the judiciary from other branches of government;
- developed the role of judicial review (see pp. 167–8)
- ensured that the Court's decisions were supreme over all courts in the land. He firmly believed in the importance of upholding national power over that of the states, and from this it followed that it was the duty of the Court to see that states did not infringe on the sovereignty of the federal government.

Size and composition

The Constitution is silent on the qualifications for judges. There is no requirement that judges be lawyers, although, in fact, all federal judges and Supreme Court justices have been members of the bar. Since the creation of the Court more than two hundred years ago, 120 justices have been appointed. The original Court comprised a Chief Justice and five associates. Thereafter, the number varied until, in 1869, the total was fixed at one Chief Justice and eight associates, and nine has been the figure ever since. Each justice has one vote, and rulings do not have to be decided unanimously. The Chief Justice is *primus inter pares* (first among equals) in relation to his colleagues.

Prior judicial service is not essential for service in the Court, and some 40% of all appointees since 1789 have had no kind of previous judicial experience in federal or state courts. Some leading figures on the bench have had a mainly political background. Earl Warren was a Californian politician, state attorney-general and governor before his elevation, and several others have been actively (some controversially) involved in political struggles before they gained recognition. It can be argued that such a background is more of an asset than a liability, for many of the decisions to be taken by the justices are essentially political ones.

In making appointments to the Court, it follows that presidents have not been primarily concerned with the judicial expertise of their nominees. They want to choose people who share a broadly similar political outlook and judicial philosophy to their own, so that the passage of contentious legislation has an easier ride both now and in the future. John Adams did not appoint John Marshall solely because of the brilliance of Marshall's mind, but because they shared a number of beliefs. Ever since then, presidents have been interested in finding people who broadly share their own opinions.

Appointments are an opportunity to change the direction of the Court's approach, and thereby to influence the evolution of public policy. For any president, therefore, the primary concern is to find someone who represents his own thinking (almost certainly someone of the same party) and who will be acceptable to the congressmen who have to confirm the appointment. Beyond these considerations, other factors may come into play, all of which have the merit of maximising the president's political advantage. Presidents may wish:

1 to make a gesture of recognition to some disadvantaged group, by appointing someone who is a member of, or sympathetic to, that community. In the past, it was sometimes considered prudent to ensure that there was a Catholic or Jew on the Court, and in 1967 Lyndon Johnson saw the advantage of appointing a black justice (Thurgood Marshall). In 1981, President Reagan appointed the first woman, Sandra Day O'Connor. In such

a way, the president might hope to boost his standing with the underrepresented group;

2 directly to influence the Court's direction, as did Roosevelt with his Court-packing scheme, and Reagan with his attempt to curtail **judicial activism**;

3 to give favours in recognition of some past service. Warren backed Eisenhower at the 1952 Republican Convention, and in return was given a seat on the bench.

Richard Nixon consciously set out to change the balance of the Court, for like many conservatives he had become increasingly irritated by the persistent judicial activism of many who sat on the bench. He wanted to tip the balance by appointing people who would exercise **judicial restraint**: whose interest was in interpreting the Constitution and the law, rather than in breaking new ground via their adventurous decisions. 'Strict constructionists' were his preferred type of judges: in his words, those who would be 'caretakers of the Constitution ... not super-legislators'. He was fortunate in having the opportunity to nominate four out of the nine justices on the Court at the time of his departure, and indeed if he had continued his presidency in the normal manner he would have been able to make another choice, and thereby gain a theoretical majority in his favour.

> **judicial activism**
> The view that the courts should be active partners in shaping government policy – especially in sensitive cases, such as those dealing with abortion and desegregation. Supporters are more interested in justice, 'doing the right thing', than in the exact letter of the text. They see the courts as having a role in looking after the groups with little political influence, such as the poor and minorities.

> **judicial restraint**
> The idea that the courts should not seek to impose their views on other branches of government, except in extreme cases. Supporters of this view are constructionists: those who want the courts to limit themselves to implementing legislative and executive intentions. They want a passive role for the courts.

The plans of presidents do not always work out in the ways intended. In the Nixon years, two of his nominees – Harold Carswell and Clement Haynsworth – fell foul of Senate approval, the first time this had happened since the 1920s. Carswell had been involved in a conflict of interest, and Haynsworth was seen as a mediocre figure with a marked tendency towards racial bias. In 1987, Robert Bork, a distinguished former professor of law and later a well-known judge of conservative persuasion, was rejected following heated battles over his confirmation. The Senate Judiciary Committee questioned him for five days before it came to its verdict. The choice proved to be too controversial, for he had been associated with the dismissal of the special prosecutor during the Watergate scandal, and was seen as having contentious views and too partisan a past. Bork aroused deep suspicion among American liberals, who pledged millions of dollars in an attempt to fight the nomination; conservatives were willing to spend freely to defend his cause.

Other Republican nominees also had difficulties. The preferred replacement for Bork, Douglas Ginsberg, was rejected and then withdrawn by President Reagan, when it became apparent that many senators were worried about his earlier use of marijuana. Clarence Thomas – accused by Anita Hill, a professor of law at Oklahoma Law School, of sexual harassment – was confirmed only after twelve days of embarrassing revelations at the Senate hearings in 1991, as graphic descriptions of his sexual habits were laid before the national television audience.

Altogether, twenty-eight presidential nominees have failed to receive the necessary majority vote in the Senate, approximately 20% of the total. Timing is often a consideration, for whereas most nominations in the first three years of a presidency are confirmed, the chances are less favourable in the fourth. The general trend is for hearings to be longer than was once the case, and in the more intensive scrutiny that takes place a candidate needs to have a very clean record to get an easy passage. Controversial nominations inevitably are more likely to fail.

President Clinton was aware of the importance of his decision when his first opportunity arose to make an appointment. The existing Court had been chosen entirely by Republican presidents, and he faced a body that had become markedly conservative in character. He wanted to arrest the rightward drift of the Court's membership, and find someone who would take a pro-choice line on abortion as he had pledged to do in his campaign. Yet he was aware that an overtly liberal person could easily be 'Borked' by conservative opponents in either party.

When Byron White retired from the court in 1993, this was the first opportunity for a Democrat to make an appointment for twenty-six years, and Clinton set out to find 'a person that has a fine mind, good judgement, wide experience of the law, and in the problems of real people, and someone with a big heart'.[2] His selection of Ruth Bader Ginsburg was readily confirmed by the Senate, for she had a reputation for fairness and moderation, was obviously well qualified, and was seen as someone who would interpret the law rather than become an advocate of special causes. A Carter nominee to the Court of Appeals in the District of Columbia, she had been a professor of law and an active supporter of women's advancement. Clinton's second nominee, Stephen Breyer, similarly survived the hearings without damage to his reputation or credibility.

Sometimes presidents find that the choice they have made turns out to be a wrong one from their own point of view. Harry Truman claimed that his biggest mistake was putting 'that damn fool from Texas' (Tom Clark) on the bench. Earl Warren proved to be a talented and innovative chief justice, but Eisenhower had not selected him as such, and never imagined that the Court

The number of Supreme Court appointments made by recent presidents

President	Period in office	Number of nominations	Number of appointments
Kennedy	Under 3 years	2	2
Johnson	Over 5 years	3	2
Nixon	Over 5 years	6	4
Ford	Over 2 years	1	1
Carter	4 years	0	0
Reagan	8 years	6	4
Bush	4 years	2	2
Clinton	8 years	2	2

would move in such a liberal direction under his leadership when he appointed him. 'Ike' was equally disenchanted with another of his appointments, Justice Brennan. Nixon was similarly disappointed with the performance of his appointees, Blackmun and Powell. Appointed primarily for short-term political reasons, justices have a habit of becoming more independent and sometimes more creative when they are safely installed in office.

George W. Bush and judicial nominations: a change of direction for the Supreme Court?

Much media interest centres on the nominations for judicial office made by modern presidents. In the 2000 election campaign, commentators speculated on the differing approaches to nomination that George W. Bush and Al Gore might adopt. It was realised that the impact of a Bush or Gore presidency on abortion rights and other controversial issues could be considerable, if a vacancy arose in the Supreme Court.

Since January 2001, the new president has shown signs of seeking to adjust the composition of the judiciary in a more conservative way. In so doing, he has taken advice from the Federalist Society for Law and Public Policy, which was formed in the early 1980s. The Federalists draw inspiration from James Madison, one of the Founding Fathers, who on occasion railed against the power of central government. Members played an influential role in the impeachment proceedings against President Clinton and in the Florida legal offensive that brought Bush to power in 2001. Federalists are trying to steer the judiciary away from the liberalism of the past, and as a means of fulfilling this agenda they seek out ideologically acceptable candidates who might become suitable judges. Most members of George W. Bush's vetting panel for nominees belong to the organisation.

The president did not have an opportunity to make any nominations to the Supreme Court in his first Administration. However, following his victory in 2004, he is likely to be able to appoint from two to four new members, including the chief justice. Aware of the prospect of achieving generational change, Bush is likely to seize the opportunity to put a more conservative imprint on American public life that will endure long beyond his presidency.

Procedure

The Court term begins in early October and runs through until June or July, depending on the workload. Throughout the term, it alternates between two weeks of open court, known as sessions, and two weeks of recess, during which the justices read petitions and write opinions. In the period when the Court is in session, the justices attend from Monday to Wednesday to hear oral arguments presented by the attorneys, whose presentations are strictly time-limited. **Briefs** (written documents) will have been presented before the hearing, so that in the oral sessions attorneys are supposed to discuss the case rather than read from a prepared text.

The more crucial stage is the **conference work**, during which the justices meet on two occasions a week to discuss and decide cases. The chief justice will initiate the discussion of each case, by outlining and commenting on the main issues as he or she sees them. Then, in order of seniority, the other eight members of the court are invited to comment. If the position of some justices is not clear at this stage, a formal but still preliminary vote will be taken. After the vote, the chief justice assigns the writing of the opinion to one of his or her colleagues. Others may decide to write **concurring opinions** (in agreement with the conclusion but not the reasoning of the majority) or **dissenting opinions** (that disagree with the majority conclusion). As the drafts are completed, the other justices comment upon them and may suggest changes in wording and reasoning. Sometimes this is a time-consuming procedure, for opinions may sharply diverge. The opinion-writing stage is only completed when all the justices have decided which opinion they support. When this has happened, the Court judgement is announced.

Role

The Supreme Court stands at the apex of the federal court system and is the only one specifically created by the Constitution. A decision of the Supreme Court cannot be appealed to any other court. Congress has the power to fix the number of judges sitting on the Court and, within limits, decide what kind of cases it may hear – but it cannot change the powers given to the Supreme Court by the Constitution itself.

The Supreme Court has original jurisdiction in only two kinds of cases – those involving foreign dignitaries, and those in which a state is a party. In all other cases, the Court is involved on appeal from lower courts or from the supreme courts of the fifty states. It decides on around 160–70 cases a year, although thousands are filed annually. Most of them are concerned with the interpretation of a particular law, or the intentions of Congress in passing it.

Case-load

Ten thousand cases are tried annually by the American courts, 2% of them by federal ones. Of these, around 8,000 reach the Supreme Court. In an average year, around 90 are the subject of oral argument, and 70 or 80 are decided by a signed, written opinion.

However, an important part of the work of the Supreme Court involves the determination of whether executive acts or legislation conform to the Constitution. This is the power of **judicial review**, which is not specifically referred to in the original document. However, it is a doctrine inferred by the Court from its reading of the Constitution, and it was propounded very clearly in the Marbury v. Madison case (1803): 'A legislative act contrary to the Constitution is not law . . . it is emphatically the province and duty of the judicial department to say what the law is.'

> **judicial review**
> The power of any federal court to refuse to enforce a law or official act based on law, because in the view of the judges it conflicts with the Constitution.

Judicial review is necessary because the Constitution provides only broad and rather vague principles for the organisation and operation of government. It establishes three branches based on the principle of the separation of powers, and it sets out a federal structure and guarantees certain individual rights. These rules have remained largely unaltered, but they require elaboration and interpretation. Somebody has to decide what the Constitution actually means, and then interpret its relevance to specific cases. The Supreme Court acts as the arbiter of the constitutionality of the acts of the legislature and the executive. In the words of Alexander Hamilton in the *Federalist Papers* (no. 78), the duty of the Court 'must be to declare all acts contrary to the manifest tenor of the Constitution void'.

After the 1803 case, the authority of the courts to act as the final arbiter on constitutional matters was confirmed in other cases in 1810 and 1821, and it has been accepted ever since. Maidment and McGrew[3] have calculated that some 80 federal statutes and more than 700 pieces of state legislation have been struck down in the subsequent period as 'unconstitutional'. The frequency of such rulings may be an indication that the federal and state governments have too often acted without due recognition of the constitutional proprieties involved, or of the assertive stance taken by Supreme Court justices. But two other possible explanations are:

1 that the Constitution has not proved to be a straightforward document to interpret. Maidment and McGrew ask whether the First Amendment ('Congress shall make no law . . . abridging the freedom of speech, or of the press') literally means that Congress cannot legislate on matters such as libel or pornography. Was the intention of those who devised the Consti-

tution really to prevent Congress from passing any legislation at all in such areas, or was it really meant to be a safeguard of political liberty, to prevent undue exercise of governmental power which might curb beliefs and the expression of ideas on matters political, social and economic?

2 that the courts have had to deal with a changing country. Even if the intention of the framers of the Constitution was to create a system that would last indefinitely, a society in rapid development clearly needs some machinery to accommodate the pace of change. The Court has had to be faithful to the original document, yet seek to interpret its provisions in a way relevant to the times. The increased role of government in the social and economic lives of the people has posed a clear challenge to those on the bench. From after the Civil War through to the Great Depression of the early 1930s, the regulation of economic activity by the government became a key issue. From the presidency of Franklin D. Roosevelt, the scale of federal intervention has grown dramatically, and the Supreme Court found much of the New Deal legislation unacceptable in its original form.

The Supreme Court has made decisions affecting every aspect of American life, decisions which have shaped the course of development in every sphere of governmental activity. The earliest ones were often concerned with the division of responsibility between the federal and state governments at a time when the nation was rapidly expanding in size. The question of slavery was relevant to that discussion. Thereafter, the degree of economic regulation by the government was a controversial subject, as was later the massive expansion of federal activity in the New Deal in the 1930s. Since World War II, the issues tackled by the Court have often been of a different type, for by then the debates over the degree of economic regulation and intervention had been resolved. The issues of the postwar era have been ones of civil liberties and rights.

The Court and political controversy

The Supreme Court is a complex body, for it is neither a completely judicial nor a completely political/policy-making body. As Grant[4] observes: 'Politics play a crucial role in the appointment, working and decision-making of the . . . Court, and many of its judgements have broad policy implications.' Yet if its work and personnel are involved in political controversy at various times, the court is also supposed to interpret the Constitution, a function which places it above the everyday political fray.

The Court has constantly been involved in political matters, even though in theory it has generally stayed clear of questions of direct political controversy. Its rulings can and often have had political implications, so that when, in *Dred Scott v Sandford* (1857), the Court declared that a slave was a property and had no rights, this was a serious blow to those campaigning for an end to slavery. In other words, a judicial judgement had impacted on the political process.

In the 1930s, a Court reflecting the conservatism of the 1920s overturned programmes aimed at fighting the economic devastation of the Great Depression. Roosevelt was dissatisfied with the Court's performance, for its members posed a threat to the New Deal by their willingness to strike down key measures as 'unconstitutional'. The broad objection raised was that the federal government was exceeding its authority, and that the president and his advisers were too willing to downplay constitutional considerations. Since then, there has been much debate about the rights and wrongs of the issue, some writers believing that legislation should have been more carefully drafted, others taking the view that political malice was involved. Four of the nine justices were hostile to the New Deal, seeing it as a threat to property rights and the powers of the states. Several of them were elderly and conservative.

As a result, FDR came up with a Court-packing scheme, which would have enlarged its size and curtailed the power of older members. The plan ran into opposition, for it seemed to some Americans to be a bending of the rules. However, in the end Roosevelt got his way, for after 1937 the president had no further problems with the Court, as its members – reinforced by new appointments – began to allow legislation to pass onto the statute book ('a switch in time saved nine').

In the 1950s and 1960s, the judgements of the Warren Court (see pp. 170–2) ushered in one of the most liberal periods in the history of the Supreme Court. Some of its decisions aroused intense controversy, as indicated by the abortive movement at one time during Warren's stewardship to replace the existing Court with a new Constitutional Court of fifty members.

The decisions of the Court are not mere exercises in constitutional exegesis (interpretation). They are related to the great questions of the day, and the verdicts delivered impinge upon the nation's economic, political and social life. Can a tax be levied? Can an abortion be performed? If so, under what conditions? Can pornography be banned? Can races be segregated? These are all issues of primary concern to many Americans, and decisions broadly seen as liberal or conservative can greatly affect the tone of political debate. On some controversial questions, such as church–state relations, affirmative action programmes and abortion, the Court was evenly balanced, often voting 5–4 one way or the other, until the early 1980s. The choice of justices was therefore a highly significant one. It had political, as much as judicial, implications.

The political role of the Court is well established, and the justices play an important part in the political process. They are appointed for political reasons, and after their appointment they inhabit an intensely political atmosphere. It may seem strange to many people that matters affecting the fate of society are ultimately decided by nine unelected justices who, once on the bench, have no direct contact with public opinion. But as has often been pointed out, 'they read the election returns, too'. In other words, they understand prevailing pressures, and react to changing moods among the population, as in their decisions on affirmative action in recent years.

At various times, the Court runs into difficulties with the left and the right, for both liberals and conservatives sometimes find its decisions controversial and unacceptable. This is because it is charged with handling issues that are of vital importance to democracy and society at large. Yet justices use their powers sparingly, for they realise that if they allow themselves to become out of step with popular opinion for too long then the reputation of the Court will be damaged. They also wish to avoid open confrontation with the other branches of government. They understand the need to interpret the Constitution in the light of the requirements of today's industrialised society, and thus ensure that it remains a living document which continues to command general assent. The Court has performed its role rather well, and Professor Archibald Cox,[5] the Watergate special prosecutor, has explained the reasons for this success:

> The Court must know us better than we know ourselves ... the roots of its decisions must already be in the nation. The aspirations voiced by the Court must be those the community is willing not only to avow but in the end to live by, for the power of the constitutional decisions rests upon the accuracy of the Court's perceptions of this kind of common will and upon the Court's ability, by expressing its perception, ultimately to command a consensus.

Three Chief Justices and their Courts

The Warren Court, 1953–69

At the time of his appointment, Earl Warren was not thought of as being progressive. He was widely expected to be a consolidator, so Eisenhower could feel comfortable with his choice. Yet the Warren Court was to be noted for its judicial activism. Decisions taken in that era were of fundamental importance, and concerned such things as the rights of individuals, especially minorities, equal representation and equality before the law. This was an innovative Court, one of the most liberal in its history. It made a huge impact on many aspects of American life, so that the years 1953–69 witnessed what has widely been seen as a constitutional revolution.

It was in the field of civil rights that Warren made his greatest impact. Segregation had developed in the United States under the constitutional doctrine laid down in *Plessey* v. *Ferguson* (1896), when it was decided that it was constitutional to segregate people according to colour on the railways, as long as the separate facilities were equal in quality. In the landmark judgement in *Brown v Board of Education, Topeka, Kansas* (1954), it was declared that segregation in schools was unconstitutional, for separate facilities were seen as inherently unequal, and thus a breach of the Fourteenth Amendment, which declared that no state could 'deny to any person within its jurisdiction the equal protection of the laws'. The verdict applied only to segregation in schools, but it soon became apparent in other judgements that no service offered by the state could be provided on a segregated basis. The Court later ruled that it was constitutional to bus children across school district lines to achieve racial equality, a decision which upset many northerners, just as the 1954 ruling was greeted with dismay in the South.

The Warren Court also:
1 produced what was criticised as the 'criminals' charter'. Justices took the view that, in criminal cases, the balance of opinion had swung too much in the direction of the prosecution rather than those on trial. New guidelines were imposed upon the police, especially over powers of search and detention, and in interrogations a code of conduct limited the possibility of unfair behaviour by those in charge of the case. Those opposed to such measures were often moved to outrage, as indicated by the posters which appeared – 'Impeach Earl Warren.' Some used 'Hang' instead of 'impeach'!
2 was willing to show a new spirit of tolerance on other issues of civil liberty. The press was rendered less vulnerable to prosecutions for libel, and the state of New York was prevented from allowing a prayer to be recited in schools, as this was deemed to be a violation of the First Amendment.

Such judgements aroused dismay and opposition, and many felt that via the new liberal line the Court was becoming too immersed in political controversy. In the 1968 election, the performance of the Warren Court came under much scrutiny, and Richard Nixon promised to appoint **strict constructionists**: those who would confine themselves to the task of interpretation, rather than engage in 'political meddling'. When Warren resigned shortly afterwards, Nixon (as president) had his opportunity. He nominated Warren Burger as Earl Warren's successor.

strict constructionists
Supporters of the view that judges must examine the exact wording of the Constitution and identify its plain, literal meaning. Generally conservative, they are supporters of judicial restraint and tend to be strongly in favour of the rights of individual states.

THE WARREN COURT AT WORK

Roth v United States (1957)

In this, the first of the modern obscenity cases, Justice Brennan tried to determine a legal test for obscenity that would provide protection of the right to deal with sexual matters and yet reserve to the government the right to prohibit that which was truly obscene. His test was 'whether to the average person, applying contemporary community standards, the dominant theme of the material taken as a whole appeals to prurient interest (exciting lustfulness)'. The judgement liberalised the laws on obscenity in such a way that only 'hard-core' pornography was unprotected by the First Amendment. The verdict was denounced as 'overly permissive' by Richard Nixon, in his 1968 election campaign.

Gideon v Wainwright (1963)

Under the Sixth Amendment, the accused has a right to representation by a lawyer. But states were not required to provide attorneys to poor defendants until 1932, when this right was established for capital offences. In 1963, the Court ruled that states would have to pay to ensure legal representation for everyone on low incomes who was a defendant in a case of serious crime.

Griswold v Connecticut (1965)

The Court struck down a Connecticut state law banning the use of contraception even by married couples, basing the judgement on a 'right to privacy' that Justice Douglas decided could be inferred from the Bill of Rights. This was **loose constructionism** in practice, and the new right established was to be quoted more controversially a few years later in *Roe v Wade* (1973).

The Burger Court, 1969–86

The Burger Court was again intended to be a consolidating one, but the counter-revolution which Nixon favoured never really took place, for although the new nominees made in this period were generally conservative they did not seek to undo the work of the Warren Court in their decisions. The Court may not have been as innovative as its predecessor, but it produced some surprisingly bold judgements. If its decisions on the criminal law were more cautious than those of the Warren era, none the less on racial matters, on abortion and over Watergate it acted adventurously.

loose constructionists

Tend to interpret the Constitution more loosely or liberally. They do not feel bound by the exact meaning of particular words or phrases and tend to be sympathetic to notions of judicial activism. They are broadly willing to extend the scope of federal governmental power.

In matters of criminal justice, the approach leaned more towards police powers, although there was no attempt to return to the pre-Warren era, but on civil rights and abortion, the stand was adventurous. The Court decided that affirmative action could be constitutional (e.g. the Baake case of 1978 – see p. 327), and in favour of legalising abortion. In *Roe v Wade* (1973), it struck down state anti-abortion laws, and ruled in favour of the right of women to control what happened to their own bodies – in the words of Gillian Peele,[6] 'a liberal interpretation of the Constitution, based on a right to privacy which is not to be found in the text of the document'.

THE BURGER COURT AT WORK

Swann v Mecklenberg Board of Education (1971)

De jure (legal) segregation had been outlawed in 1954, but de facto segregation was still in place, in that if blacks lived in one part of the town, then the local school would be overwhelmingly black, and if whites lived in one part, the local school would be white. Busing was a way round this dilemma. It was disliked by Richard Nixon and also by Linda Brown, the black girl who was not allowed to attend a segregated school and whose name was to be immortalised in the *Brown v Board of Education, Topeka, Kansas* case. The Court's decision in 1971 permitted the busing of black and white students across cities, in order to ensure a racial balance in schools.

Furman v Georgia (1972) and *Gregg v Georgia* (1976)

In 1972, by a 5–4 vote, the Court struck down all existing death-penalty laws as being a violation of the Eighth Amendment, which prohibited 'cruel and unusual punishments'. Two justices were opposed to the death penalty outright, whereas two others objected to the way in which it was 'wantonly and freakishly' imposed. The verdict prompted several states to rewrite their laws on the death penalty.

In 1976, the Court stated that capital punishment was not always unconstitutional. It approved new death-penalty statutes that were said to be less arbitrary in their operation. This reversal of the 1972 decision seemed like a concession to popular opinion, which was strongly in favour of capital punishment.

Miller v California (1973)

Following the liberal decision in 1957 (see page opposite), the Court (by then made more conservative in composition by the four Nixon appointees) moved to limit the spread of sexually explicit materials. It decided that prosecutors no longer needed to be able to demonstrate that a work was 'utterly without redeeming social value'. They only had to show that it did not possess 'serious literary, artistic, political or scientific value' for it to lose its protection as speech under the First Amendment.

See also further details of the issues involved in the Roe v Wade *and* Baake *cases, on pp. 318 and 327*

Finally, it was the Burger Court that ruled against President Nixon in the matter of the Watergate tapes, recordings made by those around the president to provide him with a clear record of conversations that had taken place in the Oval Office. As the scandal unfolded, with its allegations of a massive cover-up and obstruction of justice following the break-in to the Watergate building, a federal district court judge issued a subpoena, ordering the president to release sixty-four tapes. The president claimed executive privilege, and refused to release them to the special prosecutor. The Supreme Court insisted unanimously that the tapes must be handed over, and Nixon complied with the decision – an illustration of the status of the Supreme Court. The executive and legislative branches of government abide by its decisions, even though it lacks any direct means of enforcement. The impact of the 'tapes issue' was enormous, and within a fortnight Nixon had resigned. The action of the Court had again been of momentous consequence.

The Supreme Court and the 2000 presidential election

The final decision of the Court in the *George W. Bush v Albert Gore Jnr* case was among the most momentous of its history. In addition to deciding this particular presidency, it could have the effect in future of pushing the nation's highest court into more election battles – an area it has traditionally avoided.

The Court was dealing with an appeal by George W. Bush against a ruling in the Florida supreme court to order a manual recount in the state. The nine justices basically had three options:

1 They could have found for Bush on the grounds that the only votes usually counted in Florida are those clearly marked, so that the state's decision to allow other votes to be included was a departure from normal practice. Justices Rehnquist, Scalia and Thomas were supporters of this viewpoint, which, if handed down, would have been final and stopped all recounts without qualification.

2 The justices could have ruled clearly for Gore, deferring – as federal courts normally would do – to state courts on matters of state law. This might have involved issuing guidance to the Florida supreme court on how the recount should proceed. Justices Breyer and Ginsburg wanted to do this. To do so would have made the process more lengthy, but would have meant that ultimately the choice lay with the voters.

3 The third option, which the justices actually took, was to seem to do the second, whilst actually doing something akin to the first. By 7–2, the Court sent the case back to the Florida supreme court 'for further proceedings not inconsistent with this opinion'. In practice, as the various dissenting opinions made clear, this meant that by 5–4 the Florida supreme court had to have the votes counted, allow sufficient time for judicial review of these proceedings and do it all by midnight, 12 December – two hours after the Supreme Court issued its ruling (the date when the Electoral College votes were

The Rehnquist court, 1986–?

Given the disappointment felt by many conservatives over the performance of the Burger Court, President Reagan was determined to appoint justices of conservative persuasion. He opted for William Rehnquist as chief justice, on Burger's retirement. It is the Rehnquist Court that is still in place in 2005. The intellect and diplomatic skill of the new incumbent were not doubted, but those of more liberal leanings saw Rehnquist as the most conservative member of the existing nine. Even though justices sometimes act in unpredictable ways – contrary to the expectations of those who appoint them – there has certainly overall been a markedly less liberal tone in the judgements delivered in recent years. However, many observers from the left and the right have praised Rehnquist for improving the Court's efficiency and for his effectiveness in dealing with colleagues.

supposed to be over). By opting for the impossible, this meant that the Court effectively handed victory to Bush.

In the Court's defence, seven justices had found serious constitutional violations in the way that the manual recounts had been conducted. Even Associate Justice Ginsburg, a Democrat appointment, called the process 'flawed'. They were uneasy about the way in which decisions on vote-counting were being taken away from the officials whom the legislature had appointed for the task of managing the election, and handed over to the judiciary. The recount was, moreover, not to include 'all ballots', although that inclusion was a requirement of state law. All in all, the Court had brought finality to a messy business and produced a result.

To Gore sympathisers, any outcome of the Court's deliberations would have been questionable, but the final decision seemed to be intellectually less than rigorous. Doubts were expressed about the reasoning and remedy that led to the verdict. The verdict expressed implied that the Supreme Court knew better than the Florida supreme court what was meant by Florida state law, a strange judgement from a generally constructionist court which has generally been very sympathetic to states' rights. As Justice Breyer pointed out, the Florida supreme court would have preferred a recount finished on 18 December (when Electoral College votes were due to be certified), for it had stressed 'the will of the voters' and its willingness to recount ballots in its decision.

By rejecting some ballots as it effectively did and acting in a way that seemed to reflect its Republican majority, the Supreme Court has involved itself in controversy. The case created intense excitement and partisan feeling, and Americans and observers worldwide were waiting to see how the verdict would go. By its judgement, the court has risked eroding public confidence in its collective wisdom and fairness, what Justice Breyer called 'a public treasure that has been built up over many years'.

Presidents Reagan and Bush had the opportunity to tilt the balance of the Court, and seized it. President Clinton was able to make two appointments, so that the reaction of the nine on controversial matters such as abortion and affirmative action is not entirely predictable. But his are the only Democrat members, and although there are two other moderates the conservative cause can muster a majority if Sandra Day O'Connor votes with it. She is the least predictable justice and her reaction in the controversies surrounding the 2000 election was watched with interest (see pp. 174–5).

In general, the Rehnquist Court has taken a notably less progressive line than its predecessor, its judgements being cautious and less spectacular than some earlier ones. It has handled fewer cases than previous courts each term and struck down fewer federal and state laws. The majority of Court justices do not

THE REHNQUIST COURT AT WORK

Bowers v Hardwick (1986)

By then rather more conservative in tone, the Court decided by 5–4 in 1986 that the 'right to privacy' did not extend to consensual gay sex. States were permitted to pass their own laws on matters relating to single-sex relationships.

Texas v Johnson (1989) and US v Eichman (1990)

In this early 5–4 ruling, the Court decided that the burning of the 'Stars and Stripes' represented a form of protected free expression under the First Amendment. Two conservatives, Kennedy and Scalia, found the action deplorable, but given the wording of the Constitution they felt that had little choice but to permit it. When Congress passed a law outlawing desecration of the national flag, the Court stepped in with another judgement. In 1990, it found the congressional statute unconstitutional, in that violated the guarantee of free speech as set out in the Bill of Rights.

Reno v American Civil Liberties Union (1997)

The Court unanimously struck down the Communications Decency Act (1996), which had prohibited 'indecent' and 'patently offensive' material on the Internet or in e-mails. It adjudged that the statute lacked precision and undermined the protection offered under the First Amendment.

Washington v Glucksberg (1997)

The justices found that euthanasia, 'mercy-killing' or 'assisted suicide' was not a constitutional right and was therefore a matter for state decision.

see it as their task to act as the guardian of individual liberties and civil rights for minority groups. But their broad approach has been to nibble away at the edges of contentious issues, rather than make a direct challenge to the whole direction of past policy in areas such as abortion and affirmative action. As Biskupic[7] and some other commentators have noted: 'Gone is the self-consciously loud voice the Court once spoke with, boldly stating its position and calling upon the people and other institutions of government to follow.'

The failure to reverse many liberal judgements of an earlier era has disappointed many conservatives, but none the less Schwartz[8] has detected in the Rehnquist Court a series of cumulative decisions 'limiting the use of habeas corpus by prisoners, broadening the power of the police to search automobiles, applying the harmless error doctrine to a constitutional error committed

---

Kansas v Hendricks (1997)

The judgement allowed states to pass legislation that required the confinement of sex offenders in mental hospitals, following a term of imprisonment.

Boy Scouts of America v Dale (2000)

By 5–4, the Court decided that the requirement that the Boy Scouts admit homosexuals as scout leaders was a violation of the rights of scouting groups to free association.

Ashcroft v The Free Speech Coalition (2002)

The Court invalidated the 1996 Child Pornography Prevention Act, that had banned computer-generated images of children.

Virginia v Black (2003)

By 6–3, the justices declared that the ritual burning of a cross (as done by the Ku Klux Klan) can be banned by states if the purpose of the event is to intimidate or terrorise. The act of burning can be interpreted as threatening and therefore cannot be regarded as protected expression.

NB Several of the judgements of the Rehnquist Court have been decided on the basis of narrow majority verdicts, often 5–4 (21/74 in 1999–2000). Many commentators have found that judgements appear to lack consistency, some extending rights under the First Amendment, others curbing them.

Judges and their role in Britain and the United States: a comparison

One of the most significant political developments in Britain in recent decades has been the growing importance of judges and the courts. Previously, the role of the courts in British politics had been restricted and sporadic, whereas it is now often said to be central and constant. Today, the power of judges to review the legality of governmental action has become an important stage in the public policy process. Its increased relevance was apparent when in 1987 government lawyers produced a document for civil servants, entitled *The Judge over your Shoulder*. It showed them how to avoid the pitfalls into which they might tumble.

Between 1981 and 1996, the number of applications for judicial review rose from just over 500 to nearly 4,000; in the latter year alone, there were 1,748 immigration applications and 340 concerning homelessness. The increasing resort to review and the decisions which judges reached in several cases ranging from criminal injuries to deportation caused resentment under John Major's government (1990–7). Tension became acute, for ministers were overtly critical of judges and complained about judicial activism, whilst some judges felt there was a campaign to discredit them. The tabloid press joined in the 'judge-bashing', complaining of the 'galloping arrogance' of the judiciary.

Opponents of a British Bill of Rights – many of whom are Conservatives – often claim that it would remove power from the hands of elected MPs and give it to the judges. Similar fears about the transfer of power to the judiciary are at the heart of much anxiety about the 1998 Human Rights Act, which incorporated the European Convention on Human Rights into British law. If today that suspicion is often voiced on the political right, in the past it was the labour movement that felt uneasy about judicial power. Its suspicion was not based solely on a number of well-documented and unfavourable verdicts. It had much to do with a feeling that these judgements derived from problems about the selection, backgrounds and attitudes of those 'on the bench'.

Many British judges have formerly practised at the bar, membership of which has long been thought to be elitist and unrepresentative. Members tend to have professional, middle-class backgrounds, and have often been educated at public school before attending Oxbridge. In other words, they are said to be conservative, wealthy and out of touch. A privileged lifestyle might not by itself render judges unsuitable to exercise greater political influence. But – it is alleged – the nature of their training, and the character of the job they do, tend to give them a preference for traditional standards of behaviour and make them particularly impressed by traditional values in matters of behaviour, family life and respect for the law. They are unlikely to be overly sympathetic to demonstrators, minority activists and those who are strident in seeking justice for their cause.

Courts of law are part of the political process in most democratic countries, for governmental decisions and acts passed by the legislature may require judicial decisions to be implemented. Courts need to be independent to be respected, but in practice this is difficult to achieve. There is rarely full independence as far as appointment is concerned, though in America the process is more overtly political.

As a broad trend the role of judges in the political system has increased in liberal democracies. Some fear that this political involvement has gone too far, and that there are dangers for the standing of judges if this is unchecked. Others worry less about the damage which may be done to their reputation, but instead place their emphasis upon fear of judicial power. In both the UK and the US, alarm is sometimes raised about the politicisation of the judiciary, and interest centres on the character and leanings of those who are appointed judges.

Nowadays, to see the judiciary purely as being preoccupied with the legal system would be to ignore its key political role. As Chief Justice Holmes once put it: 'We are under the Constitution, but the Constitution is what the judges say it is.' In Britain too, judges are now much more willing to step into the political arena, an area long inhabited by justices of the Supreme Court. The same fear about their activities is voiced in both countries: those on the bench are unelected, unaccountable and invariably rather elderly.

Some of the reasons for this 'judicialisation' of politics have been listed by Richard Hodder-Williams:[10]

1 'the failure of the political process to meet the aspirations of those who are governed under it';

2 the rise of the administrative state and a bevy of bureaucracies the decisions of which affect so much of so many people's lives';

3 the rise of 'a more educated, more challenging electorate that is less deferential to government in all its forms and is more aware of deficiencies through a lively, and often vulgar, press';

4 the development of 'an ideological shift throughout Europe and America, which has enhanced the status of rights-based demands and has redefined a substantial part of what politics is about, away from struggles between classes and religious groups towards conflict between the coercive powers of the state and the individual';

5 the influence of particular and influential individuals 'like Lord Denning in Britain and Earl Warren in the United States, who had the strength of character and self-belief to challenge the old orthodoxies and help usher in new values and expectations';

6 the increased use of international conventions in the modern world and the proliferation of international or transnational courts to enforce them, ranging from the European Court of Human Rights to the European Court of Justice, from the World Trade Organisation panels to the North American Free Trade Agreement panels. They test national law against some other body of law, usually treated as being superior. In some cases, these agreements or conventions have involved members of the bench in any member country ruling against the decisions of the party in power.

at the trial, and upholding regulations prohibiting abortion counselling, referrals or advocacy by federally funded clinics'.

This view of the Rehnquist Court and its alleged judicial restraint has been questioned. Its greater ideological conservatism is generally accepted, although its record on civil liberties is more mixed than that term might imply. Some commentators have suggested that it has been highly activist in its willingness to challenge the elected branches of government. Rosen[9] is an exponent of such thinking. Comparing the Warren and Rehnquist eras, he argues that both courts were committed to an increase in judicial power: 'Both combine haughty declarations of judicial supremacy with contempt for the competing views of the political branches.' Others too[10] have observed that for all of the lip service paid to judicial self-restraint, 'most of the current justices appear entirely comfortable intervening in all manner of issues, challenging state as well as national power, and underscoring the Court's role as final arbiter of constitutional issues'.

The Rehnquist court in January 2005

Justice	Year of birth	Year of appointment	President who made appointment
Chief justice			
William Rehnquist	1924	1986*	Reagan
Associate justices			
John Stevens	1920	1975	Ford
Sandra Day O'Connor	1930	1981	Reagan
Antonin Scalia	1936	1986	Reagan
Anthony Kennedy	1936	1988	Reagan
David Souter	1939	1990	Bush
Clarence Thomas	1948	1991	Bush
Ruth Ginsburg	1933	1993	Clinton
Stephen Breyer	1938	1994	Clinton

* Rehnquist had been an associate justice for five years, prior to becoming Chief Justice

Much interest – particularly in the *Bush* v. *Gore* case, but also in matters such as abortion – centres on the composition of the Court at any time, with the past records of the nine coming under much scrutiny.

Broadly (perhaps crudely), Breyer, Ginsburg and Stevens are liberal, O'Connor and Souter are right–centre, and Kennedy, Rehnquist, Scalia and Thomas conservative. Clinton's two appointments have made the Court a moderate one, much depending on the reactions of O'Connor and Souter, who have both sometimes been joined by Kennedy in taking a more liberal line on matters of civil liberties.

CONCLUSION

Those who serve on the Supreme Court invariably survive those who put them there. This means that there is a thread of judicial continuity from one presidential administration to another and that the Court can act as a powerful counter to the other two branches of government. As a result of its rulings over the last fifty years, it has taken a central role in the political process. The situation was summed up by an early twentieth-century president, William Taft. He observed that: 'Presidents come and go, but the Supreme Court goes on forever.'[12] True enough, but the fact that the nine justices and those who serve as judges across the country are political appointments does help to shape the development of public policy. On occasion, as in the 2000 election, it may be thought to play too large a role when the justices reach their verdicts.

Because the courts have so much power, the role they play in addressing important social issues is much discussed. Dispute centres on whether judges should confine themselves to interpreting the Constitution, implementing the letter of the existing law, or whether they should actively seek to broaden the nature of justice by identifying and redressing grievances. On occasion, as with the Warren Court, judicial activism is triumphant. Usually, and certainly more recently, judicial restraint is the norm.

REFERENCES

1 M. Vile, *Politics in the USA*, Hutchinson, 1978
2 Quoted in J. Rosen, 'The New Justice', *New Republic*, 12 April 1993
3 R. Maidment and D. McGrew, *The American Political Process*, Sage/Open University, 1992
4 A. Grant, *The American Political Process*, Dartmouth, 1994
5 A. Cox, *The Court and the Constitution*, Houghton Mifflin, 1987
6 G. Peele, C. Bailey, B. Cain and B. Peters (eds), *Developments in American Politics 4*, Palgrave, 2002
7 J. Biskupic, 'The Rehnquist Court: Justices Want to Be Known as Jurists, not Activists', *Washington Post*, 9 January 2000
8 B. Schwartz, *A History of the Supreme Court*, Oxford University Press, 1993
9 J. Rosen, 'Pride and prejudice', *New Republic*, 10/17 July 2000
10 For instance: T. Yarborough, 'The Supreme Court and the Constitution', G. Peele et al., as in 6 above
11 R. Hodder-Williams, *Judges and Politics in the Contemporary Age*, Bowedean, 1996
12 Quoted in H. Pringle, *The Life and Times of William Howard Taft*, Farrar, 1939

USEFUL WEB SITES

www.uscourts.gov Federal Judiciary Home Page. Comprehensive guide to federal court system, with court statistics, answers to frequently asked questions etc.

www.supremecourtus.gov The official site of the Supreme Court, providing information relating to its background, history and procedures.

Oyez.nwu.edu The Northwestern University site that offers information about the justices, answers frequently asked questions and provides a virtual tour of the Court buildings.

www.law.cornell.edu/supct Cornell Law School. Provides a diverse array of legal sources and full text of Supreme Court judgements.

www.findlaw.com Comprehensive guide to the US Constitution and legal system, as well as coverage of all rulings since 1893.

SAMPLE QUESTIONS

1 To what extent can presidents mould and influence the Supreme Court?

2 How 'supreme' is the Supreme Court within the American political system? Would the Founding Fathers be troubled by the way in which its role has evolved?

3 'A judicial body certainly, but its decisions often have a major impact on the political scene'. Discuss this verdict on the Supreme Court.

4 Do Supreme Court judgements follow popular opinion? Should they?

5 To what extent are the decisions of the Supreme Court influenced by its changing membership?

6 Is the Supreme Court still a strong defender of the rights of the individual?

7 'In view of the political influence it exercises, it is unacceptable that the Supreme Court is an unelected body.' Discuss

8 Does the Supreme Court exercise too much influence in American government and society?

9 'Legislatures may make laws by passing statutes, but judges have to apply them in particular situations.' To what extent do judges in Britain and the United States make the law?

Elections and voting

7

Elections, campaigns and voting are central features of democratic life. America has more elections than other democracies and voters are faced with alternative visions, programmes and personalities at all levels of administration. Many voters decline the opportunity to make up their minds about their preferred choice, even in the four-yearly presidential contests.

In this chapter we are concerned to find out why elections are so basic to thinking about democracy in the United States and to see how the various types of election are conducted, particularly that for the presidency. We ask why so many Americans do not turn out to vote and what influences those who do so. We also consider the use of 'direct democracy', examining the growth in the popularity of initiatives and referendums in recent years.

POINTS TO CONSIDER

➤ Why are there so many elections in US politics? Why are they so important?

➤ In what ways has television changed the nature of election campaigns?

➤ How is the president elected? Could the system be improved? Does it need to be improved?

➤ Which is more important in the choice of president: money, personality or any other considerations?

➤ Why do so many Americans not vote in important elections such as those for president, Congress or governors?

➤ What changes have occurred in voting behaviour since the 1980s?

➤ Why might Americans 'split the ticket' when they vote?

➤ What similarities and differences are there between voting behaviour in Britain and the United States?

➤ Is direct legislation a good thing?

➤ Why was George W. Bush successful again in 2004?

GENERAL FEATURES OF ELECTIONS AND ELECTIONEERING

The importance of elections to American democracy

Elections are basic to the American democratic process. At every tier of political life, the incumbent (occupant) is selected by election. In some states, even such offices as the municipal judge and the registrar of wills are contested. Americans who turn out to vote have the chance to choose the president (via the Electoral College), a representative, a senator, state legislators, a governor, state administrative officials, local councillors, local admin-

THE USE OF PRIMARIES

At the beginning of the twentieth century, many 'progressives' were concerned at the power exercised by party bosses and their political organisations. They wanted to curb the corruption felt to be endemic in public life, and pressed for reforms to break the control of the party machines and the 'bosses' who ran them. In this spirit, they urged the use of primary elections that would transfer power away from the party regulars meeting in smoke-filled rooms to the interested ordinary voter. This was seen as a significant step towards greater democracy.

The use of primaries gradually spread, although for many years the system was still not widely used for choosing presidential candidates. By the 1970s they had become nationwide for almost all forms of election, local, state and federal. It was not only the large city machines that lost power with the advent of primaries – party organisations everywhere lost their hold. Even where there was no suspicion of doubtful propriety, they lost a key function, that of nomination – for any candidate could stand for election, whether or not he or she had rendered some service in the local party.

Types of primary

Practice varies from the restrictive to the generous. In some states everyone can vote, whereas in others only those who are registered as members of the party who have the right. Where only registered members can vote, this is a **closed primary**. Where anyone, regardless of party affiliation can vote, then this is an **open primary**. In Connecticut and Delaware in the Northeast, only party members are eligible. In the same region, Vermont holds open primaries. So does Rhode Island, which none the less requires a voter to state his or her affiliation. By contrast, Alaska in the Northwest uses open primaries, allowing voters to vote in both parties, should they wish to so do.

istrative officials, mayors and county officials. They might also help to choose judges and party officials, and take part in referendums (votes on single issues). There are in excess of a million elected offices, though because many of these are local they fail to make headline news. When allowance is made for the primary elections that are held to determine who will represent the parties in the main contests, it is obvious that elections in America occur with considerable frequency.

The vast number of elections is a reflection of the general growth of the democratic principle since the eighteenth century. Americans have long believed that the greater the direct involvement of the citizen, the better the likely outcome in terms of the quality of output. More participation is thought

---

Open and closed primaries: the procedure

As we can see, the exact procedure for use in primary contests varies between different states, each of which makes it own regulations for the conduct of the election. Broadly, the position is as follows:

1 In **open primaries**, the elector is given two ballots, one for each party. He or she fills in one ballot to go in the ballot box, and the unused one is discarded in a sealed container. He or she cannot use both, and there is no way of knowing which one has been filled in. Some object to this process on the grounds that it is possible for voters to use their vote not to distinguish between the candidates in their favoured party, but rather to seek to 'wreck' the chances of the other party by voting for its least impressive candidate. If that weak person were to be chosen, this might increase the chances of the voter's preferred party.

2 In **closed primaries**, this 'wrecking' cannot occur, but the process is not so secret, for, on entering the polling station, the voter must express his or her affiliation. The appropriate ballot paper is then handed over, and if the party officers of one side question the allegiance it can be challenged.

The merits and disadvantages of primaries

There are obvious benefits in the use of primaries: they are more democratic than the system they replaced, they emphasise the personal qualities of the candidates rather than their party label, and they sometimes produce good candidates who would otherwise not have been chosen. They can provide a chance for the different wings of the parties to air their viewpoints, and so indicate where the preferences of members really lie. They have drawbacks, in that they are an additional expense – often the machine still fights hard to ensure victory for its favoured candidate – and they demand that the voter turns out for yet another election: the frequency of elections is one reason sometimes given for low turnouts, for many ordinary voters lack the stamina or interest.

to lead to superior government. But it has another explanation: the belief in limited government. From the days of the Founding Fathers, Americans have always had a fear of too much power residing in one pair of hands. Elected officers should not be trusted too much or for too long. It is desirable for citizens to retain as much power as possible under their own control.

How people get elected

The selection of elected representatives is done via a two-part process, comprising the nomination stage, which is carried out by the party, and the final stage (polling day), which is done by all the voters in a particular town or state.

The method of selecting candidates has evolved over the two-hundred-year history of the United States. In colonial times, the method adopted was the **caucus**, an informal meeting of party leaders at which agreement was reached on the individuals who merited support. As the country evolved, different forms of political organisation developed, and the various local caucuses began to delegate representatives to meet with representatives from other local caucuses to form county and then state groups, which finally selected candidates. These enlarged bodies were known as **conventions**, the early prototypes

---

Mid-term elections and their significance

Mid-term elections take place every two years, between presidential elections (e.g. 2002, 2006 etc.). All members of the House of Representatives are due for re-election, as are a third of the members of the Senate. There are gubernatorial contests and initiative or referendum votes taking place at the same time.

In mid-term elections, existing members usually get re-elected should they decide to stand. Even in years when there is an anti-incumbency mood (1992, 1994), many more members leave office due to retirement than to defeat at the polls. Incumbents have several advantages, among them name recognition, free publicity, ease of fund-raising and the chance to deliver benefits for the area they represent.

Mid-term elections are a chance to assess the mood of the country and the president's chance of re-election. They can inspire or demoralise the person in the White House and his would-be challengers. They can be particularly significant during some presidencies. In November 1994, the Republicans scored a convincing victory, capturing both chambers of Congress for the first time for many years and thereby dealing a blow to the future legislative and other prospects of the Clinton presidency. The Republican resurgence proved costly for the president over the following years, for a partisan House was able to pursue him vigorously over the Lewinsky and other scandals. The party's revival significantly reshaped the political agenda, moving it sharply to the right.

of the presidential nominating conventions used today. The third development was the use of the primary election. **Primaries** are state-wide, intra-party elections. Their basic purpose is to give voters the opportunity to select directly their party's candidates for various offices.

> **primaries**
> Preliminary elections held within a party to choose the candidate for that party in the general election.

In general elections, the candidates of the political parties for all positions are pitted against each other. Usually, the party candidates for all offices – federal, state and local – run as a block or 'slate'. In addition each party draws up a statement of its position on various issues, called a **platform**. Voters thus make their decisions not only for or against persons who run for office, but also on the political, economic and social philosophies of the parties they represent.

> **platform**
> A statement of party aims and policies that the candidate will officially support but by which he or she does not feel bound.

Candidates may run for office without the support of a political party, as independents. To do so, they must present a petition, signed by a specified number of voters (varying from state to state) who support the candidacy. Another device is the write-in vote: a candidate's name does not appear on the ballot, but is 'written' in by voters in a space left blank for this purpose.

In mid-term elections, some candidates benefit from a coat-tails effect. When there is a popular president, it can help their cause, for they are able to associate themselves with his glories. This has not often happened in recent years, but in 2002 many Republicans were delighted to have George W. Bush lend support to their campaign and to bask in his popularity. On that occasion, the party consciously tried to 'nationalise' the campaign, so that candidates could be associated with Bush's success in Afghanistan and the early stages of the war on terrorism. By contrast, in 1994, Democrats were keen to dissociate themselves from President Clinton, for his political stock was low at the time, after the failure of his health reform project. The president's party often suffers losses in mid-term, as the voters express disappointment or disapproval of what has been done over the previous two years.

More usually, local rather than national factors are relevant to voting in mid-term elections. They assess the performance of the incumbent in 'bringing home the bacon'. Voter's wants and needs will differ from state to state. For instance, logging is a key issue in Oregon and cross-border immigration in Texas. In all cases, voters will want to see ample evidence that their elected representative has pursued every opportunity to achieve economic advantages for the district, perhaps by gaining some defence contracts or public works projects for the area. Mid-term elections determine the fate of members of the lower chamber, for their tenure expires with them. Because of the brief period in which they can make a difference, pork-barrel politics (see pp. 140–1) assume great importance to them.

The timing of elections and the voting system

Most issues relating to elections are decided within the states, although the Constitution lays down the general requirements on how often they are to take place for each institution.

American elections are used to choose representatives for a fixed-term period of office, so that the date of future elections is known in advance. They are scheduled in such a way that every fourth year (1992, 1996, 2000 and 2004) there is a presidential election. They are always held on the Tuesday after the first Monday in November, in an even year. This contrasts with the situation in countries such as Britain and Canada, where an election can be called at any time as long as there is at least one every five years.

According to the Constitution, two years is the fixed period served by a member of the House of Representatives. The election occurs on the day of the presidential election and two years later (e.g. November 2000 and November 2002). For the Senate, the period is considerably longer – six years – and the election again occurs in November. Whereas members of the House are all elected together, this is not so with the Senate: senators are elected on a staggered basis, one third at a time. There are, then, congressional contests every two years, those in the non-presidential election years being known as mid-term elections (see pp. 186–7).

The method employed

For all elections, the method employed is the one used in Britain and Canada, the 'first past the post' or simple majority system. In other words, the candidate with the most votes in the single-member constituency is elected. This method is widely seen as making it more likely that a two-party system will result, for third parties are discouraged; they may win many votes in an area, but unless they can win in an individual constituency they get no tangible reward. By comparison, proportional methods of voting, such as those used in most of continental Europe, are said to encourage the formation and development of small parties. They have a chance of gaining representation in the legislature, even on the basis of relatively small support.

Election campaigns

In past generations, speakers have needed to be effective 'on the stump', addressing a gathering in the local marketplace or school hall. Sometimes those running for office addressed electors from a platform at the back of a train, most famously Harry Truman, whose 'whistle-stop' tours involved the train pulling up at every local station. He was the last campaigner to deploy this method of electioneering on such a scale, though others subsequently (e.g. John F. Kennedy) conducted very active speech-making tours and sometimes spoke from the rear of a railway carriage.

Today, television has taken over campaigning, but the purpose remains the same: to encourage the electorate to support the personality and policy platform on polling day. Reaching the maximum number of the electorate has always been a priority, but whereas at one time an audience could be counted in tens or hundreds, now it can be counted in millions for a single programme. The whistle-stop tour could last weeks and the candidate might see a hundred thousand altogether.

Candidate-centred campaigning

The process of electioneering has always demanded certain qualities from the person chosen – a pleasing voice, a gift for public speaking, the ability to sell one's personality and to persuade people of the merits of a particular case. However, today, deficiencies in any of these aspects can be a serious liability exposed before the whole nation, whereas previously many voters did not know about them. Other personal failings are also highlighted in the blaze of publicity surrounding a modern election campaign.

Elections are nowadays far more focused on the candidate and his or her positive qualities and/or failings than on party labels. What candidates must do is to put together a winning coalition of support – they do this by making sure that there are sufficient funds to allow them to get the message across as widely as possible, so that everyone knows who they are and what they stand for.

Whether the election is for Congress, for the presidency or for some other position, the trend has been towards far greater professionalism than ever before. Those who run election campaigns are skilled in the new campaign technology. They use the direct mail-shot, targeted to individual voters, to arouse interest and obtain funding. They use computers to analyse the voters of a particular precinct. They employ professional opinion pollsters and media gurus – specialists who are able to advise on the best means of exploiting the potential of the candidate and downplaying or destroying the qualities and reputation of an opponent.

Once candidates are chosen, parties are obviously concerned to help them to sell themselves and their message. They send out their voluntary workers to canvass on the doorstep, they use the phone to call possible voters, they arrange lifts for those who otherwise might not make it to the polling booth, as well as involving themselves in fundraising, commissioning and studying opinion polls and advertising. However, the role of parties in electioneering has been downgraded, for increasingly – with the breakdown of the party machines, after the reform of the arrangements for financial contributions in the early 1970s – it is the individual candidate and the team of supporters he or she puts together that have become important. With the backing of political action committees (PACs) whose primary function is to help finance election contests, candidates now tend to run their own campaigning.

The purpose of the campaign is not only to reach as many people as possible, but to ensure that those who are sympathetically disposed actually turn out and vote. Given the relatively low turnouts in the United States, it is important for the parties and PACs to do anything they can to assist in the process of voter registration and to encourage those who are registered to go to the polls.

Electioneering in Britain and the United States: a comparison

British election campaigns are much shorter than American ones. Even though there is much speculation and a pre-election atmosphere in the third or fourth year of the lifetime of a Parliament, the campaign proper lasts only three to four weeks. Campaigns for all elective offices in America are longer, but this is especially true of presidential ones.

Despite the increasing personalisation of British politics – for example, the emphasis on the gladiatorial aspect of the Blair versus Hague contest – it remains the case that the voter is still voting for a party rather than just one person: other key figures in the Cabinet or Shadow Cabinet play a significant role in the campaign, as do the local and national party organisations. By contrast, the American experience is more candidate-centred. More stress is placed upon the personal qualities of the candidates than on their party allegiance. 'Personal qualities' can include many things, from the superficial, such as looks and friendliness, to others including character, temperament and outlook. As the person, once elected, will make up his or her own mind on political issues, personality and views can be very significant.

The organisations that provide the contestants with support (parties and PACs) have more of a personal than a party loyalty. They are concerned especially with the funding of the campaign and political advertising, aspects which are still more developed on the other side of the Atlantic – though Britain is moving in the American direction, with increased use of public relations advisers and negative advertising on posters and via the style of some party election broadcasts.

Britain does not allow unlimited access by the parties to television time, which is strictly regulated. America does not have the British-style election broadcast, but candidate-centred structures make extensive use of the media – their access is only limited by the funds they have available.

The role of money in American elections

The role of money in American elections has long been controversial, as have been the sources of funding. Several sources exist. Money can come from the individual candidate, interested individuals, interest groups operating through PACs, and political parties. There are also several purposes for which the money is made available. It may derive from the generosity of a benefactor; it may be given out of idealistic support for a particular individual, idea or set of principles; or it may be offered in the hope of securing some goal of personal or group benefit.

Whatever the motive of the donor, what is important is that the representative – once elected to public office – does not feel unduly beholden to those who have financed the campaign, at the expense of the general public who they are there to represent. The fear is that money given is 'interested money', in that those who donate it are looking for favours from the persons they back.

Given the new technology and methods of electioneering, national elections have become very costly, whether for Congress or for the presidency. An individual is – in most cases – unlikely to be able to meet those costs on his or her own. The difficulty is all the greater if the candidate is not an incumbent Congressman, for incumbents find it easier to raise money from affluent individuals and from PACs, which prefer to contribute to sitting tenants than to challengers.

There are, then, problems surrounding the sources of money and the unequal distribution of the money available. Attempts have been made to regulate political money, for by the 1960s many commentators were concerned at the escalating costs of election campaigns, the incidence of very rich candidates who could easily outspend their rivals, and the possibility of undue influence being exercised by those who handed over money.

The first significant piece of legislation was the **Federal Election Campaign Act (FECA) of 1971**, which replaced all earlier laws on the subject. All candidates for political office, as well as the individuals, campaign committees, parties and PACs that backed them, were made to declare their contributions. As a result of evidence heard in the Watergate hearings, it was felt necessary to tighten up the restrictions by a new measure three years later.

Two main themes were tackled in 1974: the importance of tough limits on contributions and the need for public funding of election campaigning (see p. 192). The new legislation tightened up the rules for disclosure of campaign income, and restricted the influence of wealthy individuals. Strict limits were imposed on donations by individuals. However, there was no overall limit on the amount that PACs could provide in a single year, although they were restricted to $5,000 per primary and general election campaign. PACs were thus placed at an advantage over other donors, so that, as Grant[1] has pointed out, 'the law effectively increased candidates' reliance on them'.

The changes ensured greater transparency. Voters and interested commentators could now check the disclosures made, and see the resources available to candidates who also had to declare their personal wealth, their property and their debts. The legislation was monitored by the Federal Election Commission, a body widely seen as ineffectual and lacking 'teeth'.

State funding for candidates

A scheme of public financing for presidential candidates was introduced in 1971, and subsequently substantially amended in 1974, 1976 and 1979. It provided, inter alia, for funding of the primary contests and for the main election. For every candidate who could raise $5,000 across twenty states from small individual contributions (under $250), there was to be a matching sum available from the federal government. State aid was not, then, unconditional, but triggered by the decisions of private individuals.

Funds are provided for candidates by means of a tax check-off box on the declaration of income from individual income tax returns. The money collected is then distributed to those candidates who have chosen to opt for public funding. They must accept stringent restrictions upon the raising or spending of corporate money. Most accept the offer of financial assistance, even wealthy candidates such as Ronald Reagan and the two George Bushes.

The scale and control of spending in presidential elections

As we have seen, the law had been used to regulate the raising and spending of money, but there remained a significant difference in the actual provisions of the law and prevailing practice. There were ways in which the regulations can be evaded, particularly by the collection of so-called **soft money**. An amendment to FECA in 1979 allowed parties to raise and spend money to be used on party-building and get-out-the-vote activities, a purpose not easy to distinguish from supporting party candidates. As the amount of spending on these activities significantly increased, there were grounds for suspicion about the ways in which money is used.

soft money

Money contributed in ways and for purposes (such as registration and mass-mailing) which do not infringe the law, as opposed to 'hard money' contributions, which are strictly regulated. Soft money is collected at state and local level, but is often used for national purposes.

The issue of campaign finance in presidential contests periodically reappeared on the political agenda in the years after 1979. It became contentious in the 1990s, as allegations were made of abuses in the 1996 Clinton re-election campaign and in particular of his use of White House facilities for purposes of party fundraising. The Federal Election Commission failed to take action over the allegations, an indication that the earlier legislation was not doing its job. Senator John McCain, made several attempts in the late 1990s to ban the raising and spending of soft money, but the proposal was blocked in the Senate. In spite of widespread support from the public and some politicians, the idea ran into difficulties. Political opponents of further restrictions were concerned that unless there was some control over the structural costs of campaigning (e.g. over advertising), they would find their income restricted and not be able to afford to enter the race, so that the restrictions would benefit only the wealthiest of candidates. The proposals were also opposed on grounds of free speech, as an affront to the First Amendment.

McCain made the issue of further reform a plank of his unsuccessful bid for the Republican candidacy in 2000, and thereafter a momentum developed for a further tightening of the law. When the House and Senate passed a bipartisan measure of campaign finance reform, President Bush – against his earlier inclinations – did not seek to veto it. Accordingly, the McCain–Feingold Campaign Finance Reform Act passed into law in 2002, and was in use by the time of the 2004 elections.

Among other things, the McCain–Feingold reforms:
- banned the national party committees from raising or spending soft money;
- prevented business and labour unions from directly funding **issue advertisements**;
- prohibited the use of business and labour money to broadcast advertisements that named a federal candidate in the 30 days prior to a primary election and the 60 days prior to a general election;
- outlawed any fundraising activities on public property.

The costs of presidential elections have risen dramatically in recent years. In 2004, both candidates spent lavishly. They chose not to accept public finance for their pre-convention campaigns, enabling them to raise and spend as much as they could. President Bush spent approximately $266 million (at least $120 million on TV ads) and John Kerry $221 million ($80 million on advertising). Between them, candidates, parties and independent groups spent at least $1.6 billion on TV ads in 2004, more than double the previous record. (As the advertising figures are all based on ads placed in the largest 100 media markets, they are almost certainly an underestimate.)

issue advertisements

Ads that are similar to the usual political advertisements on behalf of a candidate but do not use words such as 'support' or 'vote'. Moreover, whilst candidate ads are sponsored by a candidate or his or her organisation, issue ads are sponsored by individuals not running for office, corporations, unions or other organisations. Some advocate or oppose the election of a candidate in an implied way (sham issue ads), whereas others seek to mobilise constituents, policymakers or regulators in support of or opposition to legislation (pure issue ads). By purporting to be about issues, sham or candidate-centred issue ads evade restrictions that would otherwise apply.

More could be done to control the influence of wealth in American politics. For instance, airtime could be made available freely to each party for a fixed period, so that being poor or modestly well-off would no longer be a disadvantage. This might have the effect of encouraging more black and other minority candidates to come forward, as well as introducing an element of greater fairness. Candidates could still be expected to pay for the making of their own advertisements, but this is not the problem. It is the frequency with which advertisements are repeated which makes election campaigns so expensive, for what happens is that at present one candidate with greater means available can outgun his or her opponent simply by reiterating the message over and over again.

Participation in American politics

Democracy implies participation, by which we mean that people should be able to take part in the formulation, passage or implementation of policies. Democratic standards are more likely to prevail where people are well informed and willing to get involved. In the *polis*, the city state of ancient Greece, it was considered natural that people would take part in politics; then, to be able to do so was the duty of all citizens.

The United States has always attached great importance to the ideas and values of democracy. Although the founders of the American Republic were wary of majority rule, they none the less believed that most people would be able to take part in the electoral process and thus be able to play a key role in determining the direction which government policy should take. Yet at a time when the electorate is more informed about politics than ever before in its history, we find that turnout in elections is lower than it has been for many years, and involvement in party activity is on a downward slide.

Turnout in presidential and congressional elections

In much of the twentieth century, the successful presidential candidate won an election in which less than half of the eligible electorate turned out to vote, so that the decisions about who should govern the country and the direction in which it should be led were in the hands of a minority of the population. The 1960 presidential contest had a better turnout than usual, but since then the percentage voting has declined more or less continuously, as the figures below indicate. However, in 2004 the interest of the voters was more engaged by the Bush versus Kerry contest, when there seemed to be the prospect of a close race between candidates who were dissimilar in much of their political thinking. On this occasion, the improvement represented the biggest election-to-election increase since 1952. The highest turnout was in Minnesota (77.3%), the lowest in Hawaii (48.9%).

The figures are unimpressive by European standards. They suggest that the US lags well behind Britain, which itself has a smaller turnout than most other countries. Whereas Britain has usually achieved a turnout of almost 75% in general elections (a figure that dropped decisively in 2001), 55% has been good by American standards. The comparison is not, however, an entirely appropriate one, for British figures relate to the number registered who vote, whereas American ones are based upon the number of Americans over the minimum voting age who actually do so. According to V. O. Key,[2] the difference may be worth as many as six or seven percentage points.

Turnout in presidential elections since 1960

Year	People voting (%)
1960	63.8
1968	61.0
1976	54.4
1984	53.0
1992	53.0
2000	59.4

The US presidential campaign gets massive television exposure, for it dominates the media from the time of the first primaries through to November. This might have been expected to generate interest and excitement, but yet in the media age we are faced by broad decline. This fall is the more notable if we bear in mind the increase in the size of the potential electorate since the 1970s. The passage of the 1965 Voting Rights Act added many black voters to the list of those eligible to vote. Moreover, women have become more politically involved in that period, and their turnout levels have risen to such an extent that more women turned out than men in the 1996 and 2000 elections. Finally, given the overall increase in education and living standards one might have expected that more would be inspired to vote, the more so as it is traditionally the least well-off who are the most reluctant to vote.

Yet some half of the registered electorate does not turn out even in presidential contests, and for other elections the number is considerably greater still. In an off-year (when there is no presidential contest), the average figure for turnout is 35–40% in congressional elections, and in primaries the figure is often below 30%.

Why are turnouts so low?

Several reasons for low turnouts have been given, but among them **registration** arrangements have always been seen as important. In most states it is up to individuals to register themselves as qualified voters before election day. Failure to do so disqualifies anyone from using their right, even if in other respects they are eligible to do so. Registration involves either meeting a registrar or filling out a form at the country courthouse. When allowance is made for this responsibility and for age and residential qualifications, it is evident that there is built-in discouragement to voting.

A change was introduced in 1993 when President Clinton signed the so-called **motor voter** bill, designed to ease the process of registration. Citizens are now able to register when they apply for a driving licence (hence the name) or some other form of public document. Furthermore, states must designate a public office concerned with providing help to the public, a place where assistance is also available with voter registration – such as a state welfare agency. The effects should have been to enable and encourage more people to turn out on election day, for it has long been the case that in those states with same-day or no registration, turnout is considerably above the national average.

The new legislation operated from 1995, and within eight months some 5,000,000 new voters registered. Some commentators predicted that if this momentum was maintained, almost four out of every five voters would be registered by the end of the century. It was not, and today some 66% of Americans are registered to vote, a few percentage points up on the situation before 'motor voting' was introduced. Yet in 1996 and 2000, the turnout figures were disappointingly low. As president, George Bush senior had vetoed a measure such as 'motor voting', perhaps in the belief that the Democrats would benefit more from a higher turnout. His fears seem to have been largely unjustified.

Alternative explanations include the following.

1 **Apathy**: some have used apathy as an explanation, but surveys of political interest suggest that if anything Americans are rather more politically interested than people in many other democracies. Voting does, however, require more personal effort than elsewhere for the reasons we have given, and the frequency of elections could result in voter fatigue and a loss of interest.

2 **lack of a meaningful choice between the parties**: some commentators would suggest that voters who are registered fail to detect any real difference between the parties, and that the electors feel that a choice between Tweedledum and Tweedledee is not one worth attempting to make. They say 'a plague on both your houses', and see parties as increasingly irrelevant to their lives. No party really addresses their concerns.

3 **The lack of an inspiring choice of candidates**: others say that the quality of political leaders fails to inspire, and there are too many unattractive personalities who become candidates. Discontent with the available choice was a much-discussed feature of the Bush versus Dukakis contest, the 'Wimp' v. 'the Shrimp' (1988), the Clinton versus Dole contest in 1996, and the Bush versus Gore contest in 2000.

4 **The composition of the electorate**: broadly speaking, middle-class people, those with a professional education and with a college education, are more likely to turn out than unskilled working people or those whose qualifications

are only a high-school diploma or less. Again, family influence may be significant. In those homes where there is a tradition of participation, it is more likely that future generations will turn out to vote and become more generally involved in political life.

Certain groups have persistently been more reluctant to vote. Non-voting is greater in the South and in rural areas, among the young, among the less educated, and among the minorities such as the black population and Hispanics. Young people (under 24) have regularly been less disposed to involve themselves in the electoral process, although those who claim a clear allegiance to one of the main parties are markedly more willing to vote than those who are apathetic about politics and current affairs. Whites are more likely to vote than blacks, blacks than Hispanics. Groups that shun the democratic process are ones that make up an increasing proportion of the electorate.

5 **The nature of electioneering**: it may be that negative advertising produces disillusionment with the Washington politicians and the political system in general, and that this contributes to the falling turnouts of the last generation. In the 1994 elections, it was suggested that one of the most toxic campaigns in living memory had left many people turned off politicians. American voters have become more disengaged from political strategy as the style of advertising increasingly antagonises them. Elections are seen, in Hames's words, as 'over-long, over-slick and dominated by the mass media with a premium on character attacks on political opponents'.[3]

6 **Other factors**: the theory has been advanced[4] that America is now in a post-electoral era. More and more voters see parties and elections as no longer very significant. Now, major decisions are made by investigating committees and the courts, and through media revelations. The traditional processes have had their day.

Another idea is that non-voting is broadly a sign of contentment with the political system. If Americans felt worried, because their country was in crisis, they might feel inclined to turn out to avert a national catastrophe. But in times of peace and prosperity, most Americans are happy to leave the politicians to get on with their task; there is less need to vote.

Alternative forms of participation

Political issues are not the be-all and end-all of most people's lives, and – like most people – Americans are concerned with bread-and-butter matters such as making a living, improving their family position and enjoying their leisure. The level of interest varies sharply between different groups of the community, but the findings of the 1992 American National Election Study, conducted by the University of Michigan, show that only 26% were interested for 'most of the time', 41% for 'some of the time' and 21% 'only now and then'; 11% were 'hardly at all' committed.

Many people may find politics a complicated process. Surveys of political knowledge and understanding reveal widespread public ignorance. According to a survey by the *American Political Science Review* (September 1980), 40% of those interviewed could not name one of their state's senators. Ignorance covers personalities and policies. Given such a lack of interest and information, participation in the political process is inevitably unlikely to be very high.

Those who possess knowledge and understanding tend to participate more. They are often the better-educated people who read a newspaper, watch current affairs programmes and engage in political discourse with their relatives and friends. At the other end are those who participate very little, the

---

Town meetings in New England: direct democracy in action

The purest form of direct democracy was to be found in ancient Greece. All qualified citizens were allowed to participate in the government of their city state. They were encouraged and expected to play a positive role in controlling their own lives, rather than leaving it to others to act on their behalf. Such direct democracy is no longer seen as possible in large, modern industrial societies, and the nearest approximation in most countries is the use of the referendum and/or initiative. However, in New England, town meetings have operated ever since the first British settlements.

The experience of meetings in the six states of that region has been variously described as 'the Secret Flame of democracy'[7] and 'a bedrock form of democratic expression'.[8] Of Maine's 493 incorporated municipalities, 440 have a town-meeting form of government, in which residents attend for a morning or a day to chart their communal course. Topics debated range widely, from property taxes to budgets for administration, from same-sex marriages to nuts-and-bolts issues concerning local facilities.

Town meetings are not without their critics and there are problems with the way they function today. In particular:
- Often meetings are not well attended. Rarely do more than 10% of registered voters turn out to participate, and the trend has been consistently downwards in recent years. In a recent study, Joseph Zimmerman[9] has examined figures collected for the last three decades and finds the trend is common to all six states. He sees declining attendance as a parallel to the downward trend in voter turnout in state and national elections, and as correlating with towns' increasing difficulties in finding candidates to run for local office and volunteers to run fire departments.
- Those who can attend are often self-employed, retired or otherwise not working at regular daytime jobs, and therefore are unlikely to reflect accurately the opinions of

least educated who may feel isolated from the political world, which they may see as having let them down. Many of those who are somewhere in between, having sporadic interest in politics, will join in from time to time. They will vote in certain elections that seem relevant or interesting to them – as we have seen, more often in presidential ones than the rest. These people will occasionally discuss political issues at times of peak media attention, but for much of the time choose not to read about or view what is going on.

The issue of political participation has been one of lively debate. Back in 1835, the liberal French aristocrat Alexis de Tocqueville[5] visited America and was much impressed by what he saw of the way it was governed and of how society functioned. He observed that 'Americans of all ages, all stations in life, and all types of disposition are forever forming associations'. He portrayed them as belonging to 'the most democratic country in the world', extolling their involvement in groups which helped them pursue 'the objects of common desires'.

---

local citizens. An article in a local newspaper in Maine[10] carried a report that in Kingfield '65 people are calling the shots for the entire town', and that officials in the New England towns of Eustis and Strong also reported low, unrepresentative turnouts: 'in Farmington, a town of 7,600, only 80 people attended the annual meeting'.

Several reasons have been advanced for declining turnout:
- Even at the level of a small New England town, society is now too large and complex for direct democracy to be a complete success. Towns used to be smaller, with more of a sense of community. Urbanisation has affected even New England, and people are now too busy, often travelling some distance to work. Meetings take too long for those with little time available. They can spend their spare time on various forms of entertainment.
- Voters are frustrated and disenchanted with government at all levels.
- Many people are better off than ever before and therefore feel that it is not a matter of serious personal self-interest whether they attend.
- There are no burning issues in municipal government.

Town meetings have been described[11] as 'alive, but troubled'. In some towns they have actually ceased to exist, ten out of the thirty-one towns in Rhode Island having abandoned them; turnout in the remaining towns in that state is often exceptionally low, at 4–5%. Voters are experimenting with alternatives to the traditional open town meeting. Some opt for meetings where the time is spent in directly voting on a series of referendum questions; others prefer either representative town meetings, for which residents elect representatives to vote on their behalf (anyone can stand and speak, but only the representatives can vote), straightforward town councils or citizen-initiated referendums. It is in the smaller towns and more rural areas of northern New England that town meetings continue to function best.

In a controversial study, Robert Putnam[6] suggests that the willingness of Americans to engage in political life has diminished in recent decades. He argues that there is now a 'degree of social disengagement and civic connectedness' which has damaging consequences for political life. He believes that social participation is declining in the USA, observing that today more people spend time watching *Friends* than making them! More seriously, he points to static levels of political knowledge in spite of the development of university education: in addition, fewer people engage in volunteer work (there may be more pressure groups, but average membership is only 10% of its 1962 level and members tend to take a less active role), belong to trade unions, attend church or public meetings, vote in elections or trust government.

Of course, there are more opportunities for participation than voting alone. Americans can involve themselves in election campaigns, join political parties and pressure groups, and take part in protest marches and forms of direct action (see p. 286–8). The American system also offers the citizens of some states an opportunity for direct participation in decision-making, which is generally denied to the British electorate except on rare constitutional issues. This is done via the **town meeting** (see pp. 198–9) in New England, and via the initiative and **referendum** (see pp. 222–6) in many areas of the country.

Participation in various forms of electoral activity (% of total US population)

Type of activity	% of total US population
Discuss politics from time to time	81
Try to persuade others	35
Wear badge, sport sticker or sign	10
Attend meetings, rallies	6
Do other campaign work	3
Contribute to candidate	7
Contribute to political party	6

Adapted from figures produced in the 2000 National Election Study, University of Michigan.

THE MEDIA

Democracy requires the free flow of ideas, information and comment, and the role of the mass media is central in influencing public opinion; the media both reflect it and help to mould it. For many people, it is through the media that they become acquainted with what is happening in the world and form their own viewpoint on issues. There is much academic debate as to whether television in particular actually creates opinions or reinforces them.

The media are sometimes described as 'the fourth branch of government', rivaling the three main official branches in their political influence and power. Here we are concerned to examine the ways in which they influence modern electioneering.

THE TERMINOLOGY OF MODERN ELECTIONS

Photo-opportunities

Carefully stage-managed episodes in which the leading figure is set against a particular background – perhaps to demonstrate concern for the area or its industry. For example, Ronald Reagan favoured the image of the all-American cowboy, riding on horseback into the sunset, thereby conjuring up in the mind of the electors an image of the great outdoors as part of the wholesome American dream.

Sound-bites

Short sayings, full of concentrated meaning, which consists of a few easily-remembered words, and yet convey a particular message. Examples are Reagan's 'You ain't seen nothin' yet' and George Bush senior's 'Read my lips. No new taxes' – a slogan which backfired when, as President, he found himself supporting higher taxation.

The Rev. Jesse Jackson is a master of 'soundbitese'. Recognising that he will get perhaps 15 seconds on a news bulletin, he can summarise his argument in an exciting epigram. His rhyming sound-bite 'we're going to have demonstrations without hesitation and jail without bail' was a more memorable and catchy way of saying that 'we are not going to spend a long time deciding whether to have a demonstration. We are willing to go to gaol for our cause and will not accept bail.'

Spin-doctors

Part of the media team, their task being to change the way the public perceive some happening, or to alter their expectations of what might occur. Spin-doctors try to put a favourable gloss on information and events. Spin has become an accepted feature of campaigns in the US. The term derives from the spin given to a ball in various sports, originally baseball, to make it go in a direction which confuses the opponent.

By the media, we mean the various forms of communication available. By the **mass media** we mean those which in the modern day are available on a large scale. All are concerned with the dissemination of ideas in the form of information, entertainment and persuasion. However, if the term is all-embracing, in popular usage it is applied particularly to television and the press.

mass media
Those means of communication, such as newspapers, radio and television, which permit messages to reach the mass public.

Television has now become the most important of the ways via which the candidates seek to gain popular approval and support. Although party managers may still be interviewed and seek to use the medium to promote the party cause, it is the candidates who are the focus of media attention. They and their teams of consultants are constantly on the look-out for opportunities to ensure that they gain favourable coverage, and are vigilant in watching out for any signs of bias against them. They attempt to 'manage the news'.

Media management involves ensuring that journalists get the right stories (information slanted to the candidates' particular viewpoint) backed up with good pictures. It can range from crude political arm-twisting to more subtle means. Advisers dream up sound-bites and

> **media management**
> The techniques used by politicians and their advisers to control the information given to the media.

photo-opportunities, and use their spin-doctors to put across an appropriate line (see box opposite). They try to book interviews with 'softer' interviewers, rather than undergo a potentially damaging interrogation. They seek to control the agenda, sticking to themes on which they are strong and avoiding (or downplaying) embarrassing issues.

The presidential in 2004

The 2004 televised debates followed the broad pattern established over recent years, with three 90-minute debates between the two main presidential candidates, and one contest of similar length between the vice-presidential candidates. There was much more popular interest than four years earlier, the audience for the first debate being higher than for any over the previous twelve years.

The commentators and party managers were once again on the look-out for any perceived slips by either candidate. Such lapses were likely to be mercilessly revisited in TV ads in the last stages of the campaign. In the event, challenger John Kerry turned in three confident performances and emerged with enhanced credentials. Most post-debate findings showed him to be the winner on each occasion, although importantly the president committed no serious errors. Kerry's ratings in the opinion polls markedly improved as a result, for whereas he was several percentage points behind on the eve of the first debate, by the end that lead had more or less evaporated.

In the third debate, Bush attempted to engage the audience with jokes, which mostly fell flat in the formal setting of the debate. But he did raise laughter from the audience, when an opportunity allowed him to show a flash of his sometimes self-deprecating style. When the candidates were asked by the moderator what they had learned from the strong

Presidential debates

The presidential and vice-presidential debates have been of varying quality, and the rules of engagement have differed from election to election. The one which has been endlessly quoted was that held in 1960 between Kennedy and Nixon. Kennedy looked handsome, impressive and youthful, whereas his opponent looked unshaven and untrustworthy. The debate was broadcast on radio and television, and significantly, whereas polling showed that a majority of listeners thought that Nixon had emerged on top, a majority of viewers was in no doubt that Kennedy had won. When Kennedy did win, it was by the narrowest of margins, by 0.5% of the popular vote. It may well be that television swung the outcome.

Debates did not take place for several years, but resumed in 1976. Since then, they have been a regular feature of the presidential campaign and have almost certainly made a difference to the outcome of some elections, on occasion a decisive one. In a close-run contest the importance of appearing steady and in control is supreme. If you cannot win, it is crucial to avoid mistakes. Errors have been made and some have been costly. Apart from the Nixon performance in 1960, the other famous or infamous gaffe was the moment in

---

women in their families, the president chose to respond by referring to criticisms of his performance in the first debate. He said: 'To listen to them. To stand up straight and not scowl.' Kerry also showed a self-deprecating side at that moment, by answering the moderator in this way: 'I guess the president and you and I are three examples of lucky people who married up. And [in reference to his marriage to the heiress of the Heinz fortune], some would say maybe me more so than others.'

If Kerry won the debates, he did not win the presidency. Party loyalists were confirmed in their views. Their judgement of who won on each of the three occasions was determined by the person they favoured at the beginning of the campaign. Some don't knows were probably won over to Kerry's side, and passive observers may have been turned into actual voters, because there was a prospect of a close finish. But many Americans who agreed that, on balance, Kerry won the debates and showed himself stronger on the issues still voted for Bush. Fluent debating skills are not essentials for the presidency, and the widespread perception that Bush was the man best able to provide strong national leadership, counted for more on election day. It may be also that the challenger alienated some undecided viewers by his unprompted reference to vice-president Dick Cheney's lesbian daughter in the third encounter, although the apparent blunder was unlikely to have made a significant difference.

1976 when Jimmy Carter benefited from a fatal howler committed by his opponent, Gerald Ford, the Republican president. At a time when the Cold War was still a determining factor in international diplomacy, Ford said that Poland was not then under Eastern European domination! On other occasions, comments made by one candidate have opened up an opportunity for the other to hit back and score effectively. When George Bush senior attacked Governor Clinton for protesting against the Vietnam War, the challenger was smart in his response:

> When [Senator] Joe McCarthy went around this country attacking people's patriotism, he was wrong. And a Senator from Connecticut stood up to him named Prescott Bush. Your father was right to stand up to Joe McCarthy; you were wrong to attack my patriotism. I was opposed to the war, but I love my country.

Presidential debates have become the pre-eminent media event of the campaign, and they attract a vast, if – until 2004 – generally declining, audience. At their best, they are a useful means of providing each candidate with an opportunity to reach a mass audience. Their impact is unlikely to change the allegiances of the committed voters. More often, it will confirm them in their predisposition. However, on the increasing number of non-aligned voters, a strong or weak performance may have an all-important effect. Debates help viewers to assess character and ability, and may also increase their knowledge and understanding of politics. This is why media advisers are so concerned to get the details right.

Political advertising

The quality of individuals and the image they present is also important in political advertising. Here, the emphasis is often less upon the assets of the candidate than upon the deficiencies of the opponent. Advertising can be blatantly unfair.

Political advertising began in 1952, with Eisenhower's 30-minute biographical portrait, as 'the man from Abilene'. The scale of advertising has significantly increased in recent years, and the advertisements have become much shorter. Advertisers know that the public can only take in so much information at any one time. During the vice-presidential race of that same year, Richard Nixon took 30 minutes of paid television time to answer charges of corruption in front of 58 million viewers. Nowadays, advertisers specialise in the 60-second or (more often) the 30-second or even 15-second commercial which makes a point briefly, yet dramatically.

Americans have often used advertisements which are autobiographical in style. Television is good at handling personalities and stories, and some of the most effective advertisements judiciously combine the two elements. Not all advertisements are of this form. Advertising is overwhelmingly negative. It goes for the jugular and is potentially damaging to electoral prospects (see box below). Often, it pinpoints alleged deficiencies in the moral character of an opponent, as with the candidate in Tennessee who was congratulated by his opponents for 'kicking [his] chemical dependency'. Sometimes, it highlights inconsistency, as when the Bush senior campaign team in 1992 showed two politicians expressing directly opposite views on issues ranging from the first Gulf War to drug use. As the faces became clear, a voice-over observed that: 'One of these politicians is Bill Clinton. Unfortunately, so is the other!'

In 2004, some commentators noted that the vast majority of campaign ads were reaching only a relatively small proportion of the electorate, but in the days after the conclusion of the debates there was a final blitz in which some of the content of those encounters was revisited constantly. Both sides used attack advertising, although the Bush team employed this approach more often. About a third of the Bush ads were negative ones criticising the Kerry's record, over his service record in Vietnam, his inconsistency on the Iraq War and his flip-flops over many policy areas.

The Little Girl and the Daisy

In 1964, President Lyndon Johnson's campaign used the *Little Girl and the Daisy* commercial, which has been described as 'a seminal work in the history of television propaganda'.[12] Faced with an opponent, Barry Goldwater, who had made intemperate remarks about the possibility of fighting a limited nuclear war, the advert showed a little girl picking off the petals of a daisy and counting one, two, three. As she reached ten, the picture froze and then zoomed to her eye as viewers heard a missile countdown, ten, nine, eight and so on, down to one. There followed a picture of a nuclear explosion, before the president intoned: 'This then is the choice, whether to love each other or to go into the dark. We must love each other or die.'

Without mentioning the opponent by name, the advert skilfully linked him to the prospect of nuclear war. The safety of the human race was at stake. Who would wish to harm an innocent girl playing in a field? The answer, by implication, was Barry Goldwater.

It is arguable whether ads such as this one change people's outlook or voting intention, or whether they simply reinforce existing opinions. This ad played upon and confirmed feelings and suspicions that many voters already had about Goldwater, even if they were unclear about the details of what he was saying. The charge was the more damaging because it was set out in such a way that it was difficult for him to refute. An impression was left in the voter's mind. It hurt the Goldwater campaign. He lost the election by a landslide.

Bill Schneider, an American political scientist,[12] sees negative advertising as a very efficient tool: 'For one thing, it's easier in 30 seconds to turn people off your opponent than to build a positive case for yourself – especially since

THE MEDIA IN BRITAIN AND THE UNITED STATES: A COMPARISON

In both countries, the media fulfil similar functions of entertaining and informing the public. Both have a privately owned press which is often accused of political bias, and there are similar worries about concentration of ownership in too few hands and a consequent lack of diversity of opinion. In Britain, there is a much more vigorous national press, whereas in the USA many people read a more local paper; in both countries, newspaper readership is in decline.

Television has come to dominate political coverage, especially at election time. It has tended to personalise politics, so that there is now more emphasis on the qualities of those who lead and less on serious discussion of issues. American campaigns are more candidate-centred (see pp. 189–90), but in recent years commentators have frequently portrayed British party conflict in terms of the Blair–Major, or Blair–Howard conflict. Similar allegations of trivialisation are made on both sides of the Atlantic, a recognition of the fact that television is primarily a means of entertainment.

The Americanisation of British politics?

Britain has in many ways learnt from the American experience. Campaigners have visited the United States and sometimes participated in elections there. Inevitably, their findings have been relayed to their colleagues back home. In addition, people in Britain see pictures of presidential electioneering, and there has often been discussion in the media of the techniques employed. As a result, America has been a useful source of innovation in British campaign techniques. Just as the Conservatives under Margaret Thatcher absorbed a lot from the Reagan experience in the mid-to-late 1980s, so too the Labour Party was keen to derive insights from the success of the Democrat Bill Clinton in 1992 and again in 1996.

In recent years, there has been an increasing British obsession with walkabouts, photo-opportunities and other pseudo-events created for the media. In the late 1980s and

television is a medium particularly suited for carrying negative, warning-style messages . . . you get more bang for the buck by running negative ads.'

ELECTING THE PRESIDENT: A CHOICE BY ELECTORAL COLLEGE

Running for the presidency involves three stages:
- winning the support of delegates to the party convention;
- winning the approval of the convention itself;

1990s, there were several examples of the Americanisation of politics at work, not least in the style of some party broadcasts (*Kinnock – the Movie*, 1987), and in the Sheffield Rally of 1992, a triumphalist occasion very reminiscent of the American convention.

Yet there are differences, and some safeguards from the British point of view. In Britain, we are electing a party rather than just one person, and politics is not about personality alone. The in-depth interview provides a kind of antidote to the dangers of shallow but media-friendly leaders being chosen, for their personal qualities come under heavy scrutiny, and in the Sunday lunch-time type of programme policy deficiencies can be exposed. We also can now see our representatives in action in the House of Commons, and Question Time at least is an institution which shows those in power being forced to defend their position, even if it does little to inform people of the issues. The interviews conducted in the election in *Election Call* are a reminder of how leading figures can be put on the spot by skilful members of the public who can unsettle their composure.

But most people do not watch such encounters, and the likelihood is that those people who use television the most to obtain their information may be the very ones who are least discerning and able to come to a reasonable conclusion based on knowledge. They probably don't read other sources, and therefore what they see and hear has a potent effect on the least sophisticated electors.

Party broadcasts instead of political advertisements, free airtime, vigilant journalists, in-depth political interviews, and politicians more prepared to answer questions about their proposals help to differentiate the British from the US experience in certain respects, and are some kind of protection against our adopting the worst aspects of American election-eering methods. Yet as we have seen, the party broadcasts themselves have to some degree 'gone American' in style and form.

It may be that on this side of the Atlantic we are less susceptible to the excesses of emotionalism and negative campaigning that beset American politics.

- winning in the presidential race following the autumn campaign (the general election).

Winning delegates to the convention

The first stage in the process of choosing a new president is for the parties to choose their nominee, and this consumes several months of the election year. Any person who hopes to become a presidential candidate has to decide when to launch his or her bid for the White House. Some make a decision to stand soon after the last election is over, but any announcement of the intention is not usually made until the year before the election at the earliest, even if campaign planning is already actively under way. Candidates and those who manage their campaigns know the importance of lining up support and raising funds before their declaration.

Candidates have to decide how to navigate the primaries and caucuses that take place in the early months of the presidential year, and this decision involves a number of considerations. Until the 1970s, it was not common for candidates to take the primary route, but this has become the accepted procedure for any 'hopeful' to adopt. A decision not to stand entails the risk of losing momentum whilst others secure the support of party delegations.

The arrangements vary in detail from state to state, and in some cases the parties in a particular state employ different approaches. But today the use of primaries is the accepted method by both parties in most of them. Eight states use a caucus and/or convention system, the details of which are laid down by its legislature. In those using caucuses, the party organisation is still important, whereas in those using conventions the choice of national delegates is made by people who are themselves delegates from local meetings.

The primary route

More than 80% of the delegates in 1992 were chosen as a result of primary contests, and most candidates now take the primary route. They need to decide which primaries to enter, but whereas it was once common for a candidate to miss some of the early ones this is now seen as a high-risk strategy. Jimmy Carter decided to seek the Democratic nomination by staging a nationwide primary campaign and involved himself in the early contests and as many as he could thereafter. This is now the usual policy, and most commentators believe that it is wise to enter as many as possible. Candidates tend to choose contests where they are likely to make a good showing. The number of rivals, their personal standing in the opinion polls, local interests, the timing of the contest, and their level of financial backing all play a part in the decisions made.

The first primary takes place in New Hampshire, and a strong performance in the early contests can lend a useful momentum to the campaign and help to demoralise rivals who do less well. Many states have now brought their primaries forward, hoping that this will give their voters a greater influence on the final choice of candidates. As a result of this 'front-loading', some 70% of the delegates to the convention have been selected by the end of March.

To do well in the primaries, candidates need to manoeuvre with some skill. The opposition in each primary will vary, and tactics used to defeat a strong rival in one state may not work in another. Media coverage, as well as financial and human resources, is relevant to the outcome, and candidates looking for good coverage will spend heavily on the early contests in their bid to gain popular momentum. It is important for the candidates and those who support them to use the media wisely and to downplay the expectations of what they might achieve. If they then do well, this gives their campaign a boost. If it is widely expected that they will perform well as the front runner, then a disappointing outcome (even though it is a technical victory) can cost valuable momentum.

The presidential primaries are the arena in which lively personal battles are fought, and they are conducted under intense public scrutiny by the media and commentators. Sometimes, the battles have been so savage at this stage that great damage is done to party unity.

Winning support at the convention

The national nominating conventions are held over a four-day period in July and August. By then, the outcome is usually a foregone conclusion, and normally the successful candidate is chosen on the first ballot. Delegates are now forced to pledge themselves to a definite candidate for at least the first two ballots, although in the past this was not the case and delegates arrived with varying degrees of commitment.

Once the candidate has been chosen, the nominee makes an acceptance speech and receives homage as the party's standard-bearer for the forthcoming struggle. At this point, the intra-party battle that has dominated the political scene for so many months becomes unimportant, and the concentration of those present has to be on the contest with the other party. As Malcolm Vile[14] has observed: 'This switch from the bitterness of internal conflict to the competition between parties is one of the perennial wonders of the American political scene.'

The convention comprises those delegates elected in primaries, caucuses or state conventions. Their task is to choose the presidential candidate (in effect, already done) and the vice-presidential nominee – a choice actually made by the presidential candidate and invariably ratified by those assembled. Delegates also help to write the party platform, and at this stage there is often a tussle between different factions, which seek to move the party in their direction. The policy statement is not binding on the two people chosen to run for the White House, but as it indicates prevalent feeling in the party, candidates do not usually ignore such an expression of the mood of the faithful.

The conclusion of the national convention season brings to an end a long-drawn-out process for which the candidates have been planning and working for many months – if not years. As a result, the two main presidential candidates have been chosen and are ready for the main battle ahead. But there is an alternative way by which presidential candidates can be placed on the ballot for the November election, one which shuns the primary/convention route. This involves a would-be challenger complying with the petition requirements in each individual state (difficult in Maryland, where 3% – approximately 60,000 signatures – is required; simple in Louisiana, where payment of a filing fee of $500 is sufficient).

Ross Perot fulfilled these requirements in each individual state, for his funding and voluntary support enabled his cause to be well represented across the nation. Once on the ballot paper, it is these days much more possible to achieve national prominence without the backing of a political party, as the candidacy of Perot showed. Television can provide ample exposure, via chat-show and other appearances. It was a matter of some pride to Perot that he was able to run an efficient and effective campaign without dipping too heavily into his own substantial private fortune. Without any established party organisation, he was able to launch a highly successful bid in 1992 and eventually win 19% of the popular vote in November.

Winning the presidential race

There is only a short pause between the end of the convention and the beginning of the campaign, and in this time the parties are concerned to pull together again after what can be a wounding primary process. They also devise their strategy for the final stage – the bid for the White House.

The campaign, and in particular the ever-growing importance of television, are discussed on pp. 188–90 and 200–6. Some of the important features are:
- the growing use of market research;
- the use of professional consultants and assorted media gurus;
- the increasing attention to the importance of photo-opportunities, to provide the media with pictures as well as words;
- a concentration on themes which appear appropriate for the national mood;
- the use of television opportunities, ranging from chat shows to interviews and, of course, the presidential debates.

Much depends on creating the right image for the candidate, who at this stage needs to adopt a stance that can appeal to many Americans of all social groups, well beyond the confines of traditional party support. The candidate needs to be attuned to the mood of the hour. Franklin Roosevelt caught the popular imagination in 1932 with his promise of dynamic action; John F. Kennedy seemed to embody the hopes of those who wanted to see America move forward to the challenge of New Frontiers, in 1960; Bill Clinton was presented as a man who might get America moving again in 1992, after a period in which domestic policy had been neglected.

Of course, doubts about a candidate's personal standards of behaviour can throw the strategy off course. But in Clinton's case in 1992, he was able to keep the economy in the forefront despite the attempt of the Bush team to portray him in a negative way – just as it had successfully painted a picture of Dukakis as 'soft' on issues of public concern, such as crime. In 1992, it was perhaps easier for the Democrat to stick to his emphasis on the pivotal role of the economy, for Ross Perot was also making this the central element in his campaign.

The election takes place on the first Tuesday after the first Monday in November.

The Electoral College and how it works

The method of becoming president in the United States is in many ways a clumsy and protracted process. A candidate needs to acquire 270 votes in the Electoral College, out of the 538 available. Each state is apportioned a number of votes according to the number of seats it possesses in Congress: two for the Senate and a variable number for the House of Representatives.

Because of the equal representation of each state in the Senate, the smaller states are overrepresented in the Electoral College. Delaware and Vermont, with well under a million people each, still have three votes. The electors in the college formally make the choice of the person to become president, just as they separately decide on the vice-presidency also. The choice is not made by the ordinary voter, who when he or she went to the polling station in 2004 actually voted for electors who were pledged to Kerry/Edwards or Bush/Cheney. In each state, the candidate who received the largest popular vote won all of the college vote, though Maine and Nebraska have a slightly different procedure.

If, when the electors in the college are making their choice, no candidate gains a majority, then the choice is thrown open to the House of Representatives, which chooses from among the top three candidates. If there is no majority for the position of vice-president, then the choice goes to the Senate, which chooses between the first two candidates. If it became necessary to use this process, then it is the new Congress just elected (e.g. November 2004) rather than the old one that makes the choice. Theoretically, it would be possible for the two houses to choose candidates from different parties, so that in 2000 the House could have opted for Gore, the Senate for Cheney.

From this short account, it becomes apparent that it is essential for any presidential candidate to win in the Electoral College. To achieve this, he or she needs to perform strongly in the large urban and suburban states that have so much influence. Indeed, it has often been said that to become president it is necessary to win in California; its 55 votes are a greater number than those of the 12 least populated states and the District of Columbia all combined. Texas (34), New York (31), Florida (27), Illinois (21) and Pennsylvania (21) have a significant number of votes. A candidate is likely to focus attention particularly on such large states and on those where he or she can expect to fare well.

The importance of certain individual states dictates the strategy of any would-be contender. Candidates who can win in California and other large states are at an advantage over those who can do fairly well in every state. Most do not aim to win across the nation and often fight less than enthusiastically in some hostile territory. For this reason, it is important for the main parties to have a candidate of wide appeal in the states that are liable to go one way or the other. To choose a candidate from a safe state wastes the possible bonus of choosing a local person in a state or region in which there is a chance of success. For the Democrats in 1992, the choice of Clinton was a useful way of trying to restore the party's fortunes in a region where its support had been eroded over the Reagan years.

Such considerations are in the mind of the parties and commentators as they ponder the campaign scene in a presidential year. But the other factor of great significance is television, the impact of which is enormous. It has made the country one vast constituency, and concentrated attention on the personal appeal and overall abilities of the candidate. Because of this, the campaign is increasingly in the hands of the advisers and gurus who collectively enjoy the label of 'political consultants'.

Yet as we have seen, this is not the end of the process. The result of the contest may be known within a few hours of the close of polling, but it is another month before the actual election of the president takes place – when the members of the Electoral College cast their votes. The event is largely unnoticed in the outside world, yet it is of profound importance even if the actual outcome is a formality in almost every case.

Because the smaller states are proportionally overrepresented in the college, it is possible for a candidate to win the most popular votes in the country but not the majority of the votes in the Electoral College. This has happened in the past – in 1824, in 1876 and in 1888 – and it happened again in 2000. It nearly happened in 1960 and 1976, elections that were closely contested. Neither of the men elected in those years, Kennedy or Carter, received a popular majority of the votes cast, and nor did Bill Clinton in either of his two victories.

The method of choosing the president assessed

The process of choosing an American president is long, complex and expensive, in the eyes of many outside observers. It certainly tests the mettle of any candidate for the highest office, and, particularly in an age of television, any contender who can emerge relatively unscathed after such a prolonged procedure must have considerable powers of endurance and stamina. Hence Vile's[15] reference to 'almost lethal' demands.

The system enables the person chosen to become established as a national figure. In the case of someone such as General Eisenhower, his reputation was already well known. This is not the case with many of the persons who seek to win the presidency via the primary route. Jimmy Carter was an 'outsider' from Georgia, unknown to the Washington elite in 1975, a year before he was elected to the White House. Others may be more familiar, but the way in which presidential candidates emerge does ensure that they become national figures by the time they come to take office. Either by travel in the past or especially via television today, they have been exposed to the critical gaze of millions of American voters, and have been forced to sell their personalities, to demonstrate an understanding of the needs and wishes of the voters, and to show that they are worthy of the voters' respect, trust and support as the country's leader.

Yet there are many criticisms that can be made of the way in which the US chooses its national leader. Some concern the primaries, some the Electoral College and others the system of election and the nature of the campaign. There is a heavy reliance on the media, increasing professionalism and expense, yet the result is low turnouts and mounting public cynicism.

The primary system is often criticised because of the number and timing of the various contests, a situation which forces candidates to navigate the primary season with some dexterity. They need to stand in as many contests as possible, although this can be very costly and involves putting their names down in several states which ballot on the same day; for instance, several primaries in the South are held on Super Tuesday, in early March. This makes a campaign difficult to organise and conduct.

A possible improvement would be to hold a national presidential primary, an election on a single day across the whole country, in the late spring or autumn. As an alternative, the separate state primaries could all be held on the same day. Such a one-off election would reduce the demands on the candidate, attract much media publicity (and therefore a higher turnout?) and produce a fair and representative verdict. But would it increase the role of television and emphasise the professionalism of the modern campaign, with all of its advisers, consultants and preoccupation with image-building? Would it not

What qualities make a good presidential candidate?

Ideally, candidates should represent a large, pivotal state which they will have a chance of winning. They should have broad appeal, having the ability to carry some, preferably most, key states, which means being well received in California, on the east coast and in the South. They also need the flexibility to cope with the demands of the primary struggle – requiring an ability to enthuse the party faithful – and then, having won the nomination, to seem less partisan figures who can widen their area of potential support by reaching out to many non-committed Americans.

Candidates normally have a record of public service, sometimes as senators, but recently more probably as state governors. Preferably, they will not be identified too strongly with particular views, for it is likely that on contentious issues this will create many opponents. Broad intelligence allied to vagueness on policy is a useful recipe. It is desirable, if not strictly necessary, to show an appropriate interest in and knowledge of significant topics, and by the tone of one's observations to seem to be in touch with public concern. Neither Ronald Reagan nor George W. Bush proved to be intellectually high-powered, but both managed to create the impression that their hopes and fears resonate with those of the average American.

Occasionally, a candidate comes along who is a national hero, and has not stood in the usual offices prior to candidacy. Eisenhower was a good choice for the Republicans in 1952, though retired generals do not always make strong candidates. They were more common a century ago, although from time to time the name of such a man still emerges. Colin Powell, having achieved honour and distinction in the Gulf War, has the sort of reputation that could override considerations such as lack of political experience. This is why many moderate Republicans would have liked to see his candidature in 1996 and why he might still possibly be a future runner.

favour the wealthy or well-resourced candidates who could afford to advertise their cause in every state?

It would, of course, be possible to revert to the older system, and rely more on caucuses to make the choice. We have examined the reasons for the greater use of primaries (see pp. 184–5 and 187). It is unlikely that there would be any strong support for scrapping their use today, although for those who wish to strengthen the role of political parties in the American system of government there could be a benefit in so doing.

Most of the anxiety about the American system relates to the use of the Electoral College, for it is from the use of this approach that several potential problems derive. Criticism centres on several aspects, notably:
- the overrepresentation of very small states and the excessive concentration on those which have many college votes;
- the use of the simple plurality or 'winner takes all' method of voting, whereby the candidate who gets most support obtains all the votes;

Other considerations include the desirability of being a Protestant in religion, although the choice of Kennedy in 1960 showed that a Roman Catholic could make it to the White House (the nomination of John Kerry showed that this factor has now become less important). JFK was an untypical candidate, for, apart from his religion, he was spectacularly wealthy, which could have been off putting and made him appear out of touch with ordinary Americans. He also showed no great interest in agriculture, which at the time was unusual given the political importance of the farm vote. Yet he had one obvious virtue: he was a glamorous candidate and one of the first to see the potential of television as a means of selling his personality. Today, being personable and of good appearance is especially important. Television is not a medium in which bald, fat or ugly figures fare well. The ability to speak fluently and with seeming sincerity is another asset.

Presidential elections today have become major media events and successful candidates will be subjected to the glare of the cameras and the gaze of an interested public over many months. They need to avoid negative coverage, for there are many who have fallen because of media scrutiny of some impropriety in their private life, be it sexual or financial. Bill Clinton obtained the nomination in spite of damaging allegations about his private life in 1991–1992, helped by his appearance with his supportive wife together on television, frankly admitting to their marital difficulties and their determination to overcome them. Being married is an asset. No bachelor was elected president in the twentieth century.

It requires a special stamina to endure the run for president and to withstand the pressures imposed by such endless attention. It is a long and arduous struggle, enough to tax the energies and finance of even the most dedicated and ambitious politician.

- the possibility that members of the College may vote for a person other than the one to whom they were pledged;
- the fact that it is possible to win the popular vote and yet lose the election;
- the fact that there may be no clear victor in the college, if no one emerges with a majority. This could have happened in 1992, if Ross Perot had actually managed to carry some states. It was the strategy of George Wallace in 1968 to aim for deadlock, and thereby throw the decision into the House. A choice made in Congress could be contrary to the people's will as expressed in the ballot box in November.

Why have an Electoral College? Does the system work well?

The Founding Fathers wanted a method of choosing their president that would shun 'mob politics'. Democracy was then not yet in fashion, and as they were creating an elected office they wanted to ensure that they were not handing power to demagogues who could manipulate popular opinion. They were suspicious of the mass of the people. Choice by college, after the voters had expressed their feelings, could be conducted in a more leisurely and rational manner. As Hamilton put it in the *Federalist Papers*:[16] 'The immediate election [of the President] should be made by men most capable of analysing the qualities needed for the office.' In this spirit, the Founding Fathers set up a system in which the electorate actually chooses between two competing lists or 'slates' of Electoral College candidates, although on the ballot papers it is the names of the candidates for the presidential office which are actually given.

There was never any serious likelihood that members of the Electoral College meeting in December would ignore the expression of public feeling in early November, and candidates for the college soon became pledged to cast their vote for one of the presidential challengers. In other words, they do not use their individual discretion, but reflect the feelings of voters in their state. In fact, the college does not even meet as one deliberating body. Members meet in their state capitals, and their choices are conveyed to Washington. Very rarely, an elector in the Electoral College has changed his or her mind and not voted for the person to whom he or she was pledged. In 1948 a Tennessee elector did not vote for Truman, who had carried the state, but opted instead for the states' rights candidate. Twenty years later, an elector in North Carolina switched from Richard Nixon to the Third Party candidature of George Wallace. In 1988, a Democrat voted for Lloyd Bentsen, the vice-presidential nominee, rather than Michael Dukakis, the candidate for the presidency.

Some writers have also drawn attention to the way in which balloting takes place. Instead of there being a proportional split in the Electoral College vote of a particular state to reflect the division of the popular vote, the candidate who gets the most votes carries the whole state allocation. This simple plurality or 'winner takes all' method may seem unfair, especially when the result is very close. In 1960, Kennedy obtained all of New York's 45 college votes, despite the fact that he only obtained 52.5% support; a proportional split would have given him 24 votes, to 21 for his opponent. This method makes the impact of geography on the outcome very important, for as we have seen a candidate who can carry California and other populous states has an enormous advantage. This would not be the case if the college vote were divided. The importance of urban states with dense populations is unduly emphasised under this process.

For all of its disadvantages, the system has so far worked tolerably well. When there is a close popular vote, as in 1960, the outcome in the college makes the result clear cut. Until 2000, the same was true in other contests where the gap between the main candidates was a narrow one (see p. 174–5).

Is there a better alternative to the Electoral College?

There have been many suggestions for the use of an amended college system, and others for its total abolition. Modifications could take the form of using an electoral system other than 'winner takes all'. A proportional division of the college votes is an alternative to the simple plurality.

The most obvious change would be to jettison the Electoral College and opt for a straight popular election of the president by the voters, instead of using the present indirect process of election. If it proved to be the case that no candidate could overcome a 40% hurdle on the first round of voting, then there could be a replay, a run-off between the two candidates who had scored most successfully. The person elected could then claim to have wide national backing, and not be unduly beholden to the voters in especially populous states. No longer is there the same apprehension about democracy as prevailed when the Founding Fathers made their choice.

It is true that such a method could further enhance the power of television, for few candidates could ever get across the nation to tour every state to encourage popular support. Yet effectively this is what happens now; the campaign is already organised for its television impact. More seriously for some critics of reform along these lines, it might weaken further the two main parties and encourage the candidature of third party nominees.

For defenders of states' rights, such a proposal might seem to be a threat to the federal system, for it undermines the importance of each state and region in the contest. In particular, the smaller states may feel uneasy, for their current influence in deciding the outcome would be diminished.

Is change likely?

It is far more likely that the present system will continue indefinitely, for although there is periodic unease about the Electoral College, this mainly coincides with the prospect of an indecisive outcome in the next presidential election. When a clear winner emerges, as eventually happened in 1992, much of the earlier talk of change vanishes.

There is no agreement on any alternative. Direct election was supported by Jimmy Carter early in the life of his presidency, when he described the existing arrangements as 'archaic'. Many analysts might concur with such a view, but there are strong forces ranged against it. The federal system was designed to protect the influence of the states, especially small ones, and they would not readily vote for a change, either via their congressmen or in their state legislatures. For the Dakotas or Vermont, the Electoral College gives them an influence beyond their size, and why should they wish to surrender it?

HOW AMERICANS VOTE AND WHY THEY VOTE AS THEY DO

Ever since the time of the New Deal, there has been a marked trend for urban workers with low incomes, who generally live in the poorest districts and have a lower level of formal educational qualification, to vote Democrat. In contrast, well-to-do voters, often with a higher level of educational attainment and living in suburban areas, have usually inclined to the Republican side.

The Democrats have had the support of minority groups such as blacks, who suffered in the Great Depression and regarded the party as the one that conferred benefits and was more likely to be interested in advancing their economic interests. The majority of Catholics, mainly of Irish immigrant stock, have inclined to the same party, and so have groups such as the Jews and other minorities who participated. However, just as white southern Democrats were often noted for their deeply ingrained Protestant fundamentalism, so Republicans always had some voters who were poor whites, Catholics, Jewish or black. There was never a complete racial, religious or socio-economic divide.

A changed picture in recent years

The pattern of voting behaviour in Britain and America has changed over the last generation, and some of the broad generalisations were found to be inadequate by the 1980s and 1990s. The changing class structure, with fewer people working in manufacturing industry, greater prosperity for most classes in the population and more upward social mobility, challenged some previous assumptions about the way Americans vote. Voting behaviour has become more volatile, and as Stephen Wayne[17] has written:

> While class, religion and geography are still related to party identification and voting behaviour, they are not as strongly related as they were in the past. Voters are less influenced by group cues. They exercise a more independent judgement on election day, a judgement that is less predictable and more subject to be influenced by the campaign itself.

Political scientists today talk more about partisan identification, the appeal of the candidate and issues than they did in the past. There is, of course, no clear-cut division between them, for the party one associates oneself with will often help to determine what one thinks about the candidate and the topic under discussion. By partisan identification, we mean the long-standing identification that a person has with a particular party, a preference that will have often been formed over many years. It will have been influenced by family background, education and the influence of peers in the early years, and this sense of attachment stays with people for much of their lives, modified by life experience, especially economic considerations and the impressions formed of the effectiveness of particular administrations in delivering the goods and making people feel content. The idea is that most Americans will stick by their normal party affiliation unless there are seemingly good reasons for not doing so.

Party identification is still the best guide to voting behaviour over the long term, although it is a less powerful tie than in the past. In the shorter term there are other factors that are more important, for otherwise the Democrats

---

THE TREND TO SPLIT-TICKET VOTING

By **split-ticket voting**, we mean the practice of casting ballots for the candidates of at least two different political parties at the same election.

Since the days of Democratic ascendancy, which ended in 1968, there has been a clear reduction in voter loyalty. Voters are more willing to vote differently between elections and within them – by split-ticket voting. The trend to split-ticket voting actually has a longer history, going back to 1952, but it has intensified in recent years. Whereas in 1952, 12% voted differently in their choice of party for the president and their member of the House of Representatives, 26% did so by 1968, and in 1980 the figure was 34%. Voters were enthusiastic about electing Ronald Reagan, but less willing to vote for his party in the congressional elections.

The trend is notable at all levels, with more voters behaving differently in choosing a candidate for the White House and ones for Capitol Hill, more voting one way for the Senate and a different way for the House, and – particularly marked – a larger number voting differently in their choice for state and for local representatives.

Why is split-ticket voting common?

1 Many Americans want to divide power in order to prevent an undue concentration in the hands of one person or party. For example, they may have preferred Clinton to Dole as their president in 1996, but chose to balance this choice by electing a Republican-dominated Congress.
2 Voter attachment to one party has declined, there being less strong partisan identification and more voter volatility. There are more votes 'up for grabs' and voters make a judgement on the qualities and policy positions of the candidates, both of which matter more in a media age of candidate-centred electioneering.
3 Some voters may feel that the candidate of one party is better at providing leadership in the White House, whereas in Congress they prefer to see the other party predominate. They may feel safer with a Republican president who might be expected to be tough on America's enemies, but prefer the more progressive Democrat agenda on domestic policy.

would be regularly more successful than their opponents. Over several decades the American National Election Study researchers have found that considerably more Americans describe themselves as 'strong', 'weak' or 'independent-leaning' Democrats than do so as Republicans.

Less stable factors, ones that fluctuate from election to election, include the attractiveness of the individual candidate and the issues that are in the forefront of people's minds. Martin Wattenberg[18] has argued that there has been a change of focus in recent years from party allegiance to concentration on the merits of the nominee: 'The change . . . is an important historical trend, which has been gradually taking place over the last several decades.' Voters

---

Voting behaviour in Britain and the United States: a comparison

The academic study of voting behaviour became popular in the 1960s on either side of the Atlantic. Early studies such as *The American Voter* and *Political Change in Britain*[19] showed how voting was influenced by long- and short-term influences. Since those early days, theories of voting behaviour have undergone substantial modification. Social changes have occurred in all developed countries and as a result the old certainties have vanished. Voting is now less predictable than in the past. In an age of greater volatility, short-term influences are likely to be more significant, and parties cannot count on traditional loyalties to provide them with mass support.

Short-term influences relate to a particular election, and include:
• the state of the economy;
• the personality and performance of political leaders;
• the nature of the campaign;
• the mass media;
• events leading up to the election.

Long-term influences include:
• party loyalty;
• social class;
• factors relating to the social structure such as age, gender, occupation, race and religion.

In Britain, the features most noted in the postwar years up to 1970 were:
• the stability of voting patterns, as people stayed loyal to the party they had always supported;
• the relevance of social class (Pulzer[20] could once memorably write that 'Class is the basis of British politics; all else is embellishment and detail');
• the recognition that elections were determined by a body of floating voters in key marginal constituencies;
• the uniform nature of the swing across the United Kingdom;
• the domination of the two main parties, which between them could count on the support of the majority of the electorate.

now seem to be more interested in the qualities the candidate possesses – not surprisingly, as these are now featured in the media more than ever before. Via television, voters can assess candidates' leadership ability and charisma, their honesty and experience, their knowledge or their ignorance. 'Strength' and 'leadership' are much-admired qualities, as is what George Bush senior called 'the vision thing'; many people like to be led by a person who knows where he or she wishes to lead them.

Issues are also important, but rather less so than party identification and candidate-appeal. Voters are often ambiguous about where a contender stands on a particular issue, for politicians realise that clarity can sometimes antag-

---

Since the 1970s many of these assumptions have lost their validity. The main parties can no longer anticipate the degree of support they once enjoyed, and the rise of third parties has made inroads into the share of the vote the two parties can command. In 1994, Madgwick concluded[21] that: 'Voting is still related to social class, but the relationship is complex, and there is less confidence about the significance of the term.' His conclusion was heavily influenced by Ivor Crewe,[22] whose researches showed that not only was class identification weakening, but so was party identification generally.

Crewe's research indicated that demographic changes were taking their toll of Labour, as old working-class communities were being destroyed by redevelopment schemes and the inner cities were emptying. Its traditional electoral base was being eroded, a point which led Peter Kellner to write[23] that the 'sense of class solidarity which propelled Labour to power in 1945 has all but evaporated'. Tony Blair's New Labour party recognised that Labour needed to extend its appeal, particularly in Middle England. In 1997 and 2001, Labour gained broad support across the ages, sexes and social classes.

In the US, broad trends in voting behaviour in recent years are that:
• Party identification means less today than was once the case.
• Voting has become more candidate-centred. In a television age, voters know much more about the candidates, and considerations of perceived competence, integrity and visual appeal matter more than ever before.
• Policy issues may play a greater role than in the past. Today, those who stand for office are regularly grilled about how they respond to particular issues and events.

In both countries, voters are now less committed to their long-term allegiances. Partisan dealignment has occurred, and this means that there has been a weakening of the old loyalties, and a new volatility among the electorate. Other key points of comparison are that:
• Social class, once a key determinant of voting especially in Britain, has lost much of its impact.
• The personality of the candidate has assumed greater importance in a media age, particularly in America where the party label anyway counts for less.
• Issues and the election campaign become more significant, as there are today more votes 'up for grabs'.

onise people and groups whom the candidate hopes to attract. If voters have taken the trouble to find out rival policy positions and understand them clearly, then it may be that they incline to one side on one issue, the other on a different one.

More broadly, voters think in terms of what the last Administration has done for them (**retrospective** issue voting) and what the candidates are offering for the next four years (**prospective** issue voting). In 1992, many were unimpressed by the domestic performance of the Bush presidency, particularly his handling of the economy. They felt that Bill Clinton offered a better future – reform of health care, and a new emphasis on recovering from the recession and creating jobs ('It's the economy, stupid!'). However much Bush might try to stress the 'character issue', by suggesting that his opponent was untruthful, evasive and not to be trusted, this appeared to matter less on this occasion than the promise of movement on the domestic front.

DIRECT LEGISLATION

referendum

A vote on a single issue in which all registered electors are eligible to take part. Instead of being asked to give a verdict on the administration as a whole – as in a general election – they are asked their opinion on one measure or act presented to them by the legislature.

The United States is one of only five democracies that have never held a nationwide **referendum**. However, in forty-six states and many cities there is provision for direct legislation (the initiative and the referendum), and the facility has been more widely used in several of them in the last generation.

initiative

A device by which an individual citizen (or group of citizens) can – if they collect a given number of signatures on a petition – have a proposal placed directly on the ballot in a state-wide election. As such, the initiative is particularly useful in cases where law-makers refuse to enact or even consider a law that the people want.

Early twentieth-century progressives supported the use of direct democracy and many states where it is now employed adopted it around that time, originally South Dakota in 1898 and Oregon in 1902. Most of the 'early' ones opted for the **initiative** and referendum, but as David Magleby[24] points out, the states that have incorporated direct legislation since World War I decided in several cases not to go for the whole package:

> In short, in the early going, states were much more likely to embrace all aspects of direct legislation, and provide the most direct forms of the process . . . While many states permit both the initiative and the popular referendum, it is the initiative that is much more frequently used. Since 1980, there have been roughly five initiatives for every popular referendum.

Direct democracy is most commonly used in the western states. Their political systems were still relatively undeveloped at the turn of the twentieth century, so that they were much more open to the arguments of the progressive movement. Progressivism was firmly entrenched in the region, supporters urging anti-institutional reforms that allowed for popular involvement. It never took root in the same way in the older South and Northeast, which provide less opportunity for this form of direct democracy. (NB Some towns in New England have a different form of direct democracy, the town meeting – see pp. 198–9.)

Frequency and issues

Initiatives have in recent years offered Americans tough choices on a wide array of subjects, from animal welfare to gay rights, from abortion to firearms purchases. Initiatives were used in several western states in the 1990s, among other things to test how many terms a person could serve in a state legislature or on Capitol Hill, restrict (or enhance) personal liberty, and to prohibit the trapping of black bears out of season.

In 2004, voters in 34 states were faced with 162 ballot proposals. This represented a fall in the total number of measures, far below the 202 of two years earlier. One reason for the fall in activity was a reduced interest in tax and bond measures, with 24 fewer than in 2002. Most states seem to have emerged from the fiscal crises they were then experiencing, so that legislatures were not turning to the voters for new taxes or bonds.

In 2004, as usual, the topics covered ranged in importance from minor to major. Marriage was the most popular issue, followed by gambling, education, hunting and the medical use of marijuana. Voters approved 109 (67%) of the proposals.

The state most frequently associated with the use of initiatives and referendums is California, where the protagonists on either side are allowed to draw up statements of the pro and anti cases; these are freely distributed to the voters, in weighty booklets. There were sixteen propositions in 2004. With the approval of the governor, Californians agreed to borrow another $3 billion in order to finance further stem-cell research, a cause close to Californians' hearts (Hollywood has recently experienced the death of Christopher Reeve, and Michael J. Fox has Parkinson's disease – both names were mentioned as people who might have been or might be the beneficiaries of research). In this respect, the governor was opposing the stance taken by President Bush.

Why has direct democracy become more popular?

There are several explanations for the upsurge in the popularity of initiatives and referendums since the early 1980s. Key factors include:

1 Activists have discovered their value as a means of advancing particular interests. For liberals, this might be an issue such as environmental protection, and for conservatives tax-cutting or curbing abortion.

2 Some politicians have been keen to associate themselves with initiative proposals as a useful means of raising public awareness of particular subjects and their own profile. This can win them the backing – and finance – of issue activists.

3 An industry has developed to professionalise the use of initiatives and popular referendums. Pollsters, media consultants, petition circulators and others have brought their expertise into the field and thereby made it easier to get an issue 'off the ground'. The 'initiative industry' operates not just in getting measures onto the ballot, but in challenging or defending in the courts measures that have been approved by voters.

4 The news media particularly thrive on initiatives, for the attempts to raise or block contentious issues provide good stories, often with a strong human interest and great headline potential.

Direct democracy in Britain, Europe and the United States: a comparison

Referendums are a means of giving the electorate a chance to have a direct influence over the decision-makers on specific policies. In recent years, referendums have been much more widely used in many parts of the world. As we have seen, a growing number of American states have used them to decide on contentious moral, social and constitutional issues. Some member states of the European Union have used them to confirm their membership of the EU or to ratify important constitutional developments. The new democracies of Central and Eastern Europe, particularly the fifteen republics of the former Soviet Union, have used them to decide a range of issues relating to the form of their new governments.

Britain has until recently had very little experience of voting on a single issue, even though the case was often canvassed in the twentieth century. A Conservative leader and former prime minister, Arthur Balfour, told the House of Commons back in 1911 that 'so far from corrupting the sources of democratic life [they] would only be a great education for political people'. The Conservatives held a referendum on the border issue in Northern Ireland in 1973, and the Scottish and Welsh electorates were allowed to vote on whether they wanted devolution in 1979. Yet the only occasion when all of the voters have been allowed to vote on a key national issues was four years earlier, when they were asked

Participation and turnout

Citizens are involved in direct democracy in a number of activities. For the more active, this may involve organising and circulating petitions, campaigning to maximise support, or running a fundraising lunch. For most people, the limit of their involvement is voting.

Sometimes a contentious issue may provoke an enthusiastic response, but usually turnout is high only if the initiative is being held at the same time as a general election. Magleby quotes[25] the example of Maine, which stages initiatives in general election years and in the odd-numbered years in between when there is no other vote. Far more people take part in the years when offices are being contested than when there is just an issue or issues up for election. Also, in general election years, Magleby detects a mean drop-off of 15% in the number who cast a vote on the propositions, compared with the number who cast a vote for the candidates.

Are initiatives and referendums a good thing?

There has been some discussion of the idea of initiatives for the federal government, but as yet no national vote has taken place. Many who exercise

whether or not they wished the country to remain in the European Economic Community. There have been local votes on the future status of schools and the ownership of council estates, and in Wales the issue of 'local option' on the Sunday opening of pubs has been decided in this way. Some councils are now consulting their electorates as to whether they should preserve public services by raising the level of council tax.

Since May 1997 referendums have been used to resolve the issue of devolution and the shape of London's government. Also, in concurrent votes, popular approval of the Good Friday Agreement was supported by electors on both sides of the border in Ireland. Ministers have promised a vote on electoral reform at some time in the near future, and should there be a decision for Britain to join the single European currency then this too will be submitted to the people for popular backing.

Whereas the British have embraced the referendum slowly and with some reluctance, Americans have been more enthusiastic about direct legislation, though not at the national level. In a country in which the proper role of government is much discussed, issues of public spending and taxation, matters of public morality and governmental or political reform, have all been seen as suitable subjects for popular consultation, whereas the British have been wary of resolving controversial matters such as drug use or abortion in this way.

power are reluctant to opt for more direct democracy, and argue that whilst it may be appropriate for deciding local and state issues it has disadvantages in national politics. Conservatives tend to fear its use on key questions of defence and foreign affairs. Liberals worry about the repercussions for minority groups. Many members of both categories feel safer with traditional methods of representative democracy.

In favour of votes on single issues, it may be said that:
1 They give people a chance to take decisions that affect their lives, whereas in a general election voters can only offer a general verdict.
2 They stimulate interest and involvement in public policy.
3 They may exert pressure on the legislature to act responsibly and in the public interest.
4 They help counter the special interests to which legislators can be beholden.
5 They help overcome the obstructionism of out-of-touch legislators and therefore make reform more likely.

Against:
1 Proposals can be ill thought out and badly drafted.
2 Campaigns can be expensive and therefore to the advantage of well-funded groups. Money is too dominant in the process. Business interests have far more scope to influence the outcome.
3 There are too many issues for voters to handle – they elect representatives to decide. This is what representative democracy is all about. If the voter dislikes the decisions made, he or she can turn against the controlling party in the next election.
4 Initiatives and allied devices undermine political parties and therefore weaken the democratic process.
5 They encourage single-issue politics, rather than debate based on a conflict of broad principles.
6 They can work to the disadvantage of minorities who can be persecuted by the majority, such as blacks and gays.

Despite all of the reasons that may be used to oppose direct democracy, no state that possesses the provision for initiatives and/or referendums has ever repealed it. The process is likely to continue to be a major factor in the political life of many states.

ELECTION 2004: A CASE STUDY

Some commentators said that the election on 2 November 2004 would be about terrorism and the war in Iraq, a divisive issue that split the nation. Others said that the shaky recovery of the economy would prove decisive. For another group, it was going to be an election about the image of the president and the support and antagonism he inspired. All of these issues played a part, but in the end the result owed a great deal to Bush's much-proclaimed personal faith. The religious fervour aroused by his support for measures to uphold and strengthen moral values helped to mobilise the Christian Right.

A close-run contest

As polling day approached, the Democrats had some reason for encouragement in the opinion polls, which showed Kerry very close to Bush or in some cases marginally ahead. The party had been successful in securing registrations of voters in 2004, more so than the Republicans. If turnout was high, then the Democrats could hope that this would indicate that first-time voters – many of whom were sympathetic to the party – had cast their vote. The Democrats were looking for a turnout of more than 120 million – 60% plus of registered voters.

When the results were in, things had not turned out that way. In some respects, the outcome of the contest in November 2004 was strikingly similar to that of November 2000. For a brief time after the polls closed, there were some indications that it was going to be the same sort of close and bitterly contested struggle all over again, with everything depending on what happened in a single state and the legal challenges that might be mounted. Exit polls taken as voters left the polling station indicated Kerry as the likely winner. By lunchtime on voting day, they were predicting that Kerry would win the crucial swing states of Florida, Ohio and Pennsylvania, giving him certain victory. Voting closed in most of the eastern states at 7 o'clock, and by then some Democrats were already taking a Kerry victory for granted. In the event, the exit polls got the result badly wrong.

As the results came in, everything turned on Ohio. It looked as though recounts of disputed ballots could prevent the emergence of a clear winner. Democrats hoped that 150,000 provisional ballots (those votes cast in the wrong precincts, requiring further legal confirmation) would determine the outcome in their favour, for in total they exceeded the margin by which Bush was ahead in the state (135,000). But Kerry would have needed 90% of these outstanding votes to be decided in his favour for his side to win. Given the experience of the Bush–Gore struggle of four years before, he conceded that on this occasion the outcome 'should be decided by voters, not a protracted legal battle'.

The scale of victory

The votes cast for the presidential candidates

Presidential candidate	Running mate	Party	Electoral vote	Popular vote	Ballot access
George W. Bush	Richard Cheney	Republican	286	62,019,033 (50.74%)	50+DC
John Kerry	John Edwards	Democrat	251	58,994,923 (48.26%)	50+DC
Ralph Nader	Peter Miguel Camejo	Independent, Reform	0	460,650 (0.38%)	34+DC
Michael Badnarik	Richard Campagna	Libertarian	0	396,778 (0.32%)	48+DC
Michael Peroutka	Chuck Baldwin	Constitution	0	143,940 (0.12%)	36
David Cobb	Patricia LaMarche	Green	0	119,579 (0.10%)	27+DC
Totals			537	122,191,867 (100.00%)	N/A

NB Others stood as candidates: these were the only persons that had a theoretical possibility of achieving a majority in the Electoral College. One Minnesota elector voted for John Edwards as president, in the electoral college. Ballot access refers to the number of states for which the candidate was on the ballot paper. DC = District of Columbia. The total popular vote is that for all candidates.

As the provisional results turned into final outcomes, it was clear that George W. Bush had won four more years, winning approximately 51% of the popular vote to Kerry's 48%. Bush's victory was carved out of a bigger electorate than ever before, with approximately 122.2 million voting, a considerable increase on 2000. It was based on a 59.4% turnout, a higher figure than in any presidential election since 1968, when 61% voted in the election won by Richard Nixon. The turnout was good, but the increase owed more to Bush's success in mobilising his base than to the potential young Democrat voters, who did not turn out in significantly greater numbers than in the Bush versus Gore contest.

Similarities and differences between 2000 and 2004

In 2004, the voting blocks were similar to what they were in 2000, with the two main candidates between them drawing the overwhelming number of votes cast, and the gap between them being relatively small. The movement of states supporting either candidate was very small, even if the margin in the Electoral College was greater in 2004. However, there were two significant differences that enabled the president to win once more:

- The Republicans fought a much better campaign than they had last time, getting their tactics right in almost every important respect. In particular, they had realised the significance of mobilising the four million evangelical Christians who had not voted in 2000. The victory owed much to the support of the conservative Christian community, for Bush secured the support of many Americans whose politics begin – but do not end – in church.

- The background against which the election was contested had dramatically changed, because of the events post-September 11. This time, there was an ongoing war against global terrorism, and American troops were involved in the fighting in Iraq.

Aspects of the outcome in the presidential contest

- George Bush was the first candidate since 1988 to win a majority of the votes cast.
- He received the largest number of votes of any presidential candidate in US history. Kerry also received more votes than any candidate in any previous election.
- Bush won with the smallest margin of victory for a sitting president in US history in terms of the percentage of the popular vote. (Bush received 2.48 percentage points more than Kerry; the closest previous margin won by a sitting president was 3.2% for Woodrow Wilson in 1916.) In terms of absolute number of popular votes, the victory margin (approximately 3.02 million) was the smallest of any sitting president since Truman in 1948.
- Apart from the 2000 election (which Bush won by just five votes in the Electoral College), it was the smallest margin of victory won in the Electoral College since 1916.
- Nearly 17 million more votes were cast than in the 2000 election. The increase may have been caused by intense candidate or party rivalry, and enthusiastic voter registration and get-out-the-vote campaigns.
- Only three states picked a winner from a different party to their choice 2000. Bush took Iowa and New Mexico (combined twelve electoral votes), both won by Al Gore in 2000, while Kerry took New Hampshire (four votes), which Bush had won four years earlier.
- The counties where Bush led in the popular vote amount to 83% of the geographic area of the US (excluding Alaska, which did not report results by county).
- As in 2000, electoral votes split along sharp geographical lines: the west coast, Northeast and most of the Great Lakes region for Kerry, and the Southeast, Great Plains and mountain states for Bush.
- Minor-party candidates received many fewer votes, dropping from a total of 3.5% in 2000 to approximately 1%. As in 2000, Ralph Nader finished in third place, but his total declined from 2.9 million to 40,000, leaving him with fewer votes than Pat Buchanan had received in finishing fourth in 2000. The combined minor-party total is the lowest since 1988.
- The election marked the first time since Franklin Delano Roosevelt's re-election in 1936 that an incumbent president was re-elected and his political party also increased its representation in both houses of Congress. For the Republicans, it was the first time this had happened since William McKinley in the 1900 election.

The Republican victory in 2004 went far beyond the presidential election. Membership of the closely divided Congress moved in a distinctly conservative direction in both chambers, not just because more Republicans were elected but also because many of the new members are economically and socially conservative. Moderate Republicans are becoming a rarity in either chamber.

The 109th Congress: final outcome

Party	House	Senate
Republicans (R)	233	55
Democrats (D) independent	201 + 1 pro-D independent	44 + 1 Pro-D
Net change	R up 4, D down 4	R up 4, D down 4

The tide of social conservatism in the nation was a key factor in determining the outcome in several congressional contests. The party fared well in the House, helped by some redistricting in the apportionment process and also by the power of incumbency. In the Senate, the Republican Party also increased its majority. Successful candidates often succeeded in portraying their opponents as 'liberal', whilst highlighting their own socially conservative credentials. In Louisiana, the Republicans picked up their first senate seat for more than a hundred years, not least because of the uncompromising populist stance taken by the victorious David Vitter. Catholics and evangelicals liked his message that there should be no legal abortion allowable on any grounds whatsoever. In South Carolina too, a strongly conservative message was successfully conveyed to the voters, Jim deMint proclaiming that neither homosexuals nor unmarried pregnant women should be able to teach in public schools. The most high-profile Democrat loss in the Senate was the minority leader, Tom Daschle, the first party leader to lose a re-election vote for more than fifty years. The best Democrat peformance was in Illinois, where the Afro-American Barack Obama won a resounding victory. An ex-journalist and civil rights lawyer, he is a skilful communicator with prospects of a bright political future.

How and why Bush won

According to Gallup poll findings (5 November 2004), Bush owed his victory to support from conservative-leaning groups, notably men, whites, southerners, married voters, churchgoers, Protestants, gun owners and veterans. He did well in states that he had won in 2000, which offset Kerry's slightly better performance in the showdown states. In general, Bush's support was similar to what it was in 2000, but slightly higher, mainly because the two major party candidates took 99% of the vote in 2004 compared with 96% in 2000. But Bush improved on his 2000 performance among conservatives, urban residents and regular churchgoers, while he did less well among younger voters.

Who backed Bush and who backed Kerry?

Category	Bush voter	Kerry voter
Male	54	45
Female	47	52
White	57	42
African American	11	89
Hispanic	42	55
Asian	41	59
18–29	44	54
30–44	51	47
45–59	50	49
60+	53	46
Low income	36	63
Middle income	55	44
High income	62	37
Weekly churchgoer	58	41
Infrequent churchgoer	44	55
Non-attender at church	34	64
Gun owner	60	40
Gay/bisexual	23	77

Figures adapted from those in a CNN exit poll.

The skilful Republican campaign

The Bush campaign team, spearheaded by the clever strategist Karl Rove, who has masterminded the president's entire political career, ran a highly successful campaign. They allowed the president to speak only at strictly controlled, ticket-only rallies, with the result that the mass of television viewers repeatedly saw him being cheered and whooped, apparently by wildly enthusiastic hordes of voters. He was not allowed to stray from scripts that were provided for him. He kept to empty, populist slogans that were repeated over and over again, and which gradually started to hit home outside the **Beltway**. The results said it all: this was an election that was decided in the vast heartlands of America, well away from the Republican old guard, who feel decidedly less sanguine about their leader.

> **Beltway**
> The American term for what in the UK is called a ring road: a circumferential highway around a major city – in this case the federal capital, Washington, DC.

Rove and the president carefully targeted the white evangelical Christian vote, by emphasising issues such as the constitutional amendment on same-sex marriages and opposing the use of embryonic stem cells for medical research. They understood that the election would be won in the heartlands rather than in the urban areas, and that beliefs such as the sanctity of life and of marriage played well with this group (see pp. 318–19 and 331):

- 'Values vans' – basically Christian-centred political operatives on wheels – toured the areas where the religious vote needed to be galvanised.
- In the swing state of Ohio, 2.5 million anti-gay-marriage leaflets were distributed to 17,000 churches one week before the election.
- In Colorado, the campaign reached frenzied levels, with religious supporters handing out masses of badges saying 'I'm a values voter.'

Positive feelings about George Bush, doubts about John Kerry

As he left the polling station at Crawford in Texas, the president was asked about the polarised feelings he arouses in people, and said: 'I take that as a compliment. It means I'm willing to take a stand.' He saw his task as leading and never looking back. Many Americans admired a display of strength in the White House and felt that even if they did not agree with or like him, they could trust him to do what he felt was right and necessary for his country. In their eyes, he looked and sounded like presidential material. Bush was always going to be a difficult man to beat against a background of concerns about national security and with a war being waged, unless either of those areas suddenly went badly wrong.

By comparison, there were doubts about John Kerry. It wasn't that he had fought a bad campaign. His performance in the debates had been assured and impressive, and in the last few weeks he had done well and appeared credible, confirming his reputation as a 'strong finisher'. But there were doubts about him, ones that were ruthlessly exploited by the Republican campaign team. What really damaged him was the Swift Boat Veterans for Truth onslaught that dominated the campaign back in August. Funded by Bush supporters in Texas, it discredited Kerry's record in Vietnam and thereby succeeded in raising doubts about his character. Kerry's involvement, as against the president's evasion of active service, should have been a plus point for the challenger. Those who served on Kerry's swift boat testified to his heroism in winning three Purple Hearts and a Silver Star. By contrast, not one of the Vietnam veterans featured in the 'Truth' onslaught had served with Kerry. But that did not stop them from claiming to know what happened and presenting it in an unflattering light. Apparently Kerry thought the claims too far-fetched to take them seriously, seemingly overestimating the ability of the American electorate to sift fact from fiction. By hesitating in his counter-attack in those early days, he made a fatal miscalculation

The innuendo of the Bush camp created doubts about Kerry's presidential calibre, by questioning his recall and his veracity. They asked which Kerry voters would be getting, as they pointed to the changes in his positions on various issues, the so-called 'flip-flops'. Having originally voted in favour of the Iraq invasion, he then made the anti-war message his strongest suit. But he often failed to make clear exactly what he would do differently from the president.

Elements in the Bush–Cheney team, particularly Cheney himself, waged an aggressive – some would say dishonest – campaign, appropriating the tragedies of September 11, 2001, as their own exclusive property. Cheney repeated time and time again that there would be more terrorist attacks on the country and that Kerry could not be trusted to defend Americans, painting him as an elitist flip-flopper who was incapable of taking firm, coherent positions – exactly the same charges levelled successfully against Al Gore four years earlier.

Moral values: being in tune with conservative and Christian America

The mood of America appears to have moved further to the right in recent years. In 2000, half of the voters described themselves as moderates and 29% as conservatives. In 2004, the former group fell to 45% and the latter rose to 33%. Republicans were able to capitalise on this mood and were successful in persuading their potential supporters to turn out and vote in impressive numbers.

Exit polls showed that a fifth or more of voters named moral issues as their top concern, and four fifths of those voters backed Bush overwhelmingly. He won easily in the Bible Belt states such as West Virginia, Kentucky and Arkansas, which were a few years ago seen as natural Democrat territory. Bill Clinton captured all three in 1992 and 1996. These areas are relatively poor and the Democrats touted the economy as the key issue in them. But evangelical Christian belief and a conservative approach to issues of gun control were more pressing in the minds of many voters, and Bush's stance on them resonated with their own.

What did voters mean by moral values?

Those who cited moral values as a major factor offered varying interpretations of the concept. Fourty-four % of them thought the term related to specific concerns over social issues, such as abortion and gay marriage. However, others pointed to factors such as the candidates' personal qualities (e.g. trustworthiness) or made general allusions to religion and values.

In the presidential and congressional elections and in the initiatives (see p. 225), the same evidence emerged of concern at some of the trends in American society. There was a widespread wish to place renewed emphasis on the sanctity of marriage and the family, and to support candidates and campaigns that were pro-life and anti-gay marriage. Of course, not all Americans share such an agenda. Polls continue to show that a majority of

Americans feel that abortion should be always or mostly legal and that 35% or thereabouts support gay civil unions (rather fewer support gay marriages). But the causes stressed by the Bush campaigners were successful in mobilising the missing evangelical Protestants of four years earlier.

The Bushite moral majority does not just comprise right-wing evangelical Christians. Rather, it includes traditionalist and observant churchgoers of every kind. The president made gains among Hispanic Catholics and mainline Protestants, as well as evangelicals, Mormons and elements within the Jewish community. (He managed to swing crucial Jewish votes in Florida with his unquestioning support for Israeli leader Ariel Sharon.)

What issues mattered most?

Interviewees were asked: What one issue mattered most to you in deciding how you voted for president?

Issue	All voters (%)	Bush voters (%)	Kerry voters (%)
Moral values	27	44	7
Iraq	22	11	34
Economy/jobs	21	7	36
Terrorism	14	24	3
Health care	4	1	8
Education	4	2	6
Taxes	3	4	2

Information adapted from survey conducted for the Pew Research Center, 5–8 November 11 2004. Excluding 'others', 'unsure'.

CONCLUSION

There are various ways in which Americans can participate in political life. Many choose not to do so, having only a limited interest in politics. The vast majority never engage in any political activity between elections and pay little attention to what is going on.

Elections and election campaigns are the processes by which voters in any democracy choose the direction they wish to take in the future. They are the opportunity for voters to have their say. Americans are called upon to participate with great frequency, for there is a theoretical enthusiasm for the ballot box in public life. Yet many of them choose not to take advantage of this.

Those who do vote do so under various influences, of which their long-term party identification has traditionally been the most important. However, in a television age, in which campaigning is conducted in a more visible way than ever before and in which the amount of information available has dramatically increased, the merits of the candidate and the issues of the time have become particularly relevant.

REFERENCES

1 A. Grant, *Contemporary American Politics*, Dartmouth, 1995
2 V. O. Key, *Politics, Parties and Pressure Groups*, Crowell, 1964
3 T. Hames and N. Rae, *Governing America*, Manchester University Press, 1996
4 B. Ginsberg and M. Shefter, *Politics by Other Means*, WW Norton, 1999
5 A. de Tocqueville, *Democracy in America*, vol. 2, reissued by Vintage, 1954
6 R. Putnam, *Bowling Alone: The Collapse and Revival of American Community*, Simon & Schuster, 2000
7 F. Bryan (University of Vermont), as quoted in a Vermont Public Television video, *Town Meeting: A Day in the Life*, 2000
8 J. Rankin, *Morning Sentinel* (Maine), 26 March 2000
9 J. Zimmerman, *The New England Town Meeting: Democracy in Action*, McGraw-Hill, 1999
10 J. Rankin, as in 8 above
11 F. Bryan, as in 7 above
12 L. Rees, *Selling Politics*, BBC Books, 1992
13 B. Schneider, as quoted in L. Rees as in 12 above
14 M. Vile, *Politics in the USA*, Hutchinson, 1978
15 M. Vile, as in 14 above
16 J. Madison, A. Hamilton and J. Jay, *The Federalist Papers*, New American Library, 1961
17 S. Wayne, *The Road to the White House 1996*, St Martin's Press, 1996
18 M. Wattenberg, *The Rise of Candidate-Centred Politics*, Harvard University Press, 1991
19 A. Campbell, P. Converse, W. Miller and D. Stokes, *The American Voter*, John Wiley, 1960; D. Butler and D. Stokes, *Political Change in Britain*, Macmillan, 1966
20 P. Pulzer, *Political Representation and Elections in Britain*, Allen and Unwin, 1968
21 P. Madgwick, *A New Introduction to British Politics*, Thorne, 1994
22 B. Sarlvik and I. Crewe, *Decade of Dealignment*, Cambridge University Press, 1983
23 P. Kellner, *New Society*, 2 June 1983
24 D. Butler and D. Magleby, *Referendums around the World*, Macmillan, 1994
25 D. Butler and D. Magleby, as in 24 above.

USEFUL WEB SITES

On elections

www.fec.gov The Federal Election Commission. Provides data on
the financing of election campaigns.

www.pollingreport.com The Polling Report. Gives data on elections
and campaigning events.

On the media

www.appcpenn.org The Annenburg Policy Center. Provides
analyses of television coverage of politics.

www.neeewsuem.org The Freedom Forum; museum of journalism. Provides insight
into changes in the reporting of news over the years.

In addition, most newspapers and television channels have web sites, for example:

www.washingtonpost.com The *Washington Post*.

www.cnn.com CNN cable network.

SAMPLE QUESTIONS

1 Why does America have so many elections and why are many
   Americans so unwilling to vote in them?

2 'Nowadays, American election campaigns are geared to the
   requirements of television.' Discuss.

3 'Vast amounts of money are spent on elections and
   electioneering in the US, more than in any other democracy.' Are
   the elections better for all this expenditure?

4 Evaluate the strengths and weaknesses of the way in which presidential candidates are
   chosen.

5 Should the Electoral College now be abolished?

6 To what extent does the method of selection determine the kind of person who will
   become president of the United States?

7 Account for the changes in American voting behaviour since the 1980s.

8 Account for the growth in popularity of methods of direct legislation in recent decades.
   Are initiatives and referendums a reliable guide to what Americans think?

9 Compare the conduct of elections and the methods of electioneering in Britain and the
   United States.

Political parties

8

In any modern democracy, political parties play an important role, in that they organise elections and provide voters with a choice of ideas and personalities. The part played by parties in America, however, is far smaller than that in Britain. American constitutional arrangements impede the development of strong parties and were designed to do so. Many academics and commentators see their role as less important now than it was in the past. This has led to talk of 'the decline of American parties'. Other commentators detect signs of a resurgence.

Here, we are concerned with the development of parties, how the party system operates today, what the main parties stand for, whether there are substantial differences between them, and the ways in which they are organised. We can then decide whether or not their role has diminished in recent years.

POINTS TO CONSIDER

➤ Why were the Founding Fathers suspicious of political parties?

➤ What role do parties play in American politics?

➤ Can America be said to have a two-party system?

➤ What problems beset third parties in America?

➤ Why have socialist ideas not taken firmer root in the USA?

➤ What are the main ideas and beliefs associated with the two main parties and whom do they represent?

➤ What do we mean by describing American parties as decentralised?

➤ Are American parties in decline or undergoing a resurgence?

➤ In what respects are British and American parties similar and different?

The role and value of parties

American history reveals a long-standing distrust of **political parties**, which have been portrayed as factions by some writers ever since the days of the Founding Fathers. James Madison defined a faction in unflattering terms: 'By a faction, I mean a number of citizens, whether amounting to a majority of a minority of the whole, who are united and actuated by some common impulse or passion, or of interest, adverse to the rights of other citizens or to the permanent aggregate interest of the community.'

> **political party**
> A group of people of broadly similar views who organise themselves and recruit candidates for election, with a view to achieving office so that they can carry out their ideas and programme. They are not people with identical attitudes and interests, for parties are inevitably coalitions of individuals whose approach on some issues can be widely divergent.

George Washington too made clear his anxieties about 'the baneful effects of the spirit of party generally [with] its alternate domination of one faction over another, sharpened by the spirit of revenge natural to party dissension'. For him, parties 'kindle[d] the animosities of one part against another'.[1] But his warnings were delivered too late to influence the course of events. Since his time, they have been accepted as a 'necessary evil', in that they help to organise the democratic process and present Americans with a choice of candidates and policies.

The main functions of parties are concerned with fighting and winning elections:

1 **They arrange for the choice of candidates.** This was once done in 'smoke-filled rooms' by party bosses who selected their preferred choice, but in the US today it is in most states the voters who choose their preferred candidate in primary elections. By the time of the party nominating conventions the choice is normally clear cut.

2 **They support the candidates.** Once chosen, by whatever method, candidates need to have a supporting organisation to handle their campaign. Traditionally, the parties have arranged door-to-door canvassing to put their candidate's message across; they also establish phone-banks, arrange lifts to the polling station, assist in fundraising and advertising, and commission the carrying out of private polls. Again, this role has been downgraded in recent years, for with the decline in influence of the 'party machines' candidates have increasingly organised the running of their own campaign. Moreover, the growth of political action committees has meant that parties have a lower profile in fundraising and advertising than was formerly the case. The 'supportive' function has its uses, however, and at the national conventions the parties are keen to ensure that the presidential campaign attracts the maximum of favourable publicity. They attempt to

'sell' their chosen candidates for the presidency and vice-presidency, and may arrange for 'endorsements' of the ticket by well-respected party dignitaries.

3 **They organise the contest.** Throughout the nation, parties at every level conduct the useful tasks of helping to register voters and arouse their enthusiasm for the contest. Parties help arrange candidate training, research into policy issues, and the publicity that is so helpful in getting the name and message across.

4 **They clarify the issues.** Parties help to simplify the choice that is offered to the voter, for they provide them with information and help to organise the discussion of issues into a 'for' and 'against' format. The arguments on either side are reduced to an appropriate level of public comprehension.

5 **They involving the electorate in the democratic process.** Parties give the individual American a chance to participate in the democratic process. A relative few work as party activists; others who are party members have a chance to vote in primary elections and attend any local meetings. This enables the voter to rally around the party that best fits his or her vision of how American life should be organised. In other words, parties are an outlet for people's interests and enthusiasms, a focal point for their allegiances and loyalties. In providing this outlet, parties are a useful intermediary between the governed and the government – for through parties, the individuals can make their views known and conveyed to those who seek to win and retain their support.

The two-party system

America is a country of great diversity, with marked ethnic, social and regional differences, which one might expect to see represented by parties concerned with their specific interests. Yet it has a system in which only two main parties seriously compete for political influence and in particular every four years seek to capture the presidency. This has always been the case except for rare moments in the country's history. As V. O. Key[2] put it: 'While minor parties have arisen from time to time and exerted influence on governmental policy, the two major parties have been the only serious contenders for the presidency. On occasion, a major party has disintegrated, but in due course the bi-party system has reasserted itself.'

A two-party system does not preclude the existence of other parties, and in the United States as in most other Western democracies several other third and minor parties continue to operate. What it does mean is that only the main parties, the Republicans and Democrats, have a meaningful chance of achieving the highest office or gaining a majority in Congress. In a two-party system, the two parties may change or adapt; the American Republican Party replaced an established one, as did the British Labour Party. But although there may be transitional phases in which one party is giving way to another, usually within a generation there is a return to normality. In the United States, small parties find it difficult to achieve a breakthrough nationally, although in various states some are well established (see pp. 244–51).

The phrase 'two-party system' is misleading in some respects, for the American pattern of party activity could also be viewed as an 'agglomeration of many parties centred around the governments of the 50 states and their subdivisions',[3] whilst from another point of view it is a four-party system based upon Congress and the presidency. Writers such as Vile[4] have stressed that although the system nominally operates via two parties, this obscures the fact that for most purposes 'America operates under a multi-party system which coalesces into two great **coalitions** for strictly limited purposes'. As he puts it:

> **electoral coalitions**
> Groups of loyal supporters who agree with the party's stand on most issues and vote for its candidates for office.

> The nature of the Constitution, spreading power as it does to different levels of government, tends to have a disintegrating effect on party structure so that national parties tend to be coalitions of state and local parties forming and reforming every four years, so that what we have is not a single party system. We have 50 state party systems. Politics operate in a framework of 50 systems, for much decentralisation has occurred.

There is a variety of forms of party competition throughout the country. Politics in Minnesota is different to politics in New York, for inevitably, given the size of the country and the constitutional arrangements, political life varies from state to state. In most, two parties compete for power, although the intensity and effectiveness of competition depend on the individual case. There may well be a genuine alternation of power, with both Republicans and Democrats having a chance to capture the governorship and control of the legislative chamber. In other states, only one party normally ever wins, and there is never the prospect of a change of control. A number of major cities – such as Chicago and Detroit – are regular strongholds of the Democrats, just as Kansas, Utah and Wyoming are traditionally loyal to the Republicans. There are also still several non-competitive congressional districts in which one of the two major parties always wins. In 1992, twelve candidates for the House were elected without opposition, and several others faced only a token battle. The same is true of several state legislatures, a number of which have regularly been controlled by the Democrats. Where one party dominates, the battle is between different factions and individuals within the organisation.

By contrast with the one-party dominance we have been discussing, the New York scene is very different. It is not unusual for several parties to take part in any contest. When there is a multi-party situation, there are often candidates from the two regular parties and also from the American Labour Party and the Liberal Party.

If federalism is one reason why use of the term 'a two-party system' can be misleading, the separation of powers is another. The strict division of constitutional responsibility means that each of the two parties has a congressional and a presidential wing. This led James MacGregor Burns[5] to describe the American scene as a 'four-party system' with 'separate though overlapping parties', each with its own distinctive style:

> Presidential Democrats are seen as different from congressional ones, in that they have a different electoral base and appeal to different sections of the people. The presidential party seeks its major support in the urban areas of large industrialised states, whilst the majority of Democratic Senators and Congressmen are responsive to rural and suburban influences.

Congressmen are inevitably concerned with the narrow interests of the locality they represent, whereas presidential candidates must appeal in a much wider constituency. The presidential party is either in office (having captured the presidency) or else in a state of oblivion for much of the intervening period between elections, whereas the congressional party, Republican or Democrat, is permanently active. The presidential wings of both parties tend to be closer together doctrinally than they are to the respective congressional wings of their own parties.

All of these considerations make it difficult to label the American system straightforwardly as a two-party one, but for most observers it remains meaningful to talk in such language. When people think of the parties in America, they think of the battle between the Democrats and the Republicans, and (especially on this side of the Atlantic) they think primarily of the contest for the presidency.

Why does America have a two-party system?

Several factors may be advanced to explain the American system, some institutional, some cultural or historical. Key[6] has suggested that once the basis of the two-party divide had come about at the time of the formation of the Republic, then it was always likely that it would be retained, for 'there is a tendency in human institutions for a persistence of [the] initial form'. Discussion of the form of the Constitution resolved itself into a battle between two opposing viewpoints, and events thereafter in American history – such as slavery and the Civil War – perpetuated this pattern. Once the two-party system was established, the parties did all that they could to keep it that way and prevent a fractious section of either party from breaking away. In other words, a two-party system tends to be self-perpetuating.

Some would stress the natural tendency for opinion on issues to divide into 'for' and 'against' positions which often follow the basic distinction between people who generally favour retaining the status quo (the conservatives) and those who wish to see innovation and a quicker pace of change (the progressives). Duverger[7] long ago argued that a two-party system conformed to the basic division in society between those who wish to keep it broadly unchanged, and those who wish to see change and improvement. However, the liberal–conservative, progressive–stay-put distinction has not always been appropriate to American politics, and in either party there have always been those who are more forward-looking and those who oppose social advance.

The approach based on social class has not fitted the picture accurately either. The idea that one party represents the working class and the other the middle and upper class (as in the traditional view of the Labour and Conservative clash in Britain) has never had much relevance as an explanation in a country where class plays a less significant part in the political process. In several countries, there is a clear conflict between a socialist and an anti-socialist party, but in the United States there is no large party committed to transforming the social and economic order.

There are more fundamental explanations of the continued dominance of two parties at national and state level:

1 **A single executive** There is only one vacancy at the highest level, the presidency. The nature of the position means that it is not possible for coalitions of more than one party to share it, as can happen with a cabinet system. To win the presidency is the focus of a party's aspirations, for the office is the focal point of all national political life. The campaigning involved is costly and needs to be planned over a long haul, as candidates today seek to make progress and win support via the primary system. It requires substantial organisational and financial backing. In these circumstances, the best means of winning is to create a coalition behind one person, for any splintering of support makes success unlikely. The method of election makes a two-party system more desirable, for to win a majority of votes in the Electoral College it is necessary to avoid divisions. As Vile[8] has argued: 'The ability of a party to master the technique of coalition-building is the measure of its ability to command the presidency.'

2 **The broad appeal of the existing parties** As there is only one supreme prize, it is necessary for any party to appeal as widely as possible. Once the presidential candidate is chosen, the leading parties seek to show that they are attractive to many interests in the country, and this makes it difficult for any smaller party to carve out a distinctive identity that is not already catered for. Both the Republican and Democratic parties are essentially coalitions: large organisations under whose umbrella a variety of groupings can more or less comfortably co-exist.

Between them, they cater for all sections of society, being sufficiently flexible to assimilate new ideas that come along and assume importance.

The reasons advanced above (1 and 2) explain why there are only two main parties at the presidential level. They do not entirely explain why it is that in the battle for Congress the various states tend to have two-party competitions.

3 **The mechanics of the electoral system** The electoral system discourages the formation of third or minor parties. For presidential, congressional and other elections, the British simple plurality or 'first past the post' ('winner takes all') method is employed. Candidates need more votes than their rivals, not an overall majority of the votes cast in any state. A candidate carries any state on election night in which he or she has the highest number of votes. Small parties may total a considerable number of votes nationally or within the region, but it is winning in individual constituencies that counts. Under a proportional electoral system, they would have more chance of gaining some representation in the legislature.

4 **Barriers to third or minor party advancement** In many states, there are real barriers to the formation, progress and survival of third parties. The US is the only nation in which the rules for ballot access in national elections – for Congress as well as the presidency – are written not by the national government but by the states. In several states, legal hurdles have been constructed by the major parties which place third groupings at a serious disadvantage. Many states either prohibit 'subversive' groupings altogether or make life difficult for them.

Where there is no ban on particular parties, states may require that they have to be of a certain size to get their name on the ballot paper. In a few states, the hurdle is so small that it becomes a formality, so that in Arkansas a grouping of at least fifty only needs to hold a convention to qualify. In others, the barrier is so large that it poses a totally unrealistic obstacle. In certain states, there is no procedure whatever for enthusiasts to qualify to get on a ballot under their own party label. They must either run as independents or not at all. Georgia and Texas made it very difficult for the veteran consumer rights and environmental campaigner Ralph Nader to get on the ballot paper in 2000.

These statutes have often been challenged in the court as a denial of 'equal protection' under the law, and as a violation of the general right of a party to exist. But it has been consistently upheld that restrictions are constitutional, and that there is no requirement to extend to small or new parties the same privileges that are granted to others.

5 **Fear of a wasted vote** Even if they get off the ground, it is difficult for third parties to sustain any momentum over a period, for to stay in business a party needs to be able to raise funds, maintain an organisation and reward its

supporters with the prospect of office or influence. As voters know that small parties will have difficulty in gaining power, they tend to regard a vote for them as a 'wasted vote'. If these parties cannot eventually win a majority of the votes, they are devoid of real influence; they will not get that majority if people think that they have little chance of achieving it and accordingly fail to vote for them.

Third parties

The late Clinton Rossiter[9] referred to the 'persistent, obdurate two party system', and went on to note that:

> There exists in this country today the materials – substantial materials in the form of potential leaders, followers, funds, interests and ideological commitments – for at least three important third parties, any one of which could, under the rules of some other system, cut heavily and permanently into the historic Democrat–Republican monopoly. There is no reasonable expectancy, under the rules of our system, that any such party could make a respectable showing in two successive elections. Indeed, if a new party were to make such a showing in just one election, the majority party closest to it would move awkwardly but effectively to absorb it.

Types of third party

Although the American political system is basically a two-party one, at various times third parties have had a significant impact. Many have existed throughout American history. In recent years, some third-party candidates have won election to public office, and in 1990 Alaska and Connecticut both elected independents in the battle for the state governorships. Vermont re-elected a socialist to the House in the same year. In 1996, Jesse Ventura, a former professional wrestler known as 'the body', was elected as governor for Minnesota, on behalf of the Reform Party (see opposite).

By a third party, we usually mean one that is capable of gathering a sizeable percentage of popular support and regularly gains seats in the legislature. On occasion, it may win – or threaten to win – enough support to influence the outcome of an election and the control of government, and in particular regions or constituencies it may break consistently through the usual two-party system. We do not usually refer to one that polls only a tiny percentage of the vote and almost never gains representation as a third party. Such organisations are really minor parties.

Most small parties in America are minor ones that may or may not be permanent; they rarely gain more than a minute percentage of the popular vote. From time to time, however, there are those that do erupt on to the national scene, and make headline news as they bid for the presidency. These are truly third parties. The terms are often used interchangeably in textbooks, and whether we describe them as third parties, minor parties or small parties we are here concerned with all of those bodies which are parties, but which operate outside the mainstream of the two-party battle.

These small parties differ considerably in type and permanence. They range from those formed to propagate a particular doctrine over a long duration to those that are more or less transient. The Prohibition and Socialist parties have over long periods been kept alive by bands of dedicated enthusiasts, and regularly contest elections of all types and in several states. But American party history is noted for the turbulence generated by the rapid rise and equally rapid decline of minor parties; they may play a significant role at a particular time, and then become extinct.

In the 2000 batch of elections, some fifty minor parties had candidates standing in one or more states. In 2005, sixty-five such parties had candidates for political office across America.

Third parties in presidential campaigns

Some third parties arise during presidential elections and continue to have an impact. Often they are based largely on a single person, as with Theodore Roosevelt (Bull Moose) and Perot (United We Stand, America in 1992, the Reform Party in 1996). In 1992, Perot created a high-profile campaign, and won the support of activists normally associated with the two main parties. Given his substantial wealth, he could afford to buy extensive advertising on television. For all of the resources at his disposal, he did not win a single state, although he gained an impressive 19% of the popular vote and a couple of good seconds, in Maine and Utah.

Perot's was at first more a personal movement than a formal political grouping, but by 1996 it had been transformed into the Reform Party. The party made little impact in 2000, despite running an expensive campaign. There was a serious clash between hard-line conservative nationalists such as Pat Buchanan (the official candidate) and more socially liberal figures such as Jesse Ventura. Elements among the Reformists seceded and cast their vote elsewhere and the internal schism has continued, with further splintering of the membership. Such events suggest that the party is now in deep trouble.

Some third parties break away from one of the main parties because of disagreement over aspects of the platform that the party currently adopts. John Anderson stood aside from the Republicans in 1980 because he disagreed with the conservative line taken on social issues by the Reaganites, even though he liked the economic approach of the Republican candidate.

Other third parties are more long-standing, such as the Libertarians and the Greens. In 2000, the highly visible consumerist Ralph Nader was the Green candidate. He managed to win 3% of the vote and was subsequently blamed by the Democrats for Al Gore's defeat by George W. Bush. In spite of being under pressure to withdraw from the contest in 2004, Nader stood again, but this time mustered less support.

A CASE STUDY OF THREE THIRD PARTIES, THEIR OUTLOOK AND IMPACT

The Green Party

The Green Party of the United States is an informal US affiliate of the left-wing environmentalist European Greens movement. In 1996, it persuaded the prominent consumer advocate Ralph Nader to run as its first presidential nominee. In 2000, he raised millions of dollars, mobilising leftist activists and grabbing national headlines with an anti-corporate message. He finished third with an impressive 2,878,000 votes, a performance that upset many Democrats, who felt that his intervention ruined Al Gore's chances of victory. Nader was under pressure not to stand in 2004, but persisted. His impact was less significant and his vote well down on four years earlier. Nader stresses that he is seeking to build a permanent third party and therefore needs to contest every election.

The Greens have in the past been a largely autonomous collection of local and state-based entities, with only a weak and sometimes splintered national leadership structure. In 2001, they voted to convert from an umbrella co-ordinating body into a formal and unified national party organization. Strong local Green parties – with ballot status – exist in a number of states.

The Libertarian Party

Americans are deeply attached to the ideas of personal liberty and limited government. Some are attracted to the Libertarian Party, formed in 1972. Claiming to be neither left nor right, Libertarians feel that neither left nor right can be trusted to defend the rights of individuals. Libertarians:
- espouse a classical laissez-faire (leave-alone) philosophy which, they argue, means 'more freedom, less government and lower taxes';
- wish to see most services run on a private basis, so that there is unrestricted freedom in commerce;
- disapprove of federal and state welfare programmes, and policies which offer subsidies to any group – farmers, business people and others;
- dislike any regulatory bodies of a federal nature such as the FBI or the CIA, and laws that curb individual freedom such as those on the wearing of seat belts and motor-bike helmets.

Whereas most conservatives take a socially restrictive view and wish to limit the sale of marijuana and other soft drugs, gambling, prostitution and pornography, Libertarians would leave such things unrestricted. They would abolish all legislation designed to

The role and importance of third parties

A source of new ideas

Third parties can think more of principles than power, for they are unlikely ever to have to implement their proposals. They can 'think the unthinkable', before it later becomes the fashion of the day. Through them, ideas and

---

promote a particular view of morality. On abortion, there is some division, though the founders of the party were more committed to allowing free choice. As might be anticipated, they oppose gun control and are pro-home schooling.

Libertarians traditionally billed themselves as 'America's largest third party' and still usually field more state and local candidates than any other third force. However, their claim has been undermined in recent years by the growth of the Greens, who have a larger following and attract more media attention. The Reform party too attracts more votes. In 2000 and again in 2004, both parties out-polled the Libertarians.

The New York Liberal Party

The Liberal Party of New York state claims to be the longest-existing third party in the history of the United States. It was founded in 1944 as an alternative to a state Democratic Party dominated by local party machines that were rife with corruption, and a Republican Party controlled by special interests. It has a history of nominating – or more often supporting – candidates on the basis of independence, merit and a progressive viewpoint, regardless of party affiliations; it is interested primarily in whether they are likely to provide good, effective and forward-looking government. Past nominees have included Governor Mario Cuomo, Senator Robert Kennedy and New York City Mayors Fiorello LaGuardia, John Wagner and Rudolph Giuliani.

Adopting a broadly centre-left stance, the Liberal Party has been for many years an influential force in New York politics, campaigning on such things as:
- reproductive freedom – a woman's right to choose abortion;
- health care – the need for a system which is well run and affordable;
- involvement in democracy – encouraging popular participation in civic life;
- environmental progress – a serious attempt to place environmental considerations at the forefront of policy-making;
- civil rights – comprehensive legislation to ensure that discrimination on grounds of race, ethnicity, religion, gender, sexual orientation, disability and economic class does not restrict people's lives.

The Liberal Party has declined in influence in recent years. Following a poor showing in the 2002 gubernatorial election, it lost its state recognition and ceased operations at its state offices. It is currently struggling to keep going, although dedicated enthusiasts are still proud to label themselves as Liberals. Internal dissension and secession have damaged their prospects of making a return to recognised party status. The Working Families Party (formed in 1998) has drawn away much of the Liberals' support, particularly among the trade unions.

interests that are not catered for within the main parties may find expression politically. Third parties can handle contentious issues on which neither major party can take or is willing to take a clear and decisive line. They provide new ideas and issues for the voters to consider. They are not faced with the difficulty of reconciling several views under one umbrella; they can be clear cut in the solutions they offer. They suffer no particularly serious consequences if their solutions are, on analysis, found to be wanting, for they are not putting them into effect. If the ideas do capture the public imagination, then they may well be adopted by one or other of the main parties. The policy is then translated into established public practice.

At various times the Socialists, Prohibitionists and Progressives have taken up controversial matters, and thereby acted as vehicles for the expression of political discontent. Some of the best ideas have been originally advanced by those outside the political mainstream. The point was well made by the historian Richard Hofstadter.[10] Writing of third parties, he observed that their function 'has not been to win or govern, but to agitate, educate [and] generate new ideas. When a third party's demands become popular enough, they are appropriated by one or both of the major parties and the third party disappears . . . [They] are like bees; once they have stung, they die.'

A healthy democratic outlet

Even if they do not see their ideas adopted and rarely or never win a congressional seat (let alone the ultimate prize of the presidency), small parties have at the very least drawn attention to the way people feel. They form an outlet for those who dislike the character and attitudes of both the main parties, and for those who reject the party battle they provide a haven. They articulate the thoughts of a section of society, and represent a segment of public sentiment. However incoherent or impractical their view may at times be, they have something to say which needs to be considered if only to be rejected. In a democracy, they have a right to exist and put forward their ideas, however weird they may seem to the majority of people.

Holding the balance

At rare times, a third party can be in an influential position, holding the balance of power and/or affecting the outcome of an election. This is unusual, but in 1992 the Perot intervention probably cost George Bush senior the presidency, just as the votes won by Nader in states such as Florida kept Al Gore out of the White House in 2000.

Socialism in America: its failure to take root

America has not proved to be fertile ground for socialist thinkers and their ideas. The main writers and philosophers of socialism have been Europeans, and their ideas and their approach have been developed from European experience. Perhaps because of the influence of German and Jewish believers, socialism has often been regarded as an alien import unsuited to the conditions of American life.

Socialism in its various forms is traditionally associated with the wish to replace private ownership of the means of production, distribution and exchange with a system of greater public ownership. In the ultimate socialist utopia, property is owned by the state on behalf of the people, and in Marx's phrase, each receives what is necessary for his or her needs: 'From each according to his ability, to each according to his needs.' In America, there is more discussion of the rights of private property than interest in public ownership.

American socialists of whatever disposition broadly favour an increased role for government, and wish to place a greater burden on the rich by higher taxation. They would use the revenue thereby obtained to introduce more redistributive policies, including public works schemes to offer work for the unemployed, and more aid to the least well-off.

Socialist doctrine has gained a small but influential following among a section of middle-class intellectuals, but the working classes have never taken up the cause with much enthusiasm or in any significant numbers. Groups have developed to represent the various shades of socialism, most notably the Socialist Party, but, as in Europe, these left-wing organisations have been prone to internal schism, factional strife and secession. There have been socialists on the ballot paper in recent years, either standing as individuals or representing the Socialist party or groups such as the Socialist Workers or Workers' World.

Why has socialism failed to make headway in America?

1 **The American Dream**. Most Americans see capitalism as basic to the American way of life, for it promotes enterprise and initiative. It is part of the American Dream that a person, given the right encouragement and incentives, can strike out on his or her own and make a fortune. Working hard, earning their reward, being able to keep most of what they earn, passing on their fortune – whatever its size – to their offspring: these are features of life in which there is much faith. The belief is that people should be able to keep what they earn, use it to buy property of their choice, be it a dream home or a more humble shack, a factory or a farm.

Fundamental to all of this is a belief in free enterprise, and this means that doctrines such as communism and socialism are seen as un-American by most voters. They don't want to see a redistribution of other people's wealth, they are more interested in having the freedom to go ahead and make their own. Neither do they like the state to take their money via excessive taxation and spend it on costly welfare programmes that discourage other people from being as self-reliant as they are themselves.

2 **The relative absence of class antagonism**. There was never any feudal system in the United States, no society with a hierarchy of lords and ladies at the top, peasants at the bottom. Americans were, in the words of de Tocqueville, 'born equal'.[11] There was never an American class struggle as one group sought to displace the influence of another. There are objective class divisions, but there has rarely been any sense of class consciousness or worker solidarity as seen in Western Europe. The principle of equality is little disputed, even though there are differences of opinion over exactly what it means in policy implementation.

3 **Overriding social factors more significant than class**. Class solidarity is less important than other social distinctions; racial and religious attachments are strong, with distinctive groups such as the Jews in New York, the Irish, the Europeans and so many others. America has a very heterogeneous population, and the massive wave of early twentieth-century immigration has created an ethnic mosaic that is matched by the religious diversity of these peoples. These groups have continued to exist in their social enclaves, though many have moved from inner cities to the outer suburbs. Americans have traditionally been conscious of their roots, even if they also wish to develop an American identity, learn the language and be naturalised as citizens. There is no sense of social solidarity, such as exists in parts of Europe. In particular, race and ethnicity cut across divisions based on other economic and social considerations.

4 **The absence of a tradition of strong, left-wing trade unionism.** Trade unionism has never been particularly attractive to many Americans, and unions have consequently never gained great influence. Those that did develop rarely based their ideas on socialism as a means of overthrowing the established economic order, and inclined to individualist rather than collectivist ideas. Any attempts to foment industrial strife by militant, left-wing trade unionists have met a hostile response. Such groups have sometimes been banned or in other ways actively discouraged.

The Socialist Party USA and its fate

The Socialist Party advocates progress via the ballot box, rather than militant revolutionary change. Staunchly anti-communist, it was established in 1900 by Eugene V. Debs, who stood five times for the presidency. In the first twenty years or so of its existence, it was the third largest national party. It elected two members to Congress, was represented in several state legislatures and localities, and at its peak had more than 100,000 members. But even at its peak, it never really challenged the supremacy of the major parties.

In the decades since World War II, the Socialist Party has suffered from serious internal schism, control passing from left to right and back again. Since 1973, it has focused its attention more on grassroots and local politics, and has dealt with the issue as to whether to stand in presidential elections on a case-by-case basis. In 2004, Walt Brown and Mary Alice Herbert were the presidential candidates, standing in fifteen states. Their efforts were rewarded with a meagre national total of around 11,000 votes. The party actively campaigns against restrictive state laws that deny it ballot access. When it is able to stand, it does so primarily in order to educate the public about socialism and the need for electoral democracy in the United States.

According to its own mission statement, the party stands for

> the abolition of every form of domination and exploitation, whether based on social class, gender, race/ethnicity, sexual orientation or other characteristics . . . and is committed to the transformation of capitalism through the creation of a democratic socialist society . . . It strives to establish a radical democracy that places people's lives under their own control – a non-racist, classless, feminist, socialist society in which people cooperate at work, at home and in the community.

The two main parties: Democrats and Republicans

Policy attitudes: similarities and differences between Democrats and Republicans

To non-Americans, the policy differences between the two main parties may seem modest, at times almost non-existent. Lord Bryce[12] once suggested that they were 'two bottles, each having a label denoting the kind of liquor it contains, but each being empty'. The parties have certainly often seemed to have much in common in their policy attitudes.

In fact, the rhetoric of politicians in both parties suggests greater dissimilarity than actually exists. They wish to emphasise the differences and thereby clarify the choice for the voters, but if one looks beyond the speeches and the party literature and examines the record of the parties when they have won the presidency in recent years, then often there has been a broad acceptance of much that has been accomplished by their opponents.

Both parties agree about far more things than they disagree about. Both attach great importance to the Constitution and are committed to maintaining America's present form of government. Both accept the pioneering American values of free enterprise and individualism, on which there is little discord in society. Neither favours root-and-branch change in the economic system. There is certainly no deep ideological divide, and in particular no contest between socialism in its various Western European forms and those who oppose it.

Each party's candidates always closely resemble the others and few contests between them ever present the electorate with a clear-cut choice. Many years ago, one commentator, D. W. Brogan, observed[13] that: 'The fact that all Republicans claim to be democrats and all Democrats to be republicans makes the confusion of party names nearly complete.' Both parties recognise the need to appeal to a wide spectrum of groups and interests, and this generally keeps them near to the political centre; they have tended to offer a broad range of rather similar programmes. It is rarely the case that one party is united against the other. This is particularly true when the two parties are in a broadly consensual mould, less so when, as in the early Reagan years, one party veers off on a more distinctive ideological route.

Even when differences are more discernible, it is important to realise that the differences within parties can be more significant than those between them. A Massachusetts Democrat such as Edward Kennedy may be a very different political animal from a colleague from Arkansas or the Deep South, as is often an east-coast Republican from one out in the Midwest. However, there are differences of emphasis and style, degree and method, and distinct bases of support. It is to the differences that we now turn.

See also pp. 257 and 262–3) for lists of party mission statements in the 2004 election.

Each party has its own character and image. A 'typical Democrat' might be a member of an ethnic minority, belong to a trade union and the working class, be non-Protestant and an urban dweller. He or she would support measures of social welfare to assist the poor and needy, favour regulation of big business and a fairer distribution of wealth, and support the global role of America as leader of the free world. A 'typical Republican' might be white, male, middle class, college-educated and Protestant. He would support law and order, believe in limited government and individualism, support big business and free enterprise, be wary of American involvement overseas, and see himself as a conservative.

Yet this is too simplistic, as generalisations invariably are. The Democrats have supporters who are white and black, working class and middle class, urban and rural dwellers, combining as they do workers in the northern industrial cities and more wealthy farmers in the West. The Republicans have within their ranks business, professional and working people, many who are small-town religious fundamentalists and some who are city agnostics, many who support curbs on abortion, others who believe in free choice.

If we look at specific issues, there tend to be divergent positions on such contentious matters as:
- abortion;
- civil rights for blacks and other disadvantaged groups;
- affirmative action;
- the role of the federal government in education;
- anti-poverty policies and welfare reform;
- the provision of medical care;
- the problems of urban renewal;
- defence spending and the role of America in the post-Cold-War era.

One way of distinguishing the parties has in the past been to categorise them as 'liberal' or 'conservative' in tone and outlook, depending on how they view such controversies. Since 1932 the Democrats have generally taken a liberal position, whereas the Republicans have adopted a more conservative stance. The distinction is not always an effective one, for as we can see from the discussion on pp. 254–5 the 'l' word is one that has gone out of fashion in American politics. In recent years, the centre of gravity has moved well to the right. Nevertheless, for a long while after 1932 the division had some validity, and there are some party supporters who remain proud to be a liberal or conservative.

Examples of the likely beliefs of liberals and conservatives

Approach to policy	Liberals	Conservatives
Role of government	Important as regulator in public interest	Distrust, preference for free-market solutions
Spending	Spend more on disadvantaged	Keep spending down
Taxes	Tax the rich more	Keep taxes down
Abortion	Emphasise freedom of choice	Support right to life
Affirmative action	In favour	Wary, wish to make inroads
Crime	Look for causes of crime, respect rights of accused	Be tough on criminals, stress rights of victims
School prayer	Opposed	In favour

American liberalism

Classical liberalism emphasised liberty and individual rights, and a minimal role for state intervention. But by the twentieth century, liberalism became associated with protecting the individual by a regulatory action. Today's liberals see government as having a positive role in promoting greater justice in society and more equality of opportunity. They talk of individual rights, including the right to own private property, but they also see a need for measures to control the defects of a market economy. Most accept that inequalities of wealth are inevitable and even desirable, but they wish to ensure that everyone has a certain minimum level of wealth, so that they can enjoy life and have a fair deal.

Franklin Roosevelt was the model for American liberals, with his attempt to steer America out of the Depression via the New Deal. President Kennedy is similarly regarded as a liberal hero, one of his speeches echoing liberal values:

> I believe in human dignity as the source of national purpose, in human liberty as the source of national action, in the human heart as the source of national compassion, and in the human mind as the source of our invention and our ideas. It is, I believe, the faith in our fellow citizens as individuals and as people that lies at the heart of the liberal faith.

The problems of the twenty-first century are different, for the country operates in a more prosperous climate than the days of FDR, but there are still those who are left behind. Modern liberals want to provide better education and housing, are alarmed by inadequate and costly health care, and support progressive taxation graduated according to the individual's ability to pay. They are committed to civil rights and affirmative action to overcome the effects of past discrimination against minorities and women; many activists involved in areas ranging from the women's movement and the pro-choice campaign to the gay and disabled movements come within the liberal fold. These are all examples of the positive use of government to improve society and remove its defects.

Neo-liberalism and the passing of Rooseveltian liberalism

In the last few years there has been talk of neo-liberals, who are willing to argue the case for traditional liberal beliefs of justice and liberty, and the need for government intervention, but who do not endorse the whole liberal agenda. Neo-liberals are more suspicious of union power, welfare provision and big government with its large, Washington-based bureaucracies. Some also doubt the increasing concern for minority causes. In the words of Irving Kristol,[14] a leading proponent of the idea, they are 'liberals mugged by reality'.

The growth of neo-liberalism reflects the fact that liberalism has rather gone out of fashion. Even those who believe in it are aware of its allegedly adverse effects. Critics, mainly Republicans and southern Democrats, have portrayed liberalism as being too concerned with federal action by the government, with costly programmes which require huge bureaucracies to run them, and with penal taxation which hits voters in their pockets and tends to destroy their incentive for individual effort. Welfare is seen as damaging to the qualities that made America what it is; it undermines the work ethic and the entrepreneurial spirit. Neo-liberalism has more in common with classical liberalism – laissez-faire, the minimal state, and a strong commitment to economic freedom that is interpreted in a different way from what FDR meant by the term.

In 1992, Clinton was concerned to show himself as a new type of Democrat. In the more conservative climate of that decade, he and others were anxious to show that they too believed in the virtues of free enterprise, the perils of communism, the need for tough action against criminals, strong defence and a new emphasis upon traditional patriotism. 'Liberalism' has increasingly become a term of abuse used by those on the political right. The 'l' word was used by George W. Bush against John Kerry, whom it was easy – if in some ways misleading – to portray as a Massachusetts liberal.

Liberalism still has its advocates, and, at a time when politicians are reluctant to use the word, there have been academics and journalists who see merit in what it stands for. Thus Arthur Schlesinger could write an article entitled 'Hurray for the L-Word', in which he claimed:[15]

> The presidents we admire and celebrate most – Jefferson, Jackson, Lincoln, Theodore Roosevelt, Wilson, FDR, Harry Truman and JFK – were all, in the context of their times, vigorous and unashamed liberals. They were all pioneers of new frontiers, seeking out the ways of the future, meeting new problems with new remedies, carrying the message of constructive change in a world that never stops changing. From the start of the Republic, liberalism has always blazed the trail into the future – and conservatism has always deployed all the weapons of caricature and calumny and irrelevance to conceal the historic conservative objective of unchecked rule by those who already have far more than their fair share of the nation's treasure.

The Democrats

Rossiter[16] was right in suggesting that a usual characteristic of Democratic rule has been a willingness to embrace change. The party accepts innovation, and has since the days of Woodrow Wilson been more willing to extend governmental intervention and welfare programmes. The very names given by presidential contenders to their party platform suggests an acceptance of the need to embrace innovation and move forward with the task of reform. Woodrow Wilson offered the 'New Freedom', Franklin Roosevelt the 'New Deal', Harry

Truman the 'Fair Deal', John Kennedy the 'New Frontiers', Lyndon Johnson the 'Great Society', and Bill Clinton the 'New Covenant'.

Since the New Deal, the Democrats have been the party associated with more positive government action to promote social welfare and regulate business activity. They were seen as standing for some redistribution of income, the extension of welfare measures and increased governmental expenditure. Yet in the last decade or so, Democrats have gone some way to shed this image. Bill Clinton's programme, in 1992 sounded a far cry from the more liberal ones of some of his party predecessors. It was notably more cautious than the platform adopted by Kennedy and Johnson.

Clinton attempted to blend features of the liberal tradition of positive government with elements of the traditional Republican programme such as controlling the budget deficit. He knew that Americans were growing weary of the problems posed by the urban centres, with such things as the breakdown of law and order, the preoccupation with civil rights and the use of affirmative action. Their anxieties about particular programmes combined with a feeling that government was growing 'too big'. They disliked the spiralling cost of welfare and other public spending, and warmed to promises to 'get Washington off their backs' and lower taxes. In his New Covenant programme, Clinton was responding to profound changes in American attitudes.

Within the present Democratic Party, Nicol Rae has distinguished[17] several groupings:

1 The **New Left** is the most liberal faction and represents the minorities who inhabit the party. It supports interventionist policies to help the disadvantaged – blacks, Latinos, gays and the disabled. It is generally pacific in its approach to foreign policy, and its attitudes are popular on university campuses. Rev. Jesse Jackson belongs in this camp.

2 **Neo-liberals** broke away from the New Left and therefore have the same ancestry. Supporters stress administrative competence rather than traditional 'tax-and-spend' policies, and are generally sympathetic to civil liberties and minority rights. The neo-liberal approach appeals to professional suburbanites.

3 **Regulars** represent the mainstream party tradition, with its emphasis on governmental intervention in economic and welfare matters; they also tend to be more 'hawkish' on foreign policy. 'Regular' attitudes are more appealing to labour (unions) and to Catholics.

4 **Southerners**, such as Bill Clinton and Al Gore, tend to take a more conservative stance on a range of issues. They are less enthusiastic about government intervention and labour, are pro-free market in economics, and tend to take a robust stance in foreign policy. Traditional liberal nostrums have little appeal, but on civil rights they are more sympathetic than

southern Democrats of the past; they rely heavily on black votes. They appeal otherwise to the white working class and rural voters. After the 1984 defeat, the **Democratic Leadership Council (DLC)** was formed, largely by southern Democrats. It seeks to organise and co-ordinate the more centrist elements within the Democratic coalition. It serves as a forum for debate on policy, and has a Washington 'think-tank' – the Progressive Policy Unit (PPU) – and a magazine, the *New Democrat*.

The mission statements of state Democrat parties in 2004

Main priorities are listed.

Oregon:
- government not the enemy, but a partner in bettering ourselves and our communities;
- maximising opportunities in public education;
- the rights of workers to organise, bargain collectively and strike if necessary, as well as to earn sufficient wages to support their families;
- personal and community safety, as part of a criminal justice system which protects the rights of victims and the accused; preventing crime;
- affordable, comprehensive and confidential health care;
- environmental programme to manage resources and provide for a sustainable economy, via the use of public investment in renewable resources and emerging technologies;
- human rights and justice, enforcing anti-discrimination legislation, honouring Indian treaty rights and repealing the USA Patriot Act (p. 304);
- international action to promote peace, end terrorism and encourage democratic reforms worldwide.

Texas:
- equal opportunity for all citizens;
- rewards for honest, hard work, involving a living wage and a tax system that is fair;
- values that support and strengthen families;
- quality public education that gives all citizens the opportunity to reach their potential;
- freedom from government interference in private lives and personal decisions;
- separation of the church and state to preserve the freedom to pursue beliefs;
- the strengths inherent in a diverse population;
- security in our homes and safety on our streets; criminals should face swift and certain punishment;
- the moral, economic, diplomatic and military strength of the United States.

NB The Democrat performance in November 2004 is described on pp. 227–5.

The Republicans

Republicans have traditionally been more cautious than the Democrats in their approach. Sometimes they have been deeply conservative, their pro-business, pro-free enterprise tendencies gaining the upper hand. At other times, in the years of the New Deal and after, party spokespersons often sounded less hostile to government intervention, recognising the popularity of many Democratic initiatives. But there was always a general unease about the direction in which their opponents had taken the country. Many Republicans were lukewarm about the expanding role of the federal government in economic and social matters. These anxieties have developed since the 1980s, and the modern party wishes to curb the size and scale of governmental activity. It is more interested in economy in government, and the pursuit of the low taxation that reduced expenditure allows.

Some common Republican attitudes

- **Family** – members support conventional and God-fearing families.
- **Organised labour** – members tend to dislike union activity and resist the idea of industrial action.
- **Minorities** – many members are descendants of earlier settlers and pioneers (White, Anglo-Saxon Protestants: WASPs) and are suspicious of newer arrivals and of the countries from which they arrived.
- **Foreign policy** – members are often among the sharpest critics of active involvement overseas. Some are deeply isolationist, and even the east-coast establishment tends to be concerned about the scale of commitment made to Western Europe and the use of American troops abroad. There is a strong emphasis upon 'Americanism' and patriotic goals, involving protecting America's status in the world.

Moderate Republicans

Some Republicans continue to adhere to the party's more liberal beliefs and traditions, although in recent decades the influence of New Right thinking and of the conservative evangelicals in the Religious Right has left them beyond the mainstream. Republican congressmen who support more moderate ideas and policies may be found in two groupings:

- **The Ripon Society** was founded in 1962, taking its name from the Republican Party's birthplace in Ripon, Wisconsin. The society believes that certain Republican values are permanent, whatever the shifts in party opinion at any given time. It promotes a 'common-sense' agenda of limited government, a vibrant free market economy, strong families, civil rights, and a foreign policy guided by pursuit of America's national

In the 1980s, traditional conservatism – as described – increasingly gave way to a new variety of ultra-conservatism, its adherents often known collectively as the **New or Radical Right**. Ronald Reagan said that 'government is the problem'. True to this spirit, the Reagan years saw an emphasis upon the market economy, a relaxation of anti-business controls, hostility to organised trade unionism, and low taxation. In as much as government was accepted as necessary, there was a move towards local or state governmental action over that of the federal government. Reagan's approach appealed to many conservatives in America.

Members of the New Right shared much of the ground occupied by other conservatives, but they became associated with particular causes which they wished to see become accepted as public policy. They sought to achieve their programme via greater representation in Congress, and in November 1994 the **Contract with America** was based upon the New Right's philosophical approach.

Contract with America

The policy platform agreed by House Republican candidates in the run-up to the elections of November 1994. It consisted of ten bills that collectively indicated its conservative character.

The New Right wrapped itself in the symbols of nationalism and patriotism, and supporters took a strong stand in favour of business, the death penalty and school prayer, issues which struck a chord with many voters. Today, it has a more distinctive social agenda than its conservative forebears, and its restrictive policies include strict control over abortion, drugs and pornography. It dislikes affirmative action and forced busing, and is lukewarm in its support for any legislation to advance civil rights.

interests. It acts as a haven for Republican moderates, and via its journal, the *Ripon Forum*, it circulates its policy ideas. It stresses the need for the party to reach out to all Americans. Members are wary of the influence of the Christian Coalition and campaign against the overrepresentation of small midwestern and western states in the party, seeing these as antagonistic to moderate Republicanism.

• **The Tuesday Group** traditionally focused on fiscal matters, but today members discuss issues such as defence, the environment and science. They do not agree and act in unison on every issue, there being differences over issues such as abortion rights and gun control. But all are committed to a moderate approach to policy issues. They are willing to act alongside moderate and conservative Democrats, in a spirit of bipartisanship.

In recent years, mainstream Republican thinking has incorporated these New Right attitudes and the more moderate or liberal element of the party has been sidelined. (see, however, the adjacent box on 'Moderate Republicans'). However, whereas Reaganite conservatives saw government as 'the problem' and wished to curb its influence, Bushite supporters want to government to act as an enabling force that encourages citizens to assist themselves. The platform of George W. Bush in 2000 and 2004 was based on what he terms 'compassionate conservatism'. Whilst emphasising the party's traditional concerns, it makes reference to the need for a caring and inclusive approach that caters for those disadvantaged by the operation of the free market. 'Compassionate conservatices' or 'Comcons' envisage a triangular relationship between government, charities and faith-based organisations (churches).

The Bush platform owes much to the outlook of the so-called 'Moral Majority', for the influence of Christian fundamentalists (often known as the Religious Right) is fast growing in the United States. Its supporters have been successful at the local level in building a powerful base, and within the Republican Party their position is a strong one. They hold that religious values are the cement that holds the fabric of society together. Supporters are therefore especially concerned with what is taught in schools, for this will influence the attitudes and behaviour of coming generations.

The rise and continued rise of the Religious Right

Nicole Rae[18] has identified three key elements within the modern Republican Party, where the Religious Right has come to assume greatest importance in recent years:
1 **economic conservatives**, who favour competition and free markets, and on economic issues align with the libertarian right;
2 **the libertarian right**, which promotes a free market economy but criticises the growth of the role of government not just in economic, but in other aspects of life. Members stress the freedom of the individual, and see government as a threat to liberty;
3 **the Christian right**, which represents the hopes, fears and prejudices of 'ordinary' white families from small-town or suburban America. Its supporters are distinguished by their moral fervour. Although they are broadly conservative in their outlook, they do not always see eye to eye with economic conservatives.

The Christian Right

Members of the Religious Right (also known as the Christian Coalition) are concerned to take the American nation back to its true heritage, and they believe that to do so they must restore the godly principles that made the nation great. The telegenic Pat Robertson is a leading spokesman. Via his daily talk show, *The 700 Club* – a mixture of faith-healing, hymns and Christian-orientated news – he informs his listeners that in the outlook of 'liberals' it is wrong to ridicule Hispanics, blacks, the disabled, women, the gays and lesbians, but it is 'open season' for ridiculing and humiliating, denigrating and insulting Christians, 'as it was with the Jews in Nazi Germany'. In a compilation of answers given on *The 700 Club*,[19] he portrays the women's movement as a 'socialist, anti-family, political movement that encourages women to leave their husbands, kill their children, practise witchcraft and become lesbians'. He thunders that: 'God does not want us to turn America over to radical feminists, militant homosexuals, profligate spenders, humanists or world communists'.

Since a loss of influence in the late 1980s, the Religious Right has rethought its strategy. Its approach has become more sophisticated. It is based on building up grassroots support, by involving people at the local level on the city council and the school board – as well aiming for the more obvious congressional targets. In 2000 and 2004, enthusiasts for the cause mailed or handed out millions of 'scorecards', showing the voting records of congressmen on 'issues critical to the family'.

Evangelical Christians have directly involved themselves in the political process. They are encouraged to participate in Sunday evening sermons, with the advice usually pointing to the Republicans as the appropriate party for godly Christians to support. This is made easy, for members of the congregation are often given sample ballot papers showing how and where to mark support for the required candidates.

Once in local office, Christian representatives on school boards seek to eliminate 'irreligious' material, particularly books which mention alternative lifestyles and such things as abortion or witchcraft: for example, Roald Dahl's *The Witches* has been banned from school library shelves by some boards. Teachers have been told that they should teach 'creation science' (the story of the world's creation as told in Genesis) as well as – or in some cases instead of – Darwinian theories of evolution. The Bible is seen as literally true and to be regarded as the prime resource of learning. Other books which do not meet the necessary criteria include works by Martin Luther King, C. S. Lewis, Rudyard Kipling and A. A. Milne. There are now some 2,250 school boards in the United States, and the Religious Right reckons to control 15% of them.

Among Republicans there is a schism, for more traditional party regulars fear a takeover of the party. The Christian Coalition is similarly contemptuous of what it portrays as 'country-club' Republicans of the old type, who somewhere along the way lost their conservative agenda and became 'me-tooists', too close to the Democrats. Its policies have much appeal in middle America, which has over the last generation had to come to grips with the sexual revolution and the rise of left-wing radical activism, and doesn't like what it sees. Members wish to stress pro-life policies, and take a firm line on issues such as capital punishment. Some even talk enthusiastically of a wish to export convicts to Mexico, which is prepared to take them for a price and incarcerate them more cheaply.

Among other Christian Coalition policies are:
- the abolition of federal endorsement for the arts;
- the elimination of the federal and state departments of education;
- a cap on spending on AIDS research and treatment;
- compulsory reporting of AIDS carriers;
- the mandatory teaching of creationism;
- the abolition of abortion;
- the restriction on pre-school education;
- the rejection of gun control.

The Religious Right was temporarily in retreat after the failure of the Clinton impeachment trial, which its supporters strongly backed. But as the outcome of the 2004 presidential election indicates, (see pp. 230–4), it remains a highly potent electoral force on the American political scene. Exit polls suggested that 'moral values' had been the most important issue in determining the outcome of the 2004 vote. Eight out of ten of those for whom such values were the paramount concern voted for George W. Bush.

The mission statements of state Republican parties in 2004

Main priorities are listed.

Arkansas:
- importance of respect for religion and a strong faith in God;
- no undue government intervention; more scope for individuals and families;
- making the state serve the people better;
- governments to pursue only those policies which encourage individual initiative and responsibility for economic, political and social well-being;
- basic functions of government are protection of life, liberty and property, and equal justice under the law;
- power to be exercised at the lowest possible level;
- freedom to be inseparable from responsibilities to serve and participate in the life of the community, and work for preservation of our freedom.

Minnesota:
- cutting taxes and public spending;
- tackling crime;

- raising educational standards;
- family security and protecting life;
- property rights;
- government reform and ethics;
- health and welfare reform.

The voters and the parties: their perceptions

Ever since the New Deal, those with low incomes – particularly the urban working class, including the blacks and other racial minorities – have leaned strongly towards the Democrats. More affluent suburban voters have traditionally been keen supporters of the Republicans, other than a liberal element in the middle class.

The voters seem to know how to tell the parties apart, and most Americans are quite capable of identifying particular attitudes and approaches within the two parties which are seen as standing for something distinctive. Most of the business and professional people, and large farmers, judge that the Republican party best serves their interests, while workers tend to look to the Democrats as being more helpful to them, 'the party of the little man'. This characterisation owes much to the New Deal, and the subsequent programmes of leading Democrats such as Truman, Kennedy and Johnson. Such an easy division into working and middle class is less clear cut than it once was, and the union-orientated bias of the Democrats has become less apparent than in former years. But polls suggest that the instincts of many voters about the two main parties have not significantly changed.

The Republicans are widely seen as the party that does not wish to expand the role of government, especially in Washington. They are viewed as being more lukewarm about innovations, whereas Democrats tend to see positive action as necessary to promote social welfare and control the worst of the operations of big business. Their opponents would call this traditional 'tax-and-spend' Democrat thinking.

The roll of interest groups that are broadly supportive of the main parties also tells us something about their respective leanings. Republicans have long been more associated with the American Farm Bureau Federation, the National Association of Manufacturers, and the American Medical Association (AMA). The Democrats are preferred by many members of the National Farmers Union (NFU), the American Federation of Labor and Congress of Industrial Organisations (AFL/CIO), and the American Political Science Association.

Party organisation

Mass organisation developed soon after the Constitution was designed, and was under way in the 1790s. Since then, the grassroots has always been a significant source of power. Whereas in Britain the party headquarters has substantial control over the local party, in America it is the other way round. Indeed, at a national level, parties only come together four-yearly to bring about the election of the presidential candidate.

American parties are then, for most of the four-year cycle, loose alliances of state and local parties, and this **decentralisation** reflects the federal nature of the system of government. Indeed, parties are more decentralised than the system of government, which is why Malcolm Shaw[20] described the party system as 'confederal'.

> **decentralisation**
> Decision-making power is dispersed to local branches of the party organisation, so that the party is regulated at the state or local level rather than the national level.

There are so many offices for election in the United States at state and county level, and even lower, that the local party workers have many aspects on which to concentrate their attention. Their concern with Washington seems a far cry from this local preoccupation.

In the more centralised British system of party organisation, agents have a role at the constituency, regional and national level, and are all trained in and supervised from London. In the US, there is no comparable system. Local parties in America are not watched over in the same way. They have a free hand to choose the candidates of their choice, without any reference to headquarters. There is no list of 'approved' candidates provided from the centre, and it is highly unusual for there to be any attempt at influence or interference. The decision rests with the local party, though the system of primaries and the limitations on funding mean that the individual plays a substantial role in securing his or her own election.

The national role of parties is relatively small. Every four years, Democratic and Republican headquarters come to life; in between they contract. They do not have the powers to control local or state bodies, issue binding policy positions, or censure members or elected representatives who stray from official party policy.

The national and local structure of the two main parties

Generalisation about the organisation of the two main parties is difficult, for the situation undergoes periodic change. For instance, the balance of power between minority activists and traditional party power-brokers is liable to fluctuate. Similarly, because the party system is decentralised and the state parties can go their own way, the structural pattern is not identical throughout the nation. Nevertheless, it is broadly similar, even if it can vary in details from state to state.

The key functions of parties are concerned with choosing candidates for office, perhaps via the organisation of primaries, and especially with mobilising support behind the person who is chosen. Each tier of the party structure is therefore primarily concerned with elections in its own geographical area and is largely autonomous.

The Republican and Democratic National Committees (RNCs and DNCs) are the main national organisation in each party. The headquarters in Washington, DC, operates under the direction of the party's national chair, and is run day to day by a small paid office staff plus volunteers. Their job is to prevent the national party organisation fading away completely between presidential elections. Members meet a few times a year, survey the political scene and make pronouncements. The committees do some research work, produce occasional publications for party activists and are involved in raising money. But their main work is to clear up the finances of the party after the presidential election and plan for the next convention four years hence, choosing the location and making organisational arrangements.

The National Convention in each party is held four-yearly. Conventions are the arenas in which key players in the party seek to shape the future direction of their policy, and – if they are successful in capturing the presidency – of the nation as well. Their main task is to choose the presidential candidate. Effectively, candidates have usually already been chosen, having built up sufficient convention votes via the primaries and party caucuses (held in states where there are no primaries). However, if there was to be any uncertainty, this is where the choice would be resolved. A vice-presidential candidate is also chosen, and a platform on policy agreed. The convention then serves as the launch-pad for the bid to win the ultimate prize: the presidency itself.

Traditionally, the essential business at a Republican gathering was done behind closed doors, whereas the Democrats have been more open about their dealings and more willing to have rows in public. Things have changed in recent decades. In 1976, the Reagan supporters staged a challenge to the incumbent Gerald Ford on the convention floor, and twelve years later the proceedings were again lively and acrimonious as six challengers pleaded for the nomination.

At the state and local levels, organisation is carried out on the same lines. Each state has a state committee, headed by a state chair. Below state level, there are county committees, with varying functions and powers. At all levels, it is the choice and election of candidates for local office which are the key task. For winnable vacancies, there may be a primary contest. Where success is unlikely, it may be more a question of finding a candidate who will allow his or her name to go forward.

Recent trends

Traditionally, American parties have been decentralised coalitions of state and local parties, with a very limited role for the national organisations. However, since the 1960s, there have been a number of contradictory trends in the development of parties. In general, there has been a weakening of their role in selecting candidates, making policy, raising funds, informing the voter and channelling the demands of groups in society. But at the same time, via party reforms, there has been a strengthening of national party organisations, especially regarding the selection of delegates to the party conventions.

The reforms in party organisations originally stemmed from a desire, especially among elements in the Democratic Party, to reduce the power of party regulars from the states and increase participation by the voters in the process of choosing a presidential candidate. The Democrats introduced changes along these lines in the early 1970s, and the Republicans also tried to encourage participation by minority groups and ease access to selection meetings. These reforms strengthened the role of the national organisations, but two other developments weakened the power of national parties:

1 the increase in the number of presidential primaries, which led to the growth of more candidate-orientated campaigns;
2 a change in the type of people who participated in the nomination of presidential candidates. Party leaders at state and local levels have less weight and the role of minority groups has increased.

The theses of party decline and of continued party vitality

The thesis of decline, as developed by several commentators, suggested that the two main parties had been overwhelmed by the range of challenges that confronted them; they were unable to adapt to the changing political environment. Writing in 1972, Broder[21] contended that national parties were in retreat in areas they had traditionally dominated, particularly in their most basic function, selecting and running candidates for public office. There was widespread agreement that parties, always weak, were in a seemingly irreversible cycle of decline, unable to respond effectively to changing circumstances.

Since 1980, this sombre view has been questioned. J. Bibby and A. J. Reichley have claimed[22] that the evidence presented in the 1960s had been largely misinterpreted and that (certainly by the 1980s) parties had begun to adapt successfully. They saw evidence of party vitality, indeed of 'renewal'.

From this side of the Atlantic, Christopher Bailey[23] saw the 'most clear evidence of the continued vitality of the political parties . . . in the Republican Party', but felt that by the mid-1980s the Democrats were also 'showing signs of continued vitality'. He quoted various commentators who believed that political action committees (PACs), often seen as having 'rendered the parties obsolete', actually supplemented rather than challenged the work of parties;

indeed, they 'often follow the party's lead when deciding which candidates to support. Moreover, many PACs have aligned themselves with either the Democratic Party or the Republican Party because of shared beliefs and values.'

There has been a modest resurgence of parties in recent years. They have shown that they can perform a useful, if limited, role. Partly, this has come about because the new issues of the 1960s and 1970s have lost some of their importance, but it is mainly connected with the new emphasis on strengthening party organisation at the federal level and reviving the party role in fundraising. The Democrats weakened the power of party regulars and allowed minority activists a greater voice in party affairs. After the Watergate scandal, the Republicans too saw the need to clean up the party and make its organisation more professional and more appealing.

Both parties have developed new techniques of fundraising that make them useful and enable them to play once more a significant role in election campaigning. Candidates challenging for office have been keen to seek help from the increasingly more professional party associations, which can provide them with personal training, information networks, news clippings and research on their opponents, expertise in targeting particular precincts, and some financial help. Aldrich[24] concludes that 'they [the parties] have become more truly national parties, better financed, more professionalised and more institutionalised, with greater power to shape the actions of their state and local organisations'.

In the 1980s, Paul Hernnson[25] developed a different model, stressing the 'primacy of the individual candidate in campaigning, and seeing parties as support agencies for candidate-centred campaign organisations'. Rather than parties running candidates for office, candidates run for office and seek to attract the resources of parties and other bodies for their own use. It is still 'easier for most candidates to obtain [resources] from the parties than from alternative sources'.

In 2005, the two main parties retain their predominance in presidential elections, the challenge posed by third-party candidates having effectively been 'seen off'. Other evidence in favour of 'resurgence' includes:
- the high degree of partisanship in the era of George W. Bush, which has provoked many Democrats into uniting against the man who 'stole' the White House in 2000;
- the lack of minority representation in the past and present Congress – even those who have claimed to be independent have normally aligned themselves with one of the main parties;
- greater party unity in Congress;
- the continued importance of the parties in fundraising and campaigning;

- some evidence of more party activity at the grassroots level, in developing organisations and in campaigning.

If anything, there are today two parties competing for office that are more sharply polarised than for many years. The disappearance of the bulk of the white, conservative element among the southern Democrats, and the decline of the liberal element among the Republicans (especially in the northeastern states), have made the two parties more cohesive and provided them with a clearer ideological identity than was the case a few decades ago.

Bailey[26] provides some balance to the debate about resurgence. As he has indicated, 'it is clear that attempts to characterise the developments of the last two decades are extremely problematic'. Because of the fact that different writers draw upon different evidence – or interpret the same evidence in a different manner – some portray a picture of party decline, others one of renewal.

Party weakness and decline: a summary

American political parties are essentially weak and always have been, especially by comparison with parties in many other democracies.

Reasons for the historic weakness of parties include the following:
- The federal system places emphasis on the role of state rather than national parties.
- The concept of the separation of powers encourages members of a party in Congress to question even a president of their own party.
- The notion of broad consensus in American politics covers a range of fundamental issues.
- The ethos of individualism in American society is a feature of the widely shared American Dream.

Parties became weaker in the twentieth century because:
- The growth of the system of primary elections made candidates less beholden to the parties.

PARTIES IN BRITAIN AND THE UNITED STATES: A COMPARISON

In both democracies, parties fulfil some similar functions, notably clarifying the issues, stimulating public interest, supporting (in Britain choosing) candidates, organising the voters and providing an institutional framework for legislators. However, there are basic differences in the way in which parties operate in Britain and the United States.

Britain has party government. Under normal circumstances, a party wins an election and afterwards is in control of both the executive and the legislature. Having had its programme accepted by the electorate, it is expected to govern. To do so, it requires cohesive and disciplined parties if it is to act effectively. By contrast, America does not have party government in the same sense. Party allegiance is one factor borne in mind

Today, most people still think of politics in terms of the Democrat–Republican divide, and congressmen are almost entirely elected according to their party label. Parties do matter, both for politicians and for the electorate.

From a British perspective, it is easy to overstate the importance of parties at national level, and stress too much their decline or renewal. Commentators and academics on this side of the Atlantic sometimes place the emphasis on the national parties, especially their role in the nomination of presidential candidates, the most interesting and glamorous aspect of the process. But this is not the main arena for party activists and, as Alan Ware[27] has noted, 'in the federal structure it has always been at the local and state levels of politics that the parties have . . . had their main bases of power; contests for the presidency are merely the smallest but most highly visible apex of party politics'.

- The development of the mass media led to more candidate-orientated electioneering.
- The 'new issues' that arrived on the political agenda, such as, feminism and environmentalism often crossed party lines.
- The increasing importance of pressure groups and PACs provided a new basis of support for candidates.

Parties enjoyed some resurgence in the late twentieth century because:
- Some of the new issues went off the agenda.
- PACs and groups began to work with parties, rather than as a replacement for them.
- Internal party reforms were carried out in the 1970s and thereafter.
- Parties have adapted to the role of working with and supporting candidates and been in the forefront of adopting new electioneering techniques.
- The parties have become more cohesive, having each shed an important element in their former make-up.

---

when decisions are made about public policy, but there is no similar expectation that the 'party line' will be followed. Often, key figures in American government are admired precisely because they do not adopt the party stance on issues of the day. Parties are less disciplined, although in Congress it is true that almost without exception members are identified as belonging to one of the two main parties.

The reasons for these differences have much to do with the American Constitution, which was designed to disperse power in two ways. First, the Founding Fathers established a federal system across the country, and second, they were keen to create competitive institutions (the separation of powers). Both have the effect of making party government difficult and, as we have seen, do much to undermine tight discipline.

There are some similarities between the two systems. As well as the two main parties, several small ones exist on either side of the Atlantic, but the electoral system ensures that in most situations they are unlikely to make a significant impact on the outcome of elections; there are formidable hurdles for them to overcome. There are difficulties with labelling the American system as a two-party system (see pp. 239–41), and in Britain the presence of a sizeable third party as well as nationalist parties in Scotland and Wales leads some commentators to talk not of a two-party system, but of three- or four-party politics.

Policy attitudes

Of the two main British parties, one has often been characterised as a socialist party, whereas in America socialism has failed to take root. But in this respect, the two countries have moved closer. New Labour is not usually described as 'socialist' in any meaningful sense, other than by traditional party backers who cling to the party's past ethos. It has also gone some way to detach itself from the unions, making it more akin in style to the American Democrats. Significantly, both Bill Clinton (New Democrat) and Tony Blair (New Labour) have advocated similar 'third way' politics, shunning the old 'big government' and 'tax-and-spend' attitudes of bygone years and instead being willing to use the power of government yet also encourage personal responsibility.

Both countries have left and right, progressive and conservative, parties. Labour and the Democrats are more willing to accept governmental intervention and expand social welfare; the Conservatives and the Republicans are attracted by less government and lower taxes. As we have seen, Labour has moved nearer to the Democrats than in the

CONCLUSION

Political parties provide an important link between the voters and their elected representatives. In the US, a two-party system has evolved, dominated by the Democrats and the Republicans. Other parties have been unable to make much headway, even if some have been on the political scene a long while. Many voters no longer feel the same loyalty towards the two parties that their parents and grandparents did, and neither party can count on a permanent body of supporters. But most Americans still think in terms of the Democrat–Republican divide and are able to detect some difference between them. Parties remain important to candidates and office-holders, as well as to the voters.

Parties are essential in any democracy. They fulfil important functions such as organising the competition for public offices, simplifying the policy choices available, and helping to translate those choices – once made – into effective action. They may often be written off as being in decline, if not dead. But in many ways, they exhibit signs of renewed vitality.

past, and both parties have had to accept that the centre of gravity in the political system moved to the right in the Thatcher–Reagan-dominated 1980s, and respond to this.

In the 1950s–1970s, party differences in both countries often seemed to be more concerned with degree, emphasis and timing. The Conservatives and the Republicans then tended towards consensual, 'me-tooist' policies. Both became more ideological in the 1980s, putting forward distinctive and highly partisan programmes of the type that their traditional supporters liked to see. Since the 1990s, there has been less public appetite for overtly right-wing solutions. Divisions have been evident between those representatives who wish to pursue the preferences of party supporters and those who emphasise the need for a broad appeal to the wider electorate.

Organisation matters

British parties are not only more disciplined than American ones; they are also more centralised. Americans developed mass party organisations before Britain, partly because universal male franchise was introduced sooner than in this country. Grassroots organisation has long been well established and significant in the US and this – and the lack of strong leadership from Washington – makes for decentralisation. American state and local parties come together every four years to elect their president. At that time, the national headquarters plays an important role in electioneering, but in between presidential contests, its role is more modest. By contrast, British constituencies tend to be dominated by the party leadership and the controlling influence of central party headquarters.

REFERENCES

1 G. Washington, farewell message on retirement from the presidency, *Independent Chronicle*, 26 September 1796
2 V. O. Key, *Politics, Parties and Pressure Groups*, Crowell, 1964
3 G. Wasserman, *The Basics of American Politics*, Longman, 1997
4 M. Vile, *Politics in the USA*, Hutchinson, 1978
5 J. Burns, J. Peltason, T. Cronin and D. Magleby, *Government by the People*, Prentice Hall, 1994
6 V. O. Key, as in 2 above
7 M. Duverger, *Political Parties*, Methuen, 1962
8 M. Vile, as in 4 above
9 C. Rossiter, *Parties and Politics in America*, Signet, 1960
10 R. Hofstadter, *The Age of Reform: From Bryan to FDR*, Knopf, 1955
11 A. de Tocqueville, *Democracy in America*, reissued by Vintage, 1954
12 Lord Bryce, *Modern Democracies*, Macmillan, 1921
13 D. Brogan, *An Introduction to American Politics*, Hamish Hamilton, 1954

14 I. Kristol, *Reflections of a Neoconservative*, Basic Books, 1983

15 A. Schlesinger, *Cycles of American History*, Houghton Mifflin, 1986

16 C. Rossiter, as in 9 above

17 T. Hames and N. Rae, *Governing America*, Manchester University Press, 1996

18 T. Hames and N. Rae, as in 17 above

19 P. Robertson, *Bring It On*, W Publishing Group, 2002

20 M. Shaw, *Anglo-American Democracy*, Routledge and Kegan, 1968

21 D. Broder, *The Party's Over*, Harper and Row, 1972

22 J. Bibby, *Politics, Parties and Elections in America*, Wadsworth, 2000; A. Reichley, *The Life of the Parties: A History of American Political Parties*, Free Press, 1992

23 C. Bailey, 'Political Parties', *Contemporary Record* 3:3, February 1990

24 J. Aldrich, *Why Parties? The Origins and Transformation of Parties in America*, University of Chicago Press, 1995

25 P. Hernnson, *Party Campaigning in the 1980s*, Harvard University Press, 1988

26 C. Bailey, as in 23 above

27 A. Ware, 'Party Decline and Party Reform', in L. Robins (ed.), *The American Way*, Longman, 1985

USEFUL WEB SITES

www.democrats.org Democratic National Committee. Details of many aspects of recent election campaign and party platform; issues of interest to the party.

www.rnc.org Republican National Committee. Details of many aspects of recent election campaign and party platform; issues of interest to the party.

Several third parties have interesting sites, explaining their histories and different policy positions:

www.perot.org Official Ross Perot site.

www.greens.org Green Parties of North America.

www.liberalparty.org New York Liberal Party.

www.lp.org Libertarian Party.

www.reformparty.org Reform Party.

www.sp-usa.org Socialist Party.

www.ustaxpayers.org United States Taxpayers Party.

SAMPLE QUESTIONS

1 What are the distinctive features of American political parties?

2 In what sense does America have a two-party system?

3 Why are third parties unable to flourish in the US?

4 Why has socialism failed in the United States?

5 How might the emergence of a successful national third party change the nature and role of the two main political parties? Is such a development likely?

6 'Both American parties have a similar outlook on fundamental issues in American politics.' What are the main areas of agreement and disagreement in their ideologies and policies?

7 Discuss the paradox that although there are few differences between the main parties, they continue to dominate the American political system.

8 Assess the current state and prospects of either the Democratic or the Republican Party.

9 Assess the importance of the Religious Right in American politics.

10 'Party decline' or 'party renewal'? Do parties still play an important part in American politics?

11 Do American parties matter?

12 Compare the main British and US parties in respect of their ideas, sources of support and organisations.

Pressure groups: the lobby at work 9

In this chapter, we explore how individuals who share certain opinions come together to press their common outlook upon society and government. We have seen that this may be done via political parties. Here, we are concerned with the ways by which pressure groups lobby to propagate their views.

The leading groups are economic or occupational, but there is a huge variety of other civic, ethnic, ideological, racial and other bodies that have memberships that cut across the large economic groupings. In recent decades, many of them have moved on from lobbying alone and have become far more involved and significant in the electoral process. Concern has been expressed about some of their activities, leading to calls for greater regulation and vigilance.

POINTS TO CONSIDER

➤ Which interests in American society are best represented by pressure groups?

➤ Does it matter that some sections of society are poorly represented?

➤ Should pressure groups be subjected to greater control?

➤ How do groups seek to achieve their aims?

➤ In what respects has the nature of group lobbying changed over recent decades?

➤ To what extent has the iron gone out of 'iron triangles'?

➤ Is the influence of pressure groups generally benign or damaging to the workings of American democracy?

➤ Why are American pressure groups so powerful?

➤ Why is Congress more vulnerable to pressure-group activity than is the British Parliament?

The scale of lobbying

For many years, **lobbyists** have played a significant role in the legislative process, a role that has
increased with the enlargement of governmental
activity in the era since the New Deal. The term
'lobby' includes a vast array of groups, operating
at several levels and covering commercial and
industrial interests, labour unions, consumer
associations, ethnic and racial groups. In the mid-1950s, the *Encyclopaedia of
Associations* listed fewer than 5,000 of them. Now, it lists more than 20,000.
Representation of companies in Washington has greatly increased, but more
dramatic has been the explosion in the number of public-interest organisations
and grassroots groups. These barely existed at all before the 1960s; today, they
number in the tens of thousands and collect more than $4billion per year from
40 million individuals.[1]

lobbyists
Employees of organised groups
who exert pressure on
members of the legislature and
executive, with a view to
modifying public policy.

More than nine out of every ten Americans belong to at least one voluntary
grouping, be it a church, civil rights organisation, social club of some kind or
other public body. On average, Americans belong to four.

Under the Legislative Reorganisation Act (1946), lobbyists were required to
register with the relevant offices of the Senate and the House, and provide
details of their work and funding. At that time, there were fewer than 2,000
registered lobbyists with Congress, but now the number registered approaches
9,000. But this figure omits the vast array of individual corporations, state and
local governments, universities, think-tanks and other organisations in the
private sector that engage in lobbying at some level, as well as the myriad of
Washington representatives, ranging from lawyers to public relations
agencies, which do similar work.

The top ten highest-spending lobbying organisations, 1998

British American Tobacco
Philip Morris
Bell Atlantic
Chamber of Commerce
American Medical Association
Ford Motor Company
Business Roundtable
Edison Electric Institute
American Hospital Association
Blue Cross/Blue Shield

Organisations such as the Ford Motor Company not only belong to the appropriate interest group; they also maintain their own lobbying staff in Washington. Most other business corporations retain a sizeable lobby in the city, partly for reasons of prestige but also as a means of using any opportunity to influence laws and regulations. Similarly, labour unions and groups representing sections of society such as the elderly and causes such as the environment maintain well-staffed permanent offices. All wish to exert pressure at some level of government, many of them in Washington (either at the White House or on Capitol Hill).

In recent years there has been a marked extension of lobbying activity within the states as well. The American political culture is tolerant of pressure-group activity, and this encourages the creation of an array of organised interests. There are many access points for group representatives to explore. Because of their success, the average citizen looks as much to his or her voluntary groups for political satisfaction as to his or her elected representative.

Some relevant definitions

By the **lobby** we mean all those groups that seek to influence public policy, whether they are primarily promotional or propaganda bodies or those which seek to defend the interests of their group or organisation. The word 'lobby' originally derives from the location where the process occurred, the anteroom or lobby outside the chambers of Congress where representatives could be intercepted and urged to support a particular cause when they voted. Hotel lobbies have sometimes provided a similar venue, and lobbyists are those who wait there hoping for a chance meeting. To lobby is to seek to influence legislators and officials. Lobbyists are therefore employees of associations who try to influence policy decisions, especially in the executive and legislative branches of government.

By **pressure groups** we mean associations of people who come together on the basis of shared attitudes to try to influence public policy. This may involve lobbying governmental institutions or their representatives or seeking to influence voters at election time. Such groups are different from political parties, which are also bodies which include within their membership people who share a broadly agreed approach to the conduct of affairs.

Some writers dislike the term 'pressure groups', for the words may seem to imply the use of force rather than persuasion. American academics tend to use the term 'interest groups' instead. As we shall see, this label does not cover the whole range of associations with which we are concerned. Whichever term is used – and we will use the broader term 'pressure groups' – there is a further distinction which can be made between **interest or protective groups** (e.g.

the American Medical Association), which are primarily self-interested and seek to protect or defend the position of their members, and **promotional groups** (e.g. the American Civil Liberties Union), which are primarily concerned with advancing ideas or causes.

Pressure groups and political parties

Pressure groups are voluntary associations formed to advance or defend a common cause or interest. They are unlike political parties in that:

- They do not wish to assume responsibility for governing the country. Rather, they seek to influence those who do so.
- They have a narrower range of concerns than parties, which seek to draw together a variety of interests in order to broaden their appeal. Pressure groups have a limited focus, many of their aspirations being non-political.

Because pressure groups' concerns are liable to be affected by government decisions, they need to be organised in order to influence ministers and respond to what they propose.

The former category includes the most influential American associations, which wield substantial economic power. The latter are usually less influential, promoting as they do some cause idea or issue not of direct benefit to themselves or to those who belong to them, but of general benefit to society. Promotional groups tend to be smaller than protective ones, and comprise dedicated people who commit themselves to what are sometimes minority concerns.

The distinction above is not adopted by all writers, some preferring to speak of the lobby, others just using the terms 'interest' or 'pressure groups', to cover every type of association involved in the process. Woll and Zimmerman[2] employ the term 'interest groups' and define interests as 'concerns, needs, benefits, or rights that groups or individuals have or would like to have'. The areas in which people have interests include, among other things, business, the workplace, education, the environment, health and religion. These interests are shared by a number of people who organise into groups to mobilise their common feelings. Hence, according to the two writers, interest groups are 'associations of persons who share common concerns, needs, benefits or rights and have as their purpose the satisfaction of claims to these. Usually, the claims are made on the government, and are met as a result of pressure.'

Inevitably, there are some organisations that do not fit neatly into the division referred to. A number of them protect the interests of their members and also do a fair amount of promotional work that increases their acceptability to the community at large. One of the most prominent of these **hybrid** bodies is the

National Rifle Association (NRA). There are different motives for people who join together in this organisation. Some belong for reasons of commercial protection (they make or sell guns), others for ideological or self-interested reasons (owners of guns who see it as their constitutional right to bear them or who simply feel that they are necessary).

Distinguishable from such groups, whatever label we adopt, are **movements**. A movement is a wider and more all-embracing organisation, and it includes all those peoples and groups who are interested or involved in a particular cause. Movements often develop from local activity and become part of a larger national campaign – in the way that individual small groups of women in the United States took up particular concerns that then became national causes to which many more women were committed.

Within the women's movement today, there are several groups, which pursue their own distinctive agendas, whether peace, child welfare or low pay. These groups share some ideas and approaches, but may differ on controversial issues such as abortion, as well as over the tactics to adopt in seeking the fulfilment of their aims. The Civil Rights Movement for equal treatment for black Americans has similarly spanned several organisations, as do those on animal rights and the environment.

Categories of American pressure groups

> **The National Rifle Association (NRA)**
>
> Perhaps the best-known American pressure group and the most successful in lobbying on Capitol Hill. It has over three million members who are enthusiasts for shooting as both recreation and protection. It has successfully resisted most national attempts to limit the ownership of guns since the late 1960s, even though on occasion pressure for gun control has gained ground. In the last few years, it has paid more attention to state governments, for it is to that level that supporters of restriction have increasingly turned their attention.
>
> The NRA's Institute for Legislative Action exercises a watching brief over any attempt by the federal or state governments to introduce limitations on the manufacture and sale of guns or on gun ownership. If there are any such initiatives, members are immediately alerted so that they can mount strong resistance, by phoning or e-mailing relevant officials, writing to newspapers, appearing on television or any other appropriate method.
>
> The NRA is currently seeking to widen its appeal, so that some of its recent campaigning has been targeted at minority groups and women.

It is convenient to classify the lobby into broad groups. This can be done either by opting for the protective/promotional typology, or by categorising organisations according to the sector they claim to represent. This is the approach we will adopt here.

Business groups

Business is the most effective area of group activity, because it has the advantages or expertise, organisation and resources. It includes organisations that speak up for small firms (e.g. the National Federation of Independent Business), and much larger bodies, such as the National Association of Manufacturers, which represents big corporations. The Chamber of Commerce, with branches at state and local level, has a membership of more than 200,000 businesses. Such **umbrella or peak organisations** have not tended to stress a Washington role, for their individual members often have representatives based in the capital. General Electric, Ford, General Motors and other industrial giants such as Union Carbide are also well represented in Washington. These corporations are so large and so vital in the American economy that politicians of all persuasions will listen to their concerns.

umbrella or peak organisations
Broad-based organisations representing the interests of capital or labour to those in government. They speak for a range of similar interests, their members being other organisations rather than individuals. The National Association of Manufacturers represents many businesses across the country.

The business lobby is a powerful one, though it would be wrong to assume that the large range of groups (about 20% of all pressure groups) operate together as a powerful bargaining sector. 'Corporate America' is not a single entity with but one agreed objective. The interests of America's fifteen million businesses diverge. In the 1980s, some leading manufacturers favoured high protective tariffs to fend off foreign competition. Others who operated more in the export market feared that such an approach would invite retaliation and damage their overseas prospects. Also, as we have seen, not all of these organisations focus on the same areas of decision-making. Some operate in Washington, others elsewhere; some favour one target, others another. Because of such considerations, umbrella business organisations have much less influence in the United States than does the Confederation of British Industry in Britain.

Labour groups

Unions have always been less prominent in American politics than in Britain and other European countries, for the US workforce is less unionised than in many democracies. Unions lack the clout of many large corporations; moreover they are numerically in decline, and suffer diminishing membership. They have more influence in the industrial areas such as the Northeast than in the South, which has traditionally been dominated by agrarian interests.

The largest umbrella body representing organised labour is the loose alliance known as the American Federation of Labour and the Congress of Industrial Organisations (AFL/CIO), to which ninety-six unions belong; it represents about 12% of the workforce. In common with other union organisations, it lobbies government on workers' conditions and rights (e.g. the minimum wage and job security) and on business and trade matters of concern to the workforce. Long-standing individual unions include the United Automobile Workers (UAW), the International Brotherhood of Teamsters (lorry drivers), the International Ladies Garment Workers Union (ILGWU) and the United Steelworkers of America.

In industrial matters, unions can be militant in defence of workers' interests, but politically they play less of a role than in Britain. They carry more weight with the Democratic Party and may give it funds, although there have never been the formal, institutional links that exist between British unions and the Labour Party.

Professional groups

Professional bodies cater for the needs of accountants, doctors, educators, lawyers, scientists and others, and those groups within this category often have no interests in common other than their status. They may, as with the doctors and the lawyers, sometimes come into conflict – as, for instance, in a case concerning medical malpractice. Among the foremost professional associations in Washington, the American Bar Association and the National Education Association have been notably influential, the former having a substantial voice in the selection of judges, the latter having forced education to the forefront of national debate – to such an extent that in 1988 George Bush senior promised to run as the 'education president'. Perhaps the most effective has been the American Medical Association (AMA), a federation of fifty state associations representing about two thirds of the nation's doctors. In the early 1990s, it was much involved with other relevant interests in the struggle over the attempted reform of medical care. This led to a massive attempt to influence the thinking of congressmen and the general public, in an attempt to tone down the nature of the Clinton proposals.

Agricultural groups

Historically, farm organisations were particularly influential, for the agrarian community has been generously represented in the Senate and the House. This influence resulted in the passage of a number of emergency bills in the late 1970s. Much of the campaigning for these laws was conducted by the American Agriculture Movement, which often took a more militant line than the more conservative American Farm Bureau Federation (AFBF), whilst both often found themselves in disagreement with the National Farmers Union (NFU).

As the number of family farms declined (the owners having often got into debt), so agribusinesses – vast farms owned by large corporations – developed in their place. The arrival of business people, familiar with different and more sophisticated techniques of lobbying, has helped to change the image of agriculture. Professional lobbyists are now commonly employed in this field.

Public interest groups

Public interest groups include those that are concerned with the quality of government, consumerism and the environment. Common Cause, 'a national citizens' lobby', has both Democrat and Republican members. It seeks to 'open up' the processes of government, by such means as electoral reform and strict control over the financing of election campaigns. The League of Women Voters is also keen to promote better government, through greater public involvement. There is less disagreement between the various organisations operative in this area than in some other sectors. All are seeking to achieve goals designed to benefit the entire population.

Ideological and single-issue groups

Within the ideological sector there is a wide divergence of viewpoints between far left and far right. However, members of the groups are likely to share an interest in promoting causes and ideas, whatever the diversity of their backgrounds. The sizeable and well-known American Civil Liberties Union (ACLU) has been known to defend the rights of the American Nazi Party, a body which it abhors and which would, given power, almost certainly destroy the ACLU. The ACLU sometimes co-operates closely with very different organisations such as the National Abortion Rights Action League, which is determined to retain the right to abortion and stresses a woman's right to choose.

There is a vast array of associations that can be described as single-issue ones, and the abortion ones are currently among the most prominent (see pp. 318–21). Such issue groups have mushroomed since the 1960s, and gain public attention by a variety of techniques – ranging from writing to congressmen to taking action in the courts, from attending demonstrations to participating in other forms of direct action. Generally, these groups lack the funds available to large interest groups, and their influence often derives from their ability to show that they have the support of many voters.

How groups operate

Groups pursue their goals at various pressure points in the American system of government, partly depending on the objective to be achieved and on the location where relevant decisions are made. Any organisation wishes to concentrate its attention at the level where it can have the greatest influence.

The executive

Lobbying is a proven way of applying pressure on government, and most groups employ people full-time to perform the task; others may hire a professional lobbyist, as is necessary to represent their interests. Lobbyists are 'persuaders' who inhabit the world of Washington or the states, and they understand the functioning of the political system and often have useful personal contacts. As the seat of the federal government, Washington is the focus of much of their activity. More than 4,000 corporations are represented in the capital, and some 3,000 associations have an office there.

Some lobbyists have been lawyers, others have moved from working for the Administration into lobbying. Lobbyists are highly skilled, and are selected because they are likely to be able to gain access where others cannot. Any lobbyist wishes to know the key personnel in the various agencies and bureaus of government, for more and more legislation derives from initiatives from within the executive branch. Interest groups have much to offer by way of

---

Iron triangles

For many years, there were particularly close links in America between interest groups, committee chairpersons and government departments, an arrangement often referred to as 'iron triangles'. The three elements were often in close contact with each other and enjoyed cosy relationships based on interdependent self-interest. Sometimes, there was movement of personnel between one position within the triangle and another. Such iron triangles often dominated areas of domestic policy-making, possessing a virtual monopoly of information in their sector. One example was the smoking and tobacco triangle (the Department of Agriculture, the House and Senate agricultural committees, and the tobacco lobby of farmers and manufacturers), in which there was a focus on crop subsidies to tobacco farmers. Others covered areas such as defence, agriculture and, more specifically, the sugar industry. In all cases, there were tight bonds within the triangular relationship.

The defence triangle comprised the Pentagon; the relevant committee chairpersons of the two chambers of Congress, and members with a constituency interest in arms manufacturing and/or the armed forces; and representatives of the arms industry who were keen to see their business benefit from federal purchases of the weapons they produced. In his farewell speech on leaving the White House (1961), President Eisenhower issued a warning about the power of the bonds within the armaments industry. He felt that what was good for those with a vested interest in developing costly armaments and weapons systems was not necessarily beneficial to the country as a whole: 'We must guard against the acquisition of unwarranted influence by the military-industrial complex . . . in order to balance and to integrate these and other forces, new and old, within the principles of our democratic system.'

specialist information, and the group lobbyist and members of the bureaucracy will often seek to develop a sound working relationship. Some writers refer to so-called 'iron triangles' (see box below), to describe the networks of mutually self-supporting lobbyists, bureaucrats and members of congressional committees, where key decisions of government are made.

Americans speak of the 'revolving door' to describe the easy movement of personnel between the executive and the interest groups. Sometimes, the door – when opened – reveals a murky world of behind-the-scenes influence. In the Reagan–Bush years, there were many scandals involving doubtful ethical behaviour, and Woll and Zimmerman[3] quote as an example the way in which many of Reagan's appointees earned themselves a fortune as lobbyists in the HUD episode. For calling up old friends at the Department of Housing and Urban Development and obtaining lucrative contracts for clients, they received millions of dollars.

In recent decades, the autonomy of such triangles or sub-governments in America has been challenged by alternative centres of power, often known as 'issue networks'. Issue networks are wider and looser, and – in addition to the three elements above – describe other players involved in discussion of a policy area, including the research institutes and the media. Media scrutiny and the attentions of consumer protest groups have led to a more critical analysis of policy-making processes, so that secret deals and mutual back-scratching are now less frequent or effective. As Hague and Harrop[4] have explained, 'the iron has gone out of the triangle; now influence over decisions depends on what you know, as well as who you know'. In America, the policies supported by the tobacco triangle came under challenge from health authorities that had been excluded from the area of tobacco policy-making. In defence policy, at times when the danger to America seemed to be less evident, expenditure on weaponry was curbed – suggesting that influences other than the elements of the triangle were a factor in determining the level of military capability.

In the issue networks of today, relationships are not continuous or particularly close and there is less interdependence than was the case in the days of iron triangles. They have lost much of their stranglehold over policy-making, and new participants, be they environmental or human rights activists, research bodies or consumer groups, have come into the equation. Grant and Ashbee[5] have illustrated the vast array of groups now involved in the development of health policy, ranging from health-care providers (the AMA and the American Dental Association) to the health insurance companies (Health Insurance Association of America, HIAA), pharmaceutical and medical equipment manufacturers (Health Industry Manufacturers' Association), employers (National Federation of Independent Business) and representatives of big business (Chamber of Commerce).

The legislature

Congress is a key target for lobbyists, for the committees in the two chambers have responsibilities for certain subject areas. It is the committees which determine the nature of legislation or indeed prevent it from being passed, so that groups and lobbyists need to be familiar with the relevant congressmen and the staff who serve them. They discuss legislation with individual congressmen and provide evidence, written and oral, for committee hearings. Lobbyists are keen to develop close ties, inviting elected representatives to dinners and various entertainments. Abramson[6] has highlighted the bonds that bind together the two sides. Nearly a quarter of ex-representatives move over into lobbying, and members of their families are often similarly involved.

The dismantling of the old 'seniority system' in Congress in the 1970s increased the scope of the lobbyist; new committee chairs are more vulnerable to group activity. Moreover, party discipline has always been weak. In recent years groups have found more easier to have an impact, at a time when party labels have lost even more of their never-very-great meaning.

The courts

Some groups carry little weight with the executive or the legislature. When these avenues are closed, they may rely on the courts instead, and hope that they can use their knowledge of the law to gain a favourable interpretation in court rulings. Anti-abortion, consumer and environmental groups have sometimes used litigation, as have other groups that lack a strong congressional base. One group that gained successes via this route was the National Association for the Advancement of Colored People (NAACP). By using the courts, it was able to bring about pressure for a change in the status of African Americans. In 1954, it won a particularly significant victory in a case that resulted in the judgement that segregation was inherently unequal, and therefore illegal (see p. 307).

In countries in which the Constitution provides the courts with a formal role of judicial review, activists tend to use the courts more readily. In the USA, the method is well established, not least because Americans are traditionally a litigious (ready to go to law) people. American judges have wide constitutional powers to overrule the decisions of the executive and considerable latitude in interpreting the meaning of legislation, so that bringing test cases may prove invaluable in winning a friendly judgement. Of course, much depends on who is on the bench. US groups often seek to influence the selection of judges, pressing the claims of those whose political and social leanings they find acceptable.

It is not just campaigning promotional groups that have used this route. 'Going to law' requires substantial resources, so that it is often the large and powerful business corporations that have been successful in adopting this approach. They regularly challenge government statutes and regulations, and have their own lawyers to advise them and handle the passage of cases through the courts. In other cases where they might not be a party to the litigation, groups may submit an **amicus curiae** ('friend of the court') brief, in order to have their views represented and taken into account.

> **amicus curiae**
>
> A brief filed by an individual or group with the permission of the court. Such briefs provide information and argument additional to that presented by those immediately involved in a case. In effect, a group is acting in the privileged position of being an adviser to the court, a role popular with campaigners in the debates on abortion, consumerism, law and order, and the environment.

Main targets for group activity: a summary

Tier of government	Executive	Legislature	Judiciary
Federal	President, Cabinet, civil servants	House of Representatives, Senate, congressional committees	Supreme Court, other federal courts
State	Governor, departmental heads, officials	Two houses of legislature, committees	State Supreme Court, Courts of Appeal
Local	Mayors, elected and non-elected officials	Councils, school boards, other local boards	Other state courts

Table adapted from 'Access Points' in Alan Grant, *The American Political Process*, Dartmouth, 1994.

The public

American groups have always placed great emphasis on the use of campaigns directed at the 'man in the street'. By mailing, by advertising, and especially through television, an attempt is made to influence opinion. Propaganda is often targeted at certain groups, such as the voters in a congressman's home state, in the hope that the electorate will, in turn, pressure their representative to vote as the group wishes when he or she is in Washington. Congressmen are only too aware that their re-election could depend on keeping the electors happy.

Business organisations spend heavily on advertising, often using professional companies to organise a campaign. Many groups once employed indiscriminate mailing, based on names from the phone book. However, with the development of computers, mailing has become a more sophisticated technique, for letters can be personalised and directed at those likely to be sympathetic, such as members of environmentalist groups.

Direct action

In pursuing their aims, some groups resort to direct action. The anti-abortion associations that are prepared to injure or – at worst – kill those who carry out abortions are but one example. Others are prepared to use less dramatic forms of protest, ranging from demonstrations and strikes to law-breaking in the form of withholding tax or rioting.

Direct action, an attempt to coerce those in authority into a change of viewpoint, can be very effective. It may be militant, but peaceful; sometimes,

---

POLITICAL ACTION COMMITTEES (PACS)

PACs have mushroomed since the 1970s. They represent the political wing of pressure groups and are legally permitted to raise funds to distribute to candidates and parties. Business, labour and trade associations, among others, have PACs to further their political goals. PACs seek to persuade congressmen to vote as the group wishes, and they offer advice and information to candidates, as well as the financial assistance that is their most important contribution. Elections are expensive, and candidates need substantial funds from their backers for such things as their advertising campaigns.

Groups have always wanted to influence election results, and PACs existed as long ago as back in the 1930s. However, it was in the 1970s that they assumed a much greater significance, largely as a result of reforms introduced after Watergate. Now, there are nearly 5,000 PACs and the scale of their participation in the political process has dramatically increased.

The five PACs contributing most to candidates, 2000

Pac	Contribution ($m)
Realtors* Political Action Committee	3,423
Association of Trial Lawyers	2,656
American Federation of State, County and Municipal Employees	2,590
Dealers Election Action Committee of the National Automobile Dealers Association	2,498
Democrat Republican Independent Voter Education Committee	2,494

Based on information provided by the Federal Election Committee, 31 May 2001.
* Realtors are accredited estate agents.

The case for and against PACs

In favour:
1 They are the modern way to make money available for costly election campaigns. The methods employed are open and preferable to the situation before they became widespread, when the sources of finance were often disguised and unknown to the

it may involve ignoring or breaking the criminal law and can easily spill over into violence. What has made its use more commonplace is that extreme behaviour can get publicity and command prime television exposure in news and current affairs programmes.

History confirms that direct action can be effective, and many great social changes have come about because of the willingness of some people to resist what they see as unjust laws. The NAACP engaged in a policy of passive resistance, and Martin Luther King and his followers were ready to break laws

public. Indeed, it is the very availability of information that has led to criticism of PACs, criticism that is better directed at the whole system of campaign funding.

2 Such is the cost of campaigning that politicians cannot afford to be unduly beholden to particular PACs. They need a diversity of sources of funding, and this prevents any undue influence – the more so as the most a PAC could donate was the $5,000 fixed in the 1970s, until the passage of the 2002 act (see p. 193).

3 PACs represent a legitimate interest in a pluralist system, and the fact that there are nearly 5,000 of them serves to prevent any one of them from gaining excessive influence. Their actions are open to scrutiny, and the media are constantly on the lookout for examples of undue favours being granted.

4 As with groups in general, they offer an outlet through which people can be involved and express their ideas and opinions. They educate the voters, but also they act as a means of communicating the voters' views.

Against

1 The central allegation against PACs revolves around the idea that money can buy influence and power. A congressman who has the backing of a PAC is likely to give favours in return, so that they are associated with undue influence. In the words of one writer,[7] PACs are 'a huge coalition of special interest groups dedicated to perverting the political process for private gain'. The fact that some PACs have actually been willing to back rival candidates is seen as evidence of their determination to gain such influence.

2 Most PACs give money primarily to incumbent congressmen, and this makes it more difficult for a challenger to mount a successful campaign against a person already in office. In as much as this is true, it is seen as undermining the democratic process, for it makes a contest less meaningful and fair.

3 The costs of campaigning in congressional elections have spiralled out of control, a reflection of the easy availability of money collected by PACs. It is not due to the escalating costs of advertising, but more to the fact that congressmen have used this 'easy money' to equip themselves with needlessly large offices and staffing levels.

4 The usual criticism of pressure groups, the lack of internal democracy, is often mentioned as well. Alan Grant quotes[8] the example of the decision of the AFL/CIO to back Walter Mondale as the Democratic Presidential nominee in 1984, even though less than a quarter of union members were asked their preference.

they felt to be immoral. This could involve deliberately seeking service at a restaurant which operated a colour bar, or riding on a 'whites only' bus. Black Americans took more violent direct action in 1992, when riots broke out in Los Angeles; allegations of police racism provoked the black community into desperate action.

Groups and the electoral system

Pressure groups seek to influence the conduct of government, not to assume responsibility for administering policy. They do not contest elections, but wish to influence their outcome. In particular, they may wish to see certain candidates elected and certain ideas advanced. This may involve publishing the voting records of sitting congressmen in an attempt to show how far they fulfil the group's requirements.

The regulation of party funding in the 1971 Federal Election Campaign Act and the Campaign Act of 1974 spawned the growth of the political action committees (PACs), the political arms of pressure groups. These can assist candidates in several ways: by providing research material and publicity, by raising election funds, and by providing organisational backup to a candidate who lacks a strong personal political organisation or party machine. For a candidate lacking such party or organisational support and who lacks private funds, PACs can provide invaluable assistance. (See pp. 286–7.)

Of course, not all pressure groups so involve themselves in determining the outcome of election contests. They may wish to reach out to people associated with either party and therefore take a non-partisan approach. The American Telephone and Telegraph Company, and Western Electric, are examples of groups who prefer to concentrate on educating the voters and parties in their viewpoint.

The strength of group activity

Why pressure groups are strong in America

The American system of government offers much scope to the lobbyist. It provides many layers of government to target, and the relatively weak party system provides an opportunity for groups to step in and fill the gap. As parties do not have rigid doctrinal platforms, congressmen are less likely to follow the party line. They have to decide what is best in the national interest and for their geographical area, in the light of the information they receive from all quarters. Much of this comes from the interests that seek to persuade them.

There are other factors that serve to strengthen the influence of pressure groups. Via the Bill of Rights, the Constitution offers protection for groups, which are quick to proclaim their rights of free speech under the First Amendment; any ban on unions or restrictions of freedom of assembly and expression would be likely to be deemed 'unconstitutional'. Moreover, the freedom of information legislation provides access for group activists to relevant documentation, and a generally open system of government creates an atmosphere in which groups can flourish. Finally, in America, there are many influential bodies representing a variety of highly diverse and often ethnic and racial backgrounds (The Irish and Jewish lobbies, the Italian community etc.).

Factors making for group success

It is not easy to generalise about the factors which make group action successful, for there are exceptions to most sweeping generalisations. The party in control may be relevant, for business interests are traditionally catered for by the Republicans, who – as in the Reagan era – tend to show greater hostility to organised labour. Yet the Democrats won praise from some manufacturers, who were pleased by President Clinton's backing for the North Atlantic Free Trade Area, an issue on which the more conservative party failed to offer him much support. For many years, the Democrats have been viewed as sympathetic to the unions rather than big business, though the bargaining power of organised labour has been reduced under any Administration now that membership has so declined.

Size is relevant to influence, for an association able to claim the backing of 2 million voters is one that cannot be easily ignored. One with 20,000 supporters has less electoral clout. Much, of course, depends on the commitment and organisational skills of those involved, and sometimes an active and persistent small group can be effective.

If a body has nationwide support – such as the AMA, with its local organisation in almost every congressional district – it is likely to be more influential than a group whose support is localised, unless the concern being voiced is a purely local one. Also, as with British groups, resources (especially money and professional expertise) are important. Those groups which can present an impressive case based on soundly researched data are more likely to be listened to. This can be costly.

Sometimes, timing is the key factor. Groups arise because of a growing interest in particular concerns. The environmentalists have been important in recent years, and many associations have sprung up and flourished. In the present mood of social and political conservatism (and particularly with the growing influence of the Religious Right), anti-abortion groups are likely to be listened to with greater respect than those who advance the cause of a woman's right to choose.

Indeed, any group with a liberal agenda is likely to find present circumstances less congenial than in the pre-Reagan years. This applies especially in the area of civil liberties, where women and racial minorities find less support for affirmative action than was previously the case. The president and congressmen are mindful of election considerations. No cause is likely to be endorsed if it is potentially damaging to their popularity and therefore a threat to their chances of re-election.

The mass media can be very relevant, for favourable attention from broadcasters and journalists can help a group to project its image and address a wider audience. Moreover, if the organisation can convey via the media the impression that its outlook is in the general interest and shared by many people, then those in power or seeking to obtain office will be especially attentive.

The regulation of group activity

The First Amendment to the American Constitution guarantees the right of free speech and to petition for the remedy of grievances. This protection has been used by interest groups over many years as a defence of their activities against the threat of excessive regulation. Some controls were introduced at state level as far back as the early nineteenth century, and within a few decades there was pressure for more to be done. Public anxiety increased because of the widespread influence of big business, in particular the influence wielded by rich corporations, which were able to influence congressmen to gain valuable concessions – especially rights to land where it was hoped to build railroads.

Not until after World War II was anything done by national government to tackle the problems posed by the growth in lobbying. Then, it was felt that there was a need to regularise group activity, whilst recognising its legitimate role in the political process. This was achieved by encouraging groups to disclose details of their aims, membership and funding.

The **1946 Federal Regulation of Lobbying Act** required the registration of lobbyists and details of the concern that employs them. It was largely unenforced, and frequently the details were either not given or were incomplete. Some groups evaded registration, by arguing that lobbying was not their primary role. An attempt to stiffen the law in 1976 (the Lobby Disclosure Bill) failed, because of powerful opposition from lobbyists who felt that it would needlessly complicate their task and waste their time on pointless form-filling.

However, because of the alarm about some of their activities in the late 1960s and 1970s (notably about the cost of campaigning and the funding of candidates for elective office), further legislation was devised, in the form of the

Federal Election Campaign Act (FECA). The Act, passed in 1971, replaced all earlier statutes. In its present form, thrice amended, it requires candidates and parties to disclose details of their income and expenditure. Individuals and PACs have to declare the costs they incur in providing candidates and parties with any financial backing. The effect of tightening the control has ironically been to increase the number of PACs and the scale of their contributions.

A further attempt at reform was made by the 103rd Congress. Both houses approved legislation to amend the definition of lobbying so that more individuals would be required to register. Controls also restricted the right of lobbyists to dispense meals and gifts to legislators. Unfortunately there were differences between the proposals before the two chambers, and in spite of the president's support, nothing was accomplished.

The world of pressure groups is now more open than was formerly the case, and though there may be deals between representatives of interest groups and congressmen, they are today more likely to be exposed. Congressmen are less likely to be in the pay of any one major lobby, and should there be a suspicion of too close an arrangement then there is always another competing group willing to 'blow the whistle'. Because of these considerations, most congressmen do not recognise a need for more stringent regulation, a reflection of the prevailing American view that the influence of interest groups is generally beneficial to the process of government and in the public interest as well.

The merits and demerits of pressure groups

Most academics and politicians accept that groups have a legitimate role in American government, and recognise that it is inevitable that they will seek opportunities to advance their own interests. Many members of the general public might concede that they offer some advantages, but none the less remain perturbed by their ever-growing influence.

The case against

The names employed to describe the activity of interest groups are themselves a cause for concern to some people. The term 'pressure group' smacks of sinister and harmful behaviour, and when a small number of groups resort to violence or the threat of intimidation to achieve their ends, there is understandable alarm. The use of death threats by the anti-abortion lobby can damage the cause, by offending many Americans who themselves are perturbed by the practice of termination. In some respects, the term 'interest group' is no better. It has obvious overtones of self-interest and serves to fuel the fear that such groups are concerned to promote their own advantage rather than the general interest of the community.

Moreover, among these 'interests', some are more powerful than others. They have greater financial resources and can therefore develop highly professional organisations and great expertise. Rivals in the field cannot hope to match the funds and resources of a big corporation. Business and labour are well organised, whereas the voice of consumers was for many years less effectively conveyed. Consumers are now protected by many active individuals and associations, but other interests – the racial minorities, the disabled, the elderly and the unemployed – lack the income and bargaining power within the economy to enable them to achieve their goals, unless they can create enough public support as an election approaches. Abramson quotes[9] an analyst who regards Washington as a 'capital so privileged and incestuous in its dealings, that ordinary citizens believe it is no longer accessible to the general public'.

Concern has also been voiced about the unrepresentative character of some group leaderships. Some leaders are elected by a small percentage of the membership, others are appointed. Once in their position, they can purvey their own ideas and attitudes, irrespective of whether these reflect the views of those whom they are supposed to represent. One political scientist has noted[10] that 'the system is skewed, loaded and unbalanced in favour of a fraction of a minority' – those in the highest social economic and education categories.

Above all, much of the public anxiety is related to fear of behind-the-scenes influence. It is widely suspected that there is something distasteful about lobbying. It may not be illegal, the influence may be legitimate, but there is a suspicion of deals from which the bulk of the public are excluded. There have been enough cases involving corruption and malpractice to make people question the secrecy of lobbying activity, and assume that either side is out to maximise its own advantage.

The case in favour

As for the fears of undue influence, defenders of group activity might point to the fact that, besides the formal legal controls, there are also other interests that can exercise a countervailing pressure. There may not always be equally balanced groups on either side of some particular issue, but whatever the preponderance of views the arguments for and against a question are usually reasonably well aired. For instance, the influence of the energy companies is matched by that of the anti-nuclear groups that wish to halt the development of nuclear energy plants. The desire of management and unions in the northwest woodlands to cut down trees is countered by the complaints of the environmentalists who are active in demanding that the practice is controlled. Again, in the impassioned abortion and gun control debates, the influence of pro-lifers in the former is balanced by those who are pro-choice, just as the influence of the National Rifle Association is matched by that of Handgun Control.

Groups can provide positive benefits to the community and to those in authority. They allow large numbers of citizens to participate in the political process as members of associations. Some are passive supporters who pay their dues and do little else. Others, usually a small minority, are more deeply committed enthusiasts who try to galvanise the less active members into giving more positive support.

The presence of many groups ensures that the attitudes and outlook of all groups in society are articulated. It is surely healthier for all people to have an outlet for their views, however extreme, rather than for them to resort to underground methods. The groups also convey ideas to and from the elected and appointed officials who make decisions. As intermediaries between the government and the governed, the groups help to make government accountable. In these respects, rather than be a threat to the democratic process, they actually underpin democracy.

They also provide government with specialist information and expertise, and may help in carrying out policies that law-makers have laid down. They meet congressmen and officials of the Administration at regular intervals, and assist by providing evidence, submitting proposals and attending hearings. This flow of information to the agencies and institutions of government is again an important part of the democratic process. By becoming involved in this way, groups help to modify government decisions and public policy. Some may not like it, but that is what has come to pass.

Apart from the specific arguments quoted above, supporters of group activity often point out to the inevitability of group activity in a **pluralist society**. This view was developed by David Truman[11] in 1951 and has been widely accepted over the last fifty years. For those who belong to this school of thought, the formation of groups is an obvious method by which people with shared ideas and circumstances co-operate to achieve their goals. Groups are a natural, desirable and healthy democratic outlet. Any problems in their operation can be controlled by appropriate regulatory machinery.

pluralism and pluralist societies

Pluralism (literally, rule by the many) describes a political system in which there are numerous groups competing to exert influence over the government. New groups can easily be created, so that further competition can emerge in the marketplace. The state is more umpire than player, responding to interests expressed to it.

In pluralist societies (e.g. Australia, Canada, the UK and the USA), the power of the state is limited and there is a political marketplace in which group activity can flourish. Governments are responsive to group interest. In the words of Hague and Harrop,[12] 'politics is a competitive market with few barriers to entry'.

Recent trends: the changing pressure-group landscape

The nature and pattern of group activity have significantly altered in recent years. Today, there are far more groups than ever before. We have already noted the proliferation of cause or issue groups that seek to advance particular areas of concern – from abortion to the environment, from gender to the right to bear arms. One reason for this development is the growth of federal welfare and regulatory activities in the 1960s and 1970s. Several groups were formed in response to these initiatives, by groups of people who found their lives affected by the changes. Other factors might be the weakening of political parties and the increased opportunities for lobbying in Congress.

Lobbying is done also by various **think-tanks** that seek to convert policy-makers to their approach on a whole series of issues. The Heritage Foundation and the American Enterprise Institute are broadly conservative research bodies that have become an important part of the Washington lobbying network. So too are the state and local governments that now often employ the services of professional lobbyists to influence the federal government – again, via an office in Washington.

> **think-tanks**
> Policy institutes which carry out detailed research and provide analysis of and information on a range of policy options. They are often ideologically based, their ideas sometimes being influential with the parties that share a broad affinity of perspective. Think-tanks such as the Progressive Policy Institute have taken on much of the work of developing new policy options. The role of parties in this area has diminished.

If the range of groups has proliferated over the last generation, so has their relative importance changed (see the current rankings, listed in the box below). There are many variables that combine to determine the impact of groups at any given time, ranging from their size and the geographical distribution of their membership to their resources and the skills of their leadership. In the last few years, the American Association of Retired People (AARP) has consistently come out at or near the top. This is hardly surprising in an age when more people are living longer than ever before. The AARP ranks as America's largest pressure group, with around 35 million members, aged 50 or over, who are readily mobilised when issues affecting their life styles and prospects are up for national debate.

There are many more recent groups that compete with the traditional ones in the economic area and in the professions. In medicine, the AMA has long been a leader and remains very important – but now there are numerous other organisations operating in the medical field. Some are concerned with specialist work such as that of paramedics and nurses, some represent hospitals and clinics, whilst others speak for the insurance companies active in this sector.

For a long while, the lobbying scene in Washington was dominated by three major interests: agriculture, business and labour. These no longer carry the weight that they once did. We have seen that the AFBF and NFU, the large peak organisations, have now lost some of their influence to the product or regional associations. As with agriculture, so with business. The National Association of Manufacturers and the US Chamber of Commerce are still important players, but other organisations have developed and corporations increasingly organise more of their own lobbying. Similarly, the status and impact of unions have been in decline, and whereas their membership peaked at above 30% of the workforce in 1945, today it is approximately 15%. They remain important in the American economy, but many groups of workers – especially in newer, smaller, high-tech industries – are non-unionised.

THE MOST INFLUENTIAL GROUPS IN AMERICA TODAY

The ten most powerful groups in Washington

National Rifle Association of America
American Association of Retired Persons
National Federation of Independent Business
American Israel Public Affairs Committee
American Association of Trial Lawyers
American Federation of Labour and the Congress of Industrial Organisations
Chamber of Commerce of the United States of America
National Beer Wholesalers' Association
National Association of Realtors
National Association of Manufacturers

The top five most influential groups in the states

Schoolteachers' organisations (National Education Association)
General (umbrella) business organisations (Chambers of Commerce)
Utility companies and associations (those covering electricity, gas etc.)
Lawyers (state bar associations and trial lawyers)
Traditional labour groups (American Federation of Labour and the Congress of Industrial Organisations)

Information for the Washington scene adapted from an article in *Fortune* (a business magazine), 'The Power Twenty-five' survey, 28 May 2001. The survey was based on a questionnaire in which congressmen, professional lobbyists, White House aides and many others ranked on a scale of 0 to 100 the influence of 87 different associations. Information on the states adapted from R. Hrebenar, *Interest Group Politics*, Prentice Hall, 1997.

The days when congressmen from the industrial states were desperate to avoid offending the unions, or those from the South and Midwest had to show immense sympathy for agrarian interests, have gone. These interests are still important, but the industrial and farming vote are both less crucial than was once the case. Democrats fear being portrayed as too close to labour, and Reagan and Bush were prepared to cut agricultural subsidies in spite of the preferences of the small farmers of Iowa, Kansas and other farm states. Given the large number of groups, it is now less easy for congressional committees to be too close to one particular interest; similarly, an individual congressman cannot afford to be beholden to one group only. They are open to many influences, and would be unwise to fail to meet delegations from any association, irrespective of their private views.

For the lobbyist too, things have changed. Not only are there more of them, there are also more targets to influence at national and state level. Nationally, there are more agencies and congressional subcommittees to contact, and state governments have become a new focus of attention. Business organisations are particularly active in some states, often employing former state legislators, governors and officials to do their work. Since the days of Reagan's New Federalism, more policies are operated and financed at the state rather than the federal level, particularly in the welfare field.

Pressure groups in Britain and the United States: a comparison

In Britain and the United States, there is a widespread acceptance of group activity, although America has traditionally been particularly receptive to the operation of lobbying. The two countries have a vast array of groups, both protective and promotional, and although the causes that inspire activity on either side of the Atlantic may differ from time to time, it is striking how many organisations appear on both. In manufacturing industry, agriculture, labour and the professions, and on a variety of matters of civic and social concern, there are similar associations, and on topical issues such as abortion there is the same divide between pro-life and pro-choice bodies.

Such groups perform similar functions and have broadly the same advantages and disadvantages. The arguments surrounding their work overlap, and comment in the press and among the public echoes similar anxieties – about the unrepresentativeness of group leadership, the influence of powerful interests, and the secrecy and dangers surrounding lobbying of the legislature. There are, however, some differences in the mode of operation and the strategies adopted, for the reasons given below.

In the USA, the federal system means that pressure groups can operate at several levels, and they seek to achieve their aims in local and state governments as well as in Washington. Political power is more diffuse, partly because of the federal structure but also because of the separation of powers. For instance, the position of the American courts in pronouncing on the constitutionality of legislation makes them an obvious access point. By contrast, British groups have placed most of their emphasis on lobbying in Whitehall or Westminster (although the devolved assemblies now provide a new outlet) and

CONCLUSION

The United States has a vast array of pressure groups that operate at several access points and have highly significant influence. In recent decades, the extent of lobbying in Washington and the fifty states has increased and the role of PACs has become a key element in the financing of election campaigns. Group activity provokes much controversy and there have been regular calls for more regulation and control. Debate about groups has centred upon their contribution to the democratic process.

In particular, Washington has become a hub of pressure-group activity. On any given day, group activists will be involved in many arenas. Some will be testifying for or against proposed legislation in congressional hearings. Others will be arguing in the Supreme Court, perhaps for stricter enforcement of regulations or for the protection of the rights of a section of the American people. Yet others will be meeting with bureaucrats in government departments, perhaps discussing ideas about legislation.

made less use of the judicial system. Organisations such as the Commission for Racial Equality and the Equal Opportunities Commission do make use of legal procedures.

Given the weak party structure and the lack of party discipline in Congress, US groups make Capitol Hill the target of their work. There is much to be gained through contact with individual legislators. By contrast, the greater cohesion of British parliamentary parties means that the powerful groups are keen to gain consultative status in Whitehall, where decisions are made. The unitary system of government concentrates power in government hands, and ministers and civil servants are the people to influence.

Not only are American lobbyists concerned with a wider variety of targets, they also engage in some activities that are unfamiliar on the British scene. UK election campaigns are much more centralised, and the media campaign is run primarily from headquarters. Much of party income goes to the London headquarters, and there are strict controls over what the individual candidate can spend. American elections are more candidate-centred, and there is a significant role for PACs in assisting both financially and organisationally. America makes extensive use of political advertising, and PACs are much involved in putting out their own broadcasts as well as in helping the candidate's team to finance its operations in this field.

Pressure groups flourish in most advanced countries and in those that allow many access points at which they can employ pressure. Britain and the United States meet both criteria, although of the two the American groups have the advantage, both for institutional reasons and from factors associated with the political culture and the greater openness of American society. Above all, US groups have the protection of the Constitution, which safeguards their rights of assembly and to petition government.

There is an interesting paradox about the participation of Americans in their political system. Many are reluctant to turn out and vote in elections, yet they are willing to involve themselves in pressure-group activity. As Schlozman and Tierney[13] have written: 'Recent decades have witnessed an expansion of astonishing proportions in the involvement of private organisations in Washington politics.' They might have referred to the other outlets as well, for many groups are now very active in working the many sub-governments in the American system.

REFERENCES

1 J. Rauch, *Demosclerosis: The Silent Killer of American Government*, Times Books, 1995
2 P. Woll and S. Zimmerman, *American Government: The Core*, McGraw-Hill, 1992
3 P. Woll and S. Zimmerman, as in 2 above
4 R. Hague and M. Harrop, *Comparative Government and Politics: An Introduction*, Palgrave, 2004
5 A. Grant and E. Ashbee, *The Politics Today companion to American Government*, Manchester University Press, 2002
6 J. Abramson, 'The Business of Persuasion Thrives in Nation's Capitol', *New York Times*, 29 September 1998
7 C. Griffin, *Cleaning out Congress*, Griffin Associates, 1992
8 A. Grant, *Contemporary American Politics*, Dartmouth, 1995
9 J. Abramson, as in 6 above
10 G. Wasserman, *The Basics of American Politics*, Longman, 1996
11 D. Truman, *The Governmental Process: Political Interests and Public Opinion*, Knopf, 1958
12 R. Hague and M. Harrop, as in 4 above
13 K. Schlozman and J. Tierney, *Organised Interests and American Democracy*, Harper and Row, 1986

USEFUL WEB SITES

www.influence.biz *Influence*, a trade publication for the lobbying industry, which chronicles the relationship between lobbyists and their clients.

www.policy.com Lists various think-tanks and issue groups.

Two sites with a broadly ideological perspective are:

www.conservativenet.com Conservative Net.

turnleft.com Turn Left.

Individual pressure groups have their own sites dealing with the specific issues of interest to them. Examples are:

www.business-roundtable.com The Business Round Table.

www.commoncause.org Common Cause.

www.naacp.org National Association for the Advancement of Colored People.

www.now.org National Organisation for Women.

www.nra.org National Rifle Association.

www.sierrraclub.org The Sierra Club.

SAMPLE QUESTIONS

1 Should there be more restrictions on the activity of political action committees (PACs)?

2 Which 'access points' are most likely to provide opportunities for US pressure groups to achieve their objectives? Does influence vary according to the type of group involved?

3 Discuss the role and value of pressure groups in the American legislative process.

4 'It is possible to overestimate the effects of pressure group activity. Ultimately, groups cancel each other out.' Discuss.

5 Does lobbying play too large a part in the American political process?

6 Are pressure groups beneficial to American democracy or do they undermine it?

7 Are American pressure groups too powerful?

8 'In Britain and America, the producer lobby is far more powerful than that representing consumers.' Is this true, and if so, does it matter?

Civil liberties and civil rights   **10**

Civil liberties and civil rights have already been briefly discussed in Chapter 2. Civil liberties are areas of social life in which governmental power should rarely intrude upon the free choice of individuals. Civil rights are areas of social life where government must act to ensure that all citizens are treated fairly and enjoy equality of opportunity. This involves the protection of the rights of minorities from the unfair actions of state and local governments, individuals and groups.

In this chapter, we explore the protection offered by the Bill of Rights to all Americans. We assess how well First Amendment freedoms are protected, before proceeding to examine the rights of America's ethnic minority populations, women and (briefly) other groups, the policy of affirmative action and the conflict that it engenders.

POINTS TO CONSIDER

➤ How do civil liberties and civil rights differ?

➤ To what extent have First Amendment freedoms been upheld in the USA?

➤ What have been the significant landmarks in the campaign by black Americans to achieve their civil rights? How effectively are they protected today?

➤ Why did the Equal Rights Amendment fail?

➤ What has been the impact of the issue of abortion on the women's movement?

➤ What are the different forms of affirmative action?

➤ What problems have been experienced by gays in their bid for equal recognition?

➤ How effective is the Bill of Rights in securing the freedoms of all Americans?

Throughout American history, those in government have had to draw a line between areas of social life in which individual choice should be largely unrestricted and areas in which certain sorts of choices will be constrained or prohibited. The issue has been when and for what purpose the power of government should be brought to bear on individual citizens, to affect their patterns of choice and activity. The term **civil liberties** refers to those areas in which governmental power should rarely intrude on the free choice of individuals, such as free speech and freedom of worship. In these cases, citizens are protected against arbitrary or excessive governmental interference. The term **civil rights** covers those areas where government must act, intruding upon what individuals might otherwise choose to do, in order to see that everyone is treated fairly and that opportunities are available to all who are able and prepared to seize them. Here, government is acting positively to protect individuals against discrimination or unreasonable treatment by other individuals or groups.

civil liberties

Areas of social life such as freedom of speech, religion and the press, in which the Constitution restricts or prohibits governmental intrusion on the free choice of individuals.

civil rights

Areas of social life in which the Constitution requires government to ensure equal treatment of individuals – for example, by granting all of them the right to vote. Whereas civil liberties (sometimes known as negative rights) are legal protections against governmental restriction of First Amendment freedoms, civil rights are legal protections against discrimination on the grounds of such things as ethnicity, gender or religion. In these cases, the government positively confers rights on disadvantaged groups, by passing anti-discriminatory legislation.

Most Americans are theoretically comfortable with the two concepts of liberties and rights, which combine to ensure that they can do as they please unless they discriminate against others. Yet in a society whose Constitution proclaims the 'equal protection of the laws', some have seen their rights denied. In particular, members of ethnic minorities and women have long experienced disadvantage, even if much has been done to redress the balance in recent decades. It remains the case that on average they earn much less than white males. They also find that when they seek to advance up the occupational hierarchy, all too often they hit a 'glass ceiling' that limits their progress. As part of the attempt to reverse historical disadvantages, the Great Society programme contained measures of affirmative action. Today, critics of the idea see this as 'reverse discrimination'.

Civil liberties: First Amendment freedoms

The key freedoms to protect citizens from an abuse of governmental power are to be found in the First Amendment, which is why they are commonly referred to as **First Amendment freedoms**. The amendment states:

> Congress shall make no law respecting an establishment of religion, or prohibiting the free exercise thereof; or abridging the freedom of speech, or of the press, or the

right of the people peaceably to assemble, and to petition the Government for a redress of grievances.

These are the essential civil liberties that allow democracy to work, for they concern the right of people to communicate freely with each other and with the government. They allow the public, the press, lobbyists and congressmen to 'go public' and organise an attempt to change government policy. It was Justice Oliver Wendell

First Amendment freedoms
The basic freedoms of religion, speech, press and assembly, as set out in the First Amendment to the Constitution. These are very important civil liberties (see below).

Holmes who argued that in a democratic society there is as much need for competition among ideas as there is in an economic marketplace for competition among producers. It is through free discussion that ideas can be tested, allowing all options to be explained and erroneous ones to be challenged. In Holmes's view, good ideas would ultimately drive out bad ideas and the public could be relied upon to reject what was wrong and opt for what was true.

Inevitably, there must be restraints upon freedom of speech, but these are kept to a minimum, the emphasis being on maximum tolerance unless there is a clear threat to society or a serious violation of the rights of others. Justice Holmes is renowned for his remark that no one has a right to shout 'fire' in a crowded theatre when there is no fire. But in the overwhelming majority of circumstances, the free and uncensored expression of opinion is protected. This is because freedom of speech and expression is a vital element of any democracy. Political participation, open debate of alternatives and majority rule all depend upon it.

As we have seen, in the United States the requirement set out in the Constitution has been broadened to cover state as well as central governments. So too has it been extended to cover not only oral speech, but also gesturing, mimicking, wearing badges and armbands, raising signs and leafleting passers-by.

The First Amendment also protects the rights of Americans to refuse to utter things they do not believe. When some children of Jehovah's Witnesses objected to repeating the Pledge of Allegiance in schools – because in the view of the parents this was worship of 'graven images' (the flag) – the nine justices of the Supreme Court overturned their suspension from school, in the case of *West Virginia State Board of Education v Barnette* (1943). The ruling declared that: 'No official, high or petty, can prescribe what shall be orthodox in politics, nationalism or religion, or other matters of opinion, or force citizens to confess by word or act their faith therein.'

In *Watchtower Bible and Tract Society of New York Inc v Village of Stratton, Ohio* (2002), there was further protection for the same religious group. The Court protected the rights of people who go from door to door – whether for political, religious or other reasons. The Jehovah's Witnesses had challenged a Stratton law that required their officers to get a permit before they did so, but the ruling declared that 'it is offensive . . . to the very notion of a free society, that in the context of everyday public discourse a citizen must first inform the government of [his] or [her] desire to speak to [his] or [her] neighbours and then obtain a permit to do so'.

The Court has in the past also upheld state laws that ban seditious behaviour (any conspiracy to overthrow the government by force), but it has not allowed convictions of communists solely on account of their membership of the Communist Party, for to do so would infringe the right of freedom of association. In other words, merely to believe in the violent overthrow of those who rule is not in itself a crime, nor is membership of any body that advocates such a policy. It is actually attempting to overthrow the government that is prohibited. This position was made clear in the case of *Whitney v California* (1927). Whitney was convicted under state law of engaging in Communist Party organizational activities. The Supreme Court upheld the Californian statute, although a dissenting justice (Louis Brandeis) argued that 'only serious danger to the state . . . an emergency can justify repression', Forty-two years later, in *Brandenburg v Ohio*, the line taken by Brandeis was supported in the Court, which adopted the 'clear, present, and imminent danger' test in such cases.

Protection under the Constitution is also granted in cases of 'speech plus', those that exceed the normal understanding of what speech involves. These may concern such things as wearing badges and burning flags, **symbolic speech** or speech-related activities. The anti-war student who entered a courthouse with the words 'F. . . the draft' on the back of his jacket was held in contempt of court by the judge, but the Supreme Court did not concur. The justices ruled that: 'While the particular four-letter word being litigated here is perhaps more distasteful than most others of its genre [kind], it nevertheless is often true that one man's vulgarity is another's lyric.' Flag-burning too was protected towards the close of the twentieth century. In *Texas v Johnson* (1989), the Court took the view that: 'If there is a bedrock principle underlying the First Amendment, it is that Government may not prohibit the expression of an idea simply because society finds the idea itself offensive or disagreeable.'

> **symbolic speech**
> Speech-related acts, such as flag-burning, gestures and even the wearing of certain types of clothing, that are protected under the First Amendment, because they relate to the communication of ideas or opinions.

Legal rights: the rights of the accused

The Fifth and Fourteenth Amendments prevent national and state governments from depriving citizens of their lives, liberty or property without due process of law. Due process, a phrase used in the Fourteenth Amendment, provides the guarantee of fairness in rulings and actions of government officials, especially those in the courtroom. In criminal trials, the right of due process includes:

- the right to free counsel if you cannot afford a lawyer, and to have a legal representative present at any police questioning;
- the right to reasonable bail after being charged;
- the right to a speedy trial;
- the right to confront and cross-examine any who accuses or testifies against you, and to remain silent;
- the right to an impartial judge and a jury selected without racial bias;
- the right of appeal to a higher court if legal errors are committed by a judge;
- protection from double jeopardy ('nor shall any person be subject for the same offence to be twice put in jeopardy of life and limb').

Legal rights denied: anti-terrorist legislation

Almost every American could agree on the need to ensure greater security of the person by rooting out terrorists and preventing the danger of further attacks. But critics of the Bush Administration claim that its 2001 package of anti-terrorist measures ('Uniting and Strengthening America By Providing Appropriate Tools Required To Intercept and Obstruct Terrorism' – more usually known as 'the USA Patriot Act') – went far beyond what was necessary to achieve these objectives. Critics detected signs of a serious erosion of accepted freedoms.

Criticism centred mainly on three broad aspects of the Act:

1 The dedication to secrecy, which made it difficult to find out information relating to the six hundred or so detainees held in federal prisons.
2 The way in which new powers tilted the balance towards the executive branch and removed from the judicial system some of its power to review the actions of the Administration (for instance, immigration judges now have less opportunity to prevent unlawful detention or deportation of non-citizens).
3 The undermining of the traditional distinction between foreign intelligence-gathering and criminal investigation (for instance, information gathered by domestic law enforcement agencies can now be handed to bodies such as the CIA).

In the landmark case of *Miranda v Arizona* (1966), the Supreme Court outlined a set of procedures to be followed by the police before any individual can be questioned. Once an investigation is under way with the focus on one individual, he or she must receive the following warning:

> You have the right to remain silent.
> Anything you say may be used against you in a court of law.
> You have the right to be represented by an attorney of your choice.
> If you cannot afford an attorney, a public defender will be provided for you if you wish.

These **Miranda rules** apply when a person has been taken into custody or otherwise significantly deprived of freedom of movement by the police. Although some exceptions have been created, in essence they still govern all police interrogations. Courts have often thrown out confessions obtained where the rules have not been followed.

> **Miranda rules**
> The list of guidelines concerning the treatment of people during 'custodial interrogation', as established by the *Miranda* v *Arizona* ruling.

Civil rights: the search for equality

In the Declaration of Independence, Thomas Jefferson decreed that 'all men are created equal'. By this, he was not saying that everybody was alike and that there were no differences between human beings. Indeed, throughout his life, he clearly believed that there were differences, for he took the view that black Americans were genetically inferior to whites. But a further clue to his meaning is to be found in the same declaration, when it speaks of the 'unalienable rights' to which all were entitled. What he wanted was that everyone should have the same chance, in other words equality of opportunity. What individuals made of that chance was, in his view, a matter dependent on their abilities and efforts. He did not favour equality of outcome, with its emphasis on equal rewards, but he did think that in a moral sense all had the right to equal consideration.

The struggle for equality has been the rallying point for all groups demanding an end to discrimination against them and the attainment of their full civil rights, among them African Americans, women, and others such as gays and lesbians and the disabled. The list could be extended to cover the victims of discrimination on grounds of age (the old and the young), people with AIDS and the homeless. Here we concentrate on the campaigns for civil rights associated with ethnic minorities and women, and more briefly take on board the issue of gays and the disabled. All of these groups have presented challenges to mainstream America.

Minorities and women have achieved partial success and seen a considerable expansion of their civil rights. Other groups too have found it difficult to progress as far as they would in today's conservative social climate. In particular, gays and lesbians still feel that their campaign for the same rights as those enjoyed by heterosexual Americans has a long way to run. So too do the disabled and the growing band of American's elderly feel that their rights need greater recognition.

Civil rights for black Americans

The treatment of black Americans up until the 1950s

Until the late nineteenth century, black Americans were kept in their place primarily by custom and economic conditions rather than as a result of legislation. But around the turn of the century, several laws were enacted which allowed persecution and separation to exist. It became illegal for black and white people to travel together, or to use other public facilities such as hospitals and swimming baths together. The statutes were often known as the **Jim Crow laws**, a name derived from a runaway slave who composed a song and dance in which the name was used. It was taken up by white comics and came into general use as a label for all black Americans. As a result of this legislation, blacks were excluded from the electorate and from most worthwhile job opportunities.

> **Jim Crow laws**
> The generic name for all laws and practices that enforced segregation of the races in the American South, from the late nineteenth to the mid-twentieth centuries.

According to the Constitution, the 'equal protection' clause of the Fourteenth Amendment decreed that no state could 'deny to any person within its jurisdiction the equal protection of the laws'. Yet this requirement was easily evaded, because the *Plessy v Ferguson* ruling (1896) of the Supreme Court determined that racial segregation was not discrimination if 'equal accommodations' were provided for members of both races. In fact, there never was such equality, and for many years black Americans experienced inferior conditions, and – denied the vote – had no effective means of protest. There were a few challenges in the Supreme Court, but these never produced significant changes. The lot of the majority of African Americans was to suffer three indignities: **segregation**, discrimination and intimidation. The last came in the form of terror from the Ku Klux Klan and other secret societies, and beatings and lynchings by their members were commonplace.

> **segregation**
> The practice of creating separate facilities within the same society for the use of a minority group.

At the turn of the twentieth century, 90% of black Americans lived in the South, and the vast majority of them were employed in agriculture. But between the wars there was a drift to the North as they and their offspring looked for work in the developing towns and cities, where they hoped to make a better life for themselves and their families. Again, their social status was still low, life was hard and many were poverty-stricken. It was American involvement in World War II that created jobs for people of all colours and races. Once the fighting was over, returning black soldiers wanted a better deal for their families than they had known before. In the North, the number of blacks was growing, so that in Washington there was a black majority by

1961. They were becoming frustrated with their rate of advance. There were among them some articulate and able leaders who began to make an impact in their chosen field – business, education, the church, the law and the arts. The majority of their race had no such good fortune, and resentment was becoming more overt.

Postwar progress on civil rights to the 1960s

A major step forward had already come about by then, for in 1954 the Supreme Court reversed the 1896 'separate but equal' judgement, and declared that separate facilities were 'inherently unequal'. The case was *Brown v Board of Education, Topeka, Kansas*, and it concerned the issue of desegregation. At that stage, there were still seventeen states that segregated schools in accordance with their own laws. The Court said that segregated schools were illegal, for 'segregation is itself discrimination'. It had to be ended with 'all deliberate speed'. This judgement of the Warren Court shocked conservative America, members of which disliked such judicial liberalism. Although several states implemented it speedily, there were others where the dominant whites were determined to retain their privileged position. Governors in the Deep South sought to use the law to evade the ruling, but over the coming years the Supreme Court struck down many attempts to frustrate its will.

In 1957, President Eisenhower had to send in federal troops to Little Rock, Arkansas, to ensure that black children were allowed to enter the white school. The president saw the attitude of the governor as a challenge to federal authority, and it was probably the president's determination to insist on central power as much as his determination to enforce civil rights which influenced his action. Over the following years, segregation gradually disappeared, and in 1969 the Supreme Court decreed that 'all deliberate speed' must be interpreted as immediately. Dual schools were brought to an end.

Much of the progress in the 1960s came about as a result of the campaigning of the Civil Rights Movement. In particular, the National Association for the Advancement of Colored People (NAACP) had achieved a significant victory in 1955, when a bus boycott by blacks in Montgomery ended in the company relenting and ceasing to reserve seats for white people. This episode led to the emergence of Dr **Martin Luther King** as a leader in the crusade for racial justice.

There were many protests and demonstrations in the early 1960s, and King won over much white liberal opinion with his 'dream' of racial equality. President Kennedy was sympathetic on the issue of civil rights, but after his assassination it was Lyndon Johnson who introduced the Great Society legislation, which included many measures to end racial injustice – among them, the Voting Rights Act of 1965 and the Civil Rights Acts of 1964 and 1968 which tackled discrimination in jobs and housing. (For a listing of civil rights legislation, see pp. 316–17). The integrationist phase of the Civil Rights Movement reached its peak in the 1960s.

An important and controversial feature of the progress in that decade was the introduction of special programmes – sometimes backed by federal money – to help promote racial or gender balance, collectively known. The policy was known as **affirmative action**, which involved a set or procedures designed to correct the effects of past discrimination against minority groups (and women). Specific targets were set and quotas sometimes applied in recruitment for jobs and university places, with the intention of boosting the representation of these groups. Since the late 1960s, many affirmative programmes have been adopted by national, state and local governments, by public institutions such as state colleges and universities, and by some private employers and organisations.

NB See pp. 325–9 for further details of affirmative action programmes and the intense debated they have subsequently inspired. Much of the information in that section is highly relevant to this section on the advancement of civil rights for black Americans.

The rise of Black Power

In the 1960s, much was being done to improve the rights of black Americans and to remove some of the worst forms of discrimination, but many of them still found that their conditions in areas such as education, employment and housing were markedly worse than those of white Americans. Many felt powerless, and unrest in the underclass of black Americans was beginning to gather pace.

Martin Luther King preached passive resistance and non-violent direct action, arguing that violence stood little chance of success against the might of the American government. He disliked the 'hate whitey' language adopted by some of his

Martin Luther King

Martin Luther King (1929–68) was born into a well-educated and relatively prosperous family whose members understood the ways in which the church and the NAACP strengthened the black community.

Initially, he wanted to become a minister, but he became active in the black boycott of Montgomery's segregated buses (1955), helped establish the Southern Christian Leadership Conference, which campaigned for greater equality for American blacks (1957), and thereafter was involved in anti-segregation sit-ins and freedom rides. He stressed the importance of non-violent, passive resistance, although his activities often led to his arrest.

In 1963, he made his inspirational 'I Have a Dream' speech in the March on Washington, his actions encouraging President Johnson to obtain civil rights legislation.

Towards the end of King's life, he was increasingly criticised by some black as well as white Americans. In 1968, he was assassinated by a social misfit, James Earl Ray.

affirmative action

Better known in England as positive discrimination, affirmative action programmes are designed to increase the chances of women and minorities being selected for positions in public life, such as on university courses or in management positions. The topic became one of fierce debate in the 1990s.

younger, more militant critics, who wanted to see a different approach. They questioned the desirability of integration, the strategy on non-violence and the presence of white liberals in the leadership of the cause. King was particularly condemnatory of the tone adopted in the early 1960s by **Malcolm X**, a leader of the radical black Nation of Islam that had been established back in 1930 and had spread through some of the northern cities in the 1950s and afterwards. Many of its supporters were anti-Semitic (anti-Jewish) and sexist, Malcolm X describing the best position of women as 'horizontal'. He rejected political activity through the orthodox channels and urged racial separation.

Malcolm X (1925–65)
Born into a ghetto background, Malcolm Little spent his early life in petty crime, drug abuse and pimping, before being converted in prison to the Nation of Islam. He replaced his 'slave name' Little with X. His prominence increased in the 1950s, his preaching of black pride appealing to ghetto blacks. He denounced the 'Farce on Washington' in 1963, but left the Nation a year later to engage more fully in the civil rights struggle. In his last years, he was prepared to co-operate with whites against racism and apologised for his attacks on King. He was murdered, probably by fellow Muslims.

Local activists in the northern cities often adopted the rhetoric of the radicals and were active in the racial violence of the 'long hot summers' of 1965–67. The protest and rioting showed just how much discontent there was in the ghettos.

The assassination of King (April 1968) confirmed many blacks in their belief that society was so rotten that peaceful change would not work. Some leaders were more confrontational, among them Stokely Carmichael, who felt that the whites would never surrender their supremacy. Whereas King talked the language of integration, Carmichael was committed to separatism. He and other **Black Power** activists called on blacks to reject white society; they urged the use of the term 'blacks' rather than 'negroes', a term with overtones of past humiliations. They wanted to see black children taught pride in their black culture, so that a generation would grow up willing to challenge those who suppressed them. A more militant group was the Black Panther organisation, which believed in armed revolution, an open war with white society.

Within the black leadership, there were many divisions. Many of the older generation still believed in the methods of Martin Luther King; others believed that the pace of advance was too slow if they relied on seeking to secure white goodwill. Some of the spokespersons were unimpressive, and there was discord over personality and tactics. None the less, the emphasis upon 'Black Power for Black People' helped to make many black Americans prouder of their race and their individuality. They were gaining a personal dignity that many had never had before.

Economic and social progress since the 1960s

As we have seen, the affirmative action programmes launched in the 1960s provided special benefits to those in the community who had been traditionally disadvantaged. In providing enhanced opportunities, it was anticipated that there might also be other benefits, such as enriching the nation's economic, social and cultural life and creating greater harmony and stability. This might result from reduced tension on the part of disaffected blacks, and also from the creation of a larger black middle class, which would feel it had a stake in society and would demonstrate to others that advancement is possible.

Affirmative action programmes did assist many black Americans in improving their status and opportunities. But such was the weight of past injustice and disadvantage that in education, entrance to medical school and gaining skilled employment, access was likely to be denied to many of them for years to come. Moreover, in recent years, a succession of Supreme Court judgements has restricted the use of racial preferences in areas such as admissions to educational institutions, and awarding grants and contracts.

After the burst of activity in the 1960s, progress has been patchy. There have been legislative and other advances, but in many areas of life much remains to be done:

> **Black Power**
>
> Black Power was the demand of the militant Stokely Carmichael, who rejected the King approach to black campaigning for civil rights. Carmichael urged the burning of 'every court house in Mississippi' and proclaimed 'Black Power', a term taken up by his supporters. Enthusiasts rejected the integrationist ideas of King, who was concerned not to alienate white liberals. Black Power supporters felt that integration was no longer possible or even desirable, and instead argued for black and white separation. They believed that the only route to attaining equality in positions of power was to oppose the evils of white authority by every possible means, including violence. The Black Power movement was concerned to develop a sense of black consciousness, which is why it rejected the earlier ethnic term 'negro', associated by many white Americans with the idea of 'subservient niggers'.

- In housing, it has proved difficult to end discrimination, for white residents and estate agents in some districts combine to ensure that 'undesirable' elements are kept out.
- In employment, blacks still suffer twice as much unemployment as whites, and access to jobs can be limited by factors such as poor educational attainment and covert or indirect discrimination. Some blacks have 'made it' and done well, and act as a role model for others, but the majority who work do so in low-paid positions.
- Black poverty actually increased in the later 1970s and 1980s, and remains a serious problem. Whilst there are some examples of successful black Americans, one in three live in poverty (one half of black children), and many are very deprived. Recession, the impact of Reaganite policies and the increasing number of one-parent families were all contributory factors. The gap between black and white earnings actually increased towards the end of the century.

- The black infant mortality rate of 19% was higher than in some countries in the developing world.
- Poor ghetto living conditions and lack of employment opportunities were associated in the minds of many white Americans with black crime, contributing to a white backlash against measures designed to help promote black progress. The violence that erupted in Los Angeles in 1992 showed that race relations between black and white Americans were poor. Four white policemen used unnecessary force to arrest Rodney King in March 1991. Following their acquittal by a white jury, four days of rioting resulted, culminating in 47 deaths, more than 2,000 injuries and 9,000 arrests.

Black gains in the 1960s via legislation and affirmative action programmes did create white resentment. Many whites could accept black legal and political rights and appreciate the contribution made by black sporting celebrities, but widespread class prejudice and racism remained. If any proposed solution to black poverty involved higher taxation, many whites were not keen to hear the message.

Progress in political life

By 2000, the total number of black elected officials had exceeded 7,500, and although many of them served at the municipal level, more than 450 were in state legislatures, and more than 300 were mayors. Such figures indicate substantial progress, often the result of increased black voting in inner-city ghetto areas. But there were other areas in which a white majority was willing to elect a black representative.

Lyndon Johnson appointed the first black to a Cabinet post; Nixon appointed four African American ambassadors; Bush the elder nominated Clarence Thomas to the Supreme Court; and Bill Clinton proved himself to be more willing to put forward black appointees to the judiciary than any of his predecessors. George W. Bush selected Colin Powell as his first secretary of state and Condoleezza Rice as his national security adviser. She replaced Powell in early 2005. In the 109th Congress, there are 42 African Americans in the House, and one in the Senate, the first since 1999.

Although the scale of black political advancement can be exaggerated, its magnitude is illustrated by the prominence of Jesse Jackson within the Democratic Party. The son of an illiterate South Carolina sharecropper, he rose to prominence in the Southern Christian Leadership Conference (SCLC) and hoped to take over the leadership from Martin Luther King. He was so keen to advertise their closeness that, on the day of King's assassination, Jackson appeared on television with what he claimed was his hero's blood on his shirt. By 1984 and again in 1988, his appeal was such that he campaigned (unsuccessfully) for the Democratic nomination for the presidency, although the mainstream of the party did not consider him the man to take on Ronald Reagan. On the second occasion, he won markedly more support from white party members, his 'rainbow (all colours) coalition' faring particularly well in New York, among blacks, whites and Hispanics. Jackson remains a leading figure who commands respect and whose backing is much sought after by potential presidential candidates.

The black vote

Traditionally, it has been the Democrats who have been more active in the field of civil rights, and they have been rewarded with overwhelming support from black voters. Johnson won 94% of the black vote, the highest figure recorded for one party, but Clinton won over 80% in 1992. Clinton won massive backing from many black leaders during the impeachment process. They claimed that one of the reasons why he was under attack was because of his policies towards black Americans. He was their friend; in the words of one civil rights activist,[1] 'Someone called Bill Clinton our first black president, and I do think he is a man who understands race. He identifies with black people and has black friends outside politics.' Al Gore was unable to enthuse blacks so much, but he also scored well among them in the 2000 election. In 2004, exit surveys indicated that Kerry won 89% of the black vote.

Yet despite this traditional association, the voting behaviour of black voters is no longer as predictable as it once was. The black conservative is less of a rarity than previously, and Clarence Thomas and others are testimony to this phenomenon. Alan Keyes made history as the first African American to seek the Republican nomination for the White House for 1996. If his attempt was short-lived it none the less suggested that there is a growing willingness among more prosperous blacks to abandon past allegiances. Such voters share with middle-class whites an antipathy to the usual pro-black policies such as the welfare state and affirmative action, believing that these liberal shibboleths sap African American pride and foster a black dependency culture.

Such conservative values have begun to spread lower down the social scale. In bodies such as the anti-abortion movement and the Christian Coalition, common attitudes can be shared by Americans of different colours.

Postwar progess reviewed

The Democrats have been more committed than the Republicans to the active pursuit of racial justice in the United States. Harrry S.Truman (1945–53) was the first president to take active measures to help black Americans. He established a liberal civil rights committee to investigate violence against them and used its report, 'To Secure These Rights', as ammunition in his attack on the problems they faced. In his State of the Union address (1948), he had proclaimed that: 'Our first goal must be to secure fully the essential human rights of our citizens.' He drew attention to the disparity between the words of

America's Founding Fathers ('All men are created equal') and the actions of their descendants. He acted to end discrimination in the armed forces and to guarantee fair employment in the civil service.

Thereafter, progress followed in the Kennedy, Johnson, Carter and Clinton presidencies, whether in the appointment of black judges, the greater willingness to adopt black candidates for public office, the pursuit of policies based on affirmative action, or legislation against discrimination. Black voters recognised that the Democrats were more likely to pursue policies advantageous to them (see the box below), and the party's presidential candidates have benefited from their generally solid support over many years.

But what has been achieved? How different is the America of today from the country to which Martin Luther King addressed his 'I Have a Dream' message in Washington more than forty years ago? On that occasion, he reminded his audience of the past situation, before proceeding to outline his future vision:

> Five score years ago, a great American, in whose symbolic shadow we stand today, signed the Emancipation Proclamation. This momentous decree came as a great beacon light of hope to millions of Negro slaves who had been seared in the flames of withering injustice . . . One hundred years later, the life of the negro is still sadly crippled by the manacles of segregation and the chains of discrimination . . . we have come here today to dramatise a shameful condition . . .

> So I say to you, my friends, that even though we face the difficulties of today and tomorrow, I still have a dream. It is a dream deeply rooted in the American dream, that one day this nation will rise up and live out the true meaning of its creed – we hold these truths to be self-evident, that all men are created equal . . .

> With this faith we will be able to tear out of the mountain of despair a stone of hope. With this faith, we will be able to transform the jangling discords of our nation into a beautiful symphony of brotherhood.

Two years after that speech, for many white Americans the passage of civil rights legislation drew a line under the civil rights era. Since there were no legal barriers to black participation, some people chose to ignore the economic, social and political barriers that remained. Not only would they come to resist demands to address the legacy of segregation and slavery through affirmative action, but they would do so with King's own words, insisting that candidates for university and employment should be 'judged not on the colour of their skin but the content of their character'.

For King, the March and speech were a beginning. He told reporters shortly before his death that 'it is absolutely necessary now to deal massively and militantly with the economic problem. The grave problem facing us is the problem of economic deprivation, with the syndrome of bad housing and poor education and improper health facilities all surrounding this basic problem.'

A note on Red Power and the progress made by Native Americans

At the turn of the 1960s, the disadvantages endured by Native Americans were worse than those experienced by many African Americans. Many of the problems were the same: inadequate housing, poverty and unemployment, and a lack of educational opportunities. More than half of Native Americans lived on reservations, where life expectancy, at 44 years, was twenty years less than the national average, tuberculosis was a regular killer, and suicide rates were alarmingly high – not a problem that affected the black population. Native Americans, even more than other minority groups, suffered from low self-esteem, for they felt despised not only on account of their ethnicity but also on account of their distinctive culture.

The National Congress of American Indians (NCAI) had been established in 1944 and it had made some gains, preventing reservation rights from being terminated under the Eisenhower Administration and winning support from President Kennedy for a jobs strategy to boost employment opportunities. Like the NAACP, it used the courts to achieve social and political progress, but unlike the more famous pressure group it did not advocate racial integration. Its goal was to ensure the survival of the unique cultural identity of Native Americans.

As a group, Native Americans were inspired by the campaign for equality so ably pursued by black Americans. Also like them, many Native Americans adopted an increasingly militant approach in the 1960s. Young activists tired of the NCAI approach, which in their

Integration has won for many African Americans the right to eat in any restaurant, but only more equal facilities and opportunities can ensure that more of them have the funds to finance the meal. Further progress continues to be hampered by divisions within the black leadership, racial tension, the white backlash and the sheer difficulty of steering themselves out of the ghetto poverty trap.

The struggle for women's rights

For many years, American women experienced the same treatment as their counterparts in Europe. It was widely assumed that their responsibilities involved the domestic role of caring for their children and husbands, for whom they were expected to be attractive and dignified adornments. They were seen as goods and chattels, dependants of their fathers and husbands. They had few legal rights, and were unable to vote. Neither was there much opportunity to further their interests through educational advancement. This sense of powerlessness and dependency inspired some pioneering women to involve themselves in the women's movement. Under a hundred of them gathered in New York State in 1848, where they proclaimed the Seneca Falls Declaration

view involved too close co-operation with the Bureau of Indian Affairs (BIA). Many turned to the American Indian Movement (AIM), the most overtly confrontational organisation. It developed in the ghettos of Minneapolis-St Paul and demanded reform of ghetto conditions and an end to harassment of Native Americans by the police.

Like militant black equivalents, the AIM leaders wanted to present a more positive image of Native Americans. They spoke of Red Power, indulged in acts of civil disobedience, occupied BIA offices and committed sporadic violence. Such tactics inspired a backlash among some white Americans, as did those of Black Power supporters. However, white Americans were more sympathetic to Native Americans, seeing them as less of a threat to the white position.

In the late twentieth century, Native Americans made some progress within American society, a process begun during the Great Society years. Federal money was made available for tribal development, although some of the improvement in economic status owed more to a growing tourist influence in Native American culture than it did to government action.

Overall, there has been some modest increase in the living standards of many Native Americans, but they remain more than twice as likely to fall below the poverty level than African Americans and have a significantly lower level of educational attainment. Under 2 million in number, they are a declining proportion of the population.

of Rights and Sentiments and demanded 'the rights and privileges which belong to them as citizens of the United States'.

As elsewhere, the position of the minority of women who were striving for greater recognition was a difficult one. They were excluded from a political system dominated by men, and their chances of securing their rights and improving the lot of women in society were therefore dependent upon elected male representatives. Most men were unwilling to share the exercise of power, for they took the view that the world of politics and decision-making was one for which they were peculiarly well suited. Those women who tried to involve themselves in political action to persuade men to allow them to open up the citadels of power found themselves ridiculed, slandered or even arrested.

As in Britain, the vote was an initial target for many campaigners for female rights. Suffragists engaged in a variety of persuasive tactics to gain attention, some peaceful and educational, others militant and more intimidatory. Moderates were more willing to argue their case patiently, in countless leaflets and public meetings. Militants were more likely to cause a stir by chaining themselves to the railings of the White House. When they did such things, they were liable to be jailed and force-fed, among other indignities.

However, in the late nineteenth century, some states began to grant women the vote, and gradually it was extended across the country. In 1920, the Nineteenth Amendment made it legally binding for all states to provide for the female franchise. The right to vote was an important equality gain in itself. More than that, it empowered women, for once they had a voice in political life, they were able to use it to campaign for other rights – on matters such as child welfare, anti-lynching and prohibition.

In World War II, the labour shortage created a demand for extra workers. Although many women workers were considered expendable once hostilities were over, there were still 6 million in work, many of them wives rather single women and a number of them black. Since then, several factors have helped women advance their position in American society, similar ones to those which apply in Britain:

- the spread of education, especially higher education;
- the need for labour in the economy;
- the increased availability of labour-saving devices in the home;
- the increased ability of women to control their own fertility, via birth control;
- legislative action (see box below).

KEY CIVIL RIGHTS LEGISLATION AFFECTING MEMBERS OF ETHNIC MINORITIES AND WOMEN

Civil Rights Act (1957)

This made it a federal offence to seek to prevent persons from voting in federal elections and authorised the Attorney-General to take legal action when a person was deprived of his or her voting rights. This was targeted at ethnic minorities.

Civil Rights Act (1964)

This has been the most sweeping anti-discriminatory statute. It prohibited discrimination on grounds of race, sex, religion or national origin, and in public accommodation and federally funded programmes. It created the Equal Employment Opportunity Commission. The impact of the measure has been significant for ethnic minorities and women.

The women's movement

The women's movement today is a broad umbrella, and within it there are several groups pursuing their own agendas. Even where there is agreement on the goals to be pursued, there may be differences of opinion about the means by which they should be attained. All agree, however, on the need to advance rights for women.

Among those who come within the women's movement are some who see women's inferior treatment as part of a more general problem of social disadvantage for minority groups, others who stress the right to work or the need for greater educational opportunity, and yet more whose interest relates to a single controversial issue such as abortion or lesbianism. Even on abortion, there is a division of opinion (see box on pp. 318–19, for a fuller discussion of the issue), for whereas the majority would stress the mother's right to choose, a minority of activists emphasise the rights of the unborn child. There are also differences over tactics, a variety of approaches having been advocated by campaigners. Some want to change the Constitution. Others are content to work for concrete legislative gains, large or small. Some want to work with sympathetic men. More strident voices sometimes portray men as the enemy and see little hope of winning concessions from them – and may indeed find it demeaning to seek them.

Civil Rights Act (1991)

This placed the onus on employers to justify any practices that negatively impacted upon ethnic minorities and women. Employers were required to defend any such practices as being necessary for the job in question, there being no alternative approach available. Compensatory damages could be awarded for intentional discrimination and punitive damages in the case of employers found guilty of acting with malice or reckless indifference to rights based on sex, religion or disability (they could already be awarded in cases of racial discrimination, under earlier legislation).

The 1991 legislation also established a commission to enquire into the issue of 'glass ceilings', those invisible barriers that served to prevent minorities and women from becoming executives or assuming other important positions in management.

ABORTION: A FEMINIST AND A MORAL ISSUE

Abortion, the deliberate termination of a pregnancy, is a highly controversial issue in the United States. It has sometimes been referred to as a 'new Vietnam' because it has so sharply polarised popular opinion. What makes it different from most other questions is that it involves a clash of absolutes. To its supporters, it is a matter of a woman's fundamental right to do what she wishes with her own body. To its opponents, it is about the fundamental right to life of the as yet unborn child. Opponents, be they Catholics or supporters of the Christian right, regard abortion not just as another symptom of a general decline in moral standards, but as a sin. For them, it is a contravention of the divine law of the Scriptures and, for the more militant, one they cannot accept.

Abortion is sometimes portrayed as a defining issue between liberals and conservatives, and this is broadly true. But the degree of religious involvement in the debate makes the categorisation less clear cut. Many Catholics who might be liberal on a range of social questions concerning such things as employment rights would find themselves in the conservative camp in discussion of the rights of the unborn to life itself.

Abortion before and after the 1973 *Roe v Wade* judgement

In the nineteenth century, many states introduced laws against abortion, but by the early 1970s nineteen states permitted it. The American Law Institute and the American Medical Association came out in favour of terminations in certain situations such as foetal abnormality. Their members were also worried about the danger to desperate women who resorted to dubious back-street treatments. They were joined by elements in the growing women's movement, who also campaigned for the removal of restrictive state laws. On the other side of the argument, there were important developments too. Foremost among them was the increasing involvement of the Catholic church in the debate. Its role was crucial to the anti-abortion movement that resisted any liberalisation of the law. It established the National Right to Life Committee (NRLC) in 1971. Abortion, originally a state concern, had come to assume national importance.

Then, the Supreme Court delivered the much-quoted *Roe v Wade* judgement (1973). It found that state laws against abortion were unconstitutional, for they violated the right of a woman to terminate her pregnancy and thereby have control over her own person. This denied a woman her right to privacy, as laid down in the Fourteenth Amendment. In other words, there was a constitutional right to have an abortion. Abortion thereafter became legal across the United States.

Opponents and supporters of abortion were galvanised into action by this Court judgement. Supporters formed the National Association for the Repeal of Abortion Laws, now known as the National Abortion and Reproductive Rights Action League (NARAL). They felt it necessary to mount a defence of the newly proclaimed right, in order to fend off the attacks of those who would seek to undermine it. Many opponents were to be found in the

Catholic church, but there were soon stirrings among religious evangelicals. Opposition to abortion became a key issue in the emergence of what was to become the Christian right (see pp. 260–2).

Limitations upon abortion by the judiciary and legislature

Since 1973, there have been numerous attempts to reverse the legal position, mostly through the courts. In 1989 the Rehnquist Court made a significant inroad into the 'right to choose', in the *Webster v Reproductive Services* case. Instead of overruling the 1973 decision, the justices reduced its impact by acknowledging the constitutional right to an abortion, but also granting more power to individual states to impose restrictions (though not to ban the operation completely). In 1992, in *Casey v Planned Parenthood*, states were given the power to regulate abortion even in the first three months of pregnancy (the period in which the *Roe v Wade* judgement had denied any right of interference) and to ban it once the foetus was deemed to be 'viable'. Yet the basic right was upheld, and state regulations were not to infringe that right unduly.

Clinton's two appointments to the Supreme Court tilted its balance in a more moderate direction, making further Court restrictions less likely. In the 1990s the pressure to limit abortion further came from the legislative branch, following the change of party control in 1994. In late 1995, the House voted to ban a rare, late-term abortion procedure used in cases where there is a severe foetal abnormality or the health of the mother is under threat (partial birth abortion) and to jail doctors who carried it out. The Senate similarly gave the bill a speedy passage. Twice, Bill Clinton used his veto to prevent the measure from reaching the statute book, and in 2000 the Supreme Court ruled against a state law that sought to ban such abortions. The issue remained contentious, for the anti-abortion movement saw it as one on which it could make progress with its campaign to make further inroads into the constitutional right to have an abortion. In 2003, George W. Bush (who opposes abortion except in the most extreme cases) signed a ban on partial birth abortions into law. Because of its limited use, pro-choice groups were outraged at what NARAL called 'the most devastating and appalling attack on a woman's freedom to choose in the history of the House'. Anti-abortionists portrayed the operation as being tantamount to infanticide.

Party reactions

Polls show that Americans are more or less evenly divided on the rights and wrongs of abortion. Even women who favour women's rights in other areas may take a pro-life stance. Both parties are worried by internal fission over the issue. Democrats tend to favour the right to legal abortions and most feminists who campaign for it are committed to the party. Many Republicans – especially those associated with the Christian Right – strongly disapprove of terminations.

The National Organisation for Women (NOW) is in favour of retaining the current constitutional position and has been involved in lobbying senators to persuade them to view any new Supreme Court nominees made by the Bush Administration with caution. It is aware that George W. Bush is likely to put forward names of men and women judged to be pro-life. NOW's interest shows that abortion is central to the feminist agenda, even if the women's movement as a whole is divided. Some women believe that other issues more basic to their campaign, such as the Equal Rights Amendment, have not been followed up sufficiently because of an excessive preoccupation with a single contentious question. Others are pleased to have one cause around which to rally in defence of women's rights.

Tensions over goals and tactics are liable to surface in many campaigning organisations, but in the 1970s and 1980s there was a general recognition of the need to work for the passage of the **Equal Rights Amendment (ERA)**, which was designed to guarantee 'equality or rights' under the law for both sexes. This was an ambitious project that inevitably provoked an anti-feminist backlash, not just from men, but from socially conservative groups as a whole, including religious evangelicals and powerful business interests. Passed by Congress, it was never ratified by enough states to become part of the Constitution, and lapsed in 1982. Ultimately, many Americans were too anxious about the extent of social change that the Amendment might unleash to allow their support.

Some prominent organisations within the women's movement

Created in 1966, the **National Organisation for Women (NOW)** campaigns on a broad front, its interests spanning issues such as abortion access, child care, employment discrimination, the law on marital property and international women's rights. It is worried by the prospect of new nominations to the Supreme Court in George W. Bush's second term, aware that they are likely to include persons unsympathetic to the 'woman's right to choose'. It has over a half a million members across the US, with branches in all fifty states. They employ a variety of campaigning methods, ranging from the traditional electoral and lobbying work to bringing lawsuits, from mass marches to non-violent civil disobedience.

Several women's organisations are concerned with more specific issues, such as the relatively small number of women in key positions in public life. Among these:
• **Emily's List (EMILY = Early Money is Like Yeast)** was formed with the intention of getting more pro-choice women elected as representatives of the Democratic Party. It has been very successful at fundraising, and is currently one of the largest donors among American poliutical action committees. Other features of its work include the recruitment and training of candidates and campaign managers. It also acts as a

Working for constitutional change was successful in 1920, failed sixty-two years later and is again being proposed. NOW (see the box below) had been in the forefront of the battle for the ERA and enhanced its reputation and membership in the process. In 1995, it began its campaign for a Constitutional Equality Amendment, bolder, lengthier and more explicit than the original proposal. In article one, it demands that 'women and men shall have equal rights throughout the US and every place and entity subject to its jurisdiction: through this article, the subordination of women to men is abolished'. Elsewhere, it strikes out discrimination on account of 'sex, race, sexual orientation, marital status, ethnicity, national origin, color or indigence' and prohibits 'pregnancy discrimination and guarantees the absolute right of a woman to make her own reproductive decisions including the termination of pregnancy'. Overall, it seeks 'to bring the authority of the Constitution to work on entrenched beliefs about gender difference, as well as equality'.[2]

Despite the pressure of the women's movement for equal rights, only 7% of public offices are held by women in the early twenty-first century, and women's wages remain on average considerably lower than those of men. They are more likely to work in white-collar employment, more than a quarter of them performing clerical or office-related work. Their jobs tend to be in sectors that pay less well (such as teaching); management and industrial positions are still dominated by men. The fight to upgrade the level of female incomes is an important plank of the women's movement, whose members

---

consultancy, offering advice to those interested in its area of concern. Emily's List targets its money on winnable seats. The Republicans set up a similar (pro-choice) body, the **Wish List**.
* The **Fund for a Feminist Majority** targets all seats, whatever the chance of success. It likes to field female candidates at every opportunity.

On the other side of the fence, two right-wing organisations, **Concerned Women for America** and **Eagle Forum**, believe that feminists pose a threat to American society, the more so because of their espousal of the pro-abortion cause. Concerned Women actively opposes NOW and its proposed constitutional amendments. Relying mainly on education and use of the media, it focuses its case on biblical principles. Among its special causes are educative literature, religious liberty and the sanctity of life (for), and abortions, gay adoptions and pornography (against). Eagle Forum's mission is 'to enable Christian, conservative' pro-family men and women to participate in the political process: work to expose radical feminists, opposing their goals of federally financed and regulated child care and feminisation of the military, tax-funded abortions and same-sex marriages; and to honor the institution of marriage and the role of the fulltime homemaker'.

point out that twice as many women as men have incomes around the minimum wage.

The political involvement of women

Women in political office

The number of women in elected office has traditionally been markedly lower than the proportion of women in the American electorate. Several factors may be involved. Women are more reluctant to come forward as candidates, they have difficulty in getting nominated, and the electoral system makes it harder for them to succeed if they are chosen.

The percentage of women in elective public office, 1979–2004

Year	US Congress (%)	State-wide executive offices (%)	State legislatures (%)
1979	3	11	10
1989	5	14	17
1999	12	28	23
2005 (109th Congress)	15	25	23

THE SLOW PROGRESS IN INCREASING FEMALE REPRESENTATION IN POLITICS

Women have a long history of activism in local and community work, but their role in the partisan political arenas has not matched this degree of social participation. Some of the barriers have begun to diminish and women are entering politics in greater numbers at state and national levels. Yet in spite of this improvement, Congress remains overwhelmingly male at the beginning of the twenty-first century. There has been some progress, most obviously in 1992, which was dubbed the 'Year of the Woman', when women won a record forty-seven seats in the House. This advance has been most apparent within the Democratic Party, and it often occurs on occasions when there is an open race in which candidates for election stand in seats held by retiring male incumbents.

What have been the barriers to female representation?

As a group, women still possess obvious disadvantages compared with men. In the past, they suffered from more limited educational opportunity and from a lack of role models to emulate, for politics has traditionally been a man's world. More importantly today, opportunities for active participation continue to be limited by child-bearing and home-making responsibilities. Within the Republican party in particular, there are many women who would see these as their primary concerns. This limits the number willing to come forward

In the federal legislatures, women are better represented in the Democratic Party, which has been more willing to adopt them as candidates than the Republicans. In the 109th Congress, there are thirteen women in the Senate, and fifty-nine in the House. Within the fifty states, women fare better, so that some states that have had little female representation in either Washington chamber have had many women serving in one of their state bodies. Over the last thirty-five years, there has been a fourfold increase in the number of women in state legislatures, with Washington, Colorado, Maryland, California and Connecticut currently heading the list.

Women who hold political office in federal or state legislatures tend to view themselves not just as representatives of their local area. Rather, they see themselves as representing 'all women', not just in other parts of their state but across the country. According to one survey,[3] they tend to be actively involved in promoting legislation to improve women's position in society. They tend to prioritise women's concerns such as child care, domestic violence, health provision, reproductive rights and the welfare of family and children (even if this was not their original intention), have a strong interest in the policy agenda on equality, and work for more open and participatory government.

as candidates. Those who take this view tend to seek candidacy only at a stage in their lives when family responsibilities have diminished.

Male predominance tends to be self-perpetuating. Much political discussion is conducted in a macho manner, sometimes by sexist males. It requires great determination and self-confidence for any woman to resist the slings and arrows likely to be aimed at her, and to advance her claims. This can act as a deterrent for women who might be more willing to seek other professional positions. Some of the groups mentioned in the box on p. 000, such as Emily's List, have been active in encouraging women to come forward and in helping them overcoming likely obstacles – for example, by fundraising and offering training programmes.

Beyond these considerations, there are institutional factors that explain the underrepresentation of women. One is the electoral system. Women tend to fare better in countries that employ some variant of proportional representation. They are more likely to receive party encouragement to stand in multi-member constituencies. When voters have a choice of candidates, women are more likely to get elected in higher numbers.

The low turnover of legislators in Congress is another factor. Once elected, men tend to retain their office for several years, the feeling being that 'one good term deserves another'. With many seats being contested by male incumbents, the chances of a woman challenger are diminished. With very high rates of incumbent re-election, a bottleneck is created.

Jane Mansbridge[4] refers to 'surrogate representation' to describe the tendency of women representatives to see themselves as spokespersons for women beyond their electoral district. She notes how women in public office feel a special responsibility to represent the interests of women: 'In practice, it seems that legislators' feelings of responsibility for constituents outside their districts are considerably stronger when the legislature features few, or disproportionately few, representatives of the group in question.' This sense of surrogate responsibility has been articulated by the Democrat senator Barbara Boxer, who points out that: 'Women from all over the country really do follow what you do and rely on you to speak out for them on the issues [which matter].'[5]

Bill Clinton was more receptive to the claims for female representation in appointed offices in public life than his predecessors. He included three women in his first Cabinet, appointed a second to the Supreme Court, and made useful progress towards achieving a more balanced judiciary. George W. Bush included Condoleezza Rice as his national security adviser in his first administration. In the second, he made her his new secretary of state. In addition to her, there were three other women in the list of Cabinet appointees.

At state level, women hold 25.7% of elective executive offices across the country. To date, they have been elected to executive offices in forty-eight states, only Maine and West Virginia failing to have chosen them.

Women and voting

The traditional picture of women in politics suggests that they are less likely to vote and participate at all levels of activity, that they are more partisan and more likely to support right-wing parties. For many years, it was true that they turned out less enthusiastically, but in recent years there has been much less difference in male and female turnout. Over the period 1978–88, on average 2.3% less women voted than men, but as there are now more females than males there have actually been more female voters than male ones.

Similarly, there is little evidence today that women are more conservative in their voting allegiance, and in recent presidential elections it is the Democratic Party that has benefited from their support. Whereas in 1980, 47% voted for Ronald Reagan and 45% for Jimmy Carter, twelve years later they supported Bill Clinton over George Bush senior by 46% to 37% (17% for Ross Perot). Al Gore and John Kerry have maintained the Democrat lead among women voters, but whereas the former won 54% of the female vote, the latter achieved only 51%. President George W. Bush's ability to increase his share of the women's vote to 48% in 2004 (up from 43% in 2000) was a major reason why he substantially increased his share of the popular vote.

Defined as the difference between the proportion of women and the proportion of men voting for the winning candidate, the gender gap averaged 7.7% between 1980 and 2000, peaking in 2000 at 10%. In 2004, it was 7%.[6]

It may be that women have leaned to the left in the last few years because they associated Reagan, Bush and Speaker Gingrich with serious cuts in welfare expenditure, and in the case of Reagan with a hawkish attitude to issues of foreign policy. In contrast to Bush, Clinton appeared more interested in the domestic agenda, as well as being widely seen as a more attractive candidate. John Kerry may have benefited among some women from his generally more dovish approach to the Iraq War, although his ambivalence on the issue left others in doubt.

Women in other areas of political life

There are outlets other than voting for those who wish to play a part in politics in some capacity. Traditionally, they have been rather unwelcome in trade unions, which tend to be male-dominated institutions. However, there are other technically non-political bodies such as pressure groups in which to seek to influence public policy on social, moral and local issues. Women are often active in the anti-poverty lobby and areas where involvement can be reconciled with family ties.

The debate over affirmative action programmes

As we have seen, affirmative action programmes are those that are intended to correct the effects of individual and societal discrimination in the past. They provide special benefits to those in the community such as blacks, women and other disadvantaged groups that have traditionally been the victims of discrimination. Usually, these programmes involve a special effort to recruit and promote members of these groups. Affirmative action programmes may be of the hard or soft kind. Hard forms involve setting particular quotas for how many people of a certain type should be recruited to an organisation, irrespective of whether they have the appropriate qualifications (e.g. 20% of a police force must be black). Soft forms may involve measures to encourage minority applications. They are intended to boost minority representation by ensuring that when people of equal qualifications present themselves, then – in order to increase diversity – the member of the disadvantaged group is chosen.

The introduction of and debate surrounding affirmative action programmes

Although segregation and discrimination had already been made illegal by the mid-1960s, many supporters of equal rights saw this as insufficient. Neutral treatment would do little or nothing to equip women and racial minorities (primarily African Americans, Hispanics and native Americans) with genuine opportunities, and they would still be denied the chance to participate fully in American life. In particular, because African Americans had suffered from the continuing burden of disadvantage for so long, they would never have equal openings in areas such as access to education or medical school, skilled employment or winning government contracts. This, then, was a well-intentioned – and not unsuccessful – attempt to give modest preferences to those long denied their full citizenship and a fair chance in life. In the process, it might have other benefits, such as improving the nation's economic and social life (enriching it by bringing in a diversity of talents and experience) and removing a cause of disaffection and thereby promoting social order and stability. It might also help create a black middle class, which could provide a useful role model for any aspirational African Americans.

The affirmative action policy became highly contentious in the 1990s and remains controversial today. Its opponents believe that it is a form of reverse discrimination that replaces one form of discrimination by another. They feel that appointment, progress and promotion should be organised on the basis of merit rather than any other consideration. In particular, they dislike the quotas that are often written into programmes; these establish a target number of women or members of a minority group who must be employed. When there is work for everyone, the quota might seem more acceptable. When it is in short supply, or when a few particular jobs are much in demand, there tends to be a backlash against the concept. Similar controversy is stirred over educational provision. To achieve the target of a certain number of minority representatives in universities involves allowing some students to be enrolled who are less academically qualified than others who are being rejected.

Northern whites began to be upset by the policies designed to promote opportunities for black people, such as busing and affirmative action. Many of the programmes derived from the Civil Rights Act and the way it was to be interpreted. It was the Supreme Court that had to decide whether the act was constitutional. Could equality of treatment be obtained by providing opportunities for some groups that were themselves inherently unequal?

The legality of affirmative action

Within the Supreme Court there has been uncertainty over affirmative action, just as there has been throughout the nation. The Fourteenth Amendment to the Constitution laid down the notion of 'equal protection' before the law. The Court has, on occasion, argued that quota programmes in government or instigated by it are a violation of that idea. The Burger Court (1969–86) generally approved the principle of affirmative action (e.g. *The University of California Regents v Baake, 1978*), but was unhappy with the details of particular programmes. The details can vary and the variations may be very important in their constitutional implications. In *Firefighters v Stotts*, 1984, the Court would not accept the principle of affirmative action as the only or even most important consideration.

In subsequent cases, there has been a division of opinion in the attempt to apply the 'equal protection' clause of the Constitution. Sandra Day O'Connor, herself the first woman to make it on to the bench, has expressed grave doubts as to whether race-sensitive remedial measures can ever be justified, whereas others have taken the view that they can be necessary if the commitment to equality is to be honoured and past injustice righted.

Many votes have been very close, 5–4 or 6–3. In 1990, by 5–4, the Court upheld the right of Congress to adopt 'benign race-conscious measures' designed to increase the number of minority-held radio and television licences issued

the Baake case, 1978

A landmark judgement on affirmative action which stated that race could be taken into account in admissions decisions, as long as the institution did not set aside a specific number of seats for which only minorities were eligible.

Baake, a white American, could not get into medical school, even though his grades were higher than those of the sixteen African Americans who obtained entry because of a quota. He claimed that this was reverse discrimination. The Court ruled by 5–4 that he had been the victim of discrimination, but by the same margin judged that positive discrimination was not inherently unlawful. This was an ambiguous judgement that came to be regarded as favourable to the existence of affirmative action programmes, even if quotas were unacceptable.

by the Federal Communications Commission. Similarly, the Supreme Court has often been willing to accept policies designed to help women overcome past disadvantages. In 1987, it upheld the California county agency's scheme allowing consideration of gender in making appointments to positions where women had fared badly in earlier years. The Court recognised that there had in the past been an unfairness in representation and that it was therefore fair to use the issue of sex to correct the imbalance.

Bill Clinton was aware of the unpopularity of affirmative action, but generally resisted the temptation to trim his support and tried to encourage a 'mend it, don't end it' approach. His appointments to the judiciary helped to ensure that the policy continued, in spite of the hesitancy revealed by members of the Rehnquist Court. Rehnquist has long held doubts about the policy, once arguing in a dissenting submission that 'the Fourteenth Amendment was adopted to ensure that every person must be treated equally by each state regardless the colour of his skin . . . Today, the Court derails this achievement and places its imprimatur on the creation once again by government of privilege based on birth.'[7]

In the 1990s, there was increasing scrutiny of affirmative action at all levels in the political system. Some states meanwhile took their own line on affirmative action. Via a 1996 proposition (no.209), Californians voted to end affirmative action in education and the public services. There was a year-long delay in the state courts before the policy was enacted (1997). In 1998, Washington became the second state to outlaw affirmative action, passing the Initiative 200 law. In 2000, Governor Jeb Bush's 'One Florida' initiative succeeded in banning race as a factor in college admissions policies. Such moves reflected a growing hostility to the whole idea. Conservatives in many states were resistant to it, and his opposition was not confined to white Americans. Some successful African Americans shared the sense of resentment about programmes that tended to devalue success achieved on the basis of merit. Shelby Steele,[8] a black commentator, wrote *The Content of our Character*, in which he argued that not only was the value of qualifications being undermined, but, more seriously, affirmative action tended to reinforce feelings of black inferiority to white Americans.

From time to time, a particular instance arises that brings the issue into national prominence once again. The case of *Taxman v Township Board of Education* (1997) concerned events in Piscataway, New Jersey. The school board, faced with the need to make economies, fired a white teacher, Sharon Taxman, rather than her black colleague, and made the racial basis for the decision explicit. The Supreme Court decided that diversity was not a sufficient rationale for considering race, except 'to remedy past discrimination or as the result of a manifest imbalance in the employment of minorities'. The governmental review accepted that 'a simple desire to promote diversity for its own sake . . . is not a permissible basis for taking race into account'.

Bill Clinton had called for a modification of affirmative action programmes in the light of court judgements. But in the private sector, such programmes have continued to be popular with many large companies that see them as a means of winning or maintaining a market share for their products among minority communities. Their approach was a relevant factor in the policy of the University of Michigan over admissions (see box opposite for further details). By its rulings in 2003, the Supreme Court maintained its commitment to diversity as a laudable goal and accepted that race could be a factor, among others, in making decisions over recruitment. In *Gratz v Bollinger* and *Grutter v Bollinger*, the justices reaffirmed the spirit of the Baake judgement. They found against the admissions policy of the university (based as it was on additional points for being a member of an ethnic minority), but allowed the approach adopted by the Law School (considering issues of race and diversity on a practical basis) to continue.

Affirmative action remains contentious. Its opponents are aware of ambiguities in recent Court judgements and are likely to feel encouraged to continue their campaign to put the policy finally to rest.

The University of Michigan and its admission policies

In 2002–3, the Supreme Court had to decide its attitude in a case concerning affirmative action at the university of Michigan. Two white students claimed that the University acted unconstitutionally in denying them places in 1995 because of its race-scoring policy, and a third argued that the law school (which took race into account but did not explicitly score applicants) did the same to her in 1997. The university claimed that its policies were essential to its goal of assembling a diverse student body, 'which is critical to the quality of the educational experience students receive'. In most departments, it point-scored applicants, who needed to acquire 100 out of 150 to qualify for entry. Whilst full marks in a high school SAT test provided 12 points, membership of an ethnic minority qualified candidates for 20. Other supporters (including the NAACP) argued that affirmative action policies were needed for a different reason: 'race conscious admissions policies are justified to remedy both past and present discrimination at the University'.

As we have seen, fixed quotas have been outlawed since the Baake case, which none the less was in many ways a victory for affirmative action because it ruled that the broad goal of classroom diversity was 'a compelling state interest'. But in preparation for the Michigan ruling, the Bush Administration filed papers with the Supreme Court urging it to decide that the university policy was 'unconstitutional'. The Administration wanted a once-and-for-all decision that racial preferences had no places in admissions policy. It accepted that the goal of diversity was a worthy one, but argued it must not supersede equal rights and individual opportunity, for this was reverse discrimination. Moreover, because of the backlash created, any attempt to grant preference on minority grounds could end up harming the people it was intended to support.

The case proved to be hugely controversial. General Motors, which employs many graduates from the university, urged that diversity-admissions policies be allowed to continue. The company is a global enterprise and it argued that 'diversity equips American students to deal with people from different backgrounds, cultures and races – to be better business people'. Other supporters also pointed out that another crucial factor in Michigan admissions policies favours white students – namely, the allocation of extra points to those whose parents attended the institution.

The Bush Administration, keen to emphasise its commitment to diversity at a time when ethnic minorities in the United States were rapidly growing in numbers, talked about a third stance – it supported 'affirmative process', policies which led to diversity without specifically targeting race. This stance did not satisfy all members of the Administration, some of whom backed the then secretary of state, Colin Powell, who wanted to see a continuation of affirmative action policies geared to ending racial imbalance.

Gay rights and same-sex marriages

In recent years, the Supreme Court has supported the principle of marital privacy, but it has refused to extend recognition to gays and lesbians. In 1986, it decided that a Georgian law that criminalised 'consensual sodomy' (anal sex as practised by homosexuals) was acceptable within the Constitution. As such behaviour usually occurs in privacy, many people would argue that the state has no right to intrude into the home except in extreme circumstances. But this was not the view of a majority of the justices.

The issue of the degree of tolerance to be accorded to gays and lesbians is highly contentious in the United States and in many other democracies. Gay campaigners first began to organise to air their views in the 1970s, presenting their case in positive terms by emphasising the discrimination from which they suffered and their entitlement to the full range of civil rights. Their greater boldness in espousing the cause created a backlash from religious conservatives, who were assisted in proclaiming their arguments by the spread of AIDs in the following decade. This was portrayed by right-wing Christians as God's retribution for immoral behaviour.

Gay activists succeeded in persuading federal funding for AIDs research and treatment, although most relevant legislation included clauses designed to prevent such money from being used to advance homosexuality. Gays secured other gains in the 1990s, although they could not overturn the ban on gays serving openly in the military.

In his election campaign in 1992, Bill Clinton gave assurances to the gay community which aroused high expectations. Some advances were made by gay activists during his presidency. He established the first official liaison office for the gay community, and in 1998 signed an executive order prohibiting civilian federal departments and agencies from discriminating on the basis of sexual orientation. Other gains in the 1990s were the repeal of many state laws banning homosexual sex, and the creation of court orders and legislation in a small number of states to provide partner benefits for public employees in some areas such as health insurance.

But there were also disappointments. On the issue of the rights of gays to serve in the military, Clinton had to compromise under pressure from the Pentagon and top military brass. He came up with a fudge, the 'Don't Ask, Don't Tell' formula; officers could not ask about a soldier's sexual proclivities, but neither could a lesbian or gay man in uniform 'come out' or engage in sexual activities whilst on duty or special assignments. Gays also disliked the Defense of Marriage Act (1996), which banned people in same-sex marriages from eligibility for those federal benefits available to married couples, and allowed states not to recognise unions conducted in another state.

The issue of such same-sex liaisons was to become a controversial one in the new millennium. Religious conservatives were determined to achieve a ban on gay marriages. They campaigned to do so at national, state and even local level.

Civil unions and same-sex marriages

In 2000, Vermont became the first state to adopt a civil unions law, providing legal recognition of same-sex partnerships and most of the legal entitlements and obligations of marriage. In 2004, Massachusetts went a sizeable step beyond Vermont, by becoming the first state to recognise gay marriages, the first taking place in May of that year. The governor himself was against the initiative and invoked an old law to stop same-sex couples from outside the state from coming in to get married, although many city clerks said that they intended to ignore his move. It soon became apparent that there was a real doubt as to whether these same-sex marriages would be recognised in more conservative areas of the country, particularly in the thirty-eight states that have banned them by specifically stating that marriage can only involve a man and a woman.

The events of early 2004 unleashed powerful forces on either side of the debate. Gay marriage has become a touchstone social issue, with both 2004 presidential candidates opposed, and the president saying that he will support an amendment to change the Constitution to define marriage as a hetero-sexual institution. John Kerry argued that decisions on such matters should be taken at state level. Both men support civil unions, conferring some marriage benefits.

Cynics said that presidential advisers were pushing him to take up the case for an amendment as a political manoeuvre. He knew that the chances of securing an amendment were very small. But by so doing, he would divert attention from more difficult problems. In addition, he would be creating a 'wedge issue' that would serve to unite the Republicans and divide the Democrats and enable him to portray his opponent as a stereotypical liberal. Some commentators pointed out that a president who believes so strongly in states' rights in other contexts should be prepared to let the states do their jobs and work out their own marriage laws, before resorting to a constitutional amendment.

The rights of the disabled

Many Americans with disabilities have in the past suffered from discrimination, often being denied education, jobs and rehabilitation services. Throughout much of the country's history, the blind, deaf and mobility-impaired found buses, stairs, telephones and other necessities of life designed in such a way as to make it impossible for them to use them to full advantage, if at all. As one campaigning slogan put it: 'Once, blacks had to ride at the back of the bus. We can't even get on the bus.'

In 1973, the Rehabilitation Act (twice vetoed by President Nixon) added people with disabilities to the list of those protected against discrimination, and two years later an education act entitled all children to a free public education appropriate to their needs. However, the real breakthrough came during the presidency of George Bush senior. In 1990, Congress passed the Americans with Disabilities Act (ADA). The law defined a disabled person as anyone possessing a mental or physical impediment 'that substantially limits one or more activities of life'. It prohibited discrimination based on disability in employment, places of public accommodations and public services (e.g. buses, trains and subways); required that facilities be designed to make them accessible and usable by those with disabilities; and required them, to the extent feasible, to be redesigned to do so.

The introduction of the ADA was a key legislative achievement of the Bush era. It has resulted in dramatic improvements in wheelchair access to facilities ranging from churches to hotels, from restaurants to universities. Phone companies have provided special facilities for those with speech and hearing impairments. But the attainment of civil rights for the disabled has not been achieved without encountering substantial opposition. Whilst few people would wish to seem to be in outright opposition to a group already enduring emotional and/or physical handicaps, the goodwill has not always been apparent in their attitudes and actions. Even when passed into law (sometimes in the face of considerable opposition), enforcement has sometimes been sporadic and sluggish. The problem is the same one that influenced President Nixon: cost.

Civil liberties and civil rights: an assessment

The existence of civil liberties on paper is no guarantee that they will exist in practice. In times of peace and prosperity, they are more likely to be acted upon, although this was not true of the 1920s, when – in a 'golden decade' – those suspected of adhering to any progressive creed were liable to be branded as communists, or 'reds' and treated illiberally. Such intolerance was again apparent in the early post-1945 era, when the **McCarthyite** witchhunt against alleged 'subversives' was at its peak. In the 1960s, some of the methods used by the FBI, including the phone-tapping of Dr Martin Luther King and the surveillance of other protesting individuals and groups, suggested that the civil liberties of those who dissented from the American way of life were liable to be ignored. Few dissenters' will spring to their defence, especially when the cause is unpopular with majority opinion. In the atmosphere created by the attack on the Twin Towers of September 11, 2001, many Americans have been able to reconcile themselves to some alarming limitations of personal freedom, and the rights of many detainees have not been respected or defended.

Such cases might seem to be a violation of the Bill of Rights, yet throughout American history they have occurred. The 1960s was a decade in which interpretation of individual rights often revealed a surprising latitude, but this has been less true since the 1980s. The nation has been more conservative, as witnessed by the growing influence of the Christian Coalition and of the Religious Right, and by the advances made by the more cautious and conformist Republican Party in capturing the presidency for twelve years up to 1992 (and again in 2000) and gaining control in Congress in 1994. The Supreme Court has recognised this change of mood. On issues of individual freedom, it has been less liberal.

> **McCarthyism**
>
> The practice of making unsubstantiated accusations of disloyalty or communist leanings, associated with the Republican senator Joseph McCarthy. McCarthy led the notorious investigations into 'un-American activities' by members of the US government and other people prominent in public life, such as artists and intellectuals, between 1949 and 1954. Many Americans of socialist or even liberal persuasion were hounded from public life as a result of the hysteria of his anti-communist crusade.

This more conservative tide has not been widely reflected in rulings concerning freedom of speech. However, many Americans, alarmed by a wave of terrorism and of violent crime, are willing to accept restrictions on their lifestyle, such as greater electronic surveillance, helicopter searches, roadblocks and urine tests. A case can be made for many of these developments, but when viewed together they do suggest that respect for individual liberties and rights is less than it was a generation ago. Also, on matters involving criminal procedure, judicial opinion has moved. The liberal decisions of the Warren and Burger Courts (see pp. 170–4) have not subsequently been overruled, but their application has been reduced in scope. New rules have placed more emphasis on the need of society for public order than on the rights of the accused.

Since the 1960s, there has been a vast expansion in the civil rights of Americans. The process began with redress of the very obvious grievances of black Americans; it spread to tackle the rights of other ethnic minorities and women; more recently, it has been extended to gays and lesbians, the disabled and the elderly. The interests of women and minorities converged on the issue of affirmative action, the collective term for policies requiring a special effort to be made to help advantaged groups. But as we have seen, this has run into substantial opposition today.

The protection of freedoms in Britain and the United States: a comparison

Many Americans are aware of their liberties and rights, and can quote their Constitution in defence of them. The Bill of Rights is part of the Constitution. As we have seen in the section on the Constitution, there is no guarantee that constitutional rights are always upheld. The Puerto Ricans of New York were long excluded from voting by a literacy test, though of course they may have been perfectly literate in Spanish. Rights clearly depend on other things, such as the tradition of liberty in a country.

In Britain, we traditionally adopted a negative approach to freedoms, few of which are guaranteed by law. We could do or say something, provided that there was no law against it. There was no Bill of Rights to set out our entitlements. We relied upon what Dicey[9] referred to as 'the three pillars of liberty' for the protection of our freedoms: Parliament, the culture of liberty, and the courts. For much of our constitutional history, these arrangements seemed to serve us well, and politicians and commentators long believed that our liberties and rights rested on firmer foundations than any specific document. Ewing and Gearty[10] have pointed to the widespread British view that 'If a country enacted a bill of rights, then it was likely to be acknowledged as a written but inadequate consolation for the absence of that commitment to liberty which appeared to seep unconsciously and effortlessly through the British system of government.'

In the last few decades, some British politicians and several academic commentators have suggested that all is not well with the protection of basic freedoms in Britain. Breaches of rights are said to have occurred in many areas ranging from police powers to prisoners' rights, from immigration to official secrecy. As a result of Labour's change of heart on the adequacy of the available protection, the administration led by Tony Blair and elected in 1997 carried out one of the demands of those who seek more effective means: it incorporated the European Convention on Human Rights into British law via the 1998 Human

CONCLUSION

It would be wrong to see the United States as anything other than broadly liberal in matters of personal freedom. Few other countries have such an enviable record, whatever the occasional lapses. A human rights rating of 90% was awarded in the latest edition (1993) of the *Humana Guide*, a country-by-country analysis of the maintenance of civil and poliical rights around the world. The *Guide* argued that achieving a good record in a large, culturally heterogeneous country is inherently more difficult than doing it in a small country. The *Guide* denied points to the US only on the issue of capital punishment and the existence of widespread inequalities. It accepted that in

Rights Act. Effectively, Britain now has a Bill of Rights, although not a homegrown one devised for the circumstances of the day.

One reason for British anxiety over the introduction of any form of Bill of Rights has been that the existence of such a document would transfer power to appointed judges and away from elected, accountable politicians. Suspicion of judicial power is much greater in Britain than in the United States, for the British are not used to judges having a significant role in creating – as opposed to interpreting – the law. Americans are accustomed to the political role of the judiciary, and from the 1950s to the 1970s an activist Supreme Court played a significant role in expanding liberties and rights.

Civil libertarians on both sides of the Atlantic are alarmed by the scale of governmental action in the face of the terrorist threat following the attack on the World Trade Center in New York (see pp. 15 and 332–3). Drastic counter-terrorism measures enable those in authority to act in a way that erodes personal freedom for the sake of national security.

In both countries, the legislature has acted to promote civil rights for disadvantaged groups. The denial of opportunities in areas such as education, employment and housing has been remedied, usually at a time when parties of the centre-left have been in control. In America, in particular, the courts have played a significant role in ensuring the rights of arrested people, ethnic minorities and women. The Supreme Court has upheld entitlement to abortion, although allowing limitations that restrict its use and availability. In Britain, the House of Commons acted to confer the right to an abortion in the late 1960s (shortly before it was legalised in the United States), an era in which it also first acted to legalise homosexual relationships between consenting adults. More progressive British and American politicians have been willing to countenance civil unions between gay couples, but the issue of gay marriage remains a step too far for the majority of them.

the United States there is a widespread respect for freedom, even if the position on matters such as homosexuality and abortion varies between the fifty states.

The civil rights umbrella is a large one. Increasing numbers of groups seek protection for their rights, be they older and younger Americans, those with disabilities, homosexuals, or victims of AIDS and other chronic and debilitating conditions. It is difficult to predict what controversies the coming years will yield, but those categorised as belonging to disadvantaged minorities – blacks, Hispanics, gays, the disabled and the elderly among them – now constitute a very significant element in the population and are likely to be active in demanding greater recognition of their rights.

REFERENCES

1 The observation was originally made by black novelist Toni Morrison. Its validity is discussed by D. Wickham, *Bill Clinton and Black America*, Ballantine, 2002
2 NOW web site, mission statement
3 J. Flammang, *Women's Political Voice: How Women are Transforming the Practice and Study of Politics*, Temple University Press, 1997
4 J. Mansbridge, 'The Many Faces of Representation', working paper delivered to JFK School of Government, Harvard University, 1997
5 Quoted in S. Carroll, *Representing Women: Congresswomen's Perceptions of their Representative Role*, Rutgers University Press, 2000
6 Center for American Women and Politics (CAWP), press release, 1 January 2005
7 W. Rehnquist, dissenting opinion in *Fullilove v. Klutznick*, 1980
8 S. Steele, *The Content of our Characters*, HarperCollins, 1990
9 A. V. Dicey, *Introduction to the Study of the Law and the Constitution*, Macmillan, 1885
10 K. Ewing and C. Gearty, *Freedom under Thatcher*, Clarendon Press, 1990

USEFUL WEB SITES

There is a variety of sites providing information and/or argument about the range of social policies covered, some governmental, others belonging to pressure groups. These are some relevant ones among them:

Affirmative action:

www.www.bamn.com A forum for campaigning groups in favour of affirmative action (particularly in California).

www.acri.org The anti-affirmative action site of the American Civil Rights Institute, covering gender and racial issues.

Civil rights:

www.census.gov Information gathered from the official census on the ethnic and racial characteristics of Americans in every region and state.

www.naacp.org The official site of the National Association for the Advancement of Colored People.

SAMPLE QUESTIONS

1 Discuss the significance of ethnicity in American politics.

2 'The days of radical protest are largely over, because so many black Americans are now finding opportunities for advancement in American society.' Discuss.

3 'Black Americans have significantly improved their position in recent decades, but other groups still face formidable barriers.' Discuss

4 Assess the impact of women and the women's movement on American politics.

5 Why is abortion such a controversial issue in the United States?

6 What is meant by affirmative action and why has it proved controversial in American politics?

7 Why have the idea and practice of affirmative action gone out of fashion in recent years?

8 What does the treatment of gays and lesbians tell us about the state of civil rights in the United States?

9 Why do issues of civil rights continue to arouse so much controversy in the United States?

10 Has the existence of a Bill of Rights been effective in securing the civil liberties and rights of the American people?

11 Are civil liberties and rights better protected in the UK or the USA?

12 Examine the means and assess the effectiveness of protecting rights in the UK and USA.

Conclusion: the condition of American democracy **11**

The meaning of democracy

The ancient Greeks were the first to give a democratic answer to the question of how to organise a political system. Athenian democracy was practised in a small city state, where the citizens made some political decisions directly, and controlled others. This was **direct democracy** in action, with people coming together to make decisions whenever necessary. Debates in the assembly were free, open and wide-ranging, each citizen having a single vote.

> **direct democracy**
> Government in which citizens come together in one place to make laws; refers to populist measures such as the initiative and referendum.

After the Greeks, the notion of democracy went out of fashion, being associated in the eyes of many rulers with factional conflict and violence. Until the early nineteenth century, far from government being rule by the many, it was actually in effect rule by the very few, who were not subject to popular control. The majority of people were seen as unfit to rule, and members of the nobility who possessed governing skills did not feel that they should be subject to the whims of the illiterate and ill-informed majority. In *The Federalist*, James Madison echoed the outlook of many of his co-framers of the American Constitution when he wrote: 'Such democracies [as the Greek and Roman] have ever been found incompatible with personal security of the rights of property; and have in general been as short in their lives, as they have been violent in their deaths.'

The word 'democracy' is not used in the US Constitution. The framers preferred the term 'republic' to describe the form of government that they wished to create. It lacked the connection with direct democracy – with its possible associations with demagogues, mass rule and the mob. The vision of the Founding Fathers was of a **representative** system, a republic in the Greek philosopher Plato's sense, by which all those in power obtain and retain their position as a result of winning elections in which all free adults are allowed to take part.

> **representative democracy**
> Government in which the people rule indirectly through elected representatives.

The nineteenth century saw the spread of representative democracy, a system under which a person stands for and speaks on behalf of another. Today, it is widely accepted that this is the only viable form of democracy in a vast country. The mass of people cannot rule, in the sense of making binding decisions. Instead, representatives of the people, freely elected, decide. What is crucial is that there should be effective popular control over the rulers or decision-makers. A system is democratic to the extent that those who have power are subject to the wishes of the electorate. Abraham Lincoln put it more succinctly: 'government of the people, by the people and for the people'.

The past workings of American democracy: blemishes and virtues

Democracy is seen as a pre-eminently American value. Yet the United States has not always acknowledged the democratic rights of all its citizens, and some of the developments in the twentieth and early twenty-first-centuries have cast doubt upon the strength of the original attachment to democratic values. For instance, the existence of the right to vote is seen as a major criterion of any democracy. If broad categories of the public are denied the opportunity to express their preference between candidates, then this must be a blot on the landscape. Women obtained the vote in 1920, and in theory all men had the vote from the time the Constitution was created, subject origi- nally to a property qualification. Yet slaves were not allowed to participate in elections, and when slavery ended, ruses were adopted in various southern states to prevent blacks from exercising their democratic rights.

In the absence of an effective universal franchise, there must be doubts about the depth of the pre-twentieth-century American commitment to democracy. True, the property qualifications were pitched at a relatively modest level, and by the early nineteenth century some 80% of American men owned sufficient property to qualify. True also that the US was relatively speedy in extending the popular suffrage to include all women. But they were white men and white women, and it was not until the 1960s that the majority of black Americans were able to use their entitlement, if they so wished.

On the score of recognising and respecting minority rights, the Americans again did well in theory. Crucial liberties were granted in the Constitution, most obviously in the first ten amendments that make up the Bill of Rights. These are inviolable, unless there is a further constitutional amendment to change them. Yet, again, there have been blemishes upon the record. Two sets of factors mar the record of the Americans in protecting and respecting such rights:

1 In the 1920s and in the 1950s, anti-communist hysteria was at a high level. The 1920s was a markedly intolerant decade, in which the liberties of many individuals were infringed, and anyone whose views were mildly progressive was liable to be branded as a communist, or 'red'. Similarly, the McCarthy witchhunt against those portrayed as communists was at a fever pitch in the early 1950s. His techniques of investigation, with their emphasis upon smear and innuendo, displayed little respect for constitutional niceties. 'Un-American activity' was interpreted very widely, and there was much harassment of individuals and groups. There was in both eras a desperate desire for conformity, and those who did not conform to the American ideal of being White Anglo-Saxon Protestants (WASPs) were hounded.

2 The ideal of equality, as proclaimed in Jefferson's resounding cry 'We hold these truths to be self-evident, that all men are created equal', is seen as an American contribution to humankind. Certainly, privilege and rank count for less in America than in Western Europe, and an egalitarian fervour is in a way a part of the American Dream – that each person can go out and make a fortune, by using his or her gifts and exhibiting a pioneering spirit. But the position of black Americans until comparatively recently suggested that in practice not everyone benefited from the Jeffersonian dream.

States adopted many differing rules to prevent political and legal equality of white and black from becoming a reality. Segregation and racial discrimination may be particularly associated with the Deep South, but in many northern cities there was much *de facto* segregation well into the 1960s. Even today the opportunities available to many black Americans are more theoretical than real.

If, in several respects, reality has fallen short of the democratic ideal, yet the commitment to democracy of many Americans has always been apparent, and to their credit many have always felt uneasy about lapses from that ideal. It would also be fair to point to other areas of political life in which the theory and practice of democracy have been evident:

1 In the Progressive era (1900–14), the introduction of direct election of senators and the spread of primary elections to defeat the power of the party-machine bosses were moves which reflected a true concern for democracy.

2 The US has practised direct democracy as well as the representative form. Devices such as the referendum and the initiative are practical demonstrations of direct democracy in action, whatever their weaknesses. More unusual is the use of the town meeting in small rural areas of New England. Originally, such meetings were vehicles through which the mainly Puritan religious leaders informed and led other members of the community – a means of seeking a consensus via a guided discussion. They were not

opportunities for the expression of majority will on issues of the day, and those who declined to agree to the general will were likely to be driven out of the area. However, such meetings have developed into a more acceptable democratic form, and in them citizens gather together to make decisions for their community.

American democracy today

America has long been regarded as a model democracy, but some commentators believe that today the system is not working well. Indeed, Kenneth Dolbeare has written[1] of 'the decay of American democracy' and asks whether the condition is a terminal one. He sees the problem as one compounded by the sheer scale and power of the government in Washington, for these have meant that it is 'increasingly connected only to a steadily shrinking proportion of its affluent citizens'.

Dolbeare discerns several factors that have contributed to the 'decay':
- the decline of political parties;
- the rise of television;
- the dominance of money as a means of access to television and electioneering in general;
- the rise of political action committees;
- near-permanent incumbency in Congress;
- a general abandonment of leadership to the latest opinion poll.

More seriously than any of the above factors, however, he sees the 'long-term trend toward abandoning political participation as the most alarming indication of decay. In particular, this means a more or less continuous decline in voter participation, particularly a problem for those in the bottom one third of the social pyramid. He notes the paradox that has emerged: 'The growing underclass has rising needs for education, jobs, training, health care etc., but these very services are being held to a minimum or even cut – and yet the voting participation of this same underclass is declining faster than that of any other population group.'

Other writers have also noted that at the very time that the Soviet control of Eastern Europe has broken down and given rise to the creation of 'new democracies', the American version of that same system has shown severe signs of fatigue. Paul Taylor is an exponent of this viewpoint:[2] 'As democracy flourishes around the globe, it is losing ground in the United States.'

The threat to civil liberty

After the 2001 attacks on New York and Washington, there was widespread debate in the United States and elsewhere about the threats to freedom and security. By their actions, the terrorists involved had destroyed the most basic right of all – the right to life – of nearly 4,000 Americans, and had threatened the 'life, liberty and pursuit of happiness' of many more.

But critics of the USA Patriot Act claim that the situation created by September 11 has been used to launch an unnecessarily broad attack on civil liberties in America. This inspired the *New York Times*[3] to launch a ferocious attack on the limitations being imposed on personal freedom. In an editorial, it was claimed that: 'Civil liberties are eroding, and there is no evidence that the reason is anything more profound than fear and frustration . . .Two months into the war against terrorism, the nation is sliding toward the trap that we entered this conflict vowing to avoid.'

Detention at Guantanamo Bay

The growing anxiety about the threat to freedom came to a head in early 2002 over the issue of the treatment of terrorist suspects at Guantanamo Bay, in Cuba. The plan was to try them before special military courts, against the

Democracy in Britain and the United States: a comparison

In Britain, some of the same anxieties about the health of democracy exist. There is a disaffected underclass that is largely ignorant of and uninterested in political life. Many of its members do not turn out and vote. Indeed, turnouts generally have been in long-term decline (a trend particularly evident in the 2001 general election), although there was some improvement in that for the 2004 local and European elections. There is the same scepticism of politicians, but for many people it is more than a sensible wariness about those who exercise authority. Rather, it is a deep and cynical distrust of those who rule.

In Britain, there is concern about the existence of numerous quangos, power having been handed over to a new lay elite whose members increasingly run a wide range of services. American experience is different, for wherever there is a public office to fill across the Atlantic the tendency is to hold an election. Here, the passion for election does not extend to those who serve on various boards and trusts; neither does it (yet) extend to the second chamber.

In both countries, the media at best provide reflective analysis and commentary on national events, and expose alleged or real corruption, the abuse of power and other forms of public scandal. In so doing, they contribute to the workings of democracy. In other respects, they present a threat to its values. Concentration of ownership in too few hands, the lack of diversity of opinion, and intrusive and sometimes shamelessly biased reporting are dangers in the press.

Television can be said to aid democracy by informing voters, via news bulletins, current affairs programmes, and other scheduling which often conveys information in an entertaining form. But the tendency to trivialise, to concentrate upon personalities and personal

decision of which there would be no right of appeal. The defense secretary labelled them as 'unlawful combatants' rather than as 'prisoners of war', thus denying them the full protection of the Geneva Convention. But under international law they are not liable to torture or to inhumane treatment, and civil libertarians around the world have been disturbed by reports concerning the conditions in which they have been held.

Many people would accept that it is understandable for America to wish to glean as much information as possible from the Taliban and Al-Qaida detainees. People feel little sympathy for the detainees' alleged actions, and recognise that they may have been part of a dangerous terrorist conspiracy against Western targets. Yet detainees still have rights. If they are not covered by the Geneva 'laws of war', then they are ordinary criminals. As such, if tried in the United States they would be protected by the Sixth Amendment, which insists that in 'all criminal prosecutions' in the United States inalienable rights apply, including the right to a jury trial. But they are being held in a place beyond the remit of normal US jurisdiction.

'weaknesses', and to express serious issues in a shorthand, sound-bite form has reduced the educative role which at its best the medium can offer.

The basic liberties associated with democratic rule are written into the American Constitution, whereas Britain has traditionally had a negative approach to freedoms. Few of them were guaranteed by law, so that we could do or say something provided that there was no specific law against it. Unlike the situation in other Western democracies, there was no Bill of Rights or document setting out basic entitlements. With the passage of the Human Rights Act in 1998, the European Convention on Human Rights has been incorporated into British law, so that for the first time there is a written record of the liberties and rights of the subject.

Since the 1960s, there has been an expansion of individual rights in Britain and the United States. Positive freedoms have been proclaimed, with legislation and – in the US case – court judgements ensuring that the rights of women and minority groups have been enforced. However, in both countries, the events of September 11, 2001, have led to anti-terrorist legislation that some libertarians see as too all-embracing and out of proportion to the threat which exists.

Finally, on one freedom, that of the right of access to information, the US performance still leaves Britain trailing. America has had a freedom of information act since 1966. Whatever the doubts about the costs of its implementation or its effects on carrying out confidential investigations, most Americans and consumer groups welcome the fact that the legislation is strong and effective, giving Americans a 'right to know'. The British legislation that took effect in 2005 has been widely criticised for its timidity, even though significant concessions were extracted from ministers during its passage in 1999–2000.

Those within America who have criticised aspects of Administration policy and challenge US foreign and defence policy objectives have often been attacked as unpatriotic or anti-American. One writer[4] has written of the 'new McCarthyism' and pointed out that it sits uneasily in a country supposedly noted for its 'freedom of thought and speech, for diversity and dissent'. The case made by him and other civil libertarians was well expressed in a news release of the American Civil Liberties Union (ACLU):[5]

> Whilst we at ACLU feel as strongly as anyone that the perpetrators of these monstrous crimes [i.e. the September 11 attacks] must be brought to justice, we also feel that America's freedom – the very essence of our national character – must be protected as we respond to the threat of terrorism within our border. Americans can be safe and free. Unfortunately, the government has implemented measures that go light years beyond anything necessary to combat terrorism.

Democracy is sustained by public scepticism, and it is essential that people are allowed to challenge and express dissent. At the same time, a democracy under attack must have the means for its own defence. Getting the balance right between security and liberty is one of the most difficult tasks for any government at a time of national danger.

Future possibilities

We have examined some of the problems associated with the operation of democracy in the late twentieth century. Some fears may be overstated, and different writers and politicians have their own particular misgivings and complaints. There is general agreement among many that all is not currently well with the body politic, and that American democracy is today under strain.

As to the future, new forms of democratic involvement have become a possibility with the development of media technology. The scope for the use of e-mail as a means of transmitting opinions and exerting pressure on those in office is enormous. Such technology empowers voters, and provides new means for them to be more actively involved in political dialogue. It opens up the possibility that they will be able to pass information to one another, so that the overall level of knowledge of the American citizenry will be increased. Voters might wish to use these developments to their advantage, and those elected to public office will need to be more conscious of those whose vote placed them there. This does not mean that those affected have to be subservient to public pressure, but certainly their performances will be more effectively monitored.

In the longer term, another possible development is that the computer-literate might conduct some form of referendum on the net, giving many people a greater opportunity to participate in the political process than ever before.

There may be dangers in 'electronic populism' and 'mobocracy', but for others such as Kevin Kelly[6] 'the Internet revives Thomas Jefferson's 200–year-old dream of thinking individuals self-actualising a democracy'.

REFERENCES

1 P. J. Davies and F. A. Waldstein, *Political Issues in America: The 1990s Revisited*, Manchester University Press, 1996
2 P. Taylor, 'Democracy and Why Bother Americans', *International Herald Tribune*, 7 July 1990
3 Editorial, *New York Times*, 10 November 2001
4 G. Monbiot, *Guardian*, 16 October 2001
5 ACLU press release, 14 December 2001
6 K Kelly, *Wired* Magazine, quoted in the *Guardian*, 22 February 1995

SAMPLE QUESTIONS

1 Examine the condition of American democracy today.

2 'A flawed democracy.' Discuss this verdict on the American political system.

3 'Democratic in theory, but less impressive in practice.' Discuss the fairness of this assessment of the operation of the political system on either side of the Atlantic.

Index